ACCOUNT TITLE	NORMAL BALANCE	FINANCIAL REPORT FOUND ON	CATEGORY	PERMANENT OR TEMPORARY
Land	Debit	Balance Sheet	Plant & Equipment	Permanent
Land Improvement	Debit	Balance Sheet	Plant & Equipment	Permanent
Loss from Fire	Debit	Income Statement	Other Expense	Temporary
Loss on Sale of (Asset)	Debit	Income Statement	Other Expense	Temporary
Loss or Gain from Realization		Income Statement	Other Expense	Temporary
(Assume Loss)	Debit	Income Statement	Other Income	Temporary
(Assume Gain)	Credit	Balance Sheet	Plant & Equipment	Permanent
Machinery	Debit	Balance Sheet:	Current Asset:	Permanent
Merchandise Inventory	Debit	Income Statement	Cost of Goods Sold	
		Balance Sheet	Long-Term Liability	Permanent
Mortgage Payable	Credit	Balance Sheet	Current Liability	Permanent
Notes Payable	Credit	Balance Sheet	Current Asset	Permanent
Notes Receivable	Debit	Balance Sheet	Intangible Asset	Permanent
Organization Costs	Debit	Balance Sheet	Intangible Asset	Permanent
Patents	Debit	Balance Sheet	Stockholders' Equity	Permanent
Paid-In Capital from Treasury Stock	Credit	Balance Sheet	Stockholders' Equity	Permanent
Paid-In Capital in Excess of (. . . .)	Credit	Income Statement	Operating Expense	Temporary
Payroll Tax Expense	Debit	Balance Sheet	Current Asset	Permanent
Petty Cash	Debit	Balance Sheet	Long-Term Liability	Permanent
Premium on Bonds Payable	Credit	Balance Sheet	Current Asset	Permanent
Prepaid Insurance	Debit	Balance Sheet	Current Asset	Permanent
Prepaid Rent	Debit	Balance Sheet	Stockholders' Equity	Permanent
Preferred Stock	Credit	Income Statement	Cost of Goods Sold	Temporary
Purchases	Debit	Income Statement	Contra Cost of Goods Sold	Temporary
Purchases Discount	Credit	Income Statement	Contra Cost of Goods Sold	Temporary
Purchases Returns and Allowances	Credit	Statement of Retained Earnings;	Stockholders' Equity	Permanent
Retained Earnings	Credit	Balance Sheet		
		Income Statement	Operating Expense	Temporary
Salaries Expense	Debit	Balance Sheet	Current Liability	Permanent
Salaries Payable	Credit	Income Statement	Revenue	Temporary
Sales	Credit	Income Statement	Contra Revenue	Temporary
Sales Discount	Debit	Income Statement	Contra Revenue	Temporary
Sales Returns and Allowances	Debit	Balance Sheet	Current Liability	Permanent
Sales Tax Payable	Credit	Balance Sheet	Stockholders' Equity	Permanent
Stock Dividend Distributable	Credit	Balance Sheet	Current Asset	Permanent
Stock Subscriptions Receivable	Debit	Balance Sheet	Current Asset	Permanent
Supplies	Debit	Balance Sheet	Contra Stockholders' Equity	Permanent
Treasury Stock	Debit	Balance Sheet	Current Liability	Permanent
Unearned Revenue	Credit	Balance Sheet	Current Liability	Permanent
Vouchers Payable	Credit	Statement of Owner's Equity;	Owners' Equity	Temporary
Withdrawals	Debit	Balance Sheet		

4th

EDITION

Chapters 1–10

COLLEGE ACCOUNTING
A Practical Approach

Jeffrey Slater

North Shore Community College

Beverly, Massachusetts

PRENTICE HALL Englewood Cliffs, New Jersey 07632

Library of Congress Cataloging-in-Publication Data

Slater, Jeffrey (date)
    College accounting: a practical approach, 1–10/by Jeffrey
Slater. —4th ed.
       p.   cm.
    Includes index.
    ISBN 0-13-142043-7:
    1. Accounting.   I. Title.
HF635.S6315   1991
657′.044—dc20

90-7585
CIP

To Shelley, my best friend. Love, Jeff.

Chapter Opening Photo Credits

Chapter 1 Will/Deni McIntyre/Photo Researchers
Chapters 2, 3 Gabe Palmer/The Stock Market
Chapter 4 Richard Hutchings/Photo Researchers
Chapter 5 Charles Gupton/The Stock Market
Chapter 6 Richard Gross/The Stock Market

Chapter 7 Ted Horowitz/The Stock Market
Chapter 8 Will McIntyre, Science Source/Photo
    Researchers
Chapter 9 Murray Alcosser/The Image Bank
Chapter 10 A.M. Rosario/The Image Bank

Editorial/Production Credits

Development Editors: Joyce Perkins, Sid Zimmerman
Production Editor: Eleanor Ode Walter
Art Director: Janet Schmid
Book and Cover Designer: Linda J. Den Heyer Rosa
Page Layout: Karen Noferi
Manufacturing Buyers: Ed O'Dougherty, Mary Ann Gloriande

© 1991, 1988, 1984, 1979 by Prentice-Hall, Inc.
A Division of Simon & Schuster
Englewood Cliffs, New Jersey 07632

Printed in the United States of America
10 9 8 7 6 5 4 3 2 1

ISBN 0-13-142043-7

Prentice-Hall International (UK) Limited, *London*
Prentice-Hall of Australia Pty. Limited, *Sydney*
Prentice-Hall Canada Inc., *Toronto*
Prentice-Hall Hispanoamericana, S.A., *Mexico*
Prentice-Hall of India Private Limited, *New Delhi*
Prentice-Hall of Japan, Inc., *Tokyo*
Prentice-Hall of Southeast Asia Pte. Ltd., *Singapore*
Editora Prentice-Hall do Brasil, Ltda., *Rio de Janeiro*

CONTENTS

PREFACE

TO THE STUDENT

This text was written to introduce you to accounting, a dynamic tool of business. What is accounting, and why will you find it useful? Accounting is a planned and orderly way of keeping records for the purpose of seeing how a business is performing. It answers such questions as: Is the business profitable, or is it losing money? Which business activities are contributing most to profits, and which to losses? Which resources are well employed, and which are being wasted? Who owes the business money, and how much? What does the business owe? Accounting is also important for regulatory and tax purposes. You will be surprised at how often your understanding of accounting will work for you on the job.

Learning accounting means familiarizing yourself with many new terms and concepts. Don't be tempted to cut corners and take shortcuts; you will get the most out of your study of accounting if you follow the detailed, step-by-step directions provided in this text. Once you have learned the basic terms and concepts, the rest will quickly fall into place. Be sure to review the appendix, *Accounting Forms Sampler*. It will be a great help to you during the course.

I have set up each chapter according to a special format that I believe makes it easier to learn and remember the material in the chapter. Let's look at each component of a chapter and see why it was set up that way:

- *Broad objectives to introduce the chapter.* These objectives allow you to see where you're headed; they set the stage for the more specific objectives to be found later in the chapter. Page references are given where the material for each objective can be found.
- *Chapter broken down into learning units.* Students continually tell me that they learn best when material is broken into small, manageable units. This way, if a question comes up it can be identified and solved immediately without waiting until the whole chapter is read. And in this way you can test yourself on smaller amounts of material to be sure that you've mastered each bit before going on to the next.
- *Objectives follow each unit with page references.* After you have read the unit, the objectives give you a chance to recap what you've read. Stop to see if you can answer the objective—if not, go back to the page referred to and review the material.

- *Self-review quiz follows each unit.* This is a chance to test yourself on what you've just learned and try some hands-on applications of the theory just covered. The forms for the quizzes are in your *Study Guide/Working Papers.* The solution to the quiz follows right after the quiz in the text. Don't worry if you get something wrong in the quiz—these quizzes are for you, not for your professor. If you do have trouble with the quiz, go back to the problem area in the unit and review before going on to the next unit.

- *Summary of the key points and key terms at the end of the chapter.* The material you have covered in the chapter is reviewed by unit at the end of the chapter. The key points of the summary give you one more chance to review what you've learned and to point up any weak spots in the chapter. Accounting as a discipline is full of new vocabulary. The trick to learning this new vocabulary is to take it slowly and review it often. The terms introduced in the chapter are listed and defined at the end of the chapter by unit so that you can review them and make sure you know what they mean and how they are used in the chapter.

- *Blueprint at the end of the chapter.* Some people learn better by seeing something in chart or diagram form rather than reading about it. And we all remember things better if we learn them several different ways. The goal of the blueprint is to review visually the key concepts or procedures in the chapter. It is like a roadmap, showing you in simple steps what you have just been through in the chapter.

- *Discussion questions at the end of the chapter.* These questions cover the theory covered in the chapter. It is important to make sure you can answer them before going on to the next chapter.

- *Exercises at the end of the chapter.* Exercises review specific topics covered in the chapter. Notes in the margin identify the topic covered by each exercise— if you know you need more work on a certain topic that you feel uncertain about, seek out those exercises that deal with that topic.

- *Problems at the end of the chapter.* There are A & B problems in the text; forms for the problems are provided in your *Study Guide/Working Papers.* As with the exercises, notes in the margin identify the topic covered by each problem.

- *Practical accounting applications at the end of the chapter.* These give you a way to test your accounting knowledge in a situation that might occur on the job. They're challenging and also fun.

- *Comprehensive review problems follow certain chapters.* These problems give a list of transactions and information needed to perform certain tasks in accounting covered by a set of chapters. At the end of Chapter 5 is a problem that reviews the accounting cycle; in this problem you go through the accounting cycle twice to give you a more complete idea of the procedures involved at the end of each month. At the end of Chapter 10 there is a summary of payroll procedures. (After Chapter 13 there is a problem that deals with transactions of a sole proprietorship merchandise company.) These problems help put all the theory together in a practical way. Forms for completing the problems are provided in your *Study Guide/Working Papers.*

Some chapters also contain career boxes highlighting individuals who have used their college accounting coursework to help them attain a rewarding career. Their advice and experiences are informative, interesting, and inspiring.

If you follow this chapter layout carefully you will find that you learn the basic terms and concepts easily and remember them better, and that the many chances to apply them in a practical way help you to remember them.

TO THE INSTRUCTOR

As I mentioned in my note to the students, I have set up each chapter of this text so that students can learn small, manageable units of material followed by immediate feedback through the self-review quizzes that follow each unit. My concept of teaching is not new; it is based on over 20 years of teaching and writing experience in accounting. My major aim in preparing this text is to give you all the tools to choose from to make this course a positive experience for students and instructors alike.

An *Annotated Instructor's Edition* of this text is provided for your use. This is an easy-to-use volume that includes the complete student text as well as a number of different teaching aids for the instructor. The supplements that accompany this text are described at length in the *Annotated Instructor's Edition*; a short list is provided here for your convenience.

Study Guide/Working Papers with extra forms
Videotapes
How to Study College Accounting booklet
Computerized and Manual Practice Sets
General Ledger Package
Lotus® Templates
Excel® Templates
Electronic Working Papers
Transparencies (Solutions and Teaching)
Solutions Manuals
Electronic Transparencies
Tutorial Software
Computerized and Manual Complete Testing Package

ACKNOWLEDGMENTS

I would never have been able to undertake the daunting task of a large publishing venture such as this without the support of the many academic colleagues around the country who so generously gave their time to review the text and supplements. Special thanks go to Eugene Oliver for contributing the draft of the manufacturing chapter and to Susan Lanier for writing the computer chapter. To these and to all the others, many thanks for your help:

Helen Alkides
American Business Institute

Charles Berkmeyer
Meramec Community College

Yvonne Gallegos Bodle
Ventura College

David Booth
Essex Community College

Kenneth Brown
University of Houston

John Bulger
Brown Institute

Janet Cassagio
Nassau Community College

Dean Chambers
Riverside Community College

Rex Chapman
Rogue Community College

Jerry Funk
Brazosport College

Robert Gabridge
Macomb Community College

Rich Hamann
Des Moines Area
Community College

Sylvia Hearing
Portland College

Ken Hendershot
United College of Business

Carol Hande Holcomb
Spokane Falls Community College

Fred Jex
Macomb Community College

Susan Lanier
Baton Rouge School of Computers

Joel Lerner
Sullivan County
Community College

Ray Lewis
San Antonio College

Robert McCarter
Macomb Community College

Peter Megginson
Massasoit Community College

Michelle Moore
NEC—Allentown Business School

Kathleen Murphrey
San Antonio College

Diane Powell
Trend College

Claudia Quinn
San Joaquin Delta College

Lona Scala

Jeff Sears
Madison Business College

Elaine Simpson
Florissant Valley Community College

John Somers
Rogue Community College

James Stembridge
Monroe Business Institute

Joan Thompson
Marian Court Junior
College of Business

Bill Timberlake
San Antonio College

Al Walczak
Linn-Benton Community College

Linda Werner

I would also like to thank the Prentice Hall staff who worked with me, including Joyce Perkins and Sid Zimmerman, Development Editors; Eleanor Walter, Production Editor; Jenny Sheehan, Supplements Editor; Bob Kern, Acquisitions Editor; Michele Jay, Marketing Manager; Tina Culman, Director of Business Education Sales; Linda Rosa, Interior and Cover Designer; and Sophie Papanikolaou, Managing Editor, Supplements Production. And last but not least I would like to thank my typist, Sharon Young.

Jeffrey Slater

INTRODUCTION TO ACCOUNTING CONCEPTS AND PROCEDURES

In this chapter we will cover the following topics:

1. Defining and listing the functions of accounting. (p. 2)
2. Recording transactions in the basic accounting equation. (p. 5)
3. Seeing how revenue, expenses, and withdrawals expand the basic accounting equation. (p. 10)
4. Preparing an income statement, a statement of owner's equity, and a balance sheet. (p. 15)

Accounting is the language of business; it provides information to managers, owners, customers, investors, and other decision makers inside and outside an organization. Accounting provides answers and insights to questions like these:

- Is Disney's cash balance sufficient?
- Should Burger King expand its product line?
- Can Eastern Airlines pay its debt obligations?
- What percentage of IBM's marketing budget is for television advertisement? How does this compare with the competition? What is the overall financial condition of IBM?

Smaller businesses also need answers to their financial questions:

- Did business increase enough over the last year to warrant hiring a new assistant?
- Should we spend money to design, produce, and send out new brochures in an effort to create more business?

Accounting is as important to individuals as it is to business; it answers questions like

- Should I take out a loan to buy a car or wait until I can afford to pay cash for it?
- Would my money work better in a savings bank or in a credit union savings plan?

Think of accounting as a process that analyzes, records, classifies, summarizes, and reports financial information. The purpose of the accounting process is to provide this information to decision makers—whether individuals, small businesses, large corporations, or governmental agencies—in a timely fashion.

BOOKKEEPING, ACCOUNTING, AND THE COMPUTER

Confusion often arises concerning the difference between bookkeeping and accounting. **Bookkeeping** is the recording (record-keeping) function of the accounting process; a bookkeeper enters accounting information in the company's books. An accountant takes that information and prepares the financial reports that are used to analyze the company's financial position. Accounting involves many complex activities and often includes the preparation of tax and financial reports, budgeting, and analyses of financial information.

People sometimes wonder if the computer is taking over the accountant's job of completing financial reports. It is important to understand that *the computer is only a tool* that is doing the routine bookkeeping operations that previously took days or months to complete. To date, the computer has not caused fewer jobs but has, in fact, created more jobs because businesses are getting more information than they could previously get by manual record keeping.

It is important that students studying accounting understand the "whys" rather than the mere mechanics of the accounting process. For this reason the text illustrates manual accounting and also explains how you can apply the advantages of the computer to your manual accounting system by using your hands-on knowledge of how accounting works.

Let's begin our study of accounting concepts and procedures by looking at a small business: Frank Morse's law practice.

LEARNING UNIT 1-1

The Accounting Equation

ASSETS AND EQUITIES

At the end of August, Frank Morse decided to open his own law practice. His accountant told him that, first of all, a law practice (or any company) is considered a **business entity**, a separate unit, and its finances have to be kept distinct from Frank's personal finances. The accountant went on to say that all business transactions can be analyzed by something called the basic accounting equation. Frank had never heard of the basic accounting equation. He listened carefully as the accountant explained it:

1. Cash, land, supplies, office equipment, buildings, and other properties of value owned by a firm are called **assets**.
2. The rights or financial claims to the assets are called **equities** and they belong to those who supply the assets. If you are the only person to supply assets to the firm, you have the sole rights, or financial claims, to them. For example, if you supply the law firm with $3,000 in cash and $2,000 in office equipment, your equity in the firm is $5,000.
3. The relationship between assets and equities is

Assets = Equities

The total dollar value of the assets of the law firm will be equal to the total dollar value of the financial claims to those assets—that is, equal to the total dollar value of the equities.

The total dollar value is broken down on the left-hand side of the equation to show the specific items of value owned by the business and on the right-hand side to show the types of claims against the assets owned.

4. A firm may have to borrow money to buy more assets; when this occurs it means the firm is buying assets *on account* (buy now, pay later). Suppose the law firm purchases a desk for $200 on account from Joe's Stationery, and the store is willing to wait ten days for payment. The law firm has created a **liability**: an obligation to pay that comes due in the future. Joe's Stationery is called the *creditor.* This liability—the amount owed to Joe's Stationery—gives the store

the right, or the financial claim, to $200 of the law firm's assets. When Joe's Stationery is paid, the store's rights to the assets of the law firm will end, since the obligation has been paid off.

To best understand the various claims to a business's assets, accountants divide equities into two parts. The claims of creditors—outside persons or business—are labelled **liabilities**. The claims of the business's owner are labelled **owner's equity**. Let's see how the accounting equation looks now.

Assets = **Equities**

1. Liabilities: rights of creditors
2. Owner's equity: rights of owner

Assets = Liabilities + Owner's Equity

The total value of all the assets of a firm equals the combined total value of the financial claims of the creditors (liabilities) and the claims of the owners (owner's equity). This is known as the **basic accounting equation**. The basic accounting equation provides a basis for understanding the conventional accounting system of a business. The equation records business transactions in a logical and orderly way that shows their impact on the company's assets, liabilities, and owner's equity.

Another way of presenting the basic accounting equation is:

Assets − Liabilities = Owner's Equity

This form of the equation stresses the importance of creditors. The owner's rights to the assets of a business are determined by first subtracting the rights of the creditor(s). Creditors have first claim to assets. If a firm has no liabilities—and therefore no creditors—the owner has the total rights to the assets. Another term we will be using in this text is **capital**—the owner's current investment, or equity, in the assets of a business. For now, think of capital as one subdivision of owner's equity; we will look at other subdivisions later in the chapter.

As Frank Morse's law firm engages in business transactions (paying bills, serving customers, and so on), changes will take place in the assets, liabilities, and owner's equity (capital). Let's analyze some of these transactions.

> (A) Aug. 28: Morse invests $8,000 in cash and $100 of office equipment into the business.

On August 28 Frank Morse withdraws $8,000 from his personal bank account and deposits the money in the newly opened bank account of the law firm. He also invests $100 of office equipment in the business. He plans to open the law office on September 1, 19XX. With the help of his accountant, Frank begins to prepare his accounting records. Remember, we are analyzing the assets of a business, not the personal assets of Frank Morse.

Using accounting terminology, we say that (1) the law practice owns $8,100 worth of assets, in the form of cash and office equipment, and (2) Morse has the rights to the full $8,100 in assets, since no liabilities exist. (Remember, assets minus liabilities equals owner's equity.) We put this information into the basic accounting equation as follows:

Elements of the basic accounting equation.

The purpose of the accounting equation.

Assets
− Liabilities
= Owner's Equity

In accounting, capital does not mean cash. Capital is the owner's current investment, or equity, in the assets of the business.

FRANK MORSE
ATTORNEY AT LAW

ASSETS	= LIABILITIES +	OWNER'S EQUITY
Cash + Office Equipment =		**Frank Morse, Capital**
$8,000 + $100 =		$8,100
$8,100 = $8,100		

Note: **Capital is part of owner's equity; it is not an asset.**

Note that the total value of the assets, cash and office equipment—$8,100—is equal to the combined total value of liabilities (none, so far) and owner's equity ($8,100). Remember, Morse has supplied all the cash and office equipment, so he has the sole financial claim to the assets. Note how the heading "Frank Morse, Capital" is written under the owner's equity heading. The $8,100 is Morse's investment, or equity, in the assets of the law firm.

In our analyses, assume that any number without a sign in front of it is a +.

(B) Aug. 29: Law practice buys office equipment for cash, $300.

From the initial investment of $8,000 cash, the law firm buys $300 worth of office equipment for cash from Brooks Company. Keep in mind that equipment (such as a desk) lasts a long time, while supplies (such as pens) tend to be used up relatively quickly.

FRANK MORSE
ATTORNEY AT LAW

	ASSETS		= LIABILITIES +	OWNER'S EQUITY
	Cash + Office Equipment =			**Frank Morse, Capital**
BEGINNING BALANCE	$8,000 +	$100	=	$8,100
TRANSACTION	−300	+300		
ENDING BALANCE	$7,700 +	$400	=	$8,100
			$8,100 = $8,100	

Shift in Assets

As a result of the last transaction, the law office has less cash but has increased its amount of office equipment. This is called a **shift in assets**—the makeup of the assets has changed, but the total of the assets remains the same.

only causes left column to change

Suppose you go food shopping at the supermarket with $100 and spend $60. Now you have two assets, food and money. The composition of the assets has been *shifted*—you have more food and less money than you did—but the *total* of the assets has not increased or decreased. The total value of the food, $60, plus the cash, $40, is still $100. When you borrow money from the bank, on the other hand, you have an increase in cash (an asset) and an increase in liabilities; overall there is an increase in assets, not just a shift.

An accounting equation can remain in balance even if only one side is updated. The key point to remember is that the left-side total of assets must always equal the right-side total of liabilities and owner's equity.

> (C) Aug. 30: Buys additional office equipment on account, $400.

The law firm purchases an additional $400 worth of chairs and desks from Brooks Company. Instead of demanding cash right away, Brooks agrees to deliver the equipment and to allow up to sixty days for the law practice to pay the invoice (bill).

This liability, or obligation to pay in the future, has some interesting effects on the basic accounting equation. Brooks Company has accepted as payment a partial claim against the assets of the law practice. This claim exists until the law firm pays off the bill. This unwritten promise to pay the creditor is a liability called **accounts payable**.

When buying on Credit

FRANK MORSE
ATTORNEY AT LAW

	ASSETS		=	LIABILITIES	+	OWNER'S EQUITY
	Cash	+ Office Equipment	=	Accounts Payable	+	Frank Morse, Capital
BALANCE FORWARD	$7,700 +	$400	=			+ $8,100
TRANSACTION		+400		+$400		
ENDING BALANCE	$7,700 +	$800	=	$400		+ $8,100
			$8,500 = $8,500			

In analyzing this information, notice that the law practice has increased what it owes (accounts payable) as well as increased an asset (office equipment) by $400. The law practice gains $400 in an asset but has an obligation to pay Brooks Company at a future date.

Note that the owner's equity remains unchanged. This transaction results in an increase of total assets from $8,100 to $8,500.

Finally, note that after each transaction the basic accounting equation remains in balance.

Let us review the objectives of this unit. At this time, in your own words, you should be able to

1. List the functions of accounting.   (p. 2)
2. Compare and contrast bookkeeping and accounting.   (p. 2)
3. Explain the role of the computer as an accounting tool.   (p. 3)
4. State the purpose of the accounting equation.   (p. 4)
5. Explain the difference between liabilities and owner's equity.   (p. 4)
6. Define capital.   (p. 4)
7. Explain the difference between a shift in assets and an increase in assets.   (p. 5)

To test your understanding of this material, complete Self-Review Quiz 1-1. The blank forms you need are in the *Study Guide and Working Papers* for Chapter 1. The solution to the quiz immediately follows here in the text. If you have difficulty doing the problems, review Learning Unit 1-1 and the solution to the quiz. Videotapes are available to review these quizzes. Check with your instructor on availability.

Keep in mind that learning accounting is like learning to type—the more you practice, the better you become. You will not be an expert in one day. Be patient. It will all come together.

SELF-REVIEW QUIZ 1-1

Record the following transactions in the basic accounting equation:

1. John Sullivan invests $12,000 to begin a real estate office.
2. The real estate office buys computer equipment for cash, $400.
3. Buys additional computer equipment on account, $800.

SOLUTION TO SELF-REVIEW QUIZ 1-1

JOHN SULLIVAN REAL ESTATE

	ASSETS		= LIABILITIES	+ OWNER'S EQUITY
	Cash	+ Computer Equipment	= Accounts Payable	+ John Sullivan, Capital
1.	+$12,000			+$12,000
BALANCE	12,000		=	12,000
2.	−400	+$400		
BALANCE	11,600 +	400	=	12,000
3.		+800	+$800	
ENDING BALANCE	$11,600 +	$1,200	= $800	+ $12,000
		$12,800	= $12,800	

LEARNING UNIT 1-2

The Balance Sheet

Since Frank Morse's law firm plans to begin formal operations in September, there is a need to develop a report that will show, as of August 31, the following:

1. The amount of assets owned by the law practice.
2. The amount of claims (liabilities and owner's equity) against these assets.

This report is called a **balance sheet** or statement of financial position. The balance sheet (a report) presents the information from the ending balances of both sides of the accounting equation. Think of a balance sheet as a snapshot of the business's financial position taken on a particular date.

Let's look at the balance sheet of Frank Morse's law practice for August 31, 19XX, shown in Figure 1-1 (p. 8). The figures in the balance sheet come from the ending balances of the accounting equation for Morse's law practice as shown in Learning Unit 1-1.

Note that in Figure 1-1 the assets owned by Morse's practice appear on the left side and that liabilities and owner's equity appear on the right side. Both sides equal $8,500. This *balance* between left and right gives the balance sheet its name. In later chapters we will be looking at other ways to set up a balance sheet.

The balance sheet shows where we are now (in our example, at the end of August). This report shows us the financial position of the company as of a particular date.

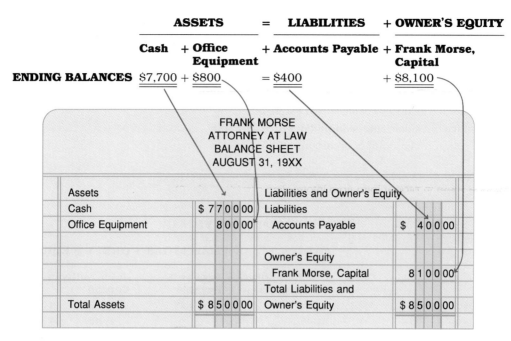

FIGURE 1-1   The Balance Sheet.

Points to Remember in Preparing a Balance Sheet

Point 1:   Note that the heading of the balance sheet answers the following three questions:

1. Who? The company's name: Frank Morse, Attorney at Law.
2. What? The name of the report: Balance Sheet.
3. When? As of a specific date, the date for which the report is prepared: August 31, 19XX.

Point 2:   In the balance sheet of Morse's law practice the dollar sign is not repeated each time a figure appears. Usually it is placed to the left of each column's top figure and to the left of the column's total.

Remember: The balance sheet is a formal report.

	FRANK MORSE ATTORNEY AT LAW BALANCE SHEET AUGUST 31, 19XX			
Assets				
Cash			$ 7 7 0 0	00
Office Equipment			8 0 0	00
Total Assets			$ 8 5 0 0	00

Do you remember the three elements that make up a balance sheet? Assets, liabilities, and owner's equity.

Point 3:   When adding numbers down a column, use a single line before the total and a double line beneath it. Also be careful to line the numbers up in the column; many errors occur because these figures are not lined up.

The balance sheet gives Frank Morse the information he needs to see the law firm's financial position before it opens for business. This information does not tell him, however, whether or not the firm will make a profit.

Let us review the objectives of Learning Unit 1-2. At this time you should be able to

1. Define and state the purpose of a balance sheet. (p. 7)
2. Identify and define the elements making up a balance sheet. (p. 8)
3. Show the relationship between the accounting equation and the balance sheet. (p. 8)
4. Prepare a balance sheet in proper form from information provided. (p. 8)

Now complete Self-Review Quiz 1-2. The solution follows. Remember that the *Study Guide and Working Papers* contains the forms needed to complete the quiz.

SELF-REVIEW QUIZ 1-2

The date is November 30, 19XX. Prepare in proper form a balance sheet for Downtown Electronics Company using the following information:

Accounts Payable	$25,000
Cash	3,000
A. Boone, Capital	8,000
Office Equipment	30,000

SOLUTION TO SELF-REVIEW QUIZ 1-2

DOWNTOWN ELECTRONICS COMPANY
BALANCE SHEET
NOVEMBER 30, 19XX

Assets		Liabilities and Owner's Equity	
Cash	$ 3 0 0 0 00	Liabilities	
Office Equipment	30 0 0 0 00	Accounts Payable	$25 0 0 0 00
		Owner's Equity	
		A. Boone, Capital	8 0 0 0 00
		Total Liabilities and	
Total Assets	$33 0 0 0 00	Owner's Equity	$33 0 0 0 00

Note: Capital does not mean cash. The capital amount is the owner's current investment of assets in the business. So Boone's $8,000 in capital means the owner may have supplied some cash and some equipment to the business.

LEARNING UNIT 1-3

The Accounting Equation Expanded: Revenue, Expenses, and Withdrawals

As soon as he opened his office, Morse began performing legal services for clients and earning revenue for his business. At the same time, as a part of doing business, he incurred various expenses, such as rent and utilities.

Morse asked his accountant to find out how to fit these transactions into the accounting equation. His accountant began by defining some terms.

1. When the law firm provides legal services to clients for legal fees, the business earns **revenue**. Revenue is a subdivision of owner's equity, so when revenue is earned, owner's equity is increased. Assets are also increased, either in the form of cash, if the client pays right away, or in the promise to pay in the future, which is called **accounts receivable**. When revenue is earned, the transaction is recorded as an increase in revenue and an increase in assets (either as cash or as accounts receivable, depending on whether it was paid right away or will be paid in the future).

2. In business there are also **expenses**, the costs the company incurs in carrying on operations in its effort to create revenue. Expenses are also a subdivision of owner's equity; when expenses are incurred, they *decrease* owner's equity. We can pay for expenses in cash or charge them.

3. When revenue totals more than expenses, **net income** is the result; when expenses total more than revenue, **net loss** is the result.

Before looking at the September transactions of Morse's law firm, we must explain one more element in the accounting equation. At some point Frank Morse may need to withdraw cash or other assets from the business to pay living or other personal expenses that do not relate to the business. The account title we will use to record these transactions is called **withdrawals**. Withdrawals is a subdivision of owner's equity that records personal expenses not related to the business. Withdrawals decrease owner's equity.

It is important to remember the difference between expenses and withdrawals. Expenses relate to business operations; withdrawals are the result of personal needs outside the normal operations of the business.

Let us now analyze the September transactions for Frank Morse's law firm, noting how we are using an **expanded accounting equation** to include withdrawals, revenue, and expenses.

(D) Sept. 1–30: Provided legal services for cash, $3,000.

Transactions A, B, and C were discussed earlier, when the law office was being formed in August. See Learning Unit 1-1.

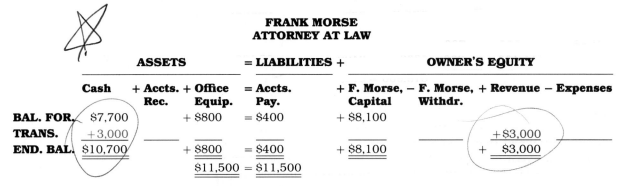

**FRANK MORSE
ATTORNEY AT LAW**

	ASSETS			= LIABILITIES +		OWNER'S EQUITY		
	Cash	+ Accts. Rec.	+ Office Equip.	= Accts. Pay.	+ F. Morse, Capital	− F. Morse, Withdr.	+ Revenue	− Expenses
BAL. FOR.	$7,700		+ $800	= $400	+ $8,100			
TRANS.	+3,000						+$3,000	
END. BAL.	$10,700		+ $800	= $400	+ $8,100		+ $3,000	
			$11,500 = $11,500					

In the law firm's first month of operation a total of $3,000 in cash was received for legal services performed. In the accounting equation the asset Cash is increased by $3,000. Revenue is also increased by $3,000, resulting in an increase in owner's equity. Notice the addition of a revenue column to the basic accounting equation. This new column will help the accountant in preparing financial reports.

Amounts are recorded in the revenue column when they are earned. They are also recorded in the assets column, either under Cash and/or under Accounts Receivable. Do not think of revenue as an asset. It is part of owner's equity. It is the revenue that creates an inward flow of cash and accounts receivable.

(E) Sept. 1–30: Provided legal services on account, $1,500.

When revenue is earned, it is recorded as an increase in owner's equity and an increase in assets.

FRANK MORSE
ATTORNEY AT LAW

	Cash	+ Accts. Rec.	+ Office Equip.	= Accts. Pay.	+ F. Morse, Capital	− F. Morse, Withdr.	+ Revenue	− Expenses
BAL. FOR.	$10,700		+$800	= $400	+ $8,100		+ $3,000	
TRANS.		+ $1,500					+1,500	
END. BAL.	$10,700	+ $1,500	+ $800	= $400	+ $8,100		+ $4,500	
			$13,000	= $13,000				

With headers: ASSETS / = LIABILITIES + / OWNER'S EQUITY

Frank Morse's law practice performed legal work on account for $1,500. The firm did not receive the cash for these earned legal fees; it accepted an unwritten promise from these clients that payment would be received in the future.

Remember: Accounts receivable results from earning revenue even when cash is not yet received.

(F) Sept. 1–30: Received $700 cash as partial payment from previous services performed on account.

FRANK MORSE
ATTORNEY AT LAW

	Cash	+ Accts. Rec.	+ Office Equip.	= Accts. Pay.	+ F. Morse, Capital	− F. Morse, Withdr.	+ Revenue	− Expenses
BAL. FOR.	$10,700	+ $1,500	+ $800	= $400	+ $8,100		+ $4,500	
TRANS.	+700	−700						
END. BAL.	$11,400	+ $ 800	+ $800	= $400	+ $8,100		+ $4,500	
			$13,000	= $13,000				

With headers: ASSETS / = LIABILITIES + / OWNER'S EQUITY

During September some of Morse's clients who had received services and promised to pay in the future decided to reduce what they owed the practice by $700 when their bills came due.

Note in the columns of the accounting equation that the law firm increased the asset Cash by $700 and reduced another asset, Accounts Receivable, by $700. The *total* of assets does not change. Also notice that the right-hand side of the expanded accounting equation has not been touched. The revenue was recorded when it was earned. *Do not record the same revenue twice.* This transaction is analyzing the situation *after* the revenue has been previously earned and recorded. What is really happening is a shifting of the composition of the assets—more cash and less accounts receivable.

Revenue is recorded *once*—when it is earned. In this situation no new revenue has been earned.

Since one asset (Cash) went up by $700 and another (Accounts Receivable) went down by $700, the total of the left side of the accounting equation has not changed at all. Therefore, the right side of the equation does not need to change.

(G) Paid salaries expense, $800.

**FRANK MORSE
ATTORNEY AT LAW**

	ASSETS			= LIABILITIES +		OWNER'S EQUITY		
	Cash	**+ Accts. Rec.**	**+ Office Equip.**	**= Accts. Pay.**	**+ F. Morse, Capital**	**− F. Morse, Withdr.**	**+ Revenue**	**− Expenses**
BAL. FOR.	$11,400	+ $800	+ $800	= $400	+ $8,100		+ $4,500	
TRANS.	−800							+$800
END. BAL.	$10,600	+ $800	+ $800	= $400	+ $8,100		+ $4,500	− $800
			$12,200	= $12,200				

As expenses increase, they decrease owner's equity. This incurred expense of $800 reduces the cash by $800. Although the expense was paid, the total of our expenses to date has *increased* by $800.

(H) Paid rent expense, $200.

**FRANK MORSE
ATTORNEY AT LAW**

	ASSETS			= LIABILITIES +		OWNER'S EQUITY		
	Cash	**+ Accts. Rec.**	**+ Office Equip.**	**= Accts. Pay.**	**+ F. Morse, Capital**	**− F. Morse, Withdr.**	**+ Revenue**	**− Expenses**
BAL. FOR.	$10,600	+ $800	+ $800	= $400	+ $8,100		+ $4,500	− $800
TRANS.	−200							+200
END. BAL.	$10,400	+ $800	+ $800	= $400	+ $8,100		+ $4,500	− $1,000
			$12,000	= $12,000				

During September the practice incurred rent expenses of $200. This rent was not paid in advance; it was paid when it came due. The payment of rent reduces the asset Cash by $200 as well as increases the expenses of the firm, resulting in a decrease in owner's equity. The firm's expenses are now $1,000.

(I) Incurred advertising expenses of $150, to be paid next month.

FRANK MORSE
ATTORNEY AT LAW

	ASSETS			= **LIABILITIES** +		**OWNER'S EQUITY**		
	Cash	+ **Accts. Rec.**	+ **Office Equip.**	= **Accts. Pay.**	+ **F. Morse, Capital**	− **F. Morse, Withdr.**	+ **Revenue**	− **Expenses**
BAL. FOR.	$10,400	+ $800	+ $800	= $400	+ $8,100		+ $4,500	− $1,000
TRANS.				+150				+150
END. BAL.	$10,400	+ $800	+ $800	= $550	+ $8,100		+ $4,500	− $1,150
			$12,000	= $12,000				

Frank Morse ran an ad in the local newspaper and incurred an expense of $150. Morse's expenses are thus increased by $150, which causes owner's equity to decrease. Since Morse has not paid the newspaper for the advertising yet, he *owes* them the $150 and, thus, his liabilities (Accounts Payable) increase by $150. Eventually, when the bill comes in and is paid, both Cash and Accounts Payable will be decreased.

(J) Morse withdrew $40 for personal use.

Record an expense when it is incurred, whether it is paid then or is to be paid later.

FRANK MORSE
ATTORNEY AT LAW

	ASSETS			= **LIABILITIES** +		**OWNER'S EQUITY**		
	Cash	+ **Accts. Rec.**	+ **Office Equip.**	= **Accts. Pay.**	+ **F. Morse, Capital**	− **F. Morse, Withdr.**	+ **Revenue**	− **Expenses**
BAL. FOR.	$10,400	+ $800	+ $800	= $550	+ $8,100		+ $4,500	− $1,150
TRANS.	−40					+$40		
END. BAL.	$10,360	+ $800	+ $800	= $550	+ $8,100	−$40	+ $4,500	− $1,150
			$11,960	= $11,960				

By taking $40 for personal use, Frank has *increased* his withdrawals from the business by $40 and the asset Cash in the business has been decreased by $40. Note that as withdrawals increase, they will *decrease* the owner's equity. Keep in mind that a withdrawal is *not* a business expense. It is a subdivision of owner's equity that records money or other assets an owner withdraws from the business for *personal* use.

Withdrawal decreases owner's equity.

Take a moment to review the subdivisions of owner's equity:

As capital increases, owner's equity increases
As withdrawals increase, owner's equity decreases
As revenue increases, owner's equity increases
As expenses increase, owner's equity decreases

Let us review the objectives of Learning Unit 1-3. At this time you should be able to

1. Define and explain the difference between revenue and expenses. (p. 10)
2. Define and explain the difference between net income and net loss. (p. 10)
3. Explain the subdivisions of owner's equity. (pp. 10–13)

4. Explain the effects of withdrawals, revenue, and expenses on owner's equity. (p. 13)

5. Record transactions in an expanded accounting equation and balance the basic accounting equation as a means of checking the accuracy of your calculations. (pp. 10–13)

Now complete Self-Review Quiz 1-3.

SELF-REVIEW QUIZ 1-3

Record the following transactions into the expanded accounting equation. Note that all titles have a beginning balance.

1. Received cash revenue, $2,000.
2. Billed customers for services rendered, $6,000.
3. Received a bill for telephone expenses (to be paid next month), $125.
4. Abby Ellen withdrew cash for personal use, $500.
5. Received $1,000 from customers in partial payment for services performed in transaction 2.

SOLUTION TO SELF-REVIEW QUIZ 1-3

ABBY ELLEN CO.

	ASSETS			= LIABILITIES +		OWNER'S EQUITY		
	Cash	+ Accts. Rec.	+ Clean. Equip.	= Accts. Pay.	+ A. Ellen, Capital	− A. Ellen, Withdr.	+ Revenue	− Expenses
BEG. BAL.	$10,000 +	$2,500 +	$6,500 =	$1,000	+ $11,800 −	$800	+ $9,000	− $2,000
1.	+2,000						+2,000	
BALANCE	12,000 +	2,500 +	6,500 =	1,000	+ 11,800 −	800	+ 11,000	− 2,000
2.		+6,000					+6,000	
BALANCE	12,000 +	8,500 +	6,500 =	1,000	+ 11,800 −	800	+ 17,000	− 2,000
3.				+125				+125
BALANCE	12,000 +	8,500 +	6,500 =	1,125	+ 11,800 −	800	+ 17,000	− 2,125
4.	−500					+500		
BALANCE	11,500 +	8,500 +	6,500 =	1,125	+ 11,800 −	1,300	+ 17,000	− 2,125
5.	+1,000	−1,000						
END. BAL.	$12,500 +	$7,500 +	$6,500 =	$1,125	+ $11,800 −	$1,300	+ $17,000	− $2,125

$26,500 = $26,500

LEARNING UNIT 1-4

Preparing Financial Reports

Frank Morse is in business to make money. To find out if the operation is making a profit, Morse asks his accountant how he can measure the financial performance of the law practice on a monthly basis. His accountant replies that there are a number of financial reports that he can prepare for Frank, one of which is the income statement, which shows how well the law firm has performed in a specific period of time. From the income statement, the accountant will get the information needed to prepare other reports.

THE INCOME STATEMENT

The income statement is prepared from data found in the revenue and expense columns of the expanded accounting equation.

The **income statement** is an accounting report that shows business results in terms of revenue and expenses. If revenues are greater than expenses, the result is net income. If expenses are greater than revenues, the result is net loss. An income statement can cover one, three, six, or twelve months, but never more than one year. The income statement is shown in Figure 1-2.

Points to Remember in Preparing an Income Statement

Point 1: Note that the heading of the income statement answers the following three questions:

1. Who? The company's name: Frank Morse, Attorney at Law
2. What? The name of the report: Income Statement
3. When? The period of time covered by the report: month of September. (Can be one, three, six, or twelve months; never more than a year. The report shows the results of all revenue and expenses throughout the entire period and not just as of a specific date.)

Point 2: As you can see on the income statement, the inside column of numbers ($800, $200, and $150) is used to subtotal all expenses ($1,150) before subtracting them from revenue ($4,500 − $1,150 = $3,350).

Point 3: Operating expenses may be listed in several ways: in alphabetical order, in order of largest amounts to smallest, or in a set order established by the accountant.

Point 4: Finally, as we noted with the balance sheet earlier, the dollar signs are not repeated for every number, but only for the first number in a column and the final total. A single line is used when adding numbers before the total and a double line beneath the total. As before, be careful to line the numbers up properly in the column to avoid errors in adding.

As we said, the income statement is a business report that shows business results in terms of revenue and expenses. But how does net income or net loss affect owner's equity? To find that out we have to look at a second type of report, the **statement of owner's equity**.

FIGURE 1-2
The Income Statement.

FRANK MORSE
ATTORNEY AT LAW
INCOME STATEMENT
FOR MONTH ENDED SEPTEMBER 30, 19XX

Revenue:		
Legal Fees		$ 4 5 0 0 00
Operating Expenses:		
Salaries Expense	$ 8 0 0 00	
Rent Expense	2 0 0 00	
Advertising Expense	1 5 0 00	
Total Operating Expenses		1 1 5 0 00
Net Income		$ 3 3 5 0 00

The inside column of numbers ($800, $200, $150) is used to subtotal all expenses ($1,150) before subtracting from revenue.

FRANK MORSE ATTORNEY AT LAW STATEMENT OF OWNER'S EQUITY FOR MONTH ENDED SEPTEMBER 30, 19XX		
Frank Morse, Capital, September 1, 19XX		$ 8 1 0 0 00
Net Income for September	$ 3 3 5 0 00	
Less Withdrawals for September	− 4 0 00	
Increase in Capital		3 3 1 0 00
Frank Morse, Capital, September 30, 19XX		$11 4 1 0 00

FIGURE 1-3
Statement of Owner's Equity.

THE STATEMENT OF OWNER'S EQUITY

The statement of owner's equity shows for a certain period of time what changes occurred in Frank Morse, Capital. The statement of owner's equity is shown in Figure 1-3.

The capital of Frank Morse can be

Increased by: Owner Investments   Net Income (Revenue − Expenses)
Decreased by: Owner Withdrawals   Net Loss

Keep in mind that a withdrawal is *not* a business expense and thus is not involved in the calculation of net income or net loss on the income statement. It appears on the statement of owner's equity. The statement of owner's equity summarizes the effects of all the subdivisions of owner's equity (revenue, expenses, withdrawals) on beginning capital. The ending capital figure of $11,410 will be the beginning figure in the next statement of owner's equity.

Suppose that Frank Morse's law firm had operated at a loss in the month of September. Suppose that instead of net income there was a net loss, and Frank also made an additional investment of $600 on September 15. This is how the statement would look if this had happened.

FRANK MORSE ATTORNEY AT LAW STATEMENT OF OWNER'S EQUITY FOR MONTH ENDED SEPTEMBER 30, 19XX		
Frank Morse, Capital, September 1, 19XX		$ 8 1 0 0 00
Additional Investment, September 15, 19XX		6 0 0 00
Total Investment for September		$ 8 7 0 0 00
Less: Net Loss for September	$ 3 5 0 00	
Withdrawals for September	4 0 00	
Decrease in Capital		3 9 0 00
Frank Morse, Capital, September 30, 19XX		$ 8 3 1 0 00

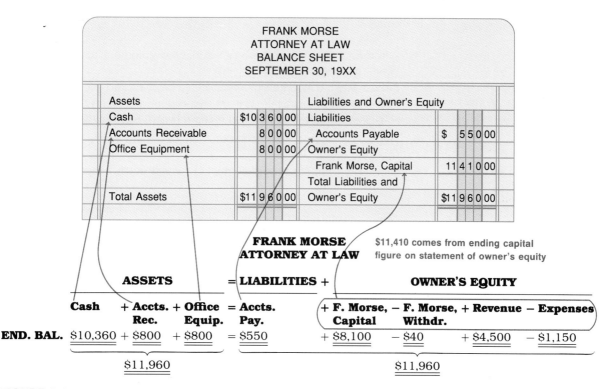

FIGURE 1-4   The Accounting Equation and the Balance Sheet.

In this chapter we have discussed three financial reports: the income statement, the statement of owner's equity, and the balance sheet.* Let us review what elements of the expanded accounting equation go into each report, and the usual order in which the reports are prepared. Figure 1-4 presents a diagram of the accounting equation and the balance sheet. Figure 1-5 summarizes the following three points:

If this statement of owner's equity is omitted, the information will be included in the owner's equity section of the balance sheet.

1. The income statement is prepared first; it includes revenues and expenses and shows net income or net loss. This net income or net loss is used to update the next report, the statement of owner's equity.

2. The statement of owner's equity is prepared second; it includes beginning capital and any additional investments, the net income or net loss shown on the financial statement, withdrawals, and the total, which is the **ending capital**. The ending capital is used on the third report, the balance sheet.

3. The balance sheet is prepared last; it includes the final balances of each of the elements listed in the accounting equation under Assets and Liabilities. The balance in Capital come from the statement of owner's equity.

FIGURE 1-5   What Goes on Each Financial Report.

	INCOME STATEMENT 1	STATEMENT OF OWNER'S EQUITY 2	BALANCE SHEET 3
assets			X
liabilities			X
capital† (beg)		X	
capital (end)		X	X
withdrawals		X	
revenues	X		
expenses	X		

† Note Additional Investments go on the Statement of Owner's Equity.

* There is a fourth report called the statement of cash flows that will not be covered at this time.

Let us review the objectives of Learning Unit 1-4. At this time you should be able to

1. Define and state the purpose of the income statement, the statement of owner's equity, and the balance sheet.   (p. 17)
2. Discuss why the income statement should be prepared first.   (p. 17)
3. Compare and contrast these three financial reports.   (p. 17)
4. Calculate a new figure for capital on the statement of owner's equity.   (p. 17)
5. Prepare an income statement, statement of owner's equity, and balance sheet. (pp. 15–17)
6. Show what happens on a statement of owner's equity if there is a net loss. (p. 16)

Now complete Self-Review Quiz 1-4.

SELF-REVIEW QUIZ 1-4

From the following balances for Assure Realty, prepare

1. Income statement for month ended November 30, 19XX.
2. Statement of owner's equity for month ended November 30, 19XX.
3. Balance sheet as of November 30, 19XX.

Cash	$4,730	Bill Ryan, Capital, November 1, 19XX	$5,000
Accounts Receivable	640	Bill Ryan, Withdrawals	100
Store Furniture	1,350	Commissions Earned	1,360
Accounts Payable	900	Rent Expense	200
		Advertising Expense	150
		Salaries Expense	90

SOLUTION TO SELF-REVIEW QUIZ 1-4

ASSURE REALTY
INCOME STATEMENT
FOR MONTH ENDED NOVEMBER 30, 19XX

Revenue:		
Commissions Earned		$ 1 3 6 0 00
Operating Expenses:		
Rent Expense	$ 2 0 0 00	
Advertising Expense	1 5 0 00	
Salaries Expense	9 0 00	
Total Operating Expenses		4 4 0 00
Net Income		$ 9 2 0 00

ASSURE REALTY
STATEMENT OF OWNER'S EQUITY
FOR MONTH ENDED NOVEMBER 30, 19XX

Bill Ryan, Capital, November 1, 19XX		$ 5 0 0 0 00
Net Income for November	$ 9 2 0 00	
Less Withdrawals for November	1 0 0 00	
Increase in Capital		8 2 0 00
Bill Ryan, Capital, November 30, 19XX		$ 5 8 2 0 00

```
                              ASSURE REALTY
                              BALANCE SHEET
                            NOVEMBER 30, 19XX

  Assets                          Liabilities and Owner's Equity
  Cash                 $ 4 7 3 0 00  Liabilities
  Accounts Receivable      6 4 0 00    Accounts Payable    $    9 0 0 00
  Store Furniture      1 3 5 0 00
                                     Owner's Equity
                                       Bill Ryan, Capital       5 8 2 0 00
                                     Total Liabilities and
  Total Assets         $ 6 7 2 0 00  Owner's Equity       $ 6 7 2 0 00
```

SUMMARY OF KEY POINTS AND KEY TERMS

LEARNING UNIT 1-1

1. The functions of accounting involve analyzing, recording, classifying, summarizing, and reporting financial information.

2. Bookkeeping is the recording part of accounting.

3. The computer is a tool to use in the accounting process.

4. Assets = Liabilities + Owner's Equity is the basic accounting equation that aids in analyzing business transactions.

5. Liabilities represent amounts owed to creditors while capital represents what is invested by the owner.

6. Capital does not mean cash. Capital is the owner's current investment. The owner could have invested equipment that was purchased before the new business was started.

7. In a shift of assets, the composition of assets changes, but the total of assets does not change. For example, if a bill is paid by a customer, the firm increases cash (an asset) but decreases accounts receivable (an asset), so there is no overall increase in assets; total assets remain the same. When you borrow money from the bank, on the other hand, you have an increase in cash (an asset) and an increase in liabilities; overall there is an increase in assets, not just a shift.

Revenue

Accounts payable: Amounts owed creditors that result from the purchase of goods or services on account; a liability.

Assets: Properties (resources) of value owned by a business (cash, supplies, equipment, land).

Basic accounting equation: Assets = Liabilities + Owner's Equity.

Bookkeeping: The recording function of the accounting process.

Business entity: In *accounting* it is assumed that a business is separate and distinct from the personal assets of the owner. Each unit or entity requires separate accounting functions.

Capital: The owner's investment or equity in the company.

Equities: The interest or financial claim of creditors (liabilities) and owners (owner's equity) who supply the assets to a firm.

Liabilities: Obligations that come due in the future. Liabilities result in increasing the financial rights or claims of creditors to assets.

Owner's equity: Rights or financial claims to the assets of a business (in the accounting equation, assets minus liabilities).

Shift in assets: A shift that occurs when the composition of the assets has changed, but the total of the assets remains the same.

Supplies: One type of asset acquired by a firm; has much shorter life than equipment.

LEARNING UNIT 1-2

1. The balance sheet is a report written as of a particular date. It lists the assets, liabilities, and owner's equity of a business. The heading of the balance sheet answers the questions Who, What, and When (as of a specific date).

2. The balance sheet is a formal report of a financial position.

Balance sheet: A report, as of a particular date, that shows the amount of assets owned by a business as well as the amount of claims (liabilities and owner's equity) against these assets.

LEARNING UNIT 1-3

1. Revenue generates an inward flow of assets. Expenses generate an outward flow of assets or a potential outward flow. Revenue and expenses are subdivisions of owner's equity. Revenue is not an asset.

2. When revenue totals more than expenses, net income is the result; when expenses total more than revenue, net loss is the result.

3. Owner's equity can be subdivided into four elements: capital, withdrawals, revenue, and expenses.

4. Withdrawals decrease owner's equity; revenue increases owner's equity; expenses decrease owner's equity. A withdrawal is *not* a business expense; it is for personal use.

Accounts receivable: An asset that indicates amounts owed by customers.

Expanded accounting equation: Assets = Liabilities + Capital − Withdrawals + Revenue − Expenses.

Expense: A cost incurred in running a business by consuming goods or services in producing revenue; a subdivision of owner's equity. When expenses *increase*, there is a *decrease* in owner's equity.

Net income: When revenue totals more than expenses, the result is net income.

Net loss: When expenses total more than revenue, the result is net loss.

Revenue: An amount earned by performing services for customers or selling goods to customers; can be in the form of cash and/or accounts receivable; a subdivision of owner's equity—as revenue increases, owner's equity increases.

Withdrawals: A subdivision of owner's equity that records money or other assets an owner withdraws from a business for personal use.

LEARNING UNIT 1-4

1. The income statement is a report written for a specific period of time that lists earned revenue and expenses incurred to produce the earned revenue. The net income or net loss will be used in the statement of owner's equity.

2. The statement of owner's equity reveals the causes of a change in capital. This report lists any investments, net income (or net loss), and withdrawals. The ending figure for capital will be used on the balance sheet.

3. The balance sheet uses some of the ending balances of assets and liabilities from the accounting equation and the capital from the statement of owner's equity.

4. The income statement should be prepared first because the information on it as to net income or net loss is used to prepare the statement of owner's equity, which in turn provides information about capital for the balance sheet. In this way one builds upon the next, and it begins with the income statement.

Ending capital: Beginning Capital + Additional Investments + Net Income − Withdrawals = Ending Capital. Or: Beginning Capital + Additional Investments − Net Loss − Withdrawals = Ending Capital.

Income statement: An accounting report that details the performance of a firm (revenue minus expenses) for a specific period of time.

Statement of owner's equity: A financial report that reveals the change in capital. The ending figure for capital is then placed on the balance sheet.

Blueprint of Financial Reports

1. Income Statement

Measuring performance

Revenue		XXX
Operating	XX	
Expenses	XX	XXX
Net Income		XXX

2. Statement of Owner's Equity

Calculating new figure for capital

Beginning Capital		XXX
Additional Investments		XXX
Total Investments		XXX
Net Income	XXX	
Less Withdrawals	XXX	
Increase in Capital		XXX
Ending Capital		XXX

3. Balance Sheet

Where do we now stand

Assets		Liabilities and Owner's Equity	
	XXX	Liabilities	XXX
	XXX	Owner's Equity	
	XXX	Ending Capital	XXX
Total Assets	XXX	Total Liab. + OE	XXX

DISCUSSION QUESTIONS

1. What are the functions of accounting?
2. What is the relationship of bookkeeping to accounting?
3. List the three elements of the basic accounting equation.
4. Define capital.
5. The total of the left side of the accounting equation must equal the total of the right side. True or false? Please explain.
6. A balance sheet tells a company where it is going and how well it will perform. True or false? Please explain.
7. Revenue is an asset. True or false? Please explain.

8. What is owner's equity subdivided into?

9. A withdrawal is a business expense. True or false? Please explain.

10. As expenses increase they cause owner's equity to increase. Defend or reject.

11. What does an income statement show?

12. The statement of owner's equity only calculates ending withdrawals. Defend or reject.

EXERCISES

1. Complete the following table:

The accounting equation.

ASSETS = LIABILITIES + OWNER'S EQUITY

A. $ 9,000 = ? + $2,000
B. ? = $2,000 + $8,000
C. $14,000 = $4,000 + ?

2. Record the following transactions in the basic accounting equation. Treat each one separately.

Recording transactions into the accounting equation.

ASSETS = LIABILITIES + OWNER'S EQUITY

A. Al invests $30,000 in company
B. Bought equipment for cash, $400
C. Bought equipment on account, $600

Preparing a balance sheet.

3. From the following, prepare a balance sheet for Ralph's Cleaners at the end of November 19XX: Cash, $19,000; Cleaning Equipment, $8,000; Accounts Payable, $7,000; A. Ralph, Capital,??

Recording transactions into the expanded accounting equation.

4. Record the following transactions into the expanded accounting equation. (A running balance may be omitted for simplicity.)

ASSETS			= LIABILITIES +	OWNER'S EQUITY			
Cash + Accounts Receivable	+ Computer Equipment		= Accounts Payable	+ Al Roe, Capital	– Al Roe, Withdrawals	+ Revenue	– Expenses

A. Al Roe invested $30,000 in the computer company.
B. Bought computer equipment on account, $8,000.
C. Al Roe paid personal telephone bill from company checkbook, $100.
D. Received fees for services rendered, $11,000.
E. Billed customers for services rendered for month, $40,000.
F. Paid current rent expense, $2,800.
G. Paid supplies expense, $1,400.

5. From the following account balances, prepare in proper form (a) an income statement for June, (b) a statement of owner's equity, and (c) a balance sheet for Katz Realty.

Preparing the income statement, statement of owner's equity, and balance sheet.

Cash	$2,000
Accounts Receivable	1,290
Office Equipment	6,700
Accounts Payable	2,000
Abby Katz, Capital, June 1	7,700
Abby Katz, Withdrawals	50
Professional Fees	1,700
Salaries Expense	500
Utilities Expense	360
Rent Expense	500

GROUP A PROBLEMS

1A-1. Jane Rang decided to open Jane's Realty. The following transactions resulted:

    A. Jane invested $14,000 cash from her personal bank account into the business.

    B. Bought equipment for cash, $1,500.

    C. Bought additional equipment on account, $900.

    D. Paid $500 cash to partially reduce what was owed from transaction C.

Based on the above information, record these transactions into the basic accounting equation.

The accounting equation.

1A-2. Ronda French is the accountant for Wells' Advertising Service. From the following information, her task is to construct a balance sheet as of September 30, 19XX, in proper form. Could you help her?

Preparing a balance sheet.

Cash	$16,000
Equipment	12,000
Building	18,000
Accounts Payable	25,000
Melissa Wells, Capital	21,000

1A-3. At the end of November, Alvin Hass decided to open his own typing service. Analyze the following transactions by recording their effects on the expanded accounting equation.

    A. Alvin Hass invested $15,000 in his typing service.

    B. Bought new office equipment on account, $6,000.

    C. Received cash for typing services rendered, $250.

    D. Performed typing services on account, $1,800.

    E. Paid secretary's salary, $450.

    F. Paid office supplies expense for the month, $190.

    G. Rent expense for office due but unpaid, $700.

    H. Alvin Hass withdrew cash for personal use, $300.

Recording transactions in the expanded accounting equation.

1A-4. Amy Peel, owner of Peel's Stenciling Service, has requested that you prepare from the following balances (a) an income statement for June 19XX, (b) a statement of owner's equity for June, and (c) a balance sheet as of June 30, 19XX.

Preparing an income statement, statement of owner's equity, and balance sheet.

Cash	$1,115
Accounts Receivable	280
Equipment	290
Accounts Payable	310
Amy Peel, Capital, June 1, 19XX	950
Amy Peel, Withdrawals	200
Stenciling Fees	1,550
Advertising Expense	110
Repair Expense	25
Travel Expense	350
Supplies Expense	190
Rent Expense	250

1A-5. Bob Fran, a retired army officer, opened Fran's Catering Service. As his accountant, analyze the transactions listed below and present to Mr. Fran the following information, in proper form.

Comprehensive problem.

    1. The analysis of the transactions by utilizing the expanded accounting equation.

    2. A balance sheet showing the position of the firm before opening on November 1, 19XX.

    3. An income statement for the month of November.

    4. A statement of owner's equity for November.

    5. A balance sheet as of November 30, 19XX.

Oct. 25 Bob Fran invested $15,000 in the catering business from his personal savings account.
   27 Bought equipment for cash from Munroe Co., $800.
   28 Bought additional equipment on account from Ryan Co., $700.
   29 Paid $400 to Ryan Co. as partial payment of the October 28 transaction.

(You should now prepare your balance sheet as of October 31, 19XX)

Nov. 1 Catered a graduation and immediately collected cash, $1,800.
    5 Paid salaries of employees, $650.
    8 Prepared desserts for customers on account, $180.
   10 Received $60 cash as partial payment of November 8 transaction.
   15 Paid telephone bill, $39.
   17 Fran paid his home electric bill from the company's checkbook, $69.
   20 Catered a wedding and received cash, $1,600.
   25 Bought additonal equipment on account, $150.
   28 Rent expense due but unpaid, $500.
   30 Paid supplies expense, $280.

GROUP B PROBLEMS

The accounting equation.

1B-1. Jane Rang began a new business called Jane's Realty. The following transactions resulted:

   A. Jane invested $17,000 cash from her personal bank account into the realty company.
   B. Bought equipment on account, $1,800.
   C. Paid $800 cash to partially reduce what was owed from transaction B.
   D. Purchased additional equipment for cash, $3,000.

Record these transactions into the basic accounting equation.

Preparing a balance sheet.

1B-2. Ronda French has asked you to prepare a balance sheet as of September 30, 19XX, for Wells' Advertising Service. Could you assist Ronda?

Melissa Wells, Capital	$19,000
Accounts Payable	70,000
Equipment	41,000
Building	16,000
Cash	32,000

Recording transactions in the expanded accounting equation.

Preparing an income statement, statement of owner's equity, and balance sheet.

1B-3. Alvin Hass decided to open his own typing service company at the end of November. Analyze the following transactions by recording their effects on the expanded accounting equation.

   A. Alvin Hass invested $9,000 in the typing service.
   B. Purchased new office equipment on account, $3,000.
   C. Received cash for typing services rendered, $1,290.
   D. Paid secretary's salary, $310.
   E. Billed customers for typing services rendered, $2,690.
   F. Paid rent expense for the month, $500.
   G. Alvin Hass withdrew cash for personal use, $350.
   H. Advertising expense due but unpaid, $100.

1B-4. Amy Peel, owner of Peel's Stenciling Service, has requested that you prepare from the following balances (a) an income statement for June 19XX, (b) a statement of owner's equity for June, and (c) a balance sheet as of June 30, 19XX.

Cash	$2,043
Accounts Receivable	1,140
Equipment	540
Accounts Payable	45
Amy Peel, Capital, June 1, 19XX	3,720
Amy Peel, Withdrawals	360

Stenciling Fees	1,098
Advertising Expense	135
Repair Expense	45
Travel Expense	90
Supplies Expense	270
Rent Expense	240

1B-5. Bob Fran, a retired army officer, opened Fran's Catering Service. As his accountant, analyze the transactions and present to Mr. Fran the following information, in proper form:

Comprehensive Problem.

1. The analysis of the transactions by utilizing the expanded accounting equation.
2. A balance sheet showing the financial position of the firm before opening on November 1, 19XX.
3. An income statement for the month of November.
4. A statement of owner's equity for November.
5. A balance sheet as of November 30, 19XX.

Oct. 25 Bob Fran invested $17,500 in the catering business.
27 Bought equipment on account from Munroe Co., $900.
28 Bought equipment for cash from Ryan Co., $1,500.
29 Paid $300 to Munroe Co. as partial payment of the October 27 transaction.

Nov. 1 Catered a business luncheon and immediately collected cash, $2,000.
5 Paid salaries of employees, $350.
8 Provided catering services to North West Community College on account, $4,500.
10 Received from North West Community College $1,000 cash as partial payment of November 8 transaction.
15 Paid telephone bill, $95.
17 Fran paid his home mortgage from the company's checkbook, $650.
20 Provided catering services and received cash, $1,800.
25 Bought additonal equipment on account, $300.
28 Rent expense due but unpaid, $750.
30 Paid supplies expense, $600.

PRACTICAL ACCOUNTING APPLICATION #1

You have just been hired to prepare, if possible, an income statement for the year ended December 31, 19XX, for Logan's Window Washing Company. The problem is that Bill Logan kept only the following records (on the back of a piece of cardboard).

Money in:
Window cleaning — $11,376
My investment — 1,200
Loan from brother in law — 4,000

Money out:
Salaries — $5,080
Withdrawals — 6,200
Supplies expense — 1,400

What I owe or they owe me
A. People that worked for me but I still owe Salaries to $1,800
B. Owe bank interest of $300
C. Work done but clients still owe me $2,900
D. Advertising bill due but not paid $95

Assume that Logan's Window Washing Company records all revenues when earned and all expenses when incurred.

PRACTICAL ACCOUNTING APPLICATION #2

While Jon Lune was on a business trip, he asked Abby Slowe, the bookkeeper for Lune Co., to try to complete a balance sheet for the year ended December 31, 19XX. Abby, who had been on the job only two months, submitted the following.

LUNE CO. FOR YEAR ENDED DECEMBER 31, 19XX					
Building	$44 6 0 0 00	Accounts Payable	$127 6 0 4 00
Land	72 9 3 5 00	Accounts Receivable	104 3 3 7 00
Notes Payable	75 3 2 8 00	Auto	14 2 6 8 00
Cash	10 0 1 6 00	Desks	6 8 2 5 00
J. Lune, Capital	?	Total Equity	$250 0 3 4 00

1. Could you help Abby fix as well as complete the balance sheet?
2. What recommendations would you make about the bookkeeper? Should she be retained?
3. Suppose that (a) Jon Lune invested an additional $20,000 in cash as well as additional desks with a value of $8,000, and (b) Lune Co. bought an auto for $6,000 that was originally marked $8,000, paying $2,000 down and issuing a note for the balance. Could you prepare an updated balance sheet? Assume that these two transactions occurred on January 4.

DEBITS AND CREDITS:
Analyzing
and Recording
Business Transactions

1. Setting up and organizing a chart of accounts. (p. 31)
2. Recording transactions in T accounts according to the rules of debit and credit. (p. 33)
3. Preparing a trial balance. (p. 40)
4. Preparing financial reports from a trial balance. (p. 43)

Can you imagine the problems IBM or Holiday Inn would have keeping track of their accounting records if they used the expanded accounting equation? Even though we used it in the last chapter with only a few transactions, the cash column quickly developed into a long list of pluses and minuses. There was no quick system of recording and summarizing the increases and decreases of cash or other items. Imagine how inefficient this accounting equation would become, and how much space it would require, as hundreds and thousands of transactions occurred. Luckily, there is a better way, as we will see in this next section.

Let's look at the problem a little more closely. Each business transaction is recorded in the accounting equation under a specific **account**. There are different accounts for each of the subdivisions of the accounting equation—there are asset accounts, liability accounts, expense accounts, revenue accounts, and so on. What is needed is a way to record the increases and decreases in specific account *categories* and yet keep them together in one place. And that is the subject of Learning Unit 2-1, The T Account.

LEARNING UNIT 2-1

The T Account

What we need is a way to record the increases and decreases of business transactions in specific account categories (such as salaries expense, advertising expense, and rent expense) and yet keep them together in one place. The answer is the **standard account** form (see Figure 2-1). In this system, each account has a separate form. All transactions affecting that account are recorded on the form. All the account forms are then placed in a **ledger**, which may be in the form of a bound or a loose-leaf book.

FIGURE 2-1
The Standard Account Form.

Account Title							Account No.	
Date	Item	PR	Debit	Date	Item	PR	Credit	

Each page of the ledger contains one account, along with an assigned account number. Where computers are used, the ledger may be part of a computer printout.

We will talk more about account forms and ledgers in the next chapter. Here, for simplicity's sake, we will use the **T account** form, so called because it looks like the letter T.

Each T account contains three basic parts:

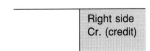

All T accounts have this structure. In accounting, the left side of any T account is called the **debit side**.

```
Left side
Dr. (debit)
```

Debit **defined:**
1. **The** *left* **side of any account.**
2. **A number entered on the left side of any account is said to be** *debited* **to an account.**

Just as the word *left* has many meanings, the word *debit* for now in accounting means a position, the left side of an account. Don't think of it as good (+) or bad (−).

Amounts entered on the left side of any account are said to be *debited* to an account. The abbreviation for debit (Dr.) is from the Latin *debere*.

The right side of any T account is called the **credit** side.

```
Right side
Cr. (credit)
```

Credit **defined:**
1. **The right side of any account.**
2. **A number entered on the right side of an account is said to be** *credited* **to an account.**

Amounts entered on the right side of an account are said to be *credited* to an account. The abbreviation for credit (Cr.) is from the Latin *credere*.

Note: At this point do not associate the definition of debit and credit with the words *increase* or *decrease*. Think of debit or credit as only indicating a *position* (left side or right side) of a T account.

BALANCING AN ACCOUNT

A T account with no heading follows. The heading is omitted to emphasize that, no matter which individual account is being balanced, the procedure used to balance it will be the same.

Dr.		Cr.	
4/2	2,000	4/3	200
4/20	300	4/25	300
	2,300		500
Bal. 1,800			

Notice that on the debit (left) side the numbers add up to $2,300. On the credit (right) side the numbers add up to $500. The numbers 4/2, 4/20, 4/3, and 4/25 are the dates when the amounts were debited or credited.

The $2,300 and the $500 written in small type are called **footings**. These figures help us calculate the new balance of $1,800. This is called the ending balance. Notice that the ending balance, $1,800, is placed on the debit or left side, since the balance of the debit side is greater than that of the credit side.

Remember, the ending balance of $1,800 does not tell us anything about increase or decrease. What it does tell us is that we have an ending balance of $1,800 on the debit side.

Footings aid in balancing an account. The ending balance is the difference between the footings.

Let us review the objectives of Learning Unit 2-1. At this time you should be able to

1. Define ledger. (p. 28)
2. State the purpose of a T account. (p. 29)
3. Identify the three parts of a T account. (p. 29)
4. Define debit. (p. 29)
5. Define credit. (p. 29)
6. Explain footings and calculate the balance of an account. (p. 30)

Now Complete Self-Review Quiz 2-1.

SELF-REVIEW QUIZ 2-1

Respond True or False to the following:

1.

Dr.	Cr.
2,000	100
50	50

The balance of the account is $1,900 (Cr.)

should be Dr. because balance of Dr side is greater

2. A credit always means increase.
3. A debit is the left side of any account.
4. A ledger can be prepared manually or by computer.
5. Footings replace the need for debits and credits.

SOLUTIONS TO SELF-REVIEW QUIZ 2-1

1. False **2.** False **3.** True **4.** True **5.** False

LEARNING UNIT 2-2

Recording Business Transactions: Debits and Credits

Do you drive your car on the left-hand side of the road? Do you drive through red lights? Can you get a queen in checkers? In a baseball game does a runner rounding first base skip second base and run over the pitcher's mound to get to third? No—most of us don't do such things because we follow the rules. Usually we learn the rules first and reflect on the reasons for them afterward. Think back on how you first learned to play the game of Monopoly.

Instead of first trying to understand all the rules of debit and credit and how they were developed in accounting, it will be easier to "play the game" first and then reflect on the whys.

ACCOUNT CATEGORY	INCREASE	DECREASE	NORMAL BALANCE
Assets	Debit	Credit	Debit
Liabilities	Credit	Debit	Credit
Owner's Equity			
Capital	Credit	Debit	Credit
Withdrawals	Debit	Credit	Debit
Revenue	Credit	Debit	Credit
Expenses	Debit	Credit	Debit

The rules of debit and credit are arbitrary. The rules will aid us in recording information in the ledger.

FIGURE 2-2
Rules of Debit and Credit.

Have patience. Learning the rules of debit and credit is like learning to play any game—the more you play, the easier it will become. Figure 2-2 shows the rules for the side on which you enter an increase or a decrease for each of the separate accounts in the accounting equation. For example, an increase is entered on the debit side in the asset account, but on the credit side for a liability account.

A **normal balance of an account** is the side that increases by the rules of debit and credit. For example, the normal balance of cash is a debit balance, because an asset is increased by a debit. In Chapter 3 we will discuss normal balance further.

It might be easier to visualize these rules of debit and credit if we show them in the T account form, using + to show increase and − to show decrease.

ASSETS	= LIABILITIES +		OWNER'S EQUITY			
			Capital −	**Withdrawals** +	**Revenue** −	**Expenses**
Dr. | Cr.	Dr. | Cr.	+	Dr. | Cr.	Dr. | Cr.	Dr. | Cr.	Dr. | Cr.
+ | −	− | +		− | +	+ | −	− | +	+ | −

Insight to the rules: First of all, note that the rules for assets work in the opposite direction to those for liabilities. As for owner's equity, the rules for withdrawals and expenses, which decrease owner's equity, work in the opposite direction to the rules for capital and revenue, which increase owner's equity.

Second, it is important to remember that any amount(s) entered on the debit side of a T account or accounts must also be entered on the credit side of another T account or accounts. This will make certain that the total amount added to the debit side will equal the total amount added to the credit side, thereby keeping the accounting equation in balance.

Our job now is to analyze Frank Morse's business transactions—the transactions we looked at in Chapter 1—using a system of accounts guided by the rules of debits and credits that will summarize increases and decreases of individual accounts in the ledger. The goal is to prepare an income statement, statement of owner's equity, and balance sheet for Frank Morse. Sound familiar? If this system works, the rules of debits and credits and the use of accounts will provide us with the same answers as in Chapter 1, but with greater ease and accuracy.

The accountant for Morse developed what is called a **chart of accounts** (see Figure 2-3). The chart of accounts is a numbering system for all Morse's accounts. It allows Morse to locate and identify accounts quickly; for example, 100s are assets, 200s are liabilities, and so on. As companies grow or as changes occur, the chart may be expanded as needed.

The chart of accounts aids in locating and identifying accounts quickly.

Balance Sheet Accounts

1. Assets
111 Cash
112 Accounts Receivable
121 Office Equipment

2. Liabilities
211 Accounts Payable

3. Owner's Equity
311 Frank Morse, Capital
312 Frank Morse, Withdrawals

Large companies may have up to four digits assigned to each title.

Income Statement Accounts

4. Revenue
411 Legal Fees

5. Expenses
511 Salaries Expense
512 Rent Expense
513 Advertising Expense

FIGURE 2-3   Chart of Accounts for Frank Morse, Attorney at Law.

In the next section we will present a handy chart to use for analyzing these transactions more easily.

THE TRANSACTION ANALYSIS: FIVE STEPS*

There are five steps to analyzing each business transaction of Frank Morse's law practice. We will use a device called a *transaction analysis chart* to record these five steps. (Please keep in mind that the transaction analysis chart is a *teaching device*, not part of any formal accounting system.) The five steps include determining the following:

Steps to analyze and record transactions. Note: Steps 1 and 2 will come from the chart of accounts.

1. Which accounts are affected? Example: cash, accounts payable, rent expense. A transaction always has at least two accounts affected, but may have more.
2. Which categories do the accounts belong to? You have six choices: assets, liabilities, capital, withdrawals, revenue, and expenses. Example: cash is an asset.
3. Are the accounts increasing or decreasing? Example: If you receive cash, that account is increasing.
4. What is the rule? Go to rule chart. (p. 31)

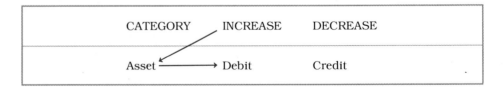

5. Where do the amounts belong? Place amounts into accounts (in our case, T accounts) either on the left or right side depending on the rules from the rule chart.

Note again that every transaction affects at least two T accounts, and that the total amount added to the debit side(s) must equal the total amount added to the credit side(s) of the T accounts of each transaction.

ANALYSIS OF TRANSACTIONS OF FRANK MORSE'S LAW PRACTICE

> (A) August 28: Frank Morse invests $8,000 cash and $100 of office equipment in the business.

The transaction analysis chart is a teaching technique to aid you in learning how to record debits and credits.

1 Accounts Affected	2 Category	3* ↓ ↑	4 Rules	5 Appearance of T Accounts
Cash	Asset	↑	Dr.	Cash 111 (A) 8,000
Office Equipment	Asset	↑	Dr.	Office Equipment 121 (A) 100
Frank Morse, Capital	Capital	↑	Cr.	Frank Morse, Capital 311 8,100 (A)

Note: ↑ means increase, ↓ means decrease.

Let us go through the transaction analysis for this transaction step by step:

Note in column 3 of the chart: It doesn't matter if both arrows go up, as long as the sum of the debits equals the sum of the credits in the T accounts in column 5.

1. Which accounts are affected? The law firm receives cash and office equipment. Are other accounts involved in this transaction? The law firm receives cash and office equipment through Frank Morse's investment, so a third account is involved—Frank Morse, Capital. Note these titles come from the chart of accounts.
2. Which categories do these accounts belong to? (The categories are assets, liabilities, capital, withdrawals, revenue, or expenses.) Cash and office equipment are assets and Frank Morse, Capital, is capital.
3. Are the accounts increasing or decreasing? The cash and office equipment, both assets, are increasing in the business. The rights or claims of Frank Morse, Capital, are also increasing, since he invested money and office equipment in the business.
4. What do the rules say? According to the rules of debit and credit, an increase in assets (cash and office equipment) is a debit. An increase in capital is a credit. Note that the total dollar amount of debits will equal the total dollar amount of credits when T accounts are updated in column 5.
5. Where do the amounts belong? Place the amounts into the T accounts. Enter the amount for cash and office equipment on the debit side and the amount for Frank Morse, Capital, on the credit side.

If a transaction involves more than one credit or more than one debit we call it a **compound entry**. This first transaction of Frank Morse's law firm is a compound entry; it involves a debit of $8,000 to Cash and a debit of $100 to Office Equipment (as well as a credit of $8,100 to Frank Morse, Capital).

Let us now emphasize a major point: *Do not try to debit or credit an account until you have gone through the first three steps of the transaction analysis:*

1. Which accounts are affected (from the chart of accounts)?
2. Which categories do the accounts belong to (Assets, Liabilities, Capital, Withdrawals, Revenue, Expenses)?
3. Are the accounts increasing or decreasing?

Having completed these steps, go to the rules of debit and credit before updating the individual accounts.

As we continue, the explanations will be brief, but do not forget to apply the five steps in analyzing and recording each business transaction.

> The rules of debit and credit only tell us on which side to place information. Whether the debit or credit represents increases or decreases depends on the account category—assets, liabilities, capital, etc. Think of a business transaction as an exchange—you get something and you give or part with something.

(B) August 29: Law practice bought office equipment for cash, $300.

---

1 Accounts Affected	2 Category	3 ↑ ↓	4 Rules	5 T Account Update
Office Equipment	Asset	↑	Dr.	Office Equipment 121 (A) 100 (B) 300
Cash	Asset	↓	Cr.	Cash 111 (A) 8,000 300 (B)

Analysis of Transaction B

1. What did the law firm receive? Office equipment. How did the firm get it? It paid cash. These are the accounts involved in the transaction.
2. Which categories do the accounts belong to? Office Equipment is an asset. Cash is an asset.
3. Are the accounts increasing or decreasing? The asset Office Equipment is increasing. The asset Cash is decreasing—it is being reduced in order to buy the office equipment.
4. What is the rule? An increase in the asset Office Equipment is a debit; a decrease in the asset Cash is a credit.
5. Where do the amounts belong? Place the amounts into the T accounts. Enter the amount for office equipment on the debit side and the amount for cash on the credit side.

(C) August 30: Bought more office equipment on account, $400.

---

1 Accounts Affected	2 Category	3 ↑ ↓	4 Rules	5 T Account Update
Office Equipment	Asset	↑	Dr.	Office Equipment 121 (A) 100 (B) 300 (C) 400
Accounts Payable	Liability	↑	Cr.	Accounts Payable 211 400 (C)

Analysis of Transaction C

1. The law firm receives office equipment by promising to pay in the future. An obligation or liability, Accounts Payable, is created.
2. Office Equipment is an asset. Accounts Payable is a liability.
3. The asset Office Equipment is increasing; the liability Accounts Payable is increasing because the law firm is increasing what it owes.
4. An increase in the asset Office Equipment is a debit. An increase in the liability Accounts Payable is a credit.
5. Enter the amount for office equipment on the debit side and the amount for the accounts payable on the credit side.

(D) September 1–30: Provided legal services for cash, $3,000.

---

1 Accounts Affected	2 Category	3 ↑ ↓	4 Rules	5 T Account Update
Cash	Asset	↑	Dr.	Cash 111 (A) 8,000 | 300 (B) (D) 3,000
Legal Fees	Revenue	↑	Cr.	Legal Fees 411 | 3,000 (D)

Analysis of Transaction D

1. The firm has earned revenue from legal services and receives $3,000 in cash.
2. Cash is an asset. Legal Fees are revenue.
3. Cash, an asset, is increasing. Legal Fees, or revenue, are also increasing.
4. An increase in Cash, an asset, is debited. An increase in Legal Fees, or revenue, is credited.

(E) September 1–30: Provided legal services on account, $1,500.

---

1 Accounts Affected	2 Category	3 ↑ ↓	4 Rules	5 T Account Update
Accounts Receivable	Asset	↑	Dr.	Accounts Receivable 112 (E) 1,500 |
Legal Fees	Revenue	↑	Cr.	Legal Fees 411 | 3,000 (D) | 1,500 (E)

Analysis of Transaction E

1. The law practice has earned revenue but has not yet received payment (cash). The amounts owed by these clients are called accounts receivable. Revenue is

earned at the time the legal services are provided, whether payment is received then or will be received sometime in the future.

2. Accounts Receivable is an asset. Legal Fees are revenue.

3. Accounts Receivable is increasing because the law practice has increased the amount owed to it for legal fees that have been earned but not paid. Legal Fees or revenue are increasing.

4. An increase in the asset Accounts Receivable is a debit. An increase in revenue is a credit.

(F) September 1–30: Received $700 cash from clients for services rendered previously on account.

---

1 Accounts Affected	2 Category	3 ↑ ↓	4 Rules	5 T Account Update	
Cash	Asset	↑	Dr.	**Cash 111**	
				(A) 8,000 (D) 3,000 (F) 700	300 (B)
Accounts Receivable	Asset	↓	Cr.	**Accounts Receivable 112**	
				(E) 1,500	700 (F)

Analysis of Transaction F

1. The law firm collects $700 in cash from previous revenue earned. Since the revenue is recorded at the time it is earned, and not when the payment is made, in this transaction we are concerned only with the payment, which affects the Cash and Accounts Receivable accounts.

2. Cash is an asset. Accounts Receivable is an asset.

3. Since clients are paying what is owed, cash (asset) is increasing and the amount owed (accounts receivable) is decreasing (the total amount owed by clients to Morse is going down). This transaction results in a shift in assets, more cash for less accounts receivable.

4. An increase in Cash, an asset, is a debit. A decrease in Accounts Receivable, an asset, is a credit.

(G) September 1–30: Paid salaries expense, $800.

---

1 Accounts Affected	2 Category	3 ↑ ↓	4 Rules	5 T Account Update	
Salaries Expense	Expense	↑	Dr.	**Salaries Expense 511**	
				(G) 800	
Cash	Asset	↓	Cr.	**Cash 111**	
				(A) 8,000 (D) 3,000 (F) 700	300 (B) 800 (G)

Analysis of Transaction G

1. The law firm pays $800 worth of salaries expense by cash.
2. Salaries Expense is an expense. Cash is an asset.
3. The salaries expense of the law firm is increasing, which results in a decrease in cash.
4. An increase in Salaries Expense, an expense, is a debit. A decrease in Cash, an asset, is a credit.

(H) September 1–30: Paid rent expense, $200.

---

1 Accounts Affected	2 Category	3 ↑ ↓	4 Rules	5 T Account Update
Rent Expense	Expense	↑	Dr.	Rent Expense 512
				(H) 200
Cash	Asset	↓	Cr.	Cash 111

Cash 111
(A) 8,000	300 (B)
(D) 3,000	800 (G)
(F) 700	200 (H)

Analysis of Transaction H

1. The law firm rent expenses are paid in cash.
2. Rent is an expense. Cash is an asset.
3. The rent expense increases the expenses, and the payment for the rent expense decreases the cash.
4. An increase in Rent Expense, an expense, is a debit. A decrease in Cash, an asset, is a credit.

(I) September 1–30: Received a bill for Advertising Expense (to be paid next month), $150.

---

1 Accounts Affected	2 Category	3 ↑ ↓	4 Rules	5 T Account Update
Advertising Expense	Expense	↑	Dr.	Advertising Expense 513
				(I) 150
Accounts Payable	Liability	↑	Cr.	Accounts Payable 211

Accounts Payable 211
	400 (C)
	150 (I)

Analysis of Transaction I

1. The advertising bill has come in and payment is due but has not yet been made. Therefore the accounts involved here are Advertising Expense and Accounts Payable; the expense has created a liability.

2. Advertising Expense is an expense. Accounts Payable is a liability.

3. Both the expense and the liability are increasing.

4. An increase in an expense is a debit. An increase in a liability is a credit.

(J) Morse withdrew cash for personal use, $40.

---

1 Accounts Affected	2 Category	3 ↑↓	4 Rules	5 T Account Update
Frank Morse, Withdrawals	Withdrawals	↑	Dr.	Frank Morse, Withdrawals 312
				(J) 40
Cash	Asset	↓	Cr.	Cash 111
				(A) 8,000 300 (B)
				(D) 3,000 800 (G)
				200 (H)
				(F) 700 40 (J)

Analysis of Transaction J

1. Morse withdraws cash from business for *personal* use. This withdrawal is not a business expense.

2. This transaction affects Withdrawal and Cash accounts.

3. Morse has increased what he has withdrawn from the business for personal use. The business cash has been decreased.

4. An increase in withdrawals is a debit. A decrease in cash is a credit. (*Remember:* Withdrawals go on the statement of owner's equity; expenses go on the income statement.)

Let us review the objectives of Learning Unit 2-2. At this time you should be able to

1. State the rules of debit and credit. (p. 31)
2. Explain the difference between an expense and a withdrawal. (p. 31)
3. List the five steps of a transaction analysis. (p. 32)
4. Show how to fill out a transaction analysis chart. (p. 33)

Now complete Self-Review Quiz 2-2.

Withdrawals are always increased by debits.

SELF-REVIEW QUIZ 2-2

Revon Company uses the following accounts from its chart of accounts: Cash (111), Accounts Receivable (112), Equipment (121), Accounts Payable (211), Ann Roe, Capital (311), Ann Roe, Withdrawals (312), Professional Fees (411), Utilities Expense (511), and Salaries Expense (512).

Record the following transactions into transaction analysis charts.

A. Ann Roe invested in the business $400 cash and equipment worth $500 from her personal assets.

B. Billed clients for services rendered, $8,000.

C. Utilities bill due but unpaid, $90.

D. Ann Roe withdrew cash for personal use, $50.

E. Paid salaries expense, $100.

SOLUTION TO SELF-REVIEW QUIZ 2-2

A.

1 Accounts Affected	2 Category	3 ↑ ↓	4 Rules	5 T Account Update
Cash	Asset	↑	Dr.	Cash 111 (A) 400 |
Equipment	Asset	↑	Dr.	Equipment 121 (A) 500 |
Ann Roe, Capital	Capital	↑	Cr.	Ann Roe, Capital 311 | (A) 900

B.

1 Accounts Affected	2 Category	3 ↑ ↓	4 Rules	5 T Account Update
Accounts Receivable	Asset	↑	Dr.	Acc. Rec. 112 (B) 8,000 |
Professional Fees	Revenue	↑	Cr.	Prof. Fees 411 | (B) 8,000

C.

1 Accounts Affected	2 Category	3 ↑ ↓	4 Rules	5 T Account Update
Utilities Expense	Expense	↑	Dr.	Utilities Exp. 511 (C) 90 |
Accounts Payable	Liability	↑	Cr.	Acct. Pay. 211 | (C) 90

D.

1 Accounts Affected	2 Category	3 ↑ ↓	4 Rules	5 T Account Update
Ann Roe, Withdrawals	Withdrawals	↑	Dr.	Ann Roe, Withd. 312 (D) 50 |
Cash	Asset	↓	Cr.	Cash 111 (A) 400 | (D) 50

E.

1 Accounts Affected	2 Category	3 ↑ ↓	4 Rules	5 T Account Update
Salaries Expense	Expense	↑	Dr.	Salaries Expense 512 (E) 100 |
Cash	Asset	↓	Cr.	Cash 111 (A) 400 | (D) 50 | (E) 100

The Trial Balance and Preparation of Financial Reports

Let us now look at all the transactions we have discussed, arranged by T accounts and recorded using the rules of debit and credit.

Cash 111	
(A) 8,000	300 (B)
(D) 3,000	800 (G)
(F) 700	200 (H)
11,700	40 (J)
10,360	1,340

Accounts Receivable 112	
(E) 1,500	700 (F)
800	

Office Equipment 121	
(A) 100	
(B) 300	
(C) 400	
800	

Accounts Payable 211	
	400 (C)
	150 (I)
	550

Frank Morse, Capital 311	
	8,100 (A)

Frank Morse, Withdrawals 312	
(J) 40	

Legal Fees 411	
	3,000 (D)
	1,500 (E)
	4,500

Salaries Expense 511	
(G) 800	

Rent Expense 512	
(H) 200	

Advertising Expense 513	
(I) 150	

Double-entry bookkeeping system: the *total* of all debits is equal to the *total* of all credits.

As mentioned earlier, the ending balance of cash, $10,360, is a *normal balance* because it is on the side that increases the asset account.

Notice how this grouping of accounts gives a much better organization than the expanded accounting equation. As previously mentioned, and as shown in each of the transactions analyzed in the past unit, the total of all the debits must be equal to the total of all the credits (columns 4 and 5 of the transaction analysis chart). For example, when Morse invested $8,100 in the business, the debits ($8,000 to Cash and $100 to Office Equipment) were equal to the credit ($8,100 to Frank Morse, Capital). This double-entry analysis of transactions, where two or more accounts are affected and the total of debits and credits is equal, is called **double-entry bookkeeping**. This double-entry system helps in checking the recording of business transactions.

When all the transactions are recorded in the accounts, the total of all the debits should be equal to the total of all the credits.

THE TRIAL BALANCE

As discussed earlier, *footings* are used to obtain the balance of each side of each T account (unless there is only one entry in the account, and then there is no need for a footing). Then the *ending balance* is found. For example, in

Lori Lievre:
Full-Charge Bookkeeper

Lori Lievre started out to be a secretary, but, she says, "I really didn't like the work at all. When I was working for a major supermarket chain, I was put in charge of the books. Even though I didn't know much about bookkeeping, I learned that I loved to work with numbers. But I was very slow because I didn't have the background. So I decided to *get* a background in the field."

At Nassau Community College, Lori found a 1-year certificate program in accounting that had evening classes. She studied bookkeeping, college accounting, business writing, economics, and other subjects. "The certificate program helped me enormously," she says. "It gave me the theoretical background I needed. I was working by intuition before. The courses taught me to think things through and follow correct procedures. They also built up my confidence. I know what I'm talking about, and I use the right terminology."

Now working as a full-charge bookkeeper for a paper-converting company in Long Island, New York, Lori goes through all journals, including cash receipts, disbursements, sales, receivables, payables, and expenses. "I love this job," Lori says. "I got it through an employment agency, and one of the best things about it is that I get to do so many different things."

What advice does Lori offer to people starting out in a college accounting course? "If you're working in bookkeeping already, a course like this can be a lifesaver. It fills in the gaps in your knowledge. If you don't have a job in the field yet, the course gives you a combination of practical skills and a strong theoretical foundation. It gives you a sense of what you will be doing in the future. It really does prepare you for the workplace."

the Cash account, the footing for the debit side is $11,700 and the footing for the credit side is $1,340. Since the debit side is larger, we subtract $1,340 from $11,700 to arrive at an *ending balance* of $10,360. When this has been done for all the accounts, we should be able to show that the total of all debits equals the total of all credits. To do this we prepare a **trial balance**, which is a listing of all the accounts in the ledger with their ending balances.

A trial balance of Frank Morse's accounts is shown in Figure 2-4 (p. 42). Keep in mind that the trial balance is *not* a formal report. It is used as an aid in preparing the financial statement and in proving the accuracy of the recording of transactions into accounts. The trial balance lists all the accounts with their balances in the same order as they appear in the chart of accounts. Keep in mind that the figure for capital might not be the beginning figure if any additional investment has taken place during the period. You can tell this by looking at the capital account in the ledger.

A more detailed discussion of the trial balance will be provided in the next chapter. For now, notice the heading, how the accounts are listed, the debits in the left column, the credits in the right, and the fact that the total of debits is equal to the total of credits. Note also that since this is not a

FRANK MORSE
ATTORNEY AT LAW
TRIAL BALANCE
SEPTEMBER 30, 19XX

	Dr.	Cr.
Cash	10 3 6 0 00	
Accounts Receivable	8 0 0 00	
Office Equipment	8 0 0 00	
Accounts Payable		5 5 0 00
Frank Morse, Capital		8 1 0 0 00
Frank Morse, Withdrawals	4 0 00	
Legal Fees		4 5 0 0 00
Salaries Expense	8 0 0 00	
Rent Expense	2 0 0 00	
Advertising Expense	1 5 0 00	
Totals	13 1 5 0 00	13 1 5 0 00

FIGURE 2-4   A Trial Balance.

formal report, there is no need to use dollar signs; however, the single and double lines under subtotals and final totals are still used for clarity.

From the trial balance we can now go on to prepare the financial reports.

PREPARING FINANCIAL REPORTS

In Chapter 1 we prepared financial reports using the expanded accounting equation. Now look at the diagram in Figure 2-5 carefully. It shows how financial reports can be prepared from a trial balance. A key point to remember is that *there are no debit or credit columns on financial reports.* The information is entered in the ledger by debits and credits to eventually supply the amounts (ending balances) needed to prepare financial reports, but the financial reports themselves do not use debit or credit columns. The left columns are used only to subtotal numbers.

At this point you should be able to

1. Explain double-entry bookkeeping.   (p. 40)
2. Explain the role of footings.   (p. 40)
3. Prepare a trial balance from a set of accounts.   (p. 41)
4. Prepare financial reports from a trial balance.   (p. 43)

Now complete Self-Review Quiz 2-3.

SELF-REVIEW QUIZ 2-3

As the bookkeeper of Mel's Hair Salon you are to prepare from the following accounts on June 30, 19XX (1) a trial balance as of June 30; (2) an income statement for June; (3) a statement of owner's equity for the month ended June 30; and (4) a balance sheet as of June 30, 19XX.

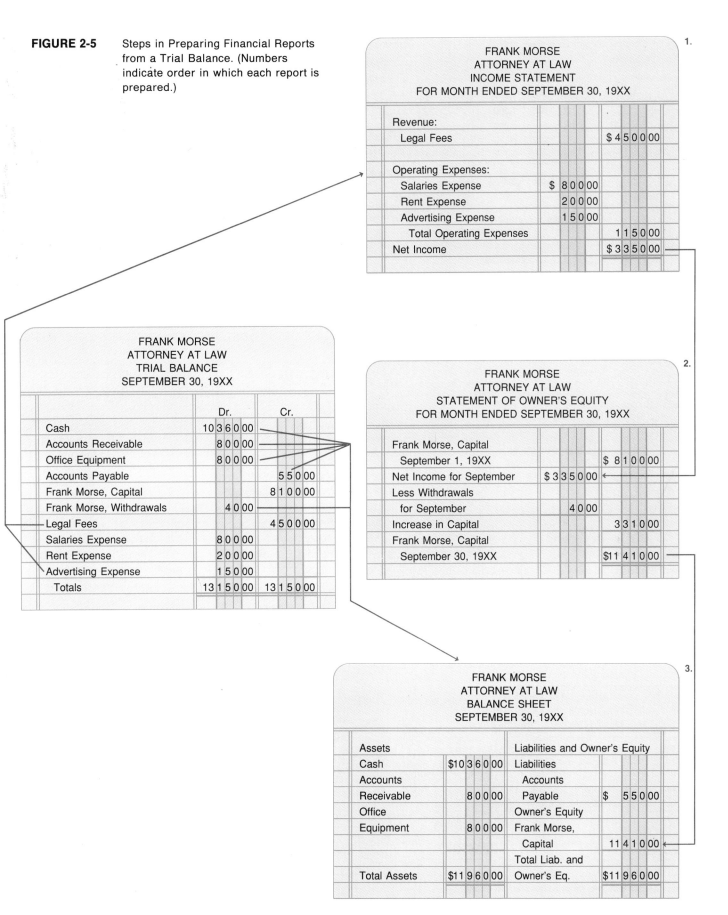

FIGURE 2-5 Steps in Preparing Financial Reports from a Trial Balance. (Numbers indicate order in which each report is prepared.)

1.

FRANK MORSE
ATTORNEY AT LAW
INCOME STATEMENT
FOR MONTH ENDED SEPTEMBER 30, 19XX

Revenue:			
Legal Fees		$ 4 5 0 0 00	
Operating Expenses:			
Salaries Expense	$ 8 0 0 00		
Rent Expense	2 0 0 00		
Advertising Expense	1 5 0 00		
Total Operating Expenses		1 1 5 0 00	
Net Income		$ 3 3 5 0 00	

FRANK MORSE
ATTORNEY AT LAW
TRIAL BALANCE
SEPTEMBER 30, 19XX

	Dr.	Cr.
Cash	10 3 6 0 00	
Accounts Receivable	8 0 0 00	
Office Equipment	8 0 0 00	
Accounts Payable		5 5 0 00
Frank Morse, Capital		8 1 0 0 00
Frank Morse, Withdrawals	4 0 00	
Legal Fees		4 5 0 0 00
Salaries Expense	8 0 0 00	
Rent Expense	2 0 0 00	
Advertising Expense	1 5 0 00	
Totals	13 1 5 0 00	13 1 5 0 00

2.

FRANK MORSE
ATTORNEY AT LAW
STATEMENT OF OWNER'S EQUITY
FOR MONTH ENDED SEPTEMBER 30, 19XX

Frank Morse, Capital		
September 1, 19XX		$ 8 1 0 0 00
Net Income for September	$ 3 3 5 0 00	
Less Withdrawals		
for September	4 0 00	
Increase in Capital		3 3 1 0 00
Frank Morse, Capital		
September 30, 19XX		$11 4 1 0 00

3.

FRANK MORSE
ATTORNEY AT LAW
BALANCE SHEET
SEPTEMBER 30, 19XX

Assets		Liabilities and Owner's Equity	
Cash	$10 3 6 0 00	Liabilities	
Accounts		Accounts	
Receivable	8 0 0 00	Payable	$ 5 5 0 00
Office		Owner's Equity	
Equipment	8 0 0 00	Frank Morse,	
		Capital	11 4 1 0 00
		Total Liab. and	
Total Assets	$11 9 6 0 00	Owner's Eq.	$11 9 6 0 00

T-Accounts

Cash 111	
4,000	300
2,000	100
1,000	1,200
300	1,300
	2,600

Accounts Payable 211	
300	700

Salon Fees 411	
	3,000
	1,000

Accounts Receivable 121	
1,000	300

Mel Harris, Capital 311	
	4,000*

Rent Expense 511	
1,200	

Salon Equipment 131	
700	

Mel Harris, Withdrawals 321	
100	

Salon Supplies Expense 521	
1,300	

Salaries Expense 531	
2,600	

* No additional investment.

SOLUTION TO SELF-REVIEW QUIZ 2-3

1.

MEL'S HAIR SALON
TRIAL BALANCE
JUNE 30, 19XX

	Dr.	Cr.
Cash	1 8 0 0 00	
Accounts Receivable	7 0 0 00	
Salon Equipment	7 0 0 00	
Accounts Payable		4 0 0 00
Mel Harris, Capital		4 0 0 0 00
Mel Harris, Withdrawals	1 0 0 00	
Salon Fees		4 0 0 0 00
Rent Expense	1 2 0 0 00	
Salon Supplies Expense	1 3 0 0 00	
Salaries Expense	2 6 0 0 00	
Totals	8 4 0 0 00	8 4 0 0 00

2.

MEL'S HAIR SALON
INCOME STATEMENT
FOR MONTH ENDED JUNE 30, 19XX

Revenue:		
Salon Fees		$ 4 0 0 0 00
Operating Expenses:		
Rent Expense	$ 1 2 0 0 00	
Salon Supplies Expense	1 3 0 0 00	
Salaries Expense	2 6 0 0 00	
Total Operating Expenses		5 1 0 0 00
Net Loss		$ 1 1 0 0 00

3.

MEL'S HAIR SALON
STATEMENT OF OWNER'S EQUITY
FOR MONTH ENDED JUNE 30, 19XX

Mel Harris, Capital		
June 1, 19XX		$ 4 0 0 0 00
Less: Net Loss for June	$ 1 1 0 0 00	
Withdrawals for June	1 0 0 00	
Decrease in Capital		1 2 0 0 00
Mel Harris, Capital,		
June 30, 19XX		$ 2 8 0 0 00

Note: The net loss results in a decrease to Capital

4.

MEL'S HAIR SALON
BALANCE SHEET
JUNE 30, 19XX

Assets		Liabilities and Owner's Equity	
Cash	$ 1 8 0 0 00	Liabilities	
Accounts Receivable	7 0 0 00	Accounts Payable	$ 4 0 0 00
Salon Equipment	7 0 0 00		
		Owner's Equity	
		Mel Harris, Capital	2 8 0 0 00
		Total Liabilities and	
Total Assets	$ 3 2 0 0 00	Owner's Equity	$ 3 2 0 0 00

SUMMARY OF KEY POINTS AND KEY TERMS

LEARNING UNIT 2-1

1. A T account is a simplified version of a standard account.

2. A ledger is a group of accounts.

3. A debit is the left position (side) of an account and a credit is the right position (side) of an account.

4. A footing is the total of one side of an account; the ending balance is the difference between the footings.

Account: An accounting device used in bookkeeping to record increases and decreases of business transactions relating to individual assets, liabilities, capital, withdrawals, revenue, expenses, etc.

Credit: The right side of any account. A number entered on the right side of any account is said to be credited to an account.

Debit: The left side of any account. A number entered on the left side of any account is said to be debited to an account.

Ending balance: The difference between footings in a T account.

Footings: The totals of each side of a T account.

Ledger: A group of accounts that records data from business transactions.

Standard account: A formal account that includes columns for date, explanation, posting reference, debit and credit.

T account: A skeleton version of a standard account, used for demonstration purposes.

LEARNING UNIT 2-2

1. A chart of accounts lists the account titles and their numbers for a company.

2. The transaction analysis chart is a teaching device, not to be confused with standard accounting procedures.

3. A compound entry is a transaction involving more than one debit or credit.

Chart of accounts: A numbering system of accounts that lists the account titles and account numbers to be used by a company.

Compound entry: A transaction involving more than one debit or credit.

Normal balance of an account: The side of an account that increases by the rules of debit and credit.

LEARNING UNIT 2-3

1. In double-entry bookkeeping, the recording of each business transaction affects two or more accounts, and the total of debits equals the total of credits.

2. A trial balance is a list of the ending balances of all accounts, listed in the same order as on the chart of accounts.

3. Any additional investments during the period result in capital on the trial balance not being the beginning figure for capital.

4. There are *no* debit or credit columns on the three financial reports.

Double-entry bookkeeping: An accounting system in which the recording of each transaction affects two or more accounts, and the total of the debits is equal to the total of the credits.

Trial balance: A list of the ending balances of all the accounts in a ledger. The total of the debits should equal the total of the credits.

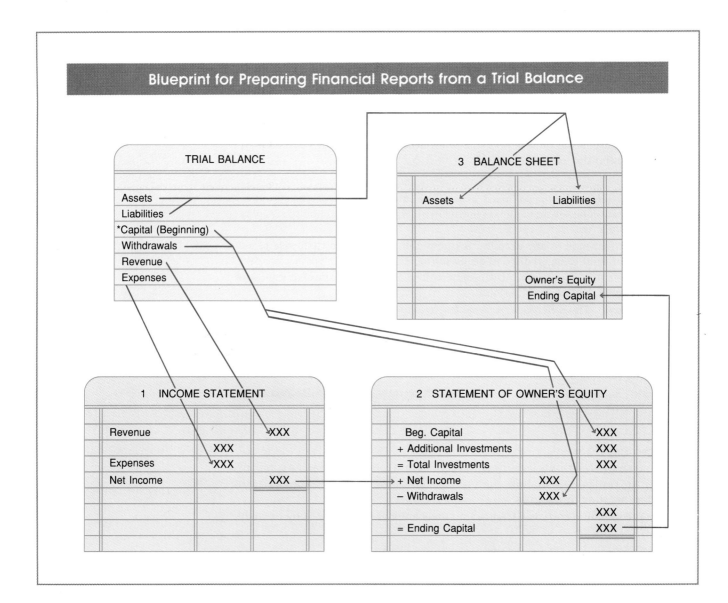

Blueprint for Preparing Financial Reports from a Trial Balance

TRIAL BALANCE

Assets
Liabilities
*Capital (Beginning)
Withdrawals
Revenue
Expenses

3 BALANCE SHEET

Assets	Liabilities
	Owner's Equity
	Ending Capital

1 INCOME STATEMENT

Revenue		XXX	
	XXX		
Expenses	XXX		
Net Income		XXX	

2 STATEMENT OF OWNER'S EQUITY

Beg. Capital		XXX	
+ Additional Investments		XXX	
= Total Investments		XXX	
+ Net Income	XXX		
− Withdrawals	XXX		
		XXX	
= Ending Capital		XXX	

DISCUSSION QUESTIONS

1. Define a ledger.

2. Why is the left side of an account called a debit?

3. Footings are used in balancing all accounts. True or false? Please explain.

4. What is the end product of the accounting process?

5. What do we mean when we say that a transaction analysis chart is a teaching device?

6. What are the five steps of the transaction analysis chart?

7. Explain the concept of double-entry bookkeeping.

8. A trial balance is a formal report. True or false? Please explain.

9. Why are there no debit or credit columns on financial reports?

10. Compare the financial statements prepared from the expanded accounting equation with those prepared from a trial balance.

EXERCISES

Preparing a chart of accounts.

1. From the following, prepare a chart of accounts, using the same numbering system used in this chapter.

Office Equipment *121*
Rent Expense *512*
Accounts Payable *211*
Accounts Receivable *112*
Repair Expense *513*

Professional Fees *411*
J. Deen, Capital *311*
Cash *111*
Salaries Expense *511*
J. Deen, Withdrawals *312*

2. Record the following transaction into the transaction analysis chart: Alice Flynn bought a new piece of office equipment for $7,000, paying $500 down and charging the rest.

3. Complete the table: For each account listed on the left, fill in what category it belongs to, whether increases and decreases in the account are marked on the debit or credit sides, and which financial report the account appears on. A sample is provided.

Account	Category	↑	↓	Appears on which Financial Report
Cash	**Asset**	**Dr.**	**Cr.**	**Balance Sheet**
Professional Fees Earned	*Revenue*	*CR*	*Dr*	*Income Statement*
B. Blank, Withdrawals	*W/D*	*Dr*	*CR*	*Statement of Owners Equity*
Accounts Payable	*Liability*	*CR*	*DR*	*Balance Sheet*
Rent Expense	*Expense*	*Dr*	*CR*	*Income Statement*
Truck	*Asset*	*Dr*	*CR*	*Balance sheet*

4. Given the following accounts, complete the table by inserting appropriate numbers next to the individual transaction to indicate which account is debited and which account is credited.

(1) Cash
(2) Accounts Receivable
(3) Equipment
(4) Accounts Payable
(5) K. Ray, Capital

(6) K. Ray, Withdrawals
(7) Plumbing Fees Earned
(8) Salaries Expense
(9) Advertising Expense
(10) Supplies Expense

		RULES	
TRANSACTION		**Dr.**	**Cr.**
Example: A. Paid salaries expense.		8	1
B. Ray paid personal utilities bill from company checkbook.		6	1
C. Advertising bill received but unpaid.		9	4
D. Received cash from plumbing fees.		1	7
E. Paid supplies expense.		10	1
F. Ray invested additional equipment into the business.		3	5
G. Billed customers for plumbing services rendered.		2	7
H. Received one-half the balance from transaction G.		1	2
I. Bought equipment on account.		3	4

Preparing a transaction analysis chart.

Accounts: categorizing, rules, and which reports they appear on.

Rules of debits and credits.

Preparing financial reports.

5. From the following trial balance of Lee Cleaners, prepare the following:

1. Income Statement
2. Statement of Owner's Equity
3. Balance Sheet

LEE CLEANERS TRIAL BALANCE JULY 31, 19XX		
	Dr.	Cr.
Cash	337 00	
Equipment	692 00	
Accounts Payable		242 00
B. Lee, Capital		800 00
B. Lee, Withdrawals	198 00	
Cleaning Fees		458 00
Salaries Expense	160 00	
Utilities Expense	113 00	
Totals	1500 00	1500 00

GROUP A PROBLEMS

Use of a transaction analysis chart.

2A-1. The following transactions occurred in the opening and operation of Amy's Bookkeeping Service.

A. Amy opened the bookkeeping service by investing $3,000 from her personal savings account.
B. Purchased office equipment on account, $2,000.
C. Rent expense due but unpaid, $300.
D. Received cash for bookkeeping services rendered, $550.
E. Billed a client on account, $600.
F. Amy Rice withdrew cash for personal use, $100.

Complete the transaction analysis chart in the *Study Guide and Working Papers.* The chart of accounts includes Cash; Accounts Receivable; Office Equipment; Accounts Payable; Amy Rice, Capital; Amy Rice, Withdrawals; Bookkeeping Fees Earned; and Rent Expense.

Recording transactions into ledger accounts.

2A-2. Rick Cerone opened a travel agency, and the following transactions resulted:

A. Rick Cerone invested $20,000 in the travel agency.
B. Bought office equipment on account, $4,000.
C. Agency received cash for travel arrangements that it completed for a client, $2,500.
D. Rick Cerone paid a personal bill from the company checkbook, $50.
E. Paid advertising expense for the month, $700.
F. Rent expense for the month due but unpaid, $500.
G. Paid $800 as partial payment of what was owed from transaction B.

As Rick Cerone's accountant, analyze and record the tansactions in T-account form. Set up the T accounts and label each entry with the letter of the transaction.

Chart of Accounts

Assets
Cash 111
Office Equipment 121

Liabilities
Accounts Payable 211

Owner's Equity
R. Cerone, Capital 311
R. Cerone, Withdrawals 312

Revenue
Travel Fees Earned 411

Expenses
Advertising Expense 511
Rent Expense 512

2A-3. From the following T accounts of Al's Window Washing Service, (a) record and foot the balances in the *Study Guide and Working Papers* where appropriate, and (b) prepare a trial balance in proper form for May 31, 19XX.

Preparing a trial balance from the T accounts.

Cash 111			Accounts Payable 211		Fees Earned 411	
5,000 (A)	100 (D)		100 (D)	300 (C)		6,000 (B)
3,000 (G)	200 (E)					
8,000	400 (F)					
	200 (H)					
6200	900 (I) *1,800*			*200*		*6,000*

Accounts Receivable 112			Al Hart, Capital 311		Rent Expense 511	
6,000 (B)	3,000 (G)			5,000 (A)	400 (F)	
3,000				*5000*	*400*	

Office Equipment 121			Al Hart, Withdrawals 312		Utilities Expense 512	
300 (C)			900 (I)		200 (E)	
200 (H)						
500			*900*		*200*	

2A-4. From the trial balance of Janet Foss, Attorney at Law, prepare (a) an income statement for the month of May, (b) a statement of owner's equity for the month ended May 31, and (c) a balance sheet as of May 31, 19XX.

Preparing financial reports from the trial balance.

JANET FOSS
ATTORNEY AT LAW
TRIAL BALANCE
MAY 31, 19XX

	Dr.	Cr.
Cash	1 8 0 0 00	
Accounts Receivable	7 5 0 00	
Office Equipment	7 5 0 00	
Accounts Payable		1 2 0 0 00
Salaries Payable		6 7 5 00
Janet Foss, Capital		1 2 7 5 00
Janet Foss, Withdrawals	3 0 0 00	
Revenue from Legal Fees		1 3 5 0 00
Utilities Expense	3 0 0 00	
Rent Epense	4 5 0 00	
Salaries Expense	1 5 0 00	
Totals	4 5 0 0 00	4 5 0 0 00

Comprehensive Problem

2A-5. The chart of accounts for Pete's Delivery Service is as follows:

Chart of Accounts

Assets
Cash 111
Accounts Receivable 112
Office Equipment 121
Delivery Trucks 122

Liabilities
Accounts Payable 211

Owner's Equity
Pete Jean, Capital 311
Pete Jean, Withdrawals 312

Revenue
Delivery Fees Earned 411

Expenses
Advertising Expense 511
Gas Expense 512
Salaries Expense 513
Telephone Expense 514

The following transactions resulted for Pete's Delivery Service during the month of March:

A. Pete Jean invested $25,000 in the delivery service from his personal savings account.

B. Bought delivery trucks on account, $20,000.

C. Bought office equipment for cash, $400.

D. Paid advertising expense, $250.

E. Collected cash for delivery services rendered, $2,600.

F. Paid drivers' salaries, $900.

G. Paid gas expense for trucks, $1,200.

H. Performed delivery services for a customer on account, $800.

I. Telephone expense due but unpaid, $700.

J. Received $300 as partial payment of transaction H.

K. Pete Jean withdrew cash for personal use, $300.

As Pete's newly employed accountant, your task is to

1. Set up T accounts in a ledger.

2. Record transactions in the T accounts. (Place the letter of the transaction next to the entry.)

3. Foot the T accounts where appropriate.

4. Prepare a trial balance at the end of March.

5. Prepare from the trial balance, in proper form, (a) an income statement for the month of March, (b) a statement of owner's equity, and (c) a balance sheet as of March 31, 19XX.

GROUP B PROBLEMS

Use of a transaction analysis chart.

2B-1. Amy Rice decided to open a bookkeeping service. Record the following transactions into the transaction analysis charts:

A. Amy invested $1,500 in the bookkeeping service from her personal savings account.

B. Purchased office equipment on account, $900.

C. Rent expense due but unpaid, $250.

D. Performed bookkeeping services for cash, $1,200.

E. Billed clients for bookkeeping services rendered, $700.

F. Amy paid her home heating bill from the company checkbook, $275.

The chart of accounts for the shop includes Cash; Accounts Receivable; Office Equipment; Accounts Payable; Amy Rice, Capital; Amy Rice, Withdrawals; Bookkeeping Fees Earned; and Rent Expense.

Recording transactions into ledger accounts.

2B-2. Rick Cerone established a new travel agency. Record the following transactions for Rick in T-account form. Label each entry with the letter of the transaction.

A. Rick Cerone invested $18,000 in the travel agency from his personal bank account.

B. Bought office equipment on account, $6,000.

C. Travel agency rendered service to Jensen Corp. and received cash, $1,200.

D. Rick Cerone withdrew cash for personal use, $200.

E. Paid advertising expense, $600.

F. Rent expense due but unpaid, $500.

G. Paid $400 in partial payment of transaction B.

The chart of accounts includes Cash, 111; Office Equipment, 121; Accounts Payable, 211; R. Cerone, Capital, 311; R. Cerone, Withdrawals, 312; Travel Fees Earned, 411; Advertising Expense, 511; and Rent Expense, 512.

Preparing a trial balance from the T accounts.

2B-3. From the following T accounts of Al's Window Washing Service, (1) record and foot the balances in the *Study Guide* where appropriate, and (2) prepare a trial balance for May 31, 19XX.

Cash 111

Debit	Credit
10,000 (A)	4,000 (C)
4,000 (F)	310 (D)
2,000 (G)	50 (E)
	600 (I)

Accounts Receivable 112

Debit	Credit
2,000 (G)	

Office Equipment 121

Debit	Credit
2,000 (B)	
4,000 (C)	

Accounts Payable 211

Debit	Credit
	2,000 (B)

Al Hart, Capital 311

Debit	Credit
	10,000 (A)

Al Hart, Withdrawals 312

Debit	Credit
600 (I)	

Fees Earned 411

Debit	Credit
	4,000 (F)
	4,000 (G)

Rent Expense 511

Debit	Credit
310 (D)	

Utilities Expense 512

Debit	Credit
50 (E)	

2B-4. From the trial balance of Janet Foss, Attorney at Law, prepare (1) an income statement for the month of May, (2) a statement of owner's equity for the month ended May 31, and (3) a balance sheet as of May 31, 19XX.

Preparing financial reports from the trial balance.

JANET FOSS
ATTORNEY AT LAW
TRIAL BALANCE
MAY 31, 19XX

	Debit	Credit
Cash	6 0 0 00	
Accounts Receivable	2 4 0 0 00	
Office Equipment	2 4 0 0 00	
Accounts Payable		2 0 0 00
Salaries Payable		6 0 0 00
Janet Foss, Capital		4 0 0 0 00
Janet Foss, Withdrawals	2 0 0 0 00	
Revenue from Legal Fees		8 8 0 0 00
Utilities Expense	1 0 0 00	
Rent Epense	3 0 0 00	
Salaries Expense	4 0 0 00	
Totals	13 6 0 0 00	13 6 0 0 00

2B-5. The chart of accounts of Pete's Delivery Service includes the following: Cash, 111; Accounts Receivable, 112; Office Equipment, 121; Delivery Trucks, 122; Accounts Payable, 211; Pete Jean, Capital, 311; Pete Jean, Withdrawals, 312; Delivery Fees Earned, 411; Advertising Expense, 511; Gas Expense, 512; Salaries Expense, 513; and Telephone Expense, 514. The following transactions resulted for Pete's Delivery Service during the month of March:

Comprehensive Problem

A. Pete invested $40,000 in the business from his personal savings account.
B. Bought delivery trucks on account, $25,000.
C. Advertising bill received but unpaid, $800.
D. Bought office equipment for cash, $2,500.
E. Received cash for delivery services rendered, $13,000.
F. Paid salaries expense, $1,850.
G. Paid gas expense for company trucks, $750.
H. Billed customers for delivery services rendered, $5,500.
 I. Paid telephone bill, $400.
J. Received $1,600 as partial payment of transaction H.
K. Pete paid home telephone bill from company checkbook, $88.

As Pete's newly employed accountant, your task is to

1. Set up T accounts in a ledger.
2. Record transactions in the T accounts. (Place the letter of the transaction next to the entry.)
3. Foot the T accounts where appropriate.
4. Prepare a trial balance at the end of March.
5. Prepare from the trial balance, in proper form, (a) an income statement for the month of March, (b) a statement of owner's equity, and (c) a balance sheet as of March 31, 19XX.

PRACTICAL ACCOUNTING APPLICATION #1

Andy Leaf is a careless bookkeeper. He is having a terrible time getting his trial balance to balance. Andy has asked for your assistance in preparing a correct trial balance. The following is the incorrect trial balance.

RANCH COMPANY
TRIAL BALANCE
JUNE 30, 19XX

	Dr.	Cr.
Cash	5 1 0 00	
Accounts Receivable		6 3 5 00
Office Equipment	3 6 0 00	
Accounts Payable	1 1 0 00	
Wages Payable	1 0 00	
H. Clo, Capital	6 3 5 00	
H. Clo, Withdrawals	1 4 4 0 00	
Professional Fees		2 2 4 0 00
Rent Expense		2 4 0 00
Advertising Expense	2 5 00	
Totals	3 0 9 0 00	3 1 1 5 00

Facts you have discovered:

1. Debits to the Cash account were $2,640; credits to the Cash account were $2,150.
2. Amy Hall paid $15 but was not updated in Accounts Receivable.
3. A purchase of office equipment for $5 on account was never recorded in the ledger.
4. Revenue was understated in the ledger by $180.

Show how these errors would have affected the ending balances for the accounts involved, and show how once they are corrected the trial balance will indeed balance.

PRACTICAL ACCOUNTING APPLICATION #2

Given the following six independent situations, Alice Groove, owner of Lonton Company, has asked her bookkeeper how each situation would have affected the totals of the trial balance as well as individual ledger accounts. As the bookkeeper, could you respond to Alice's concerns: Be specific in telling whether accounts are overstated, understated, or correctly stated.

1. An $850 payment for a desk was recorded as a debit to Office Equipment, $85, and a credit to Cash, $85.

2. A payment of $300 to a creditor was recorded as a debit to Accounts Payable, $300, and a credit to Cash, $100.
3. The collection of an Accounts Receivable for $400 was recorded as a debit to Cash, $400, and a credit to J. Ray, Capital, $400.
4. The payment of a liability for $400 was recorded as a debit to Accounts Payable, $40, and a credit to Supplies, $40.
5. A purchase of equipment of $800 was recorded as a debit to Supplies, $800, and a credit to Cash, $800.
6. A payment of $95 to a creditor was recorded as a debit to Accounts Payable, $95, and a credit to Cash, $59.

BEGINNING THE ACCOUNTING CYCLE:
Journalizing, Posting, and the Trial Balance

The example of Frank Morse, Attorney, gave you some insights into accounting terms and basic procedures as well as the preparation of the three financial reports. Now our attention will shift to Brenda Clark, who is planning to open a word processing business. In this chapter, and in Chapters 4 and 5, we will follow step by step the normal accounting procedures that her business, Clark's Word Processing Services, performs over a period of time.

FIGURE 3-1
Steps of the Accounting Cycle.

STEPS	NOTES
1. Business transactions occur and generate source documents.	Source documents are cash register tapes, sales tickets, bills, checks, payroll cards.
2. Analyze and record business transactions into a journal.	Called journalizing.
3. Post or transfer information from journal to ledger.	Copying the debits and credits of the journal entries, placing them into the ledger accounts.
4. Prepare a trial balance.	Summarizing each individual ledger account and listing these accounts and their balances to test for accuracy in recording transactions.
5. Prepare a work sheet.	A multicolumn form that summarizes accounting information to complete the accounting cycle.
6. Prepare financial statements.	Income statement, statement of owner's equity, balance sheet.
7. Journalize and post adjusting entries.	Refers to adjustment columns of work sheet.
8. Journalize and post closing entries.	Refers to income statement columns of work sheet.
9. Prepare a post-closing trial balance.	Prove the equality of debits and credits after adjusting and closing entries are posted.

Use this as a reference table in your study of Chapters 3, 4, and 5.

The normal accounting procedures that are performed over a period of time are called the **accounting cycle**. The accounting cycle takes place in a period of time called an **accounting period**—it can be a month, three months, one year, etc. An accounting period is the period of time covered by the income statement. The norm for accounting periods is one year.

A **fiscal year** is an accounting period that runs for any 12 consecutive months. Clark has chosen to use a fiscal year of January 1 to December 31, which also is the **calendar year**. A fiscal year can be a calendar year but does not have to be; a business can choose any fiscal year that is convenient. For example, some companies, such as retail furniture companies, may decide to end their fiscal year when inventories and business activity are at a low point (in this case, Feb. 28). This is called a natural business year. It allows the business to count year-end inventory at the time when it is easiest to do so.

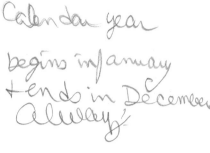

Whether we are talking about a calender year or a fiscal year, financial reports can be prepared monthly, quarterly, or every six months. These reports are called **interim reports**.

To keep things simple, we will look at an accounting cycle for one month for Clark's Word Processing Services. Please keep in mind that her actual accounting cycle is 12 months.

The blueprint shown in Figure 3-1 on page 55 is a list of the steps of the accounting cycle for Clark's Word Processing Services. Please do not try to memorize this blueprint. It will be repeated frequently in the next three chapters. Simply use it as a reference table. By the end of Chapter 5 all the steps and the notes of the blueprint will have been explained and illustrated.

This chapter covers Steps 1 to 4 of the accounting cycle.

LEARNING UNIT 3-1

Analyzing and Recording Business Transactions into a Journal: Steps 1 and 2 of the Accounting Cycle

THE GENERAL JOURNAL

In the last chapter we analyzed and recorded business transactions of Frank Morse's law practice into T accounts, or ledger accounts. Dealing only with accounts, however, makes it difficult to locate errors (because a debit may be in one account—on one page of the ledger—and a credit in another account—on another page of the ledger). We need a place where the entire transaction (debit and credit) can be found. For this reason we record business transactions in a **journal**. The simplest form of journal is the **general journal**. Transactions are entered in the journal in chronological order (January 1, 8, 15, etc.), and then this recorded information is used to update the ledger accounts. In computerized accounting, a journal may be recorded on disk or tape.

A business uses a journal to record transactions in chronological order. A ledger accumulates information from a journal. The journal and the ledger are in two different books.

The general journal, the simplest form of a journal, will be used to record the transactions of Clark's Word Processing Services (see Figure 3-2). A transaction (debit(s) + credit(s)) that has been analyzed and recorded in a journal is called a **journal entry**. The process of recording the journal entry into the journal is called **journalizing**.

Journal—book of original entry.

The journal is called the **book of original entry**, since it will contain the first formal information about the business transactions. The ledger, a

CLARK'S WORD PROCESSING SERVICES
GENERAL JOURNAL

Page 1

Date		Account Titles and Description	PR	Dr.	Cr.

FIGURE 3-2
The General Journal.

group of accounts, will be known as the **book of final entry**, since the information in the journal will eventually be transferred to the ledger. Like the ledger, the journal is a bound or loose-leaf book. The journal pages are each like the one illustrated in Figure 3-2. The journal is numbered by page (1, 2, 3, and so on), while the ledger is set up with one or more pages for each account, and each account in order according to the account number assigned. Keep in mind that the journal and the ledger are separate books.

Ledger—book of final entry.

Relationship of journal to chart of accounts.

Before the accountant can journalize the business transactions of Clark's Word Processing Services, a chart of accounts is needed to identify what account name to use for each debit and each credit. Most companies have their own "unique" chart of accounts. Seldom do two companies have exactly the same chart. Don't worry about accounts in the chart we haven't talked about or seen—you will learn about them by the end of the accounting

In a journal
debit's done first –

Clark's Word Processing Services
Chart of Accounts

Assets (100–199)
111 Cash
112 Accounts Receivable
114 Office Supplies
115 Prepaid Rent
121 Word Processing Equipment
122 Accumulated Depreciation, Word Processing Equipment

Liabilities (200–299)
211 Accounts Payable
212 Salaries Payable

Owner's Equity (300–399)
311 Brenda Clark, Capital
312 Brenda Clark, Withdrawals
313 Income Summary

Revenue (400–499)
411 Word Processing Fees

Expenses (500–599)
511 Office Salaries Expense
512 Advertising Expense
513 Telephone Expense
514 Office Supplies Expense
515 Rent Expense
516 Depreciation Expense, Word Processing Equipment

cycle. The chart of accounts of Clark's Word Processing Services is presented on p. 57.

Journalizing the Transactions of Clark's Word Processing Services

With a chart of accounts available, we can proceed to record business transactions in chronological order in the general journal. (Note that we are still using the transaction analysis charts as a teaching aid in the journalizing process.)

> May 1, 19XX: Brenda Clark began the business by investing $7,000 in cash.

1 Accounts Affected	2 Category	3 ↑↓	4 Rules
Cash	Asset	↑	Dr.
Brenda Clark, Capital	Capital	↑	Cr.

CLARK'S WORD PROCESSING SERVICES
GENERAL JOURNAL

Page 1

Date	Account Titles and Description	PR	Dr.*	Cr.
19XX May 1	Cash		7 0 0 0 00	
	Brenda Clark, Capital			7 0 0 0 00
	Initial investment of cash by owner			

* You may, if you prefer, use dashes instead of zeros (for example, 7,000.00 or 7,000—) be sure to check with your instructor.

Let's now look at the stucture of this journal entry. The entry contains the following information:

1. Year of the journal entry   19XX
2. Month of journal entry   May
3. Day of journal entry   1
4. Name(s) of accounts debited   Cash
5. Name(s) of accounts credited   Brenda Clark, Capital
6. Explanation of transaction   Investment of cash
7. Amount of debit(s) $7,000
8. Amount of credit(s) $7,000

For now the PR (posting reference) column is blank; we will discuss it later. Notice the following in this journal entry:

Debit is listed *first*, next to date column.

1. The location of the year, month, and day.
2. The account name Cash is written on the first line next to the date column in the account titles and description section. The amount of the account is entered

in debit column. *Note:* The debit portion of the transaction is always recorded in the journal first.

Credit is listed second and is indented $\frac{1}{2}$-inch to right of date column.

3. The account B. Clark, Capital, is written on the second line, indented one-half inch from the left side of the account titles and description (or date column). The credit portion of a transaction is placed below the debit portion.
4. The explanation of the journal entry follows immediately after the debit and credit account titles, indented 1 inch from the date column.
5. Following each transaction and explanation leave a 1 line space. This makes the journal easier to read, and there is less chance of mixing transactions.
6. The total amount of debits ($7,000) is equal to the total amount of credits ($7,000).

> May 1: Purchased word processing equipment from Ben Co. for $8,000, paying $2,000 and promising to pay the balance within 30 days.

1 Accounts Affected	2 Category	3 ↑ ↓	4 Rules
Word Processing Equipment	Asset	↑	Dr.
Cash	Asset	↓	Cr.
Accounts Payable	Liability	↑	Cr.

Note that in this compound entry we have one debit and two credits—but the total amount of debits equals the total amount of credits.

Note that there are three accounts affected here.

		1	Word Processing Equipment		8 0 0 0 00		
			Cash			2 0 0 0 00	
			Accounts Payable			6 0 0 0 00	
			Purchase of equipment from Ben Co.				

Notice that only the day is entered in the date column. Since the year and month are entered at the top of the page from the first transaction, there is no need to repeat the month until a new page is needed or a change of month occurs. Note again that the debit is listed first, and then the two credits are indented and listed below the debit. When a journal entry has more than two accounts, it is called a **compound journal entry**. We discussed this in Chapter 1.

A journal entry that requires three or more accounts is called a compound journal entry.

> May 1: Rented office space, paying $900 in advance for the first three months.

Since he owns the space for three months, it is an asset.

1 Accounts Affected	2 Category	3 ↑ ↓	4 Rules
Prepaid Rent	Asset	↑	Dr.
Cash	Asset	↓	Cr.

Rent paid in advance is an asset.

In this transaction Clark gains an asset called prepaid rent but gives up an asset, cash. When the rent *expires*, it will become an expense. In the last chapter the rent for Frank Morse had expired; thus we recorded it as an expense. However, for now prepaid rent is an asset.

1	Prepaid Rent		9 0 0 00		
	Cash			9 0 0 00	
	Rent paid in advance-3 mo.				

> May 3: Purchased office supplies from Norris Co. on account, $400.

1 Accounts Affected	2 Category	3 ↑ ↓	4 Rules
Office Supplies	**Asset**	↑	**Dr.**
Accounts Payable	**Liability**	↑	**Cr.**

Remember the following guidelines:

Supplies become an *expense* when used up.

1. When we purchase supplies, they are an *asset* that has not been used up.
2. When the supplies are used up or consumed in the operation of the business, they become an expense.

3	Office Supplies		4 0 0 00		
	Accounts Payable			4 0 0 00	
	Purchase of supplies on account				
	from Norris				

> May 7: Completed sales promotion pieces for a client and immediately collected $2,500.

1 Accounts Affected	2 Category	3 ↑ ↓	4 Rules
Cash	**Asset**	↑	**Dr.**
Word Processing Fees	**Revenue**	↑	**Cr.**

7	Cash		2 5 0 0 00		
	Word Processing Fees			2 5 0 0 00	
	Cash received for services rendered				

May 15: Paid office salaries, $450.

1 Accounts Affected	2 Category	3 ↑ ↓	4 Rules
Office Salaries Expense	Expense	↑	Dr.
Cash	Asset	↓	Cr.

	15	Office Salaries Expense		4 5 0 00	
		Cash			4 5 0 00
		Payment of office salaries			

May 18: Advertising bill from Al's News Co. comes in but is not paid, $175.

1 Accounts Affected	2 Category	3 ↑ ↓	4 Rules
Advertising Expense	Expense	↑	Dr.
Accounts Payable	Liability	↑	Cr.

As we noted in Chapter 1, we record an expense when it is incurred, no matter when it is paid.

	18	Advertising Expense		1 7 5 00	
		Accounts Payable			1 7 5 00
		Bill in but not paid from Al's News			

May 20: Brenda Clark wrote a check on the bank account of the business to pay her home mortgage payment of $430.

1 Accounts Affected	2 Category	3 ↑ ↓	4 Rules
Brenda Clark, Withdrawals	Withdrawals	↑	Dr.
Cash	Asset	↓	Cr.

Keep in mind that as withdrawals *increase*, the end result is to *reduce* owner's equity.

	20	Brenda Clark, Withdrawals			4 3 0 00		
		Cash				4 3 0 00	
		Personal withdrawal of cash					

May 22: Billed Morris Company for a sophisticated word processing job, $4,100.

1 Accounts Affected	2 Category	3 ↑ ↓	4 Rules
Accounts Receivable	Asset	↑	Dr.
Word Processing Fees	Revenue	↑	Cr.

As we discussed in Chapter 1, revenue is recorded when earned, no matter when the actual cash is received.

	22	Accounts Receivable			4 1 0 0 00		
		Word Processing Fees				4 1 0 0 00	
		Billed Morris Co. for fees earned					

May 27: Paid office salaries, $450.

1 Accounts Affected	2 Category	3 ↑ ↓	4 Rules
Office Salaries Expense	Expense	↑	Dr.
Cash	Asset	↓	Cr.

CLARK'S WORD PROCESSING SERVICES
GENERAL JOURNAL

Page 2

	Date		Account Titles and Description	PR	Dr.	Cr.
	19XX May	27	Office Salaries Expense		4 5 0 00	
			Cash			4 5 0 00
			Payment of office salaries			

Note that, since we are on page 2 of the journal, the year and month are repeated.

May 28: Paid half the amount owed for word processing equipment purchased May 1 from Ben Co., $3,000.

1 Accounts Affected	2 Category	3 ↑ ↓	4 Rules
Accounts Payable	Liability	↓	Dr.
Cash	Asset	↓	Cr.

28	Accounts Payable		3 0 0 0 00		
	Cash			3 0 0 0 00	
	Paid half the amount owed Ben Co.				

May 29: Paid telephone bill, $180.

1 Accounts Affected	2 Category	3 ↑ ↓	4 Rules
Telephone Expense	Expense	↑	Dr.
Cash	Asset	↓	Cr.

29	Telephone Expense		1 8 0 00		
	Cash			1 8 0 00	
	Paid telephone bill				

This concludes the journal transactions of Clark's Word Processing Services.

To review this unit, you should be able to

1. Explain the purpose of the accounting cycle. (p. 56)
2. Define and explain the relationship of the accounting period to the income statement. (p. 56)
3. Compare and contrast a calendar year to a fiscal year. (p. 56)
4. Explain the term natural business year. (p. 56)
5. Explain the function of interim reports. (p. 56)
6. Define and state the purpose of a journal. (p. 56)
7. Compare and contrast a book of original entry to a book of final entry. (p. 57)
8. Differentiate between a chart of accounts and a journal. (p. 57)
9. Explain a compound entry. (p. 59)
10. Journalize business transactions. (p. 58–63)

SELF-REVIEW QUIZ 3-1

The following are the transactions of Pete's Repair Service. Journalize the transactions in proper form. The chart of accounts includes Cash; Accounts Receivable; Prepaid Rent; Repair Supplies; Repair Equipment; Accounts Payable; P. Quick, Capital; P. Quick, Withdrawals; Repair Fees Earned; Salaries Expense; Advertising Expense; and Supplies Expense.

19XX

June 1   Pete invested $5,000 cash and $2,000 of repair equipment in the business.
       1   Paid two months' rent in advance, $900.
       4   Bought repair supplies from Melvin Co. on account, $500. (These supplies have not yet been consumed or used up.)
    15   Performed repair work, received $600 cash, and had to bill Doe Co. for remaining balance of $300.
    18   Pete paid his home telephone bill, $50, with a check from the company.
    20   Advertising bill for $400 from Jones Co. received but payment not due yet. (Advertising has already appeared in the newspaper.)
    24   Paid salaries, $1,400.

SOLUTION TO SELF-REVIEW QUIZ 3-1

PETE'S REPAIR
GENERAL JOURNAL

Page 1

Date			Account Titles and Description	PR*	Dr.	Cr.
19XX						
June	1		Cash		5 0 0 0 00	
			Repair Equipment		2 0 0 0 00	
			P. Quick, Capital			7 0 0 0 00
			Owner investment			
	1		Prepaid Rent		9 0 0 00	
			Cash			9 0 0 00
			Rent paid in advance			
	4		Repair Supplies		5 0 0 00	
			Accounts Payable			5 0 0 00
			Purchase of supplies on account			
	15		Cash		6 0 0 00	
			Accounts Receivable		3 0 0 00	
			Repair Fees Earned			9 0 0 00
			Performed repairs			
	18		P. Quick, Withdrawals		5 0 00	
			Cash			5 0 00
			Personal withdrawal			
	20		Advertising Expense		4 0 0 00	
			Accounts Payable			4 0 0 00
			Advertising bill			
	24		Salaries Expense		1 4 0 0 00	
			Cash			1 4 0 0 00
			Paid salaries			

* Note that the PR column is left blank in the journalizing process.

Posting to the Ledger: Step 3 of the Accounting Cycle

If you were asked to find the balance of the cash account from the general journal, you would not be able to find it in one place. You would have to go through the journal, look for only the cash entries, add up the debits and credits, and take the difference between the two. Thus, what we really need to do to find *balances of accounts* is to transfer, copy, or record the information from the journal to the ledger. This is called **posting**. In the ledger we will *accumulate* an ending balance for each account so that we can prepare financial statements.

The ledger accumulates information from the journal.

Before looking at how to post, let's first introduce a **four-column account** that we will be using instead of the standard two-column account. This four-column balance account will be used throughout the rest of the text and will make accumulating items in the ledger a bit easier.

The two-column account was valuable for learning debits and credits. It forced you to think of lefts and rights. In actual practice there has been a shift to forms that use a four-column account. A sample of a standard four-column account is shown in Figure 3-3. (We will explain the Post. Ref. column in a moment.) Keep in mind: in balancing two debits are added. Two credits would be added. If you have a debit and credit the difference would be taken with the balance placed on the larger side.

Advantages of the four-column account:

1. You will need only one date column.
2. It is easier to see whether the balance (or ending balance) is a debit or credit.
3. Footings will *not* be needed.

When using this account, we need to know on which side the balance is usually placed. As stated in the last chapter, the **normal balance** of an account is the side of the account where we record increases. Figure 3-4 (p. 66) reviews the rules of normal balances.

If, after an account is balanced, the last balance doesn't fall on the side that increases the account, it is said to have an *unusual balance*. If we were using a single balance column, a bracket [ ] would be placed around the number to indicate that it is an unusual balance.

Now let's look at how to post the transactions of Clark's Word Processing Service from its journal.

POSTING

The diagram in Figure 3-5 (p. 67) shows how to post the cash line from the journal to the ledger. Again, *posting* is the transferring, copying, or recording of information to the ledger from the journal.

FIGURE 3-3
Four-Column Account.

Accounts Payable						Account No. 211	
		Post.			Balance		
Date	Explanation	Ref.	Debit	Credit	Debit	Credit	
19XX May 1		GJ1		6 0 0 0 0		6 0 0 0 0	
3		GJ1		4 0 0 0		6 4 0 0 0	
18		GJ1		1 7 5 00		6 5 7 5 00	
28		GJ2	3 0 0 0 00			3 5 7 5 00	

65

FIGURE 3-4
Normal Balances

		↑	↓	NORMAL BALANCE
After balancing asset accounts, the balance will be on the debit or left side.	← Assets	Dr.	Cr.	Dr.
	Liabilities	Cr.	Dr.	Cr.
	Capital	Cr.	Dr.	Cr.
	Withdrawals	Dr.	Cr.	Dr.
	Revenues	Cr.	Dr.	Cr.
	Expenses	Dr.	Cr.	Dr.

Note how normal balance is on the side that increases the account.

Note the following key points:

- Journal and ledger are in separate books.
- PR column of general journal will be the last to be filled in.
- No new analysis is taking place in the ledger. We are just copying transactions from the journal into the ledger.

Steps to Post

These steps are numbered and illustrated in Figure 3-5.

1. In the Cash account in the ledger, record the date (May 1, 19XX) and the amount of the entry ($7,000).
2. Record the page number of the journal "GJ1" in the posting reference (Post. Ref.) column of the Cash account.
3. Record the account number of Cash (111) in the posting reference (PR) column of the journal. This is called **cross-referencing**.
4. Calculate the new balance of the account. You keep a running balance in each account as you would in your checkbook. To do this you take the present balance in the account on the previous line and add or subtract the transaction as necessary to arrive at your new balance.

The same sequence of steps occurs for each line in the journal. In a manual system like Clark's, the debits and credits in the journal may be posted in the order they were recorded, or all the debits may be posted first and then all the credits.

Using Posting References

The posting references are very helpful. In the journal, the PR column tells us which transactions have or have not been posted and also to which accounts they were posted. In the ledger, the posting reference leads us back to the original transaction in its entirety, so that we can see why the debit or credit was recorded and what other accounts were affected. (It leads us back to the original transaction by identifying the journal and the page in the journal the information came from.)

Now, at this point you should be able to:

1. State the purpose of posting.   (p. 65)
2. Discuss the advantages of the four-column account.   (p. 65)

FIGURE 3-5 How to Post from Journal to Ledger.

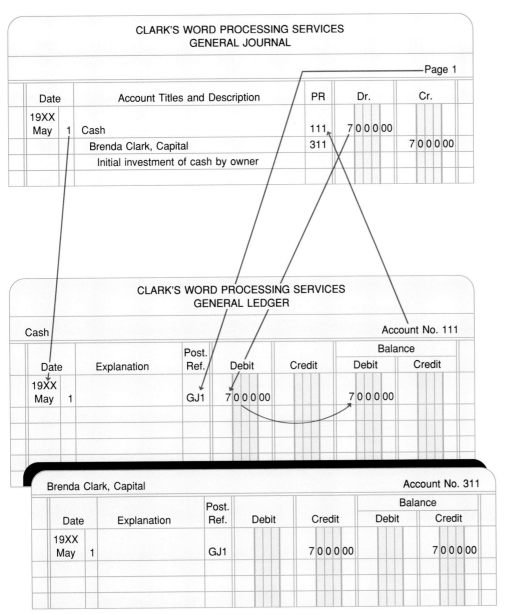

3. Define a normal balance. (p. 65)
4. Identify the elements to be posted. (p. 67)
5. From journalized transactions, post to the general ledger. (p. 66)

SELF-REVIEW QUIZ 3-2

The following are the journalized transactions of Clark's Word Processing Services. Your task is to post information to the ledger. The ledger in your workbook has all the account titles and numbers that were used from the chart of accounts on p. 57. *To keep things simple, assume in the quiz that all journal entries are "p. 1."*

CLARK'S WORD PROCESSING SERVICES
GENERAL JOURNAL

Page 1

	Date	Account Titles and Description	PR*	Dr.	Cr.
	19XX May	1	Cash		7 0 0 0 00	
			Brenda Clark, Capital			7 0 0 0 00
			Initial investment of cash by owner			
		1	Word Processing Equipment		8 0 0 0 00	
			Cash			2 0 0 0 00
			Accounts Payable			6 0 0 0 00
			Purchase of equip. from Ben Co.			
		1	Prepaid Rent		9 0 0 00	
			Cash			9 0 0 00
			Rent paid in advance (3 months)			
		3	Office Supplies		4 0 0 00	
			Accounts Payable			4 0 0 00
			Purchase of supplies on acct. from Norris			
		7	Cash		2 5 0 0 00	
			Word Processing Fees			2 5 0 0 00
			Cash received from services rendered			
		15	Office Salaries Expense		4 5 0 00	
			Cash			4 5 0 00
			Payment of office salaries			
		18	Advertising Expense		1 7 5 00	
			Accounts Payable			1 7 5 00
			Bill received but not paid from Al's News			
		20	Brenda Clark, Withdrawals		4 3 0 00	
			Cash			4 3 0 00
			Personal withdrawal of cash			
		22	Accounts Receivable		4 1 0 0 00	
			Word Processing Fees			4 1 0 0 00
			Billed Morris Co. for fees earned			
		27	Office Salaries Expense		4 5 0 00	
			Cash			4 5 0 00
			Payment of office salaries			
		28	Accounts Payable		3 0 0 0 00	
			Cash			3 0 0 0 00
			Paid half the amount owed Ben Co.			

* Note that the PR column is empty—this is because these entries have not been posted yet.

CLARK'S WORD PROCESSING SERVICES
GENERAL JOURNAL

Page 1

Date		Account Titles and Description	PR	Dr.	Cr.
19XX					
May	29	Telephone Expense		1 8 0 00	
		Cash			1 8 0 00
		Paid telephone bill			

SOLUTION TO SELF-REVIEW QUIZ 3-2

CLARK'S WORD PROCESSING SERVICES
GENERAL JOURNAL

Page 1

Date		Account Titles and Description	PR	Dr.	Cr.
19XX					
May	1	Cash	111	7 0 0 0 00	
		Brenda Clark, Capital	311		7 0 0 0 00
		Initial investment of cash by owner			
	1	Word Processing Equipment	121	8 0 0 0 00	
		Cash	111		2 0 0 0 00
		Accounts Payable	211		6 0 0 0 00
		Purchase of equip. from Ben Co.			
	1	Prepaid Rent	115	9 0 0 00	
		Cash	111		9 0 0 00
		Rent paid in advance (3 months)			
	3	Office Supplies	114	4 0 0 00	
		Accounts Payable	211		4 0 0 00
		Purchase of supplies on acct. from Norris.			
	7	Cash	111	2 5 0 0 00	
		Word Processing Fees	411		2 5 0 0 00
		Cash received for services rendered			
	15	Office Salaries Expense	511	4 5 0 00	
		Cash	111		4 5 0 00
		Payment of office salaries			

CLARK'S WORD PROCESSING SERVICES
GENERAL JOURNAL

Page 1

	Date	Account Titles and Description	PR	Dr.	Cr.
19XX May	18	Advertising Expense	512	1 7 5 00	
		Accounts Payable	211		1 7 5 00
		Bill received but not paid from Al's News			
	20	Brenda Clark, Withdrawals	312	4 3 0 00	
		Cash	111		4 3 0 00
		Personal withdrawal of cash			
	22	Accounts Receivable	112	4 1 0 0 00	
		Word Processing Fees	411		4 1 0 0 00
		Billed Morris Co. for fees earned			
	27	Office Salaries Expense	511	4 5 0 00	
		Cash	111		4 5 0 00
		Payment of office salaries			
	28	Accounts Payable	211	3 0 0 0 00	
		Cash	111		3 0 0 0 00
		Paid half the amount owed Ben Co.			
	29	Telephone Expense	513	1 8 0 00	
		Cash	111		1 8 0 00
		Paid telephone bill			

CLARK'S WORD PROCESSING SERVICES
PARTIAL GENERAL LEDGER

Cash   Account No. 111

	Date	Explanation	Post. Ref.	Debit	Credit	Balance Debit	Balance Credit
19XX May	1		GJ1	7 0 0 0 00		7 0 0 0 00	
	1		GJ1		2 0 0 0 00	5 0 0 0 00	
	1		GJ1		9 0 0 00	4 1 0 0 00	
	7		GJ1	2 5 0 0 00		6 6 0 0 00	
	15		GJ1		4 5 0 00	6 1 5 0 00	
	20		GJ1		4 3 0 00	5 7 2 0 00	
	27		GJ1		4 5 0 00	5 2 7 0 00	
	28		GJ1		3 0 0 0 00	2 2 7 0 00	
	29		GJ1		1 8 0 00	2 0 9 0 00	

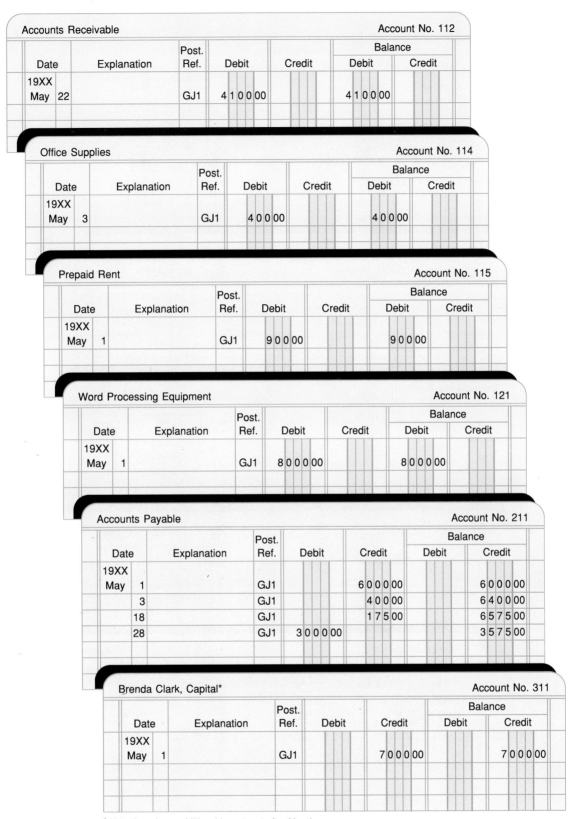

Accounts Receivable — Account No. 112

Date		Explanation	Post. Ref.	Debit	Credit	Balance Debit	Balance Credit
19XX May	22		GJ1	4 1 0 0 00		4 1 0 0 00	

Office Supplies — Account No. 114

Date		Explanation	Post. Ref.	Debit	Credit	Balance Debit	Balance Credit
19XX May	3		GJ1	4 0 0 00		4 0 0 00	

Prepaid Rent — Account No. 115

Date		Explanation	Post. Ref.	Debit	Credit	Balance Debit	Balance Credit
19XX May	1		GJ1	9 0 0 00		9 0 0 00	

Word Processing Equipment — Account No. 121

Date		Explanation	Post. Ref.	Debit	Credit	Balance Debit	Balance Credit
19XX May	1		GJ1	8 0 0 0 00		8 0 0 0 00	

Accounts Payable — Account No. 211

Date		Explanation	Post. Ref.	Debit	Credit	Balance Debit	Balance Credit
19XX May	1		GJ1		6 0 0 0 00		6 0 0 0 00
	3		GJ1		4 0 0 00		6 4 0 0 00
	18		GJ1		1 7 5 00		6 5 7 5 00
	28		GJ1	3 0 0 0 00			3 5 7 5 00

Brenda Clark, Capital* — Account No. 311

Date		Explanation	Post. Ref.	Debit	Credit	Balance Debit	Balance Credit
19XX May	1		GJ1		7 0 0 0 00		7 0 0 0 00

* Note there is no additional investment after May 1.

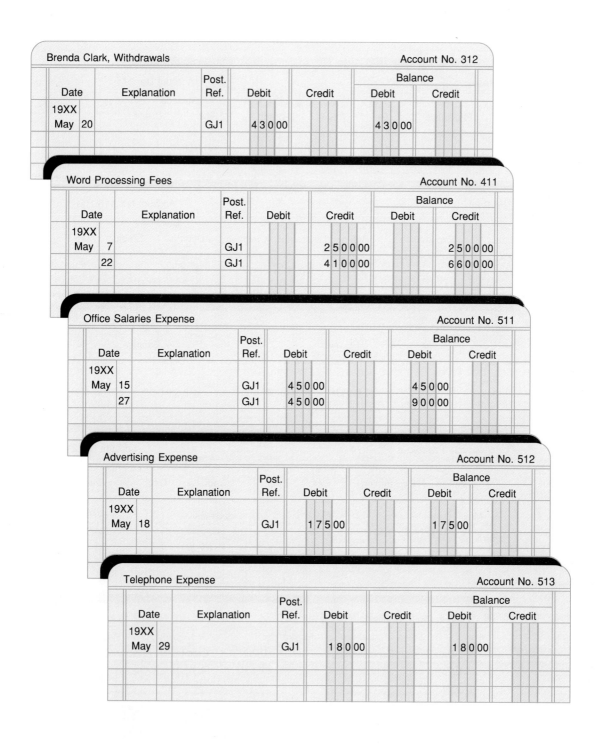

Brenda Clark, Withdrawals   Account No. 312

Date		Explanation	Post. Ref.	Debit	Credit	Balance Debit	Balance Credit
19XX							
May	20		GJ1	4 3 0 00		4 3 0 00	

Word Processing Fees   Account No. 411

Date		Explanation	Post. Ref.	Debit	Credit	Balance Debit	Balance Credit
19XX							
May	7		GJ1		2 5 0 0 00		2 5 0 0 00
	22		GJ1		4 1 0 0 00		6 6 0 0 00

Office Salaries Expense   Account No. 511

Date		Explanation	Post. Ref.	Debit	Credit	Balance Debit	Balance Credit
19XX							
May	15		GJ1	4 5 0 00		4 5 0 00	
	27		GJ1	4 5 0 00		9 0 0 00	

Advertising Expense   Account No. 512

Date		Explanation	Post. Ref.	Debit	Credit	Balance Debit	Balance Credit
19XX							
May	18		GJ1	1 7 5 00		1 7 5 00	

Telephone Expense   Account No. 513

Date		Explanation	Post. Ref.	Debit	Credit	Balance Debit	Balance Credit
19XX							
May	29		GJ1	1 8 0 00		1 8 0 00	

LEARNING UNIT 3-3

Preparing the Trial Balance: Step 4 of the Accounting Cycle

Did you note in Quiz 3-2 how each account had a running balance figure? Did you know the normal balance of each account in Clark's ledger? As we discussed in Chapter 2, the list of the individual accounts with their balances taken from the ledger is called a **trial balance**.

The trial balance shown in Figure 3-6 was developed from the ledger accounts of Clark's Word Processing Services that were posted and balanced in Quiz 3-2. If information is journalized or posted incorrectly, you can be sure your trial balance will not be correct.

It is important to remember that the capital figure on the trial balance might not be the beginning capital figure. This could happen if Brenda Clark had made additional investments during the period. This additional investment would be journalized and posted to the capital account. The only way to tell if the capital balance on the trial balance is the original balance is to check the ledger capital account to see if any additional investments have taken place. This will be important when we make financial reports.

The trial balance of Clark's Word Processing Services shows that the total of debits is equal to the total of credits. This does *not*, however, guarantee that transactions have been properly recorded. For example, the following errors would remain undetected; (1) a transaction that may have been omitted in the journalizing process; (2) a transaction incorrectly analyzed and recorded in the journal; (3) a journal entry journalized or posted twice.

Let's look at an instance of how a trial balance can be in balance, debits equaling credits, but the correct amount is not recorded in each ledger account. If a journal entry should have been a debit to cash and credit to salaries payable, but was instead recorded as a credit to accounts payable, the entry

The totals of a trial balance can balance and yet be incorrect.

The trial balance lists the accounts in the same order as in the ledger. The $2,090 figure of cash came from the ledger, p. 70.

FIGURE 3-6
Trial Balance.

CLARK'S WORD PROCESSING SERVICES TRIAL BALANCE MAY 31, 19XX	Dr.	Cr.
Cash	2 0 9 0 00	
Accounts Receivable	4 1 0 0 00	
Office Supplies	4 0 0 00	
Prepaid Rent	9 0 0 00	
Word Processing Equipment	8 0 0 0 00	
Accounts Payable		3 5 7 5 00
B. Clark, Capital		7 0 0 0 00
B. Clark, Withdrawals	4 3 0 00	
Word Processing Fees		6 6 0 0 00
Office Salaries Expense	9 0 0 00	
Advertising Expense	1 7 5 00	
Telephone Expense	1 8 0 00	
Totals	17 1 7 5 00	17 1 7 5 00

will balance, but the analysis of the transaction is incorrect. Accounts payable is thus too high and salaries payable is too low, but total liabilities are correct.

Obviously, it is of crucial importance to be accurate in the journalizing and posting process. We will look at how to specifically correct entries in a moment.

WHAT TO DO IF A TRIAL BALANCE DOESN'T BALANCE

If the total amounts of debits and credits are not equal, the following should be considered:

Correcting the trial balance: What to do if your trial balance doesn't balance.

Did you clear your adding machine?

1. If the difference is 10, 100, 1,000, etc., you have probably made a mathematical error in addition.
2. If the difference is equal to one individual account balance in the ledger, see if you omitted one by error. Possibly the figure was not posted from the general journal.
3. Divide the difference (the amount you are off) by 2; then check to see if a debit should have been a credit and vice versa in the ledger or trial balance. Example: $150 difference ÷ 2 = $75. This means you may have placed $75 as a debit to an account instead of a credit or vice versa.
4. Divide the difference by 9. If it is evenly divisible by 9, a **slide** or transposition may have occurred. A slide is an error resulting from adding or deleting zeros in writing numbers. For example, $4,175.00 may have been copied as $41.75. A **transposition** is the accidental rearrangement of digits of a number. For example, $4,175 might have been accidentally written as $4,157.
5. Compare the balances in the trial balance with the ledger accounts to check for copying errors.
6. Recompute balances in each ledger account.
7. Trace all postings from journal to ledger.
8. Take a coffee break before beginning again.

CORRECTING ERRORS IN JOURNALIZING AND POSTING

What should you do if you find an error? First, don't panic. Everyone makes mistakes, and there are accepted ways of correcting them. Only pencilled-in data can be erased. Once an entry has been made in ink, correcting an error in it must always show that the entry has been changed and who changed it. Sometimes, you must also explain why a change has been made.

Making a Correction before Posting

Before posting, error correction is straightforward. Simply draw a line through the incorrect entry, write the correct information above the line, and write your initials near the change. The following illustration shows an error and its correction in an account title:

	1	Word Processing Equipment	8 0 0 0 00			
		Cash		2 0 0 0 00		
		Accounts Payable ~~Accounts Receivable~~ *amp*		6 0 0 0 00		
		Purchase of equip. from Ben Co.				

Numbers are handled the same way as account titles, as the next change from 571 to 175 shows:

	18	Advertising Expense		1 7 5 00		1 7 5 00	
		Accounts Payable				amp 5 7 1 00	
		Bill from Al's News					

If a number has been entered in the wrong column, a straight line is drawn through it, and the number is then written in the correct column:

	1	Word Processing Equipment		8 0 0 0 00			
		Cash				2 0 0 0 00	
		Accounts Payable		amp 6 0 0 0 00		6 0 0 0 00	
		Purchase of equip. from Ben Co.					

Making a Correction after Posting

What if an amount is correctly entered in the journal but posted incorrectly to the ledger of the proper account? The first step is to draw a line through the error and write the correct figure above it. Then, the running balance must be changed to reflect the corrected posting. Here too a line is drawn through the balance and the corrected balance is written above it. Both changes are initialed.

Word Processing Fees							Account No. 411	
			Post				Balance	
Date		Explanation	Ref.	Debit		Credit	Debit	Credit
19XX								
May	7		GJ1			2 5 0 0 00		2 5 0 0 00
	22		GJ1			4 1 8 0 00 1 0 0 0 00 amp		6 6 0 0 00 2 6 0 0 00 amp

Correcting an Entry Posted to the Wrong Account

Drawing a line through an error and writing the correction above it is possible when a mistake has occurred within the proper account. But when an error involves posting to the wrong account, then a correction accompanied by an explanation must be made in the journal. The correct information is then posted to the appropriate ledgers.

Suppose, for example, that as a result of tracing postings from journal entries to ledgers you find that a $180 telephone bill has been incorrectly debited as an advertising expense. First, the journal entry should be corrected and the correction explained, like this:

	Date	Account Titles and Description	PR	Dr.	Cr.
	19XX				
	May 29	Telephone Expense	513	1 8 0 00	
		Advertising Expense	112		1 8 0 00
		To correct error in which			
		Advertising Exp. was debited			
		for charges to Telephone Exp.			

GENERAL JOURNAL — Page 3

This is what the corrected ledger account would look like:

Advertising Expense — Account No. 512

	Date	Explanation	Post Ref.	Debit	Credit	Balance Debit	Balance Credit
	19XX						
	May 18		GJ1	1 7 5 00		1 7 5 00	
	23		GJ1	1 8 0 00		3 5 5 00	
	29		GJ3		1 8 0 00	1 7 5 00	

and the Telephone Expense ledger would look like this:

Telephone Expense — Account No. 513

	Date	Explanation	Post Ref.	Debit	Credit	Balance Debit	Balance Credit
	19XX						
	May 29		GJ3	1 8 0 00		1 8 0 00	

In summary, at this point you should be able to

1. Prepare a trial balance with a ledger, using four-column accounts. (p. 73)
2. Analyze and correct a trial balance that doesn't balance. (p. 74)
3. Correct journal and posting errors. (p. 74)

SELF-REVIEW QUIZ 3-3

1.

> Interoffice Memo
>
> To: Al Vincent
>
> From: Professor Jones
>
> Re: Trial Balance
>
> You have submitted to me an incorrect trial balance. Could you please rework and turn in to me before next Friday.
> Note: Individual amounts look OK.

J. FLYNN
TRIAL BALANCE
OCTOBER 31, 19XX

	Dr.	Cr.
Cash		7 6 6 0 00
Operating Expenses		1 6 0 0 00
J. Flynn, Withdrawals		8 0 0 00
Service Revenue		5 3 0 0 00
Equipment	6 0 0 0 00	
Accounts Receivable	2 5 4 0 00	
Accounts Payable	2 0 0 0 00	
Supplies	3 0 0 00	
J. Flynn, Capital		11 6 0 0 00

2. A $4,000 debit to office equipment was mistakenly posted on June 9, 19XX to office supplies. Prepare the appropriate journal entry to correct this error.

SOLUTION TO SELF-REVIEW QUIZ 3-3

1.

J. FLYNN
TRIAL BALANCE
OCTOBER 31, 19XX

	Dr.	Cr.
Cash	7 6 6 0 00	
Accounts Receivable	2 5 4 0 00	
Supplies	3 0 0 00	
Equipment	6 0 0 0 00	
Accounts Payable		2 0 0 0 00
J. Flynn, Capital		11 6 0 0 00
J. Flynn, Withdrawals	8 0 0 00	
Service Revenue		5 3 0 0 00
Operating Expenses	1 6 0 0 00	
Totals	18 9 0 0 00	18 9 0 0 00

2.

GENERAL JOURNAL					Page 4
Date	Account Titles and Description	PR	Dr.	Cr.
19XX June 9	Office Equipment		4 0 0 0 00	
	Office Supplies			4 0 0 0 00
	To correct error in which office supplies			
	had been debited for purchase of office			
	equipment			

SUMMARY OF KEY POINTS AND KEY TERMS

LEARNING UNIT 3-1

1. The accounting cycle is a sequence of accounting procedures that are usually performed during an accounting period.

2. An accounting period is the time period for which the income statement is prepared.

3. A calendar year is from January 1 to December 31. The fiscal year is any twelve-month period. A fiscal year could be a calendar year but does not have to be.

4. Interim reports are statements that are usually prepared for a month or a quarter (a portion of the fiscal year).

5. A general journal is a book where transactions are recorded in chronological order. Here debits and credits are shown together on one page. This is the book of original entry.

6. The ledger is a collection of accounts where information is accumulated from the postings of the journal. The ledger is the book of final entry.

7. Journalizing is the process of recording journal entries.

8. The chart of accounts provides the specific titles of accounts to be entered in the journal.

9. When journalizing, the post reference column is left blank.

10. A compound journal entry occurs when more than two accounts are affected in the journalizing process of a business transaction.

Accounting cycle: For each accounting period, the process that begins with the recording of business transactions or procedures into a journal and ends with the completion of a post-closing trial balance.

Accounting period: The period of time for which an income statement is prepared.

Book of final entry: Book that receives information about business transactions from a book of original entry (a journal). Example: a ledger.

Book of original entry: Book that records the first formal information about business transactions. Example: a journal.

Calendar year: January 1 to December 31.

Compound journal entry: A journal entry that affects more than two accounts.

Fiscal year: The twelve-month period a business chooses for its accounting year.

General journal: The simplest form of a journal, which records information from transactions in chronological order as they occur. This journal links the debit and credit parts of transactions together.

Interim reports: Financial reports that are prepared for a month, quarter, or some other portion of the fiscal year.

Journal: A listing of business transactions in chronological order. The journal links on one page the debit and credit parts of transactions.

Journal entry: The transaction (debits and credits) that is recorded into a journal once it is analyzed.

Journalizing: The process of recording a transaction entry into the journal.

Natural business year: A business's fiscal year that ends at the same time as a slow seasonal period begins.

LEARNING UNIT 3-2

1. Posting is the process of transferring information from the journal to the ledger.

2. The journal and ledger contain the same information but in a different form.

3. The four-column account aids in keeping a running balance of an account.

4. The normal balance of an account will be located on the side that increases it according to the rules of debits and credits. For example, the normal balances of liabilities occur on the credit side.

5. The mechanical process of posting requires care in transferring appropriate dates, post references, titles, and amounts.

Cross-referencing: Adding to the PR column of the journal the account number of the ledger account that was updated from the journal.

Four-column account: A running balance account that records debits and credits and has a column for an ending balance (debit or credit). Replaces the standard two-column account we used earlier.

(Summary continues on p. 80.)

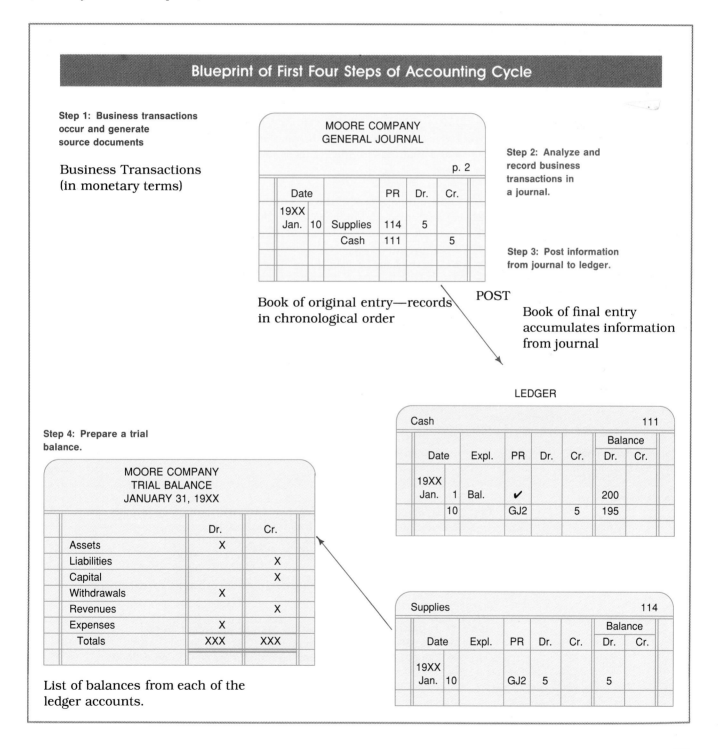

Blueprint of First Four Steps of Accounting Cycle

Step 1: Business transactions occur and generate source documents

Business Transactions (in monetary terms)

MOORE COMPANY GENERAL JOURNAL

p. 2

Date			PR	Dr.	Cr.
19XX Jan.	10	Supplies	114	5	
		Cash	111		5

Book of original entry—records in chronological order

POST

Step 2: Analyze and record business transactions in a journal.

Step 3: Post information from journal to ledger.

Book of final entry accumulates information from journal

LEDGER

Cash						111	
						Balance	
Date		Expl.	PR	Dr.	Cr.	Dr.	Cr.
19XX Jan.	1	Bal.	✔			200	
	10		GJ2		5	195	

Step 4: Prepare a trial balance.

MOORE COMPANY TRIAL BALANCE JANUARY 31, 19XX

	Dr.	Cr.
Assets	X	
Liabilities		X
Capital		X
Withdrawals	X	
Revenues		X
Expenses	X	
Totals	XXX	XXX

List of balances from each of the ledger accounts.

Supplies						114	
						Balance	
Date		Expl.	PR	Dr.	Cr.	Dr.	Cr.
19XX Jan.	10		GJ2	5		5	

Normal balance: The side of an account that is increasing according to the rules of debit and credit. For example, the normal balance of assets is on the debit side; the normal balance of liabilities is on the credit side.

Posting: The transferring, copying, or recording of information from a journal to a ledger.

LEARNING UNIT 3-3

1. A trial balance can balance but be incorrect. For example, an entire journal entry may not have been posted.

2. If a trial balance doesn't balance, check for errors in addition, omission of postings, slides, transpositions, copying errors, etc.

3. Specific procedures should be followed in making corrections in journals and ledgers.

Slide: The error that results in adding or deleting zeros in the writing of a number. Example: 79,200 → 79,20.

Transposition: The accidental rearrangement of digits of a number. Example: 152 → 125.

Trial balance: An informal listing of the ledger accounts and their balances in the ledger that aids in proving the equality of debits and credits.

DISCUSSION QUESTIONS

1. Explain the concept of the accounting cycle.
2. An accounting period is based on the balance sheet. Agree or disagree.
3. Compare and contrast a calendar year versus a fiscal year.
4. What are interim reports?
5. Why is the ledger called the book of final entry?
6. How do transactions get "linked" in a general journal?
7. What is the relationship of the chart of accounts to the general journal?
8. What is a compound journal entry?
9. Posting means updating the journal. Agree or disagree. Please comment.
10. The side that decreases an account is the normal balance. True or false?
11. The PR column of a general journal is the last item to be filled in during the posting process. Agree or disagree.
12. Discuss the concept of cross-referencing.
13. What is the difference between a transposition and a slide?

EXERCISES

Preparing journal entries.

1. Prepare journal entries for the following transactions that occurred during October:

Preparing journal entries.

19XX
Oct. 1 M. Slade invested $600 cash and $200 of equipment into his new business.
3 Purchased building for $25,000 on account.
12 Purchased from Long Co. a truck for $6,000 cash.
18 Bought supplies from Rolo Co. on account, $400.

2. Record the following into the general journal of Paul's Repair Shop:

19XX
Jan. 1 Paul Keen invested $15,000 cash in the repair shop.
5 Paid $6,000 for shop equipment.
8 Bought from Hal Co. shop equipment for $8,000 on account.
14 Received $500 for repair fees earned.
18 Billed Rusty David $400 for services rendered.
20 Paul withdrew $100 for personal use.

3. Post the following transactions to the ledger of Hester Company. The partial ledger of Hester is Cash, 111; Equipment, 121; Accounts Payable, 211; and J. Hester, Capital, 311. Please use four-column accounts in the posting process.

Posting.

Date 19XX			PR	Dr.	Cr.
Mar.	4	Cash		2 0 0 0 00	
		J. Hester, Capital			2 0 0 0 00
		Cash investment			
	9	Equipment		6 0 0 0 00	
		Cash			1 0 0 0 00
		Accounts Payable			5 0 0 0 00
		Purchase of equipment			

Page 4

4. From the following transactions for Veel Company for the month of July, (a) prepare journal entries (assume that it is p. 1 of the journal), (b) post to the ledger (use four-column account), and (c) prepare a trial balance.

Journalizing, posting, and preparing a trial balance.

July 1 Nancy Veel invested $4,000 in the business.
4 Bought from Jee Co. equipment on account, $600.
15 Billed Langley Co. for services rendered, $3,000.
18 Received $2,000 cash for services rendered.
24 Paid salaries expense, $1,600.
28 Nancy withdrew $200 for personal use.

Partial chart of accounts includes: Cash, 111; Accounts Receivable, 112; Equipment, 121; Accounts Payable, 211; N. Veel, Capital, 311; N. Veel, Withdrawals, 312; Fees Earned, 411; Salaries Expense, 511.

5. You have been hired to corect the following trial balance that has been recorded improperly from the ledger to the trial balance.

Correcting a trial balance.

POTTER CO.
TRIAL BALANCE
MARCH 31, 19XX

	Dr.	Cr.
Cash	9 8 0 0 00	
Accounts Receivable		1 2 0 0 00
Accounts Payable	1 8 0 0 00	
A. Potter, Capital		6 5 0 0 00
A. Potter, Withdrawals		3 0 0 0 00
Services Earned		4 7 0 0 00
Concessions Earned	2 5 0 0 00	
Rent Expense	4 0 0 00	
Salaries Expense	2 5 0 0 00	
Miscellaneous Expense		1 3 0 0 00
Totals	17 0 0 0 00	14 0 0 0 00

6. On February 6, 19XX, Bob Allen made the following journal entry to record the purchase on account of office equipment priced at $1,200. This transaction had not yet been posted when the error was discovered. Make the appropriate correction.

	Date		Account Titles and Description	PR	Dr.	Cr.
	19XX					
	Feb.	6	Office Equipment		9 0 0 00	
			Accounts Payable			9 0 0 00
			Purchase of office equip. on account			

GENERAL JOURNAL

GROUP A PROBLEMS

3A-1. Jessie Roy has decided to open Roy's Dog Grooming Center. As the bookkeeper, you have been requested to journalize the following transactions:

19XX
April 1 Paid rent for two months in advance, $1,600.
    3 Purchased grooming equipment on account from Rick's Supply House, $2,200.
    10 Purchased grooming supplies from Pete's Wholesale for $300 cash.
    12 Received $900 cash from grooming fees earned.
    20 Jessie withdrew $200 for her personal use.
    21 Advertising bill received from *Daily Sun* but unpaid, $75.
    25 Paid cleaning expense, $70.
    28 Paid salaries expense, $300.
    29 Performed grooming work for $1,200; however, payment will not be received from Jay's Kennel until May.
    30 Paid Rick's Supply House half the amount owed from April 3 transaction.

Your task is to journalize the above transactions. The chart of accounts for Roy's Dog Grooming Center is as follows:

Assets
111 Cash
112 Accounts Receivable
114 Prepaid Rent
116 Grooming Supplies
121 Grooming Equipment

Liabilities
211 Accounts Payable

Owner's Equity
311 Jessie Roy, Capital
312 Jessie Roy, Withdrawals

Revenue
411 Grooming Fees Earned

Expenses
511 Advertising Expense
512 Salaries Expense
514 Cleaning Expense

3A-2. On June 1, 19XX, Mike Wallace opened Mike's Dance Studio. The following transactions occurred in June:

Comprehensive Problem: Journalizing, posting, and preparing a trial balance.

19XX
June 1 Mike Wallace invested $5,000 in the dance studio.
　　 1 Paid three months' rent in advance, $900.
　　 3 Purchased $600 of equipment from Moore Co. on account.
　　 5 Received $700 cash for fitness-training workshop for dancers.
　　 8 Purchased $400 of supplies for cash.
　　 9 Billed Ranger Co. $1,800 for group dance lesson for its employees.
　　 10 Paid salaries of assistants, $600.
　　 15 Mike Wallace withdrew $200 from the business for his personal use.
　　 28 Paid electrical expense, $150.
　　 29 Paid telephone bill for June, $220.

Your task is to
　　 A. Set up the ledger based on the chart of accounts below.
　　 B. Journalize (journal is Page 1) and post the June transactions.
　　 C. Prepare a trial balance as of June 30, 19XX.
The chart of accounts for Mike's Dance Studio is as follows:

Assets
111 Cash
112 Accounts Receivable
114 Prepaid Rent
121 Supplies
131 Equipment

Liabilities
211 Accounts Payable

Owner's Equity
311 Mike Wallace, Capital
321 Mike Wallace, Withdrawals

Revenue
411 Fees Earned

Expenses
511 Electrical Expense
521 Salaries Expense
531 Telephone Expense

3A-3. The following transactions occurred in June 19XX for R. Black's Placement Agency:

19XX
June 1 R. Black invested $8,000 cash in the placement agency.
　　 1 Bought equipment on account from Rolo Co., $1,000.
　　 3 Earned placement fees of $1,400, but payment will not be received until July.
　　 5 R. Black withdrew $200 for his personal use.
　　 7 Paid wage expense, $400.
　　 9 Placed a client on a local TV show, receiving $500 cash.
　　 15 Bought supplies on account from Roger Co., $300.
　　 28 Paid telephone bill for June, $280.
　　 29 Advertising bill from Globe Co. received but not paid, $600.

The chart of accounts for R. Black's Placement Agency is as follows:

Assets
111 Cash
112 Accounts Receivable
131 Supplies
141 Equipment

Liabilities
211 Accounts Payable

Owner's Equity
311 R. Black, Capital
321 R. Black, Withdrawals

Revenue
411 Placement Fees Earned

Expenses
511 Wage Expense
521 Telephone Expense
531 Advertising Expense

Your task is to

    A. Set up the ledger based on the chart of accounts.
    B. Journalize (P. 1) and post the June transactions.
    C. Prepare a trial balance as of June 30, 19XX.

GROUP B PROBLEMS

3B-1. In April Jessie Roy opened a new dog grooming center. Please assist her by journalizing the following business transactions:

19XX
April   1   Jessie Roy invested $4,000 of grooming equipment as well as $6,000 cash in the new business.
       3   Purchased grooming supplies on account from Rex Co., $500.
     10   Purchased office equipment on account from Ross Stationery, $400.
     12   Jessie paid her home telephone bill from the company checkbook, $60.
     20   Received $600 cash for grooming services performed.
     21   Advertising bill received but not paid, $75.
     25   Cleaning bill received but not paid, $90.
     28   Performed grooming work for Jay Kennels, $700; however, payment will not be received until May.
     29   Paid salaries expense, $400.
     30   Paid Ross Stationery half the amount owed from April 10 transaction.

The chart of accounts for Roy includes: Cash, 111; Accounts Receivable, 112; Prepaid Rent, 114; Grooming Supplies, 116; Office Equipment, 120; Grooming Equipment, 121; Accounts Payable, 211; Jessie Roy, Capital, 311; Jessie Roy, Withdrawals, 312; Grooming Fees Earned, 411; Advertising Expense, 511; Salaries Expense, 512; and Cleaning Expense, 514.

3B-2. In June the following transactions occurred for Mike's Dance Studio.

19XX
June   1   Mike Wallace invested $6,000 in the dance studio.
      1   Paid four months' rent in advance, $1,200.
      3   Purchased supplies on account from A.J.K., $700.
      5   Purchased equipment on account from Reese Company, $900.
      8   Received $1,300 cash for dance-training program provided to Northwest Jr. College.
      9   Billed Long Co. for dance lessons provided, $600.
     10   Mike withdrew $400 from the dance studio to buy a new chain saw for his home.

15   Paid salaries expense, $400.

28   Paid telephone bill, $118.

28   Electric bill received but unpaid, $120.

Your task is to

A. Set up a ledger.

B. Journalize (all P. 1) and post the June transactions.

C. Prepare a trial balance as of June 30, 19XX.

Chart of accounts includes: Cash, 111; Accounts Receivable, 112; Prepaid Rent, 114; Supplies, 121; Equipment, 131; Accounts Payable, 211; Mike Wallace, Capital, 311; Mike Wallace, Withdrawals, 321; Fees Earned, 411; Electrical Expense, 511; Salaries Expense, 521; Telephone Expense, 531.

3B-3.   In June, R. Black's Placement Agency had the following transactions:

19XX

June   1   R. Black invested $6,000 in the new placement agency.

2   Bought equipment for cash, $350.

3   Earned placement fee commission, $2,100, but payment from Avon Co. will not be received until July.

5   Paid wages expense, $400.

7   R. Black paid his home utility bill from the company checkbook, $69.

9   Placed Jay Diamond on a national TV show, receiving $900 cash.

15   Paid cash for supplies, $350.

28   Telephone bill received but not paid, $185.

29   Advertising bill received but not paid, $200.

The chart of accounts includes: Cash, 111; Accounts Receivable, 112; Supplies, 131; Equipment, 141; Accounts Payable, 211; R. Black, Capital, 311; R. Black, Withdrawals, 321; Placement Fees Earned, 411; Wage Expense, 511; Telephone Expense, 521; Advertising Expense, 531.

Your task is to

A. Set up a ledger based on the chart of accounts.

B. Journalize (all P. 1) and post transactions.

C. Prepare a trial balance for June 30, 19XX.

PRACTICAL ACCOUNTING APPLICATION #1

Paul Regan, bookkeeper of Hampton Co., has been up half the night trying to get his trial balance to balance. Here are his results:

HAMPTON CO.
TRIAL BALANCE
JUNE 30, 19XX

	Dr.	Cr.
Office Sales		5 7 2 0 00
Cash in Bank	3 2 6 0 00	
Accounts Receivable	5 6 6 0 00	
Office Equipment	8 4 0 0 00	
Accounts Payable		4 1 6 0 00
D. Hole, Capital		11 5 6 0 00
D. Hole, Withdrawals		7 0 0 00
Wage Expense	2 6 0 0 00	
Rent Expense	9 4 0 00	
Utilities Expense	2 6 00	
Office Supplies	1 2 0 00	
Prepaid Rent	1 8 0 00	

Ken Small, the accountant, compared Paul's amounts in the trial balance with those in the ledger, recomputed each account balance, and compared postings. Ken found the following errors:

1. A $200 debit to D. Hole, Withdrawals, was posted as a credit.
2. D. Hole, Withdrawals, was listed on the trial balance as a credit.
3. A Note Payable account with a credit balance of $2,400 was not listed on the trial balance.
4. The pencil footings for Accounts Payable were debits of $5,320 and credits of $8,800.
5. A debit of $180 to Prepaid Rent was not posted.
6. Office Supplies bought for $60 was posted as a credit to Supplies.
7. A debit of $120 to Accounts Receivable was not posted.
8. A cash payment of $420 was credited to Cash for $240.
9. The pencil footing of the credits to Cash was overstated by $400.
10. The Utilities Expense of $260 was listed in the trial balance as $26.

Assist Paul Regan by preparing a correct trial balance. What advice could you give Ken about Paul? Can you explain the situation to Paul?

PRACTICAL ACCOUNTING APPLICATION #2

Lauren Oliver, an accounting lab tutor, is having a debate with some of her assistants. They are trying to find out how each of the following five unrelated situations would affect the trial balance:

1. A $5 debit to Cash in the ledger was not posted.
2. A $10 debit to Computer Supplies was debited to Computer Equipment.
3. An $8 debit to Wage Expense was debited twice to the account.
4. A $4 debit to Computer Supplies was debited to Computer Sales.
5. A $35 credit to Accounts Payable was posted as a $53 credit.

Could you indicate to Lauren the effect that each situation will have on the trial balance? If a situation will have no effect, indicate that fact.

THE ACCOUNTING CYCLE CONTINUED:
Preparing Work Sheets and Financial Reports

The accompanying diagram shows the steps of the accounting cycle that were completed for Clark's Word Processing Services in the last chapter. This chapter continues the cycle with the preparation of a work sheet and then three financial reports.

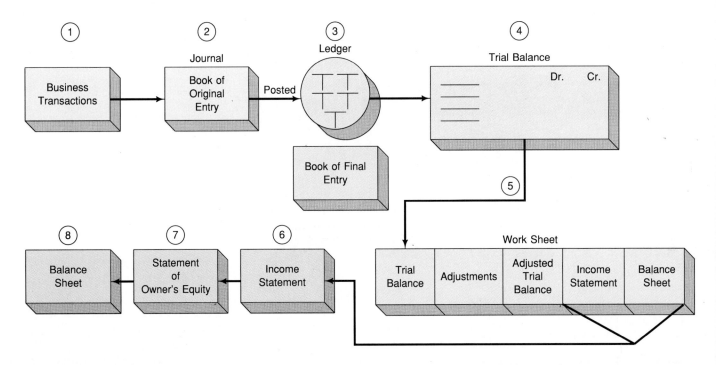

LEARNING UNIT 4-1

Step 5 of the Accounting Cycle: Preparing a Work Sheet

The work sheet helps to organize the data needed to prepare financial reports.

An accountant uses a **work sheet** like a scratch pad, in order to organize and check data before preparing the financial reports necessary to complete the accounting cycle. A sample work sheet is shown in Figure 4-1. The work sheet is not a formal report, and no dollar signs appear on it. You could compare it with the rough draft of a research paper that you prepare for a course. When the research paper is complete, in proper form, no one sees the scratch paper that made the final report possible. The most important function of the work sheet is to allow the accountant to find and correct errors before financial statements are prepared.

CLARK'S WORD PROCESSING SERVICES
WORK SHEET
FOR MONTH ENDED MAY 31, 19XX

taken from ledger

Account Titles	Trial Balance		Adjustments		Adjusted Trial Balance		Income Statement	
	Dr.	Cr.	Dr.	Cr.	Dr.	Cr.	Dr.	Cr.
Cash	2090 00							
Accounts Receivable	4100 00							
Office Supplies	400 00							
Prepaid Rent	900 00							
Word Processing Equipment	8000 00							
Accounts Payable		3575 00						
B. Clark, Capital		7000 00						
B. Clark, Withdrawals	430 00							
Word Processing Fees		6600 00						
Office Salaries Expense	900 00							
Advertising Expense	175 00							
Telephone Expense	180 00							
	17175 00	17175 00						

FIGURE 4-1 The Work Sheet.

Notice the heading on the work sheet for Clark's Word Processing Services shown here:

Clark's Word Processing Services	(Name of company)
Work Sheet	(Name of the working paper)
For Month Ended May 31, 19XX	(Date and the length of the accounting period represented by the work sheet)

The accounts listed on the far left of the work sheet are the only ones in the ledger with balances. The rest of the work sheet is made up of five sections, each divided into debit and credit columns. These five sections are the trial balance, adjustments, adjusted trial balance, income statement, and balance sheet sections. We will discuss each in turn.

THE TRIAL BALANCE SECTION

We discussed how to prepare a trial balance in Chapter 2. Some companies prepare a separate trial balance; others, such as Clark's Word Processing Services, place the trial balance directly on the work sheet. In any case, the trial balance consists of the list of the individual accounts taken from the ledger with their balances. Note that the accountant has listed only those titles in the ledger that have a balance. New titles from the ledger will be added as needed (we will be doing this in a moment).

THE ADJUSTMENTS SECTION

Before the financial reports are prepared, the accountant wants to calculate the *latest* up-to-date balances of each account. In the last few chapters we have been discussing transactions that occur with outside suppliers and companies. But there are also inside transactions that occur during the accounting cycle that must be recorded. By analyzing each of Clark's accounts, the accountant is able to identify specific accounts that must be **adjusted**, or brought up to date. The following accounts are of concern to the accountant for Clark's Word Processing Services:

Prepaid Rent
Office Supplies
Word Processing Equipment
Office Salaries Expense

Need to be adjusted so as to bring their balances up to date before financial reports are prepared.

Let's look at each account separately. After each one is analyzed, the work sheet will be reproduced to show how the adjustments columns will help to update the trial balance. And, after adjustments are completed, a new adjusted trial balance will be prepared.

Adjustment A: Office Supplies

At the end of May the accountant received information that of the $400 worth of office supplies that had been bought, only $80 worth were left (or on hand) as of May 31.

Remember, when the supplies were purchased they were considered an asset. But as supplies get used in the operation of the word processing firm, they become expenses. Let's look at office supplies:

1. Office supplies available, $400.
2. Office supplies left or on hand as of May 31, $80.
3. Office supplies used up or consumed in the operation of the business for the month of May, $320 ($400 − $80 = $320).

Therefore, the asset Office Supplies is really too high on the trial balance (it should be $80, not $400). At the same time, if we don't show the additional expense of supplies used, the *net income* of Clark's Word Processing Services will be too high.

To summarize, if the adjustment to Office Supplies does *not* take place:

1. Expenses for May will be too low.
2. The asset Office Supplies will be too high.

As a consequence:

1. On the income statement, net income will be too high.
2. On the balance sheet, both sides (assets and owner's equity) will be too high.

Now let's look at the adjustment for office supplies in terms of the transaction analysis chart.

Will go on income statement

Accounts Affected	Category	↑ ↓	Rules
Office Supplies Expense	Expense	↑	Dr. ←
Office Supplies	Asset	↓	Cr. ←

Will go on balance sheet

Office Supplies Expense comes from the chart of accounts, p. 57. Remember Office Supplies Expense records amount of supplies used up.

The account Office Supplies is called a **mixed account** because the amount entered on the trial balance is partly a balance sheet amount and partly an income statement amount. On the balance sheet, Office Supplies will be an unexpired cost. On the income statement, Office Supplies Expense will be an expired cost.

Let's see how we enter this adjustment on the work sheet (note how the letter A is used to code the adjustment):

(A) 1. An increase in Office Supplies Expense, $320.
2. A decrease in Office Supplies, $320.

handwritten note: this is the amount of office supplies used up (it decreases)

CLARK'S WORD PROCESSING SERVICES
WORK SHEET
FOR MONTH ENDED MAY 31, 19XX

Account Titles	Trial Balance Dr.	Trial Balance Cr.	Adjustments Dr.	Adjustments Cr.
Cash	2 0 9 0 00			
Accounts Receivabe	4 1 0 0 00			
Office Supplies	4 0 0 00			(A) 3 2 0 00
Prepaid Rent	9 0 0 00			
Word Processing Equipment	8 0 0 0 00			
Accounts Payable		3 5 7 5 00		
B. Clark, Capital		7 0 0 0 00		
B. Clark, Withdrawals	4 3 0 00			
Word Processing Fees		6 6 0 0 00		
Offic Salaries Expense	9 0 0 00			
Advertising Expense	1 7 5 00			
Telephone Expense	1 8 0 00			
	17 1 7 5 00	17 1 7 5 00		
Office Supplies Expense			(A) 3 2 0 00	

Note: All accounts listed *below* the trial balance will be *increasing*.

Since the account Office Supplies Expense is not listed in the account titles, we must list it below the trial balance. Place $320 in the debit column of the adjustments section on the same line as Office Supplies Expense. Place $320 in the credit column of the adjustments section on the same line as Office Supplies. These numbers in the adjustment column show what is used, *not* what is on hand.

The Office Supplies Expense account indicates the amount of supplies used up. It is listed below other trial balance accounts, since it was not on the original trial balance. Think of the Office Supplies Expense account as office supplies used.

Adjustment B: Prepaid Rent

Back on May 1, Clark's Word Processing Services paid three months' rent in advance. The accountant realized that the rent expense would be $300 per month ($900 ÷ 3 months = $300).

Remember, when rent is paid in advance, it is considered an asset called *prepaid rent*. When the asset, prepaid rent, begins to expire or be used up, it becomes an expense. Now it is May 31, and one month's rent, which was paid in advance, has expired and thus becomes an expense.

Should the account be $900, or is there really only $600 of prepaid rent left as of May 31? What do we need to do to bring prepaid rent to the "true" or up-to-date balance? We need to increase Rent Expense by $300 and decrease Prepaid Rent by $300.

A debit will increase the account Office Supplies Expense; a credit will reduce the account Office Supplies.

Adjusting Prepaid Rent.
On p. 92 the trial balance showed a figure for Prepaid Rent of $900.
The amount of rent *expired* is the adjustment figure used to update Prepaid Rent and Rent Expense.

To summarize, if we don't adjust or bring our rent expense up to its proper amount:

1. Expenses for Clark's Word Processing Services for May will be too low.
2. The asset Prepaid Rent will be too high.

The result of this is:

1. On the income statement, net income will be too high.
2. On the balance sheet, both sides (assets and owner's equity) will be too high.

In terms of our transaction analysis chart, the adjustment would look like this:

Will go on income statement

Rent Expense 515

| 300 | |

Accounts Affected	Category	↓ ↑	Rules
Rent Expense	**Expense**	↑	**Dr.** ←
Prepaid Rent	**Asset**	↓	**Cr.** ←

Will go on balance sheet

Prepaid Rent 115

| **900** | 300 Adj. |
| *600* | |

Note that the account Rent Expense comes from the chart of accounts on p. 57. The account Prepaid Rent is also called a mixed account because its balance on the trial balance is partly a balance sheet amount and partly an income statement amount. Thus, after adjustment, Prepaid Rent will be an unexpired cost in the balance sheet, and Rent Expense will be an expired cost in the income statement.

Let's look at how we enter this adjustment on the work sheet:

Rent expense is listed below other trial balance accounts, since it was not on the original trial balance.

(B) 1. An increase in Rent Expense of $300.
2. A decrease in Prepaid Rent of $300.

CLARK'S WORD PROCESSING SERVICES
WORK SHEET
FOR MONTH ENDED MAY 31, 19XX

	Trial Balance		Adjustments	
Account Titles	Dr.	Cr.	Dr.	Cr.
Cash	2 0 9 0 00			
Accounts Receivable	4 1 0 0 00			
Office Supplies	4 0 0 00			(A) 3 2 0 00
	9 0 0 00			
Prepaid Rent				(B) 3 0 0 00
Word Processing Equipment	8 0 0 0 00			
Accounts Payable		3 5 7 5 00		
B. Clark, Capital		7 0 0 0 00		
B. Clark, Withdrawals	4 3 0 00			
Word Processing Equipment		6 6 0 0 00		
Office Supplies Expense	9 0 0 00			
Advertising Expense	1 7 5 00			
Telephone Expense	1 8 0 00			
	17 1 7 5 00	17 1 7 5 00		
Office Supplies Expense			(A) 3 2 0 00	
Rent Expense			(B) 3 0 0 00	

Again, note that accounts listed *below* the trial balance are *increasing*.

Since the account Rent Expense is not listed in the account titles, we must list it below the trial balance (and below Office Supplies Expense). Place $300 in the debit column of the adjustments section, on the same line as Rent Expense. Place $300 in the credit column of the adjustments section, on the same line as Prepaid Rent.

Debit increases rent expense and credit reduces amount of rent paid in advance.

Adjustment C: Word Processing Equipment

Did you note in the first two adjustments how the asset office supplies and the asset prepaid rent were reduced? Our next adjustment, for word processing equipment, will not be handled in quite the same way. Why not? Supplies and prepaid rent tend to be used up in a relatively *short* period of time, but equipment is assumed to have a long life and thus helps to produce revenue over a longer period. Thus accountants choose to keep a record on the balance sheet of the **historical cost**, or original amount of cost, of the equipment. This means that when the adjustment for the word processing equipment is complete, the original cost of $8,000 will still be shown on the balance sheet, as well as reflected in the ledger.

Take this one slowly.

Original cost of $8,000 for word processing equipment remains *unchanged* after adjustments.

Our goal in making this adjustment is to allocate or spread the cost of the equipment over its expected useful life while still maintaining a record of the full original cost. This spreading is called **depreciation**. To reach this goal we must be able to figure out how much the equipment depreciates per month, and then keep a running total of how that depreciation mounts up over the years.

Our first step is to calculate the amount of depreciation that will be taken for May. (The IRS has guidelines, tables, and formulas to estimate amounts of depreciation. For the moment, we will use the straight-line method of depreciation—so called because equal amounts are taken over successive periods of time.) The calculation of depreciation for the year for Clark's Word Processing Services is as follows:

$$\frac{\text{cost of equipment} - \text{residual value}}{\text{estimated years of usefulness}}$$

Think of **residual value** as the estimated value of the equipment at end of the fifth year. For Clark the equipment has an estimated residual value of $2,000.

$$\frac{\$8,000 - \$2,000}{5 \text{ years}} = \frac{\$6,000}{5} = \$1,200 \text{ per year}$$

Assume equipment has a 5-year life.

Clark will record $1,200 of depreciation each year.

Depreciation is an expense reported on the income statement.

Since the adjustment for May is only for *one* month, we further calculate the depreciation as follows:

$$\frac{\$1,200}{12 \text{ months}} = \$100 \text{ depreciation per month}$$

This $100 is known as *Depreciation Expense* and will be shown on the income statement.

The question now is, how can we keep this running total of the depreciation amount and yet still keep a record of the full original cost of the equipment? To do this we have to create a new account, called **Accumulated Depreciation**. This is a **contra asset** account; it has the opposite balance of an asset such as equipment. Accumulated Depreciation will summarize, accumulate, or build up the amount of depreciation that is taken on the word processing equipment over its estimated useful life.

The purposes of Accumulated Depreciation are to

1. Let the amount listed on Clark's books for word processing equipment remain at the original cost of $8,000.
2. As of May 31, summarize or accumulate the amount of depreciation taken on the equipment to that date.

Accumulated Depreciation	
Dr.	Cr.
−	+

is a contra-asset account found on the balance sheet.

Let's see how this would look on a partial balance sheet of Clark's Word Processing Services.

At end of June the accumulated depreciation will be $200, but historical cost will stay at $8,000.

1. Historical cost of $8,000 of equipment is not changed.
2. Amount of accumulated depreciation is $100.
3. This shows the unused amount of the equipment that may be depreciated in future periods of time. This figure, the cost of the asset less its accumulated depreciation, is often termed **book value** or carrying value.

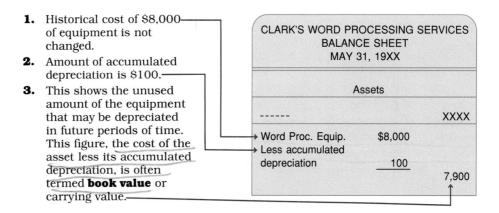

CLARK'S WORD PROCESSING SERVICES
BALANCE SHEET
MAY 31, 19XX

Assets

------   XXXX

Word Proc. Equip. $8,000
Less accumulated depreciation   100
7,900

We need an Accumulated Depreciation account to see the relationship of the original or historical cost of the equipment and the amount of depreciation that has been taken or accumulated over a period of time. Remember, Accumulated Depreciation is a contra-asset account found on the balance sheet.

Let's summarize the key points before going on to mark the adjustment on the work sheet:

Taking depreciation does not result in any new payment of cash. The result of depreciation provides some tax savings.

1. Depreciation Expense goes on the income statement, which results in
   (a) An increase in total expenses.
   (b) A decrease in net income.
   (c) Therefore, less to be paid in taxes.
2. Accumulated depreciation is a contra-asset account found on the balance sheet next to its related equipment account.
3. The original cost of equipment is not reduced; it stays the same until the equipment is sold or removed.
4. Each month the amount in the Accumulated Depreciation account grows larger while the cost of the equipment remains the same.

Now let's analyze the adjustment on the transaction analysis chart:

Accounts Affected	Category	↑ ↓	Rules	
Depreciation Expense, Word Processing Equipment	Expense	↑	Dr. ←	Will go on income statement
Accumulated Depreciation, Word Processing Equipment	Contra asset	↑	Cr. ←	Will go on balance sheet

Dep. Expense, W. P. 516

100 |

Accum. Dep., W. P. 122

| 100

Note that the accounts affected do not include the equipment account, because we leave the original cost of the equipment as is. Note also that as the Accumulated Depreciation increases (as a credit), the end result will be to lower the equipment's *book value*, but the original cost of the equipment is not changed.

We enter the adjustment for depreciation of word processing equipment on the work sheet in the following way:

Note that the original cost of the equipment on the work sheet has *not* been changed ($8,000).

(C) 1. An increase in Depreciation Expense, W. P. Equipment.
2. An increase in Accumulated Depreciation, W. P. Equipment.

CLARK'S WORD PROCESSING SERVICES
WORK SHEET
FOR MONTH ENDED MAY 31, 19XX

Account Titles	Trial Balance Dr.	Trial Balance Cr.	Adjustments Dr.	Adjustments Cr.
Cash	2 0 9 0 00			
Accounts Receivable	4 1 0 0 00			
Office Supplies	4 0 0 00			(A) 3 2 0 00
Prepaid Rent	9 0 0 00			(B) 3 0 0 00
Word Processing Equipment	8 0 0 0 00			
Accounts Payable		3 5 7 5 00		
B. Clark, Capital		7 0 0 0 00		
B. Clark, Withdrawals	4 3 0 00			
Word Processing Fees		6 6 0 0 00		
Office Salaries Expense	9 0 0 00			
Advertising Expense	1 7 5 00			
Telephone Expense	1 8 0 00			
	17 1 7 5 00	17 1 7 5 00		
Office Supplies Expense			(A) 3 2 0 00	
Rent Expense			(B) 3 0 0 00	
Depreciation Expense, W.P. Equip.			(C) 1 0 0 00	
Accum. Depreciation, W.P. Equip.				(C) 1 0 0 00

Since this is a new business, neither account that we are adjusting is listed in the account titles, we need to list both accounts below Rent Expense in the account titles section. Next month accumulated depreciation will be listed in the original trial balance. On the work sheet, place $100 in the debit column of the adjustments section, on the same line as Depreciation Expense, W. P. Equipment. Place $100 in the credit column of the adjustments section, on the same line as Accumulated Depreciation, W. P. Equipment.

In the next month, on June 30, you would enter $100 under Depreciation Expense, and Accumulated Depreciation would show a balance of $200. Remember, in May Clark was a new company, with no previous depreciation having been taken.

Now let's look at the last adjustment for Clark's Word Processing Services.

Adjustment D: Salaries Accrued

Clark's Word Processing Services paid $900 in Office Salaries Expense (see the trial balance of any previous work sheet in this chapter).

On May 27 the last salary checks were paid for the month. Since we are concerned with information as of May 31, our goal is to update the Office Salaries Expense. What is the true figure for May? Is it $900?

During the days of May 28, 29, 30, 31, John Murray worked for Clark, but his next paycheck is not due until June. For these four days he earned $250. The question is whether this $250 is an expense to Clark in May, before it is actually paid. Or should it be shown as an expense to Clark in June when it is due and is paid?

May						
S	M	T	W	T	F	S
						1
2	3	4	5	6	7	8
9	10	11	12	13	14	15
16	17	18	19	20	21	22
23	24	25	26	27	28	29
30	31					

Think back to Chapter 1, when we first discussed revenue and expenses. We noted then that revenue is recorded when it is earned, not when the money actually comes in, and expenses are recorded when they are incurred, not when they are actually paid off. This is a principle that we will be discussing in a later chapter; for now it is enough to remember that we record revenue and expenses when they occur, because we want to match earned revenue with the expenses that resulted in earning those revenues. In this case, by working those four days, John Murray was able to create some revenues for Clark in May. Although John will not be paid until June, it is important to show his office salaries expense in May when the revenue was earned.

The results are:

1. Office Salaries Expense is increased by $250. This unpaid and unrecorded expense for salaries for which payment is not due is called **accrued salaries**. In effect, we now show the true expense for salaries ($1,150 instead of $900):

Office Salaries Expense	
900	
250	

<table>
<tr><td>Accumulated Depreciation</td></tr>
</table>

Accumulated Depreciation	
Dr.	Cr.
	History of amount of depreciation taken to date

Adjusting Salaries

An expense can be incurred without being paid as long as it has helped in creating earned revenue for a period of time.

2. The second result is that salaries payable is increased by $250. Clark's has created a liability called Salaries Payable, meaning that the firm owes money for salaries. Next month, when the firm pays John Murray, it will reduce its liability, Salaries Payable, as well as decrease its cash.

In terms of the transaction analysis chart, the following would be done:

Accounts Affected	Category	↑ ↓	Rule
Office Salaries Expense	Expense	↑	Dr.
Salaries Payable	Liability	↑	Cr.

Office Salaries Exp. 511

| 900 | |
| 250 | |

Salaries Payable 212

| | 250 |

We enter the adjustment for accrued salaries in the following way:

(D) 1. An increase in Office Salaries Expense, $250.
2. An increase in Salaries Payable, $250.

CLARK'S WORD PROCESSING SERVICES
WORK SHEET
FOR MONTH ENDED MAY 31, 19XX

Account Titles	Trial Balance Dr.	Trial Balance Cr.	Adjustments Dr.	Adjustments Cr.
Cash	2 0 9 0 00			
Accounts Receivable	4 1 0 0 00			
Office Supplies	4 0 0 00			(A) 3 2 0 00
Prepaid Rent	9 0 0 00			(B) 3 0 0 00
Word Processing Equipment	8 0 0 0 00			
Accounts Payable		3 5 7 5 00		
B. Clark, Capital		7 0 0 0 00		
B. Clark, Withdrawals	4 3 0 00			
Word Processing Fees		6 6 0 0 00		
Office Salaries Expense	9 0 0 00		(D) 2 5 0 00	
Advertising Expense	1 7 5 00			
Telephone Expense	1 8 0 00			
	17 1 7 5 00	17 1 7 5 00		
Office Supplies Expense			(A) 3 2 0 00	
Rent Expense			(B) 3 0 0 00	
Depreciation Expense, W.P. Equip.			(C) 1 0 0 00	
Accum. Depreciation, W.P. Equip.				(C) 1 0 0 00
Salaries Payable				(D) 2 5 0 00

Note again that all accounts added below the trial balance are *increasing*.

Since the account Office Salaries Expense is already listed in the account titles, place $250 in the debit column of the adjustments section on the same line as Office Salaries Expense. Since Salaries Payable is not listed in the account titles, add the account title Salaries Payable below the trial balance, below Accumulated Depreciation, W. P. Equipment. Place $250 in the credit column of the adjustments section on the same line as Salaries Payable.

Now that we have finished all the adjustments that we intended to make, we total the adjustments section, as shown in Figure 4-2.

THE ADJUSTED TRIAL BALANCE SECTION

Next on the work sheet is the adjusted trial balance section. In order to fill it out, we summarize the information that has been placed in the trial balance and adjustments sections, as shown in Figure 4-3 (p. 99).

It is important to note carefully that, when bringing numbers across from the trial balance to the adjusted trial balance, two debits will be added together and two credits will be added together. If you have a debit and a credit, take the difference and place it on the side that is larger.

FIGURE 4-2
The Adjustments Section of the Work Sheet.

CLARK'S WORD PROCESSING SERVICES
WORK SHEET
FOR MONTH ENDED MAY 31, 19XX

Account Titles	Trial Balance Dr.	Trial Balance Cr.	Adjustments Dr.	Adjustments Cr.
Cash	2 0 9 0 00			
Accounts Receivable	4 1 0 0 00			
Office Supplies	4 0 0 00			(A) 3 2 0 00
Prepaid Rent	9 0 0 00			(B) 3 0 0 00
Word Processing Equipment	8 0 0 0 00			
Accounts Payable		3 5 7 5 00		
B. Clark, Capital		7 0 0 0 00		
B. Clark, Withdrawals	4 3 0 00			
Word Processing Fees		6 6 0 0 00		
Office Salaries Expense	9 0 0 00		(D) 2 5 0 00	
Advertising Expense	1 7 5 00			
Telephone Expense	1 8 0 00			
	17 1 7 5 00	17 1 7 5 00		
Office Supplies Expense			(A) 3 2 0 00	
Rent Expense			(B) 3 0 0 00	
Depreciation Expense, W.P. Equip.			(C) 1 0 0 00	
Accum. Depreciation, W.P. Equip.				(C) 1 0 0 00
Salaries Payable				(D) 2 5 0 00
			9 7 0 00	9 7 0 00

CLARK'S WORD PROCESSING SERVICES
WORK SHEET
FOR MONTH ENDED MAY 31, 19XX

Account Titles	Trial Balance Dr.	Trial Balance Cr.	Adjustments Dr.	Adjustments Cr.	Adjusted Trial Balance Dr.	Adjusted Trial Balance Cr.
Cash	2 0 9 0 00				2 0 9 0 00	
Accounts Receivable	4 1 0 0 00				4 1 0 0 00	
Office Supplies	4 0 0 00			(A) 3 2 0 00	8 0 00	
Prepaid Rent	9 0 0 00			(B) 3 0 0 00	6 0 0 00	
Word Processing Equipment	8 0 0 0 00				8 0 0 0 00	
Accounts Payable		3 5 7 5 00				3 5 7 5 00
B. Clark, Capital		7 0 0 0 00				7 0 0 0 00
B. Clark, Withdrawals	4 3 0 00				4 3 0 00	
Word Processing Fees		6 6 0 0 00				6 6 0 0 00
Office Salaries Expense	9 0 0 00		(D) 2 5 0 00		1 1 5 0 00	
Advertising	1 7 5 00				1 7 5 00	
Telephone Expense	1 8 0 00				1 8 0 00	
	17 1 7 5 00	17 1 7 5 00				
Office Supplies Expense			(A) 3 2 0 00		3 2 0 00	
Rent Expense			(B) 3 0 0 00		3 0 0 00	
Depreciation Expense, W.P. Equip.			(C) 1 0 0 00		1 0 0 00	
Accum. Depreciation, W.P. Equip.				(C) 1 0 0 00		1 0 0 00
Salaries Payable				(D) 2 5 0 00		2 5 0 00
			9 7 0 00	9 7 0 00	17 5 2 5 00	17 5 2 5 00

If no adjustment is made, just carry over amount from trial balance on same side.

Supplies were $400 but we used up $320, leaving us with an $80 balance in supplies. Note: If there are a debit and a credit, take the *difference* between the two and place it on the side that is larger.

Note: Equipment is *not* adjusted here.

Two debits are added together. If two credits, they also would have been added together.

Carry these amounts over to adjusted trial balance in the same positions.

Note: The total of the left (debit) must equal the total of the right (credit) ($17,525).

FIGURE 4-3 The Adjusted Trial Balance Section of the Work Sheet.

TABLE 4-1   Normal Balances and Account Categories

ACCOUNT TITLES	CATEGORY	NORMAL BALANCE ON ADJUSTED TRIAL BALANCE	INCOME STATEMENT Dr.	INCOME STATEMENT Cr.	BALANCE SHEET Dr.	BALANCE SHEET Cr.
Cash	Asset	Dr.			X	
Accounts Receivable	Asset	Dr.			X	
Office Supplies	Asset	Dr.			X	
Prepaid Rent	Asset	Dr.			X	
Word Proc. Equip.	Asset	Dr.			X	
Accounts Payable	Liability	Cr.				X
B. Clark, Capital	Capital	Cr.				X
B. Clark, Withdrawals	Withdrawal	Dr.			X	
Word Proc. Fees	Revenue	Cr.		X		
Office Salaries Exp.	Expense	Dr.	X			
Advertising Expense	Expense	Dr.	X			
Telephone Expense	Expense	Dr.	X			
Office Supplies Exp.	Expense	Dr.	X			
Rent Expense	Expense	Dr.	X			
Dep. Exp., W. P. Equip.	Expense	Dr.	X			
Acc. Dep., W. P. Equip.	Contra Asset	Cr.				X
Salaries Payable	Liability	Cr.				X

Now that we have completed the adjustments and adjusted trial balance sections of the work sheet, it is time to move on to the income statement section and the balance sheet section. But before we do that, take a look at the chart shown in Table 4-1. Do not try to memorize this aid, just use it as a reference to help you in filling out the next two sections of the work sheet. Keep in mind that we first carry over the numbers from the adjusted trial balance to one of the last four columns of the work sheet and then we complete the bottom section.

THE INCOME STATEMENT SECTION

The income statement section lists only revenue and expenses from the adjusted trial balance. Note how this is accomplished in Figure 4-4.

Did you notice that accumulated depreciation and salaries payable do not go on the income statement? Accumulated depreciation is a contra asset found on the balance sheet. Salaries payable is a liability found on the balance sheet.

The revenue of $6,600 and all the individual expenses are listed in the income statement section. The revenue, since it has a credit balance, is placed in the credit column of the income statement section. The expenses, since they have debit balances, are placed in the debit column of the income statement section. Once the debits and credits are placed in the columns, you should

1. Total the debits and credits.
2. Calculate the balance between the debit and credit columns and place the difference on the smaller side.
3. Total the columns.

Do not think of Net Income as a Dr. or Cr. The $4,375 is placed in the debit column to balance both columns to $6,600. In actuality the credit side is larger by $4,375.

CLARK'S WORD PROCESSING SERVICES
WORK SHEET
FOR MONTH ENDED MAY 31, 19XX

Account Titles	Adjusted Trial Balance Dr.	Cr.	Income Statement Dr.	Cr.
Cash	2090 00			
Accounts Receivable	4100 00			
Office Supplies	80 00			
Prepaid Rent	600 00			
Word Processing Equipment	8000 00			
Accounts Payable		3575 00		
B. Clark, Capital		7000 00		
B. Clark, Withdrawals	430 00			
Word Processing Fees		6600 00		6600 00
Office Salaries Expense	1150 00		1150 00	
Advertising Expense	175 00		175 00	
Telephone Expense	180 00		180 00	
Office Supplies Expense	320 00		320 00	
Rent Expense	300 00		300 00	
Depreciation Exp., W.P. Equip.	100 00		100 00	
Acc. Depreciation, W.P. Equip.		100 00		
Salaries Payable		250 00		
	17525 00	17525 00	2225 00	6600 00
Net Income			4375 00	
			6600 00	6600 00

FIGURE 4-4 The Income Statement Section of the Work Sheet.

The difference between $2,225 Dr. and $6,600 Cr. indicates a net income of $4,375. Notice on the work sheet in Figure 4-4 that the label Net Income is added in the account title column on the same line as $4,375. When there is a net income, it will be placed in the debit column of the income statement section of the work sheet. If you have a net loss, it will be placed in the credit column. The $6,600 total indicates that the two columns are in balance.

THE BALANCE SHEET SECTION

In order to fill out the balance sheet section of the work sheet, we carry over the following from the adjusted trial balance section: assets, contra assets, liabilities, capital, and withdrawals. Because the beginning figure for capital* is used on the work sheet, we have to bring over net income to the credit column of the balance sheet in order to have both columns balance. *Remember: The ending figure for capital is not on the work sheet.*

Let's now look at the completed work sheet in Figure 4-5 (p. 102) to see how the balance sheet section is completed. Note how the net income of $4,375

---

* Remember, to see if additional investments occurred for period you will have to check capital account in ledger.

CLARK'S WORD PROCESSING SERVICES
WORK SHEET
FOR MONTH ENDED MAY 31, 19XX

Account Titles	Trial Balance Dr.	Trial Balance Cr.	Adjustments Dr.	Adjustments Cr.	Adjusted Trial Balance Dr.	Adjusted Trial Balance Cr.	Income Statement Dr.	Income Statement Cr.	Balance Sheet Dr.	Balance Sheet Cr.
Cash	2 0 9 0 00				2 0 9 0 00				2 0 9 0 00	
Accounts Receiveable	4 1 0 0 00				4 1 0 0 00				4 1 0 0 00	
Office Supplies	4 0 0 00			(A) 3 2 0 00	8 0 00				8 0 00	
Prepaid Rent	9 0 0 00			(B) 3 0 0 00	6 0 0 00				6 0 0 00	
Word Processing Equipment	8 0 0 0 00				8 0 0 0 00				8 0 0 0 00	
Acct. Payable		3 5 7 5 00				3 5 7 5 00				3 5 7 5 00
B. Clark, Capital		7 0 0 0 00				7 0 0 0 00				7 0 0 0 00
B. Clark. Withdrawals	4 3 0 00				4 3 0 00				4 3 0 00	
Word Processing Fees		6 6 0 0 00				6 6 0 0 00		6 6 0 0 00		
Office Salaries Expense	9 0 0 00		(D) 2 5 0 00		1 1 5 0 00		1 1 5 0 00			
Advertising Expense	1 7 5 00				1 7 5 00		1 7 5 00			
Telephone Expense	1 8 0 00				1 8 0 00		1 8 0 00			
	1 7 1 7 5 00	1 7 1 7 5 00								
Office Supplies Expense			(A) 3 2 0 00		3 2 0 00		3 2 0 00			
Rent Expense			(B) 3 0 0 00		3 0 0 00		3 0 0 00			
Depreciation Expense W.P. Equip.			(C) 1 0 0 00		1 0 0 00		1 0 0 00			
Accum. Depreciation, W.P. Equip.				(C) 1 0 0 00		1 0 0 00				1 0 0 00
Salaries Payable				(D) 2 5 0 00		2 5 0 00				2 5 0 00
			9 7 0 00	9 7 0 00	1 7 5 2 5 00	1 7 5 2 5 00	2 2 2 5 00	6 6 0 0 00	1 5 3 0 0 00	1 0 9 2 5 00
Net Income							4 3 7 5 00			4 3 7 5 00
							6 6 0 0 00	6 6 0 0 00	1 5 3 0 0 00	1 5 3 0 0 00

FIGURE 4-5   The Completed Work Sheet.

is brought over to the credit column of the work sheet. The figure for capital is also on the credit column while the figure for withdrawals is on the debit column. By placing the net income in the credit column both sides total $15,300. If a net loss were to occur it would be placed in the debit column of the balance sheet column.

Now that we have completed the work sheet, our next goal is to complete the three financial reports. But first let's summarize our progress.

The amounts come from the adjusted trial balance, except the $4,375, which was carried over from the income statement section.

At this point you should be able to

1. Define and explain the purpose of a work sheet.   (p. 88)
2. Explain the need as well as the process for adjustments.   (p. 90)
3. Define and give an example of a mixed account.   (p. 91)
4. Explain the concept of depreciation.   (p. 94)
5. Explain the difference between depreciation expense and accumulated depreciation.   (p. 94)
6. Prepare a work sheet from a trial balance and adjustment data.   (p. 102)

SELF-REVIEW QUIZ 4-1

From the accompanying trial balance and adjustment data, complete a work sheet for B. Bass Co. for the month ended Dec. 31, 19XX.

Note: The numbers used on this quiz may seem impossibly small, but we have done that on purpose, so that at this point you don't have to worry about arithmetic, just about preparing the work sheet correctly.

B. BASS CO.
TRIAL BALANCE
DECEMBER 31, 19XX

	Dr.	Cr.
Cash	16 00	
Accounts Receivable	2 00	
Prepaid Insurance	3 00	
Store Supplies	5 00	
Store Equipment	6 00	
Accumulated Depreciation, Store Equipment		4 00
Accounts Payable		2 00
B. Bass, Capital		14 00
B. Bass, Withdrawals	3 00	
Revenue from Clients		25 00
Rent Expense	2 00	
Salaries Expense	8 00	
	45 00	45 00

Adjustment data:

(A) Depreciation Expense, Store Equipment, $1.
(B) Insurance Expired, $2.
(C) Supplies on hand, $1.
(D) Salaries owed but not paid to employees, $3.

Don't adjust this line! Store Equipment always contains the historical cost.

B. BASS COMPANY
WORK SHEET
FOR MONTH ENDED DECEMBER 31, 19XX

Account Titles	Trial Balance Dr.	Trial Balance Cr.	Adjustments Dr.	Adjustments Cr.	Adjusted Trial Balance Dr.	Adjusted Trial Balance Cr.	Income Statement Dr.	Income Statement Cr.	Balance Sheet Dr.	Balance Sheet Cr.
Cash	16 00				16 00				16 00	
Accounts Receivable	2 00				2 00				2 00	
Prepaid Insurance	3 00			(B) 2 00	1 00				1 00	
Store Supplies	5 00			(C) 4 00	1 00				1 00	
Store Equipment	6 00				6 00				6 00	
Accum. Dep., Store Equipment		4 00		(A) 1 00		5 00				5 00
Accounts Payable		2 00				2 00				2 00
B. Bass, Capital		14 00				14 00				14 00
B. Bass, Withdrawals	3 00				3 00				3 00	
Revenue from Clients		25 00				25 00		25 00		
Rent Expense	2 00				2 00		2 00			
Salaries Expense	8 00		(D) 3 00		11 00		11 00			
	45 00	45 00								
Dep. Exp., Store Equipment			(A) 1 00		1 00		1 00			
Insurance Expense			(B) 2 00		2 00		2 00			
Supplies Expense			(C) 4 00		4 00		4 00			
Salaries Payable				(D) 3 00		3 00				3 00
			10 00	10 00	49 00	49 00	20 00	25 00	29 00	24 00
Net Income							5 00			5 00
							25 00	25 00	29 00	29 00

Note that Accumulated Depreciation is listed in trial balance, since this is not a new company. Store Equipment has already been depreciated $4.00 from an earlier period.

Step 6 of the Accounting Cycle: Preparing the Financial Statements from the Work Sheet

From the work sheet completed in Unit 4-1 we will now be able to prepare the *formal* financial reports. Let's first prepare the income statement for Clark for the month of May.

PREPARING THE INCOME STATEMENT

There are several points to remember when preparing the income statement:

1. Every figure on the formal report is on the work sheet. The diagram on p. 106 shows where each of these figures goes on the income statement.
2. There are no debit or credit columns on the formal report.
3. The inside column on financial reports is used for subtotaling.
4. Withdrawals do not go on the income statement; they go on the statement of owner's equity.

Take a moment to look at the income statement in the diagram in Figure 4-6 (p. 106). Note which items go where from the income statement section of the work sheet onto the formal report.

PREPARING THE STATEMENT OF OWNER'S EQUITY

Figure 4-7 (p. 106) is the statement of owner's equity for Clark showing where the information comes from on the work sheet. When the statement of owner's equity is prepared from the work sheet you should recall that the figure on the work sheet for capital might not be the beginning figure for capital if any additional investments have taken place. You can find this out by checking the ledger account for capital. Note how net income and withdrawals aid in calculating the new figure for capital.

PREPARING THE BALANCE SHEET

In preparing the balance sheet, remember that the balance sheet section totals on the work sheet ($15,300) do *not* match the totals on the formal balance sheet ($14,770) (Figure 4-8, p. 107). This is because there are no debit or credit columns on the formal report. We must rearrange the information from the work sheet to prepare the balance sheet. For example, at the bottom of the work sheet, Accumulated Depreciation ($100) was in the column opposite Word Processing Equipment ($8,000); however, when the formal balance sheet was prepared, note how the book value was calculated on the formal report. The $7,900 on the balance sheet is not found on the work sheet. Figure 4-8 shows how to prepare the balance sheet from the work sheet.

CLARK'S WORD PROCESSING SERVICES
INCOME STATEMENT
FOR MONTH ENDED MAY 31, 19XX

Revenue		
Word Processing Fees		$6600.00
Operating Expenses:		
Office Salaries Expense	$1150.00	
Advertising Expense	175.00	
Telephone Expense	180.00	
Office Supplies Expense	320.00	
Rent Expense	300.00	
Depreciation Expense, W.P. Equipment	100.00	
Total Operating Expenses		2225.00
Net Income		$4375.00

Account Titles	Income Statement	
	Dr.	Cr.
Cash		
Accounts Receivable		
Office Supplies		
Prepaid Rent		
Word Processing Equipment		
Accounts Payable		
B. Clark, Capital		
B. Clark, Withdrawals		
Word Processing Fees		6600.00
Office Salaries Expense	1150.00	
Advertising Expense	175.00	
Telephone Expense	180.00	
Office Supplies Expense	320.00	
Rent Expense	300.00	
Depreciation Expense, W.P. Equip.	100.00	
Accum. Depreciation, W.P. Equip.		
Salaries Payable		
	2225.00	6600.00
Net Income	4375.00	
	6600.00	6600.00

FIGURE 4-6   From Work Sheet to Income Statement.

CLARK'S WORD PROCESSING SERVICES
STATEMENT OF OWNER'S EQUITY
FOR MONTH ENDED MAY 31, 19XX

Brenda Clark, Capital, May 1, 19XX		$7000.00
Net Income for May	$4375.00	
Less Withdrawals for May	430.00	
Increase in Capital		3945.00
Brenda Clark, Capital, May 31, 19XX		$10945.00

Annotations:
- Adjusted trial balance Dr. Column on work sheet (p. 102)
- From income statement Net Income on work sheet (p. 102) (or from formal report just prepared)
- Adjusted trial balance Dr. Column on work sheet (p. 102)
- This figure is *not* on the work sheet. This will be used to prepare the balance sheet.

FIGURE 4-7   Completing a Statement of Owner's Equity.

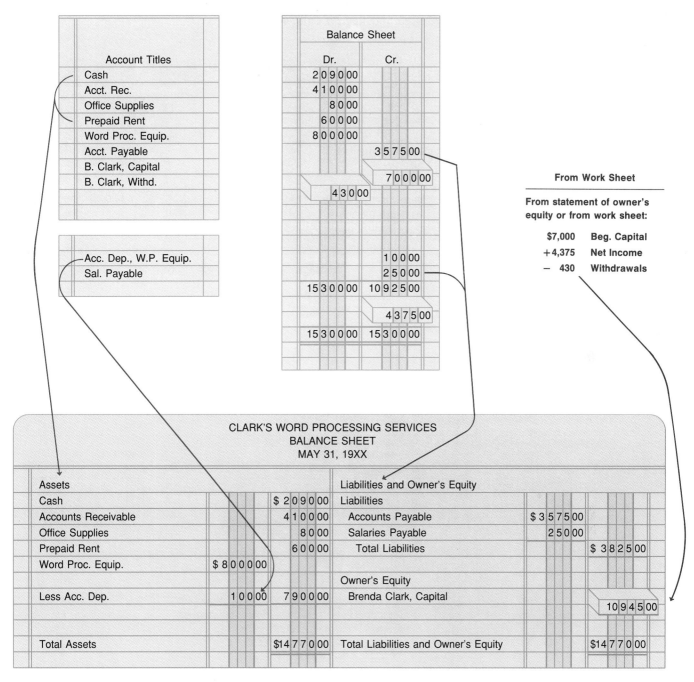

Account Titles					
Cash					
Acct. Rec.					
Office Supplies					
Prepaid Rent					
Word Proc. Equip.					
Acct. Payable					
B. Clark, Capital					
B. Clark, Withd.					

	Balance Sheet	
	Dr.	Cr.
	2 0 9 0 00	
	4 1 0 0 00	
	8 0 00	
	6 0 0 00	
	8 0 0 0 00	
		3 5 7 5 00
		7 0 0 0 00
	4 3 0 00	

Acc. Dep., W.P. Equip.	
Sal. Payable	

1 0 0 00	
	2 5 0 00
15 3 0 0 00	10 9 2 5 00
	4 3 7 5 00
15 3 0 0 00	15 3 0 0 00

From Work Sheet

From statement of owner's equity or from work sheet:

$7,000	Beg. Capital
+4,375	Net Income
− 430	Withdrawals

CLARK'S WORD PROCESSING SERVICES
BALANCE SHEET
MAY 31, 19XX

Assets				Liabilities and Owner's Equity			
Cash			$ 2 0 9 0 00	Liabilities			
Accounts Receivable			4 1 0 0 00	Accounts Payable	$ 3 5 7 5 00		
Office Supplies			8 0 00	Salaries Payable	2 5 0 00		
Prepaid Rent			6 0 0 00	Total Liabilities		$ 3 8 2 5 00	
Word Proc. Equip.	$ 8 0 0 0 00						
				Owner's Equity			
Less Acc. Dep.	1 0 0 00	7 9 0 0 00		Brenda Clark, Capital			10 9 4 5 00
Total Assets		$14 7 7 0 00		Total Liabilities and Owner's Equity		$14 7 7 0 00	

FIGURE 4-8   From Work Sheet to Balance Sheet.

Now at this point you should be able to

1. Prepare the three financial reports from a work sheet.   (pp. 105–107)
2. Explain why formal financial reports do not have debit and credit columns.   (p. 105)

SELF-REVIEW QUIZ 4-2

From the work sheet on p. 104 for B. Bass, please prepare (1) an income statement for December; (2) a statement of owner's equity; and (3) a balance sheet for December 31, 19XX. No additional investments took place during the period.

SOLUTION TO SELF-REVIEW QUIZ 4-2

B. BASS
INCOME STATEMENT
FOR MONTH ENDED DECEMBER 31, 19XX

Revenue:			
Revenue from clients			$25 00
Operating Expenses:			
Rent Expense	$2 00		
Salaries Expense	11 00		
Depreciation Expense, Store Equipment	1 00		
Insurance Expense	2 00		
Supplies Expense	4 00		
Total Operating Expenses		20 00	
Net Income		$5 00	

B. BASS
STATEMENT OF OWNER'S EQUITY
FOR MONTH ENDED DECEMBER 31, 19XX

B. Bass, Capital, December 1, 19XX		$14 00
Net Income for December	$5 00	
Less Withdrawals for December	3 00	
Increase in Capital		2 00
B. Bass, Capital, December 31, 19XX		$16 00

B. BASS
BALANCE SHEET
DECEMBER 31, 19XX

Assets			Liabilities and Owner's Equity		
Cash		$16 00	Liabilities		
Accounts Receivable		2 00	Accounts Payable	$2 00	
Prepaid Insurance		1 00	Salaries Payable	3 00	
Store Supplies		1 00	Total Liabilities		$5 00
Store Equipment	$6 00		Owner's Equity		
Less Acc. Dep.	5 00	1 00	B. Bass, Capital		16 00
			Total Liabilities and		
Total Assets		$21 00	Owner's Equity		$21 00

SUMMARY OF KEY POINTS AND KEY TERMS

LEARNING UNIT 4-1

1. The work sheet is not a formal report.

2. Adjustments update certain accounts so that they will be up to their latest balance before financial reports are prepared. Adjustments are the result of internal transactions.

3. Adjustments will affect both the income statement and the balance sheet.

4. A mixed account results in balances partly on the balance sheet and partly on the income statement.

5. Accounts listed *below* the account titles on the trial balance of the work sheet are *increasing*.

6. The original cost of a piece of equipment is not adjusted, historical cost is not lost.

7. Depreciation is the process of spreading the original cost of the asset over its expected useful life.

8. Accumulated depreciation is a contra asset on the balance sheet that summarizes, accumulates, or builds up the amount of depreciation that an asset has accumulated.

9. Book value is the original cost less accumulated depreciation.

10. Accrued salaries are unpaid and unrecorded expenses that are accumulating but for which payment is not yet due.

11. Revenue and expenses go on income statement sections of the work sheet. Assets, contra assets, liabilities, capital, and withdrawals go on balance sheet sections of the work sheet.

Accrued salaries: Salaries that are earned but unpaid and unrecorded during the period (and thus need to be recorded by an adjustment) and will not come due for payment until the next accounting period.

Accumulated depreciation: A contra-asset account that summarizes or accumulates the amount of depreciation that has been taken on an asset (such as an

Adjusting: The process of calculating the latest up-to-date balance of each account at the end of an accounting period.

Book value: Cost of equipment less accumulated depreciation

Depreciation: The allocation (spreading) of the cost of an asset (such as an auto or equipment) over its expected useful life.

Historical cost: The actual cost of an asset at time of purchase.

Mixed account: An account whose balance is partly an income statement amount and partly a balance sheet amount on the trial balance. Examples: Prepaid Rent, Supplies.

Residual value: Estimated value of an asset after all the allowable depreciation has been taken. *Salvage value.*

Work sheet: A columnar device used by accountants to aid them in completing the accounting cycle. It is not a formal report. Often called a spreadsheet.

LEARNING UNIT 4-2

1. The formal reports prepared from a work sheet do not have debit or credit columns.

2. Revenue and expenses go on the income statement. Beginning capital plus net income less withdrawals (or: beginning capital minus net loss, less withdrawals) go on the statement of owner's equity. Be sure to check capital account in ledger to see if any additional investments took place. Assets, liabilities, and the new figure for capital go on the balance sheet.

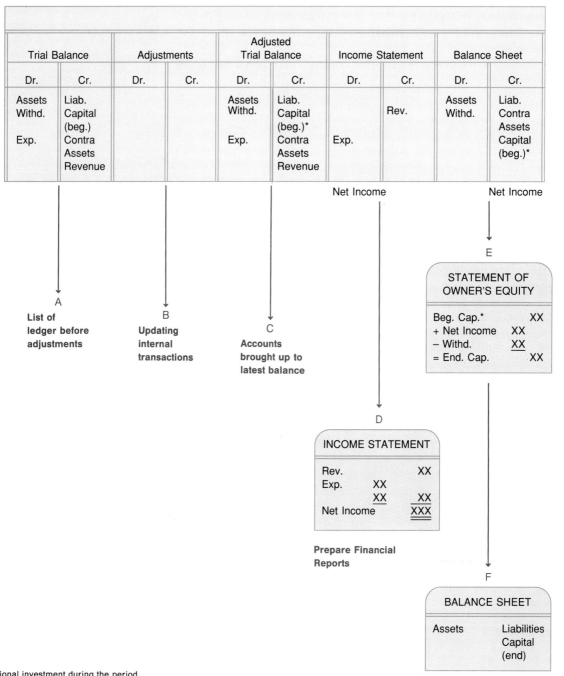

Blueprint of Steps 5 and 6 of the Accounting Cycle

Prepare Work Sheet

	Trial Balance		Adjustments		Adjusted Trial Balance		Income Statement		Balance Sheet	
	Dr.	Cr.	Dr.	Cr.	Dr.	Cr.	Dr.	Cr.	Dr.	Cr.
	Assets Withd. Exp.	Liab. Capital (beg.) Contra Assets Revenue			Assets Withd. Exp.	Liab. Capital (beg.)* Contra Assets Revenue	Exp.	Rev.	Assets Withd.	Liab. Contra Assets Capital (beg.)*

A

List of ledger before adjustments

B

Updating internal transactions

C

Accounts brought up to latest balance

Net Income

Net Income

E

STATEMENT OF OWNER'S EQUITY

Beg. Cap.*	XX
+ Net Income	XX
– Withd.	XX
= End. Cap.	XX

D

INCOME STATEMENT

Rev.		XX
Exp.	XX	
	XX	XX
Net Income		XXX

Prepare Financial Reports

F

BALANCE SHEET

| Assets | Liabilities Capital (end) |

* No additional investment during the period.

DISCUSSION QUESTIONS

1. Work sheets are required in every company's accounting cycle. Please agree or disagree and explain why.
2. What is the purpose of adjusting accounts?
3. What is the relationship of internal transactions to the adjusting process?
4. Explain how an adjustment can affect both the income statement and balance sheet. Please give an example.
5. What is a mixed account?
6. Why do we need the accumulated depreciation account?
7. Depreciation expense goes on the balance sheet. True or false. Why?
8. Each month the cost of accumulated depreciation grows while the cost of equipment goes up. Agree or disagree. Defend your position.
9. Define accrued salaries.
10. Why don't the formal financial reports contain debit or credit columns?
11. Explain how the financial reports are prepared from the work sheet.

EXERCISES

1. Complete the following table.

ACCOUNT	CATEGORY	NORMAL BALANCE	WHICH FINANCIAL REPORT(S) FOUND ON
Accounts Payable			
Prepaid Insurance			
Equipment			
Accumulated Dep.			
B. Avery, Capital			
B. Avery, Withd.			
Salaries Payable			
Advertising Expense			

Categorizing accounts.

2. Use transaction analysis charts to analyze the following adjustments:

  A. Depreciation on equipment, $400.
  B. Rent expired, $200.

Reviewing adjustments and the transaction analysis charts.

3. From the following adjustment data, calculate the adjustment amount and record appropriate debits or credits:

  A. Supplies available, $700.
     Supplies on hand, $100.
  B. Store equipment, $9,000.
     Accumulated depreciation before adjustment, $700.
     Depreciation expense, $100.

Recording adjusting entries.

4. From the following trial balance and adjustment data, complete a work sheet for B. Jay as of December 31, 19XX:

Preparing a work sheet.

  A. Depreciation expense, equipment $1.00
  B. Insurance Expired   3.00
  C. Supplies on hand   2.00
  D. Wages owed, but not paid for (they   3.00
     are an expense in the old year)

B. JAY TRIAL BALANCE DECEMBER 31, 19XX	Dr.	Cr.
Cash	8 00	
Accounts Receivable	3 00	
Prepaid Insurance	5 00	
Store Supplies	6 00	
Store Equipment	7 00	
Accumulated Depreciation, Equipment		2 00
Accounts Payable		2 00
B. Jay, Capital		1 7 00
B. Jay, Withdrawals	4 00	
Revenue from Clients		2 0 00
Rent Expense	4 00	
Wage Expense	4 00	
	4 1 00	4 1 00

Preparing financial reports from a work sheet.

5. From the completed work sheet in Exercise 4, prepare

    A. An income statement for December.

    B. A statement of owner's equity for December.

    C. A balance sheet as of December 31, 19XX.

GROUP A PROBLEMS

4A-1.

Completing a partial work sheet up to the adjusted trial balance.

VIKI'S GYM TRIAL BALANCE DECEMBER 31, 19XX	Dr.	Cr.
Cash in Bank	2 4 0 0 00	
Accounts Receivable	3 0 0 0 00	
Gym Supplies	5 4 0 0 00	
Gym Equipment	7 2 0 0 00	
Accumulated Depreciation, Gym Equipment		2 2 5 0 00
Viki Kahn, Capital		9 0 0 0 00
Viki Kahn, Withdrawals	3 0 0 0 00	
Gym Fees		10 8 0 0 00
Rent Expense	9 0 0 00	
Advertising Expense	1 5 0 00	
	22 0 5 0 00	22 0 5 0 00

Given the following adjustment data on December 31:

    A. Gym supplies on hand, $900.

    B. Depreciation taken on gym equipment, $600.

Complete a partial work sheet up to the adjusted trial balance.

4A-2. Below is the trial balance for Al's Plumbing Service for December 31, 19XX.

AL'S PLUMBING SERVICE
TRIAL BALANCE
DECEMBER 31, 19XX

	Dr.	Cr.
Cash in Bank	2 1 5 6 00	
Accounts Receivable	5 8 4 00	
Prepaid Rent	7 4 4 00	
Plumbing Supplies	7 4 2 00	
Plumbing Equipment	1 2 0 0 00	
Accumulated Depreciation, Plumbing Equipment		5 6 0 00
Accounts Payable		4 6 00
Al Sullivan, Capital		2 2 0 0 00
Plumbing Revenue		4 4 8 0 00
Heat Expense	4 0 0 00	
Advertising Expense	2 0 0 00	
Wage Expense	1 2 6 0 00	
	7 2 8 6 00	7 2 8 6 00

Adjustment data to update the trial balance:

A. Rent expired, $250.
B. Plumbing supplies on hand (left), $290.
C. Depreciation expense, plumbing equipment, $150.
D. Wages earned by workers but not paid or due until January, $100.

Your task is to prepare a work sheet for Al's Plumbing Service for the month of December.

4A-3. The following is the trial balance for Bert's Moving Co.

BERT'S MOVING CO.
TRIAL BALANCE
OCTOBER 31, 19XX

	Dr.	Cr.
Cash	5 3 7 0 00	
Prepaid Insurance	2 2 8 8 00	
Moving Supplies	1 5 1 0 00	
Moving Truck	10 6 5 8 00	
Accumulated Depreciation, Moving Truck		7 2 6 0 00
Accounts Payable		3 1 2 00
Bert Jess, Capital		5 4 4 2 00
Bert Jess, Withdrawals	2 2 4 0 00	
Revenue from Moving		14 1 6 2 00
Wage Expense	3 7 1 2 00	
Rent Expense	1 0 8 0 00	
Advertising Expense	3 1 8 00	
	27 1 7 6 00	27 1 7 6 00

Adjustment data to update trial balance:

A. Insurance expired, $350.
B. Moving supplies on hand, $300.

C. Depreciation on moving truck, $450.

D. Wages earned but unpaid, $525.

Your task is to

1. Complete a work sheet for Bert's Moving Co. for the month of October.

2. Prepare an income statement for October, a statement of owner's equity for October, and a balance sheet as of October 31, 19XX.

4A-4.

ED'S REPAIR SERVICE
TRIAL BALANCE
NOVEMBER 30, 19XX

	Dr.	Cr.
Cash	2 7 6 6 00	
Prepaid Insurance	2 0 0 0 00	
Repair Supplies	5 7 0 00	
Repair Equipment	2 8 8 6 00	
Accumulated Depreciation, Repair Equipment		6 3 4 00
Accounts Payable		1 6 2 00
Ed Clean, Capital		3 8 0 0 00
Revenue from Repairs		6 0 0 0 00
Wages Expense	1 9 0 4 00	
Rent Expense	3 6 0 00	
Advertising Expense	1 1 0 00	
	10 5 9 6 00	10 5 9 6 00

Adjustment data to update trial balance:

A. Insurance expired, $500.

B. Repair supplies on hand, $260.

C. Depreciation on repair equipment, $410.

D. Wages earned but unpaid, $350.

Your task is to

1. Complete a work sheet for Ed's Repair Service for the month of November.

2. Prepare an income statement for November, a statement of owner's equity for November, and a balance sheet as of November 30, 19XX.

GROUP B PROBLEMS

4B-1.

VIKI'S GYM
TRIAL BALANCE
DECEMBER 31, 19XX

	Dr.	Cr.
Cash in Bank	2 0 0 0 00	
Accounts Receivable	2 0 0 0 00	
Gym Supplies	4 2 0 0 00	
Gym Equipment	8 0 0 0 00	
Accumulated Depreciation, Gym Equipment		5 7 0 00
Viki Kahn, Capital		11 0 0 0 00
Viki Kahn, Withdrawals	1 0 0 0 00	
Gym Fees		1 4 0 0 00
Rent Expense	8 0 0 00	
Advertising Expense	1 0 0 00	
	18 1 0 0 00	18 1 0 0 00

Please complete a partial work sheet up to the adjusted trial balance using the following adjustment data:

    A. Gym supplies on hand, $2,600.
    B. Depreciation taken on gym equipment, $500.

4B-2. Given the following trial balance and adjustment data of Al's Plumbing Service, your task is to prepare a work sheet for the month of December.

Completing a work sheet.

AL'S PLUMBING SERVICE
TRIAL BALANCE
DECEMBER 31, 19XX

	Dr.	Cr.
Cash in Bank	3 9 6 00	
Accounts Receivable	2 8 4 00	
Prepaid Rent	4 0 0 00	
Plumbing Supplies	3 1 0 00	
Plumbing Equipment	1 0 0 0 00	
Accumulated Depreciation, Plumbing Equipment		2 0 0 00
Accounts Payable		3 4 6 00
Al Sullivan, Capital		4 5 6 00
Plumbing Revenue		4 6 8 0 00
Heat Expense	6 3 2 00	
Advertising Expense	1 2 0 0 00	
Wage Expense	1 4 6 0 00	
Total	5 6 8 2 00	5 6 8 2 00

Adjustment data:

    A. Plumbing supplies on hand, $60.
    B. Rent expired, $150.
    C. Depreciation on plumbing equipment, $200.
    D. Wages earned but unpaid, $115.

4B-3. Using the following trial balance and adjustment data of Bert's Moving Co., prepare

    1. A work sheet for the month of October.
    2. An income statement for October, a statement of owner's equity for October, and a balance sheet as of October 31, 19XX.

Comprehensive Problem

BERT'S MOVING CO.
TRIAL BALANCE
OCTOBER 31, 19XX

	Dr.	Cr.
Cash	3 9 2 0 00	
Prepaid Insurance	3 2 8 8 00	
Moving Supplies	1 4 0 0 00	
Moving Truck	10 6 5 8 00	
Accumulated Depreciation, Moving Truck		3 6 6 0 00
Accounts Payable		1 3 1 2 00
Bert Jess, Capital		17 4 8 2 00
Bert Jess, Withdrawals	4 2 4 0 00	
Revenue from Moving		8 1 6 2 00
Wages Expense	5 7 1 2 00	
Rent Expense	1 0 8 0 00	
Advertising Expense	3 1 8 00	
	30 6 1 6 00	30 6 1 6 00

Adjustment data:

    A. Insurance expired, $600.

    B. Moving supplies on hand, $310.

    C. Depreciation on moving truck, $580.

    D. Wages earned but unpaid, $410.

4B-4. As the bookkeeper of Ed's Repair Service, use the information that follows to prepare

    1. A work sheet for the month of November.

    2. An income statement for November. A statement of owner's equity for November. A balance sheet as of November 30, 19XX.

Comprehensive Problem

ED'S REPAIR SERVICE TRIAL BALANCE NOVEMBER 30, 19XX	Dr.	Cr.
Cash	3 2 0 4 00	
Prepaid Insurance	4 0 0 0 00	
Repair Supplies	7 7 0 00	
Repair Equipment	3 1 0 6 00	
Accumulated Depreciation, Repair Equipment		6 5 0 00
Accounts Payable		1 9 0 4 00
Ed Clean, Capital		6 2 5 8 00
Revenue from Repairs		5 6 3 4 00
Wages Expense	1 6 0 0 00	
Rent Expense	1 5 6 0 00	
Advertising Expense	2 0 6 00	
	14 4 4 6 00	14 4 4 6 00

Adjustment data:

    A. Insurance expired, $300.

    B. Repair supplies on hand, $170.

    C. Depreciation on repair equipment, $250.

    D. Wages earned but unpaid, $106.

PRACTICAL ACCOUNTING APPLICATION # 1

To: Hal Hogan, Bookkeeper

From: Pete Tennant, V. P.

Re: Adjustments for year ended December 31, 19XX

Hal, here is the information you requested. Please supply me with the adjustments needed ASAP.

                             Thanks

Attached to memo:

(a) Insurance data:

POLICY NO.	DATE OF POLICY PURCHASE	POLICY LENGTH	COST
100	November 1 of previous year	4 years	$480
200	May 1 of current year	2 years	600
300	September 1 of current year	1 year	240

(b) Rent data: Prepaid rent had a $500 balance at beginning of year. An additional $400 of rent was paid in advance in June. At year end, $200 of rent had expired.

(c) Revenue data: Accrued storage fees of $500 were earned but uncollected and unrecorded at year end.

PRACTICAL ACCOUNTING APPLICATION #2

Hint: Unearned Rent is a liability on the balance sheet.

On Friday, Harry Swag's boss asks him to prepare a special report, due on Monday at 8:00 A.M. Harry gathers the following material in his briefcase:

		DEC. 31	
		19X1	19X2
Prepaid Advertising		$300	$600
Interest Payable		150	350
Unearned Rent		500	300
Cash paid for: Advertising	$1,900		
Interest	1,500		
Cash received for: Rent	2,300		

As his best friend, could you help Harry show the amounts that are to be reported on the 19X2 income statement for (a) Advertising Expense, (b) Interest Expense, and (c) Rent Fees Earned.

THE ACCOUNTING CYCLE COMPLETED:
Adjusting, Closing, and Post-Closing Trial Balance

In Chapters 3 and 4 we completed the following steps of the accounting cycle for Clark's Word Processing Services:

1. Business transactions occurred and generated source documents.
2. Business transactions were analyzed and recorded into a journal.
3. Information was posted or transferred from journal to ledger.
4. A trial balance was prepared.
5. A work sheet was completed.
6. Financial statements were prepared.

Remember, for ease of presentation we are using a month as the accounting cycle for Clark.

This chapter completes the accounting cycle for Clark for the month of May by taking the following steps:

7. Journalizing and posting adjusting entries.
8. Journalizing and posting closing entries.
9. Preparing a post-closing trial balance.

LEARNING UNIT 5-1

Journalizing and Posting Adjusting Entries: Step 7 of the Accounting Cycle

RECORDING JOURNAL ENTRIES FROM THE WORK SHEET

Many students have asked the purpose of journalizing adjusting entries. They claim that the information is already on the work sheet—why do it again? They forget that the work sheet is an *informal* report. The information concerning the adjustments has not been (a) placed into the journal, or (b) posted to the ledger accounts. We may have made the financial reports, but the ledger is not up to date. It was management that needed the reports quickly. Now we need to get the books ready for the upcoming acounting period. For example, at this point the ledger shows prepaid rent for Clark at $900 (p. 71), when in reality the balance sheet we prepared in Chapter 4 revealed a $600 balance. The work sheet is a tool in preparing financial reports *before* updating the ledger. Now we must use the adjustment columns of the work sheet as a basis for **adjusting journal entries** to bring certain amounts up to date in the ledger before beginning the next accounting period (see Figure 5-1).

Purpose of adjusting entries.

Figure 5-2 shows the adjusting journal entries for Clark taken from the adjustments section of the work sheet.

Once these adjusting journal entries are posted to the ledger, the accounts making up the financial statements that were prepared from the work sheet will equal the updated ledger. (Keep in mind that this is the same jour-

At this point, many ledger accounts are *not up to date*.

| Account Titles | Trial Balance | | Adjustments | |
	Dr.	Cr.	Dr.	Cr.
Cash	2 0 9 0 00			
Accounts Receivable	4 1 0 0 00			
Office Supplies	4 0 0 00			(A) 3 2 0 00
Prepaid Rent	9 0 0 00			(B) 3 0 0 00
Word Processing Equipment	8 0 0 0 00			
Accounts Payable		3 5 7 5 00		
B. Clark, Capital		7 0 0 0 00		
B. Clark, Withdrawals	4 3 0 00			
Word Processing Fees		6 6 0 0 00		
Office Salaries Expense	9 0 0 00		(D) 2 5 0 00	
Advertising Expense	1 7 5 00			
Telephone Expense	1 8 0 00			
	17 1 7 5 00	17 1 7 5 00		
Office Supplies Expense			(A) 3 2 0 00	
Rent Expense			(B) 3 0 0 00	
Depreciation Exp., W.P. Equip.			(C) 1 0 0 00	
Accum. Depreciation, W.P. Equip.				(C) 1 0 0 00
Salaries Payable				(D) 2 5 0 00
			9 7 0 00	9 7 0 00

FIGURE 5-1   Journalizing and Posting Adjustments from the Adjustments Section of the Work Sheet.

CLARK'S WORD PROCESSING SERVICES
GENERAL JOURNAL

Page 2

Date		Account Titles and Description	PR	Dr.	Cr.
		Adjusting Entries			
May	31	Office Supplies Expense	514	3 2 0 00	
		Office Supplies	114		3 2 0 00
	31	Rent Expense	515	3 0 0 00	
		Prepaid Rent	115		3 0 0 00
	31	Depreciation Expense, W.P. Equip.	516	1 0 0 00	
		Accumulated Depreciation, W.P. Equip.	122		1 0 0 00
	31	Office Salaries Expense	511	2 5 0 00	
		Salaries Payable	212		2 5 0 00

FIGURE 5-2   Adjusting Journal Entries.

nal we have been using, but now we are on page 2.) Let's look at some simplified T accounts to show the ledger of Clark before and after posting the adjustments.

Accounts Before Adjustment Posted: Adjustment (A):

Office Supplies 114		Office Supplies Expense 514	
400			

Accounts After Adjustment Posted:

Office Supplies 114		Office Supplies Expense 514	
400	320	320	

Accounts Before Adjustment Posted: Adjustment (B):

Prepaid Rent 115		Rent Expense 515	
900			

Accounts After Adjustment Posted:

Prepaid Rent 115		Rent Expense 515	
900	300	300	

Accounts Before Adjustment Posted: Adjustment (C):

Word Processing Equipment 121		Depreciation Expense, W. P. Equipment 516		Accumulated Depreciation, W. P. Equipment 122	
8,000					

Accounts After Adjustment Posted:

Word Processing Equipment 121		Depreciation Expense, W. P. Equipment 516		Accumulated Depreciation W. P. Equipment 122	
8,000		100			100

Only the first adjustment in (C) will result in balances of Depreciation Expense and Accumulated Depreciation being the same. In subsequent adjustments the Accumulated Depreciation *balance* will be larger and larger, but the debit to Depreciation Expense and the credit to Accumulated Depreciation will be the same. We will see why in a moment.

Accounts Before Adjustment Posted: Adjustment (D):

Office Salaries Expense 511		Salaries Payable 212	
450			
450			

Accounts After Adjustment Posted:

Office Salaries Expense 511		Salaries Payable 212	
450		250	
450			
250			

Timothy Walkes: Work-Study Program Participant

When he entered Ohio's Wilberforce University, Timothy Walkes knew he wouldn't be a traditional full-time student as he worked to fulfill his educational goals. "Luckily," he says, "I was able to enter a program in which I studied one semester and worked one semester. I was very fortunate to work at General Motors, where I started as a payroll clerk and worked my way up."

Timothy liked being in the business world while he was in school. "I was able to apply what I learned in school right away. The college accounting course reinforced what I learned on the job, and for the most part the job reinforced what I learned in the course. The best part was being able to go back to the classroom and relate my work experiences to the class. In some cases, I had the opportunity to tell the professor that General Motors handled some things—straight-line depreciation, for instance—differently from the way they were taught in class. I got to explain General Motors' policy, and that was an eye-opener for the professor."

"I felt that I was a role model," he says. "The other students looked to my real-world experience, and I especially enjoyed helping the ones who wanted to work and take classes at the same time. But there's a very practical payoff, too. I've moved to a new state, and as I look for a new job, I'm finding would-be employers are impressed with my combination of business experience and academic background."

What advice does Timothy have for college accounting students? "Learn all you can about computers. Computer literacy is important in your field, whether you become a bookkeeper or are doing general-ledger accounting."

The main point to remember is that the adjusting entries are not journalized and posted until *after* the financial reports are prepared.

Now you should be able to

1. Define and state the purpose of adjusting entries.   (p. 119)
2. Journalize adjusting entries from the work sheet.   (pp. 120–121)
3. Post journalized adjusting entries to the ledger.   (pp. 120–121)
4. Compare specific ledger accounts before and after posting of the journalized adjusting entries.   (pp. 120–121)

SELF-REVIEW QUIZ 5-1

Turn to the work sheet of B. Bass (p. 104) and (1) journalize and post the adjusting entries and (2) compare the adjusted ledger accounts before and after the adjustments are posted. T accounts are provided in your study guide with beginning balances.

SOLUTION TO SELF-REVIEW QUIZ 5-1

	Date		Account Titles and Description	PR	Dr.	Cr.
						Page 2
			Adjusting Entries			
	Dec.	31	Depreciation Expense, Store Equip.	511	1 00	
			Accumulated Depreciation, Store Equip.	122		1 00
		31	Insurance Expense	516	2 00	
			Prepaid Insurance	116		2 00
		31	Supplies Expense	514	4 00	
			Store Supplies	114		4 00
		31	Salaries Expense	512	3 00	
			Salaries Payable	212		3 00

PARTIAL LEDGER

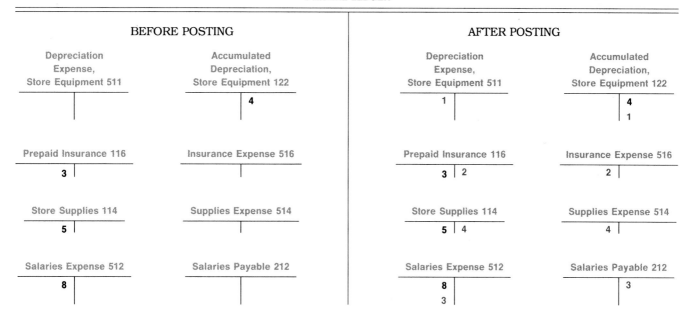

LEARNING UNIT 5-2

Journalizing and Posting Closing Entries: Step 8 of the Accounting Cycle

In order to make the recording of the next period's transactions easier, a mechanical step, called closing, is taken by Clark's accountant. Before we discuss closing, however, let's look carefully at the difference between temporary (nominal) accounts and permanent (real) accounts.

TEMPORARY AND PERMANENT ACCOUNTS

First recall the expanded accounting equation:

Assets = Liabilities + Capital − Withdrawals + Revenues − Expenses

Permanent accounts are found on the balance sheet.

Assets, liabilities, and capital are known as **real** or **permanent accounts**, because their balances are carried over from one accounting period to another.

Withdrawals, revenue, and expenses are called **nominal** or **temporary accounts**, because their balances are *not* carried over from one accounting period to another. Why not? By setting their "balances" back to zero, we will be able to accumulate new data about revenue, expenses, etc., in the new accounting period. Thus in the process called *closing*, accomplished by means of journalizing and posting **closing journal entries**, we will summarize the effects of the temporary accounts on capital for that period. When the closing process is complete, the accounting equation will be reduced to:

Goals of closing.

Assets = Liabilities + Ending Capital

All closing entries are journalized and posted to the ledger; all temporary accounts will have a zero balance in the ledger.

All revenue, expenses, and withdrawals will have a zero balance in the ledger at the end of the closing process. These balances, which are cleared to zero, are used to calculate the new or ending figure for capital at the end of the accounting period. In the next period we can gather new information about revenue, expenses, and withdrawal transactions.

Remember, closing requires mechanical steps. If you look back to p. 107 in Chapter 4 you will see that we have already calculated the new capital on the balance sheet to be $10,945 for Clark's Word Processing Services. But before the mechanical closing procedures are journalized and posted, the capital account of Clark in the ledger is only $7,000 (Chapter 3, p. 71). Let's look now at how to journalize and post closing entries.

HOW TO JOURNALIZE CLOSING ENTRIES

For our present purpose, the information needed to complete closing entries will be found in *the income statement and balance sheet sections of the work sheet.*

There are four steps to be performed in journalizing closing entries:

On p. 57 Income Summary is a temporary account located in the chart of accounts under owner's equity. It does not have a normal balance of a debit or a credit.

1. *Clear the revenue balance and transfer it to Income Summary.* **Income Summary** is a temporary account in the ledger needed for closing. At the end of the closing process there will be no balance in Income Summary.

Revenue ⟶ Income Summary

2. *Clear the individual expense balances and transfer them to Income Summary.*

Expenses ⟶ Income Summary

3. *Clear the balance in Income Summary and transfer it to Capital.*

Income Summary ⟶ Capital

4. *Clear the balance in Withdrawals and transfer it to Capital.*

Withdrawals ⟶ *Capital*

Remember, Income Summary is a temporary account in the ledger used to summarize revenue and expenses. After steps 1 and 2 are journalized and posted, the Income Summary account in the ledger will contain:

Income Summary	
Exp.	**Rev.**

Figure 5-3 summarizes these four steps in a visual form.

Keep in mind that this information must first be journalized and then posted to the appropriate ledger accounts. To do this use the work sheet presented in Figure 5-4, in which all the figures we will need for the closing process will be found.

Step 1: Clear Revenue Balance and Transfer to Income Summary

Here is what is in the ledger before closing entries are journalized and posted:

Word Processing Fees 411		Income Summary 313	
	6,600		

Notice by looking at the income statement section on the work sheet on p. 126 that the Word Processing Fees have a credit balance. To close or clear this to zero, a debit of $6,600 is needed. But if we add an amount to the debit side, we must also add a credit—so we add $6,600 to Income Summary on the credit side.

By debiting Word Processing Fees for $6,600 and then crediting Income Summary for $6,600 we will be able to

1. Bring the temporary account Word Processing Fees to a zero balance.
2. Transfer the information from Word Processing Fees to Income Summary.

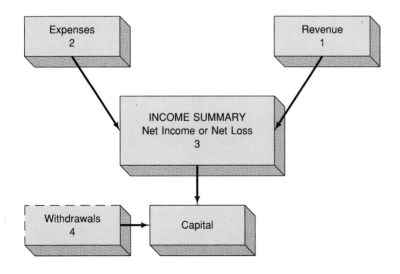

FIGURE 5-3
Four Steps in Journalizing Closing Entries.

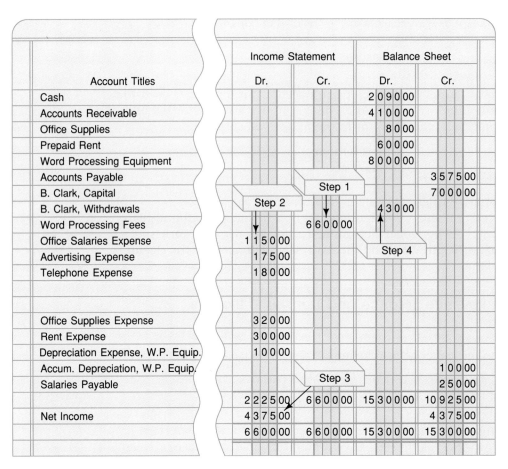

Account Titles	Income Statement		Balance Sheet	
	Dr.	Cr.	Dr.	Cr.
Cash			2 0 9 0 00	
Accounts Receivable			4 1 0 0 00	
Office Supplies			8 0 00	
Prepaid Rent			6 0 0 00	
Word Processing Equipment			8 0 0 0 00	
Accounts Payable				3 5 7 5 00
B. Clark, Capital				7 0 0 0 00
B. Clark, Withdrawals			4 3 0 00	
Word Processing Fees		6 6 0 0 00		
Office Salaries Expense	1 1 5 0 00			
Advertising Expense	1 7 5 00			
Telephone Expense	1 8 0 00			
Office Supplies Expense	3 2 0 00			
Rent Expense	3 0 0 00			
Depreciation Expense, W.P. Equip.	1 0 0 00			
Accum. Depreciation, W.P. Equip.				1 0 0 00
Salaries Payable				2 5 0 00
	2 2 2 5 00	6 6 0 0 00	15 3 0 0 00	10 9 2 5 00
Net Income	4 3 7 5 00			4 3 7 5 00
	6 6 0 0 00	6 6 0 0 00	15 3 0 0 00	15 3 0 0 00

Step 1 · Step 2 · Step 3 · Step 4

FIGURE 5-4   Closing Figures on the Work Sheet.

The following is the journalized closing entry for step 1:

May	31	Word Processing Fees	411	6 6 0 0 00		
		Income Summary	313			6 6 0 0 00

Don't forget two goals of closing:

Don't forget two goals of closing:
1. **Clear all temporary accounts in ledger.**
2. **Update capital to a new balance that reflects a summary of all the temporary accounts.**

All numbers used in the closing process can be found on the work sheet. Note that the *account* Income Summary is *not* on the work sheet.

This is what Word Processing Fees and Income Summary should look like in the ledger after the first step of closing entries is journalized and posted:

Word Processing Fees 411	
6,600	6,600
Closing	**Revenue**

Income Summary 313
6,600
Revenue

Note that the revenue balance is cleared to 0 and transferred to Income Summary, a temporary account also located in the ledger.

Step 2: Clear Individual Expense Balances and Transfer the Total to Income Summary

Here is what is in the ledger for each expense before step 2 of closing entries is journalized and posted. Each expense is listed on the work sheet in the debit column of the income statement section on p. 126.

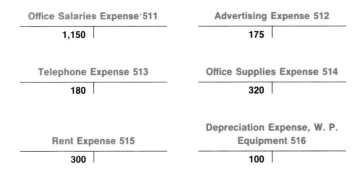

Office Salaries Expense 511 — 1,150

Advertising Expense 512 — 175

Telephone Expense 513 — 180

Office Supplies Expense 514 — 320

Rent Expense 515 — 300

Depreciation Expense, W. P. Equipment 516 — 100

In order to reach our goal, what must be done with these expenses before closing?

In the income statement section of the work sheet, all the expenses were listed as debits. If we want to reduce each expense to zero and they are all debits, we will have to credit each one.

The work sheet, once again, doesn't tell you where the total of the expenses is to be brought in the closing process, but it does give you the amount of $2,225. Remember, the work sheet is a tool. The accountant realizes that the information about the total of the expenses will be transferred to Income Summary.

By crediting each individual expense and debiting Income Summary for the total of all the expenses we will be able to:

1. Bring all expenses to a zero balance.
2. Transfer the information about the expenses to Income Summary.

The following is the journalized closing entry for step 2:

	31	Income Summary	313	2 2 2 5 00		
		Office Salaries Expense	511		1 1 5 0 00	
		Advertising Expense	512		1 7 5 00	
		Telephone Expense	513		1 8 0 00	
		Office Supplies Expense	514		3 2 0 00	
		Rent Expense	515		3 0 0 00	
		Depreciation Expense, W.P. Equipment	516		1 0 0 00	

This is what individual expenses and Income Summary should look like in the ledger after step 2 of closing entries is journalized and posted:

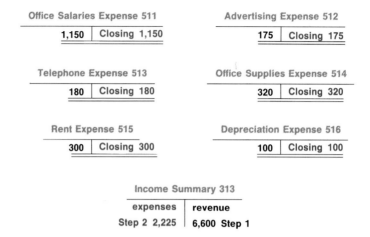

Office Salaries Expense 511			Advertising Expense 512	
1,150	Closing 1,150		175	Closing 175

Telephone Expense 513			Office Supplies Expense 514	
180	Closing 180		320	Closing 320

Rent Expense 515			Depreciation Expense 516	
300	Closing 300		100	Closing 100

Income Summary 313

expenses	revenue
Step 2 2,225	6,600 Step 1

Step 3: Clear Balance in Income Summary (Net Income) and Transfer It to Capital

This is how the Income Summary and B. Clark, Capital, accounts look before step 3:

Income Summary 313		B. Clark, Capital 311	
2,225	6,600		7,000
	4,375		

What do we have to do in order to accomplish step 3? First, note that the *balance* of Income Summary (revenue minus expenses or $6,600 − $2,225) is $4,375. It is this amount that we must clear from the income summary account and transfer to the B. Clark, Capital, account.

In order to transfer the balance of $4,375 from income summary (check the bottom debit column of the income statement section on work sheet) to capital it will be necessary to debit Income Summary for $4,375 (the difference between the revenue and expenses) and credit or increase capital of B. Clark.* The results will be to:

1. Clear Income Summary (a temporary account) to zero.
2. Summarize the effects on capital of revenue and expenses, which have been accumulated in Income Summary from steps 1 and 2 of the closing process.

The journalized closing entry for step 3 is:

	31	Income Summary	313	4 3 7 5 00		
		B. Clark, Capital	311		4 3 7 5 00	

* For a net loss, the opposite process would take place.

This is what the Income Summary and B. Clark, Capital, accounts will look like in the ledger after step 3 of closing entries is journalized and posted:

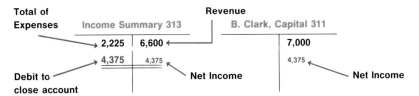

To this point the three closing journal entries when posted will have (1) cleared all revenue and expense accounts to arrive at a zero balance, and (2) summarized the effect of the revenue and expense accounts on capital.

Now let's look at how to close the withdrawals account.

Income Summary now has a zero balance. If we had a net loss the end result would be to decrease capital. Entry would be debit capital and credit income summary for the loss.

Step 4: Clear the Withdrawals Balance and Transfer it to Capital

The B. Clark, Withdrawals, and B. Clark, Capital, accounts now look like this:

B. Clark, Withdrawals 312		B. Clark, Capital 311	
430			7,000
			4,375

In order to reach the goal of bringing the Withdrawals account to a zero balance, as well as summarizing its effect on Capital, the following must be done:

1. Credit Withdrawals.
2. Debit Capital.

Remember, withdrawals are a nonbusiness expense and thus not transferred to Income Summary.

The closing entry would be journalized as follows:

31	B. Clark, Capital	311	4 3 0 00	
	B. Clark, Withdrawals	312		4 3 0 00

At this point the B. Clark, Withdrawals, and B. Clark, Capital, accounts would look like this in the ledger.

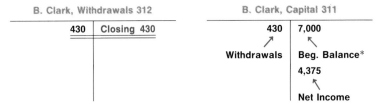

* It is beginning balance since no additional investments took place during the period.

Now let's look at the complete ledger for Clark Word Processing Services (see Figure 5-5). Note how the word "adjusting" or "closing" is written in the explanation column of individual ledgers, as for example in the one for Office Supplies. If the goals of closing have been achieved, only permanent accounts will have balances carried to the next accounting period. All temporary accounts should have zero balances.

FIGURE 5-5   Complete Ledger.

BRENDA CLARK WORD PROCESSING SERVICES
GENERAL LEDGER

Cash   Account No. 111

Date		Explanation	Post. Ref.	Debit	Credit	Balance Debit	Balance Credit
19XX May	1		GJ1	7 0 0 0 00		7 0 0 0 00	
	1		GJ1		2 0 0 0 00	5 0 0 0 00	
	1		GJ1		9 0 0 00	4 1 0 0 00	
	7		GJ1	2 5 0 0 00		6 6 0 0 00	
	15		GJ1		4 5 0 00	6 1 5 0 00	
	20		GJ1		4 3 0 00	5 7 2 0 00	
	27		GJ2		4 5 0 00	5 2 7 0 00	
	28		GJ2		3 0 0 0 00	2 2 7 0 00	
	29		GJ2		1 8 0 00	2 0 9 0 00	

Accounts Receivable   Account No. 112

Date		Explanation	Post. Ref.	Debit	Credit	Balance Debit	Balance Credit
19XX May	22		GJ1	4 1 0 0 00		4 1 0 0 00	

Office Supplies   Account No. 114

Date		Explanation	Post. Ref.	Debit	Credit	Balance Debit	Balance Credit
19XX May	3		GJ1	4 0 0 00		4 0 0 00	
	31	Adjusting	GJ2		3 2 0 00	8 0 00	

Prepaid Rent   Account No. 115

Date		Explanation	Post. Ref.	Debit	Credit	Balance Debit	Balance Credit
19XX May	1		GJ1	9 0 0 00		9 0 0 00	
	31	Adjusting	GJ2		3 0 0 00	6 0 0 00	

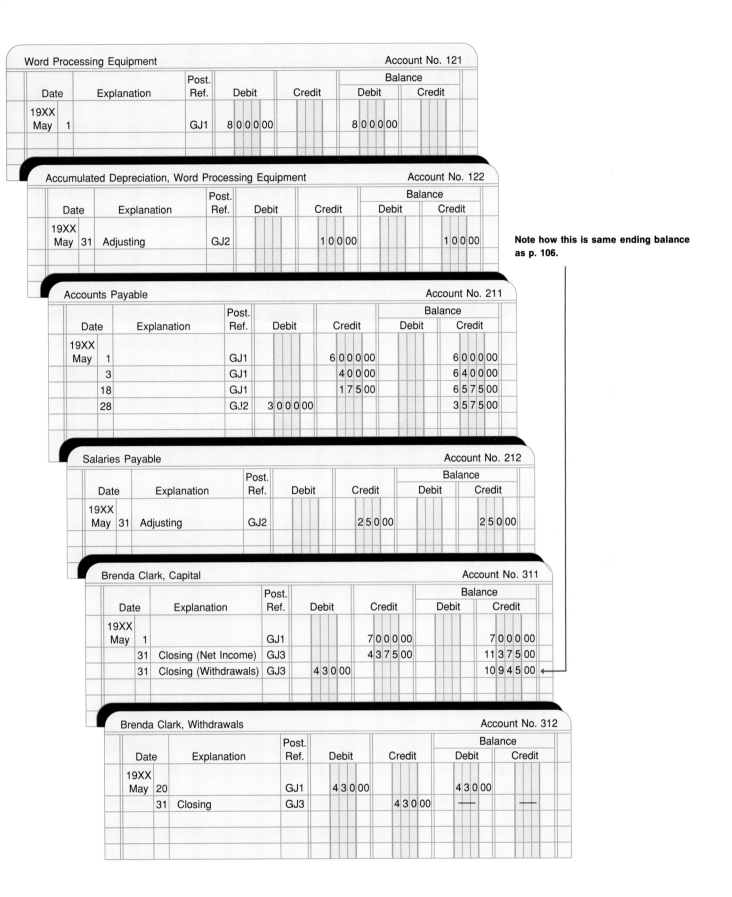

Word Processing Equipment — Account No. 121

Date	Explanation	Post. Ref.	Debit	Credit	Balance Debit	Balance Credit
19XX May 1		GJ1	8 0 0 0 00		8 0 0 0 00	

Accumulated Depreciation, Word Processing Equipment — Account No. 122

Date	Explanation	Post. Ref.	Debit	Credit	Balance Debit	Balance Credit
19XX May 31	Adjusting	GJ2		1 0 0 00		1 0 0 00

Note how this is same ending balance as p. 106.

Accounts Payable — Account No. 211

Date	Explanation	Post. Ref.	Debit	Credit	Balance Debit	Balance Credit
19XX May 1		GJ1		6 0 0 0 00		6 0 0 0 00
3		GJ1		4 0 0 00		6 4 0 0 00
18		GJ1		1 7 5 00		6 5 7 5 00
28		GJ2	3 0 0 0 00			3 5 7 5 00

Salaries Payable — Account No. 212

Date	Explanation	Post. Ref.	Debit	Credit	Balance Debit	Balance Credit
19XX May 31	Adjusting	GJ2		2 5 0 00		2 5 0 00

Brenda Clark, Capital — Account No. 311

Date	Explanation	Post. Ref.	Debit	Credit	Balance Debit	Balance Credit
19XX May 1		GJ1		7 0 0 0 00		7 0 0 0 00
31	Closing (Net Income)	GJ3		4 3 7 5 00		11 3 7 5 00
31	Closing (Withdrawals)	GJ3	4 3 0 00			10 9 4 5 00

Brenda Clark, Withdrawals — Account No. 312

Date	Explanation	Post. Ref.	Debit	Credit	Balance Debit	Balance Credit
19XX May 20		GJ1	4 3 0 00		4 3 0 00	
31	Closing	GJ3		4 3 0 00	—	—

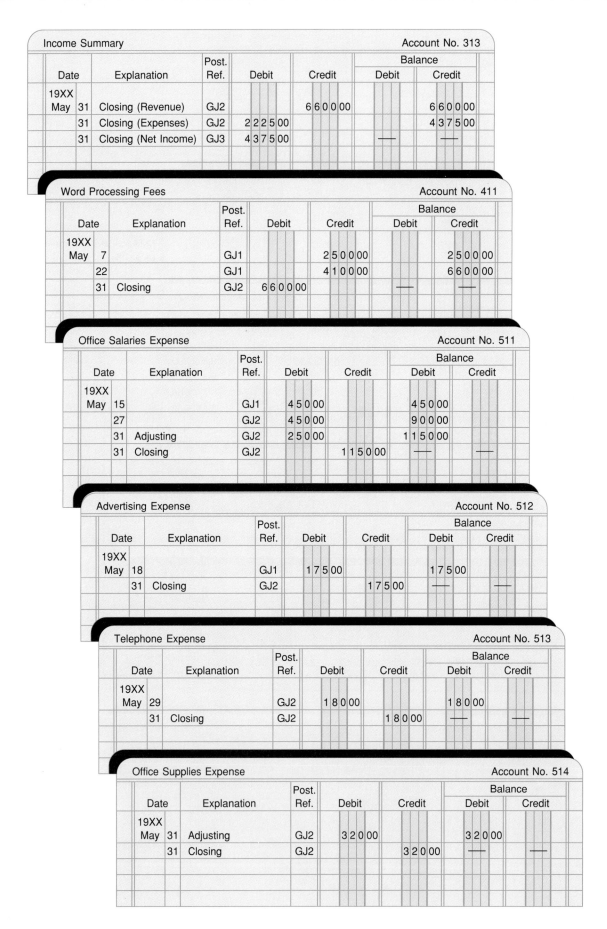

Income Summary   Account No. 313

Date		Explanation	Post. Ref.	Debit	Credit	Balance Debit	Balance Credit
19XX May	31	Closing (Revenue)	GJ2		6 6 0 0 00		6 6 0 0 00
	31	Closing (Expenses)	GJ2	2 2 2 5 00			4 3 7 5 00
	31	Closing (Net Income)	GJ3	4 3 7 5 00		—	—

Word Processing Fees   Account No. 411

Date		Explanation	Post. Ref.	Debit	Credit	Balance Debit	Balance Credit
19XX May	7		GJ1		2 5 0 0 00		2 5 0 0 00
	22		GJ1		4 1 0 0 00		6 6 0 0 00
	31	Closing	GJ2	6 6 0 0 00		—	—

Office Salaries Expense   Account No. 511

Date		Explanation	Post. Ref.	Debit	Credit	Balance Debit	Balance Credit
19XX May	15		GJ1	4 5 0 00		4 5 0 00	
	27		GJ2	4 5 0 00		9 0 0 00	
	31	Adjusting	GJ2	2 5 0 00		1 1 5 0 00	
	31	Closing	GJ2		1 1 5 0 00	—	—

Advertising Expense   Account No. 512

Date		Explanation	Post. Ref.	Debit	Credit	Balance Debit	Balance Credit
19XX May	18		GJ1	1 7 5 00		1 7 5 00	
	31	Closing	GJ2		1 7 5 00	—	—

Telephone Expense   Account No. 513

Date		Explanation	Post. Ref.	Debit	Credit	Balance Debit	Balance Credit
19XX May	29		GJ2	1 8 0 00		1 8 0 00	
	31	Closing	GJ2		1 8 0 00	—	—

Office Supplies Expense   Account No. 514

Date		Explanation	Post. Ref.	Debit	Credit	Balance Debit	Balance Credit
19XX May	31	Adjusting	GJ2	3 2 0 00		3 2 0 00	
	31	Closing	GJ2		3 2 0 00	—	—

| Rent Expense | | | | | | Account No. 515 |

| | | Post. | | | Balance | |
Date	Explanation	Ref.	Debit	Credit	Debit	Credit
19XX						
May 31	Adjusting	GJ2	300 00		300 00	
31	Closing	GJ2		300 00	—	—

| Depreciation Expense, Word Processing Equipment | | | | | | Account No. 516 |

| | | Post. | | | Balance | |
Date	Explanation	Ref.	Debit	Credit	Debit	Credit
19XX						
May 31	Adjusting	GJ2	100 00		100 00	
31	Closing	GJ2		100 00	—	—

At this point you should be able to

1. Define closing. (p. 124)
2. Differentiate between temporary (nominal) and permanent (real) accounts. (p. 124)
3. List the four mechanical steps of closing. (pp. 124–125)
4. Explain the role of the Income Summary account. (p. 125)
5. Explain the role of the work sheet in the closing process. (p. 126)

SELF-REVIEW QUIZ 5-2

Go to the work sheet of B. Bass on p. 104 and (1) journalize and post the closing entries and (2) calculate the new balance for B. Bass, Capital.

SOLUTION TO SELF-REVIEW QUIZ 5-2

			Closing				
Dec.	31	Revenue from Clients	410	25 00			
		Income Summary	312			25 00	
	31	Income Summary	312	20 00			
		Rent Expense	518			2 00	
		Salaries Expense	512			11 00	
		Depreciation Expense, Store Equip.	510			1 00	
		Insurance Expense	516			2 00	
		Supplies Expense	514			4 00	
	31	Income Summary	312	5 00			
		B. Bass, Capital	310			5 00	
	31	B. Bass, Capital	310	3 00			
		B. Bass, Withdrawals	311			3 00	

B. Bass, Capital 310		Revenue from Clients 410		Supplies Expense 514	
3	14	25	25	4	4
	5				
	16				

B. Bass, Withdrawals 311		Dep. Exp., Store Equip 510		Insurance Expense 516	
3	3	1	1	2	2

Income Summary 312		Salaries Expense 512		Rent Expense 518	
20	25	11	11	2	2
5	5				

B. Bass, Capital		$14
Net Income	$5	
Less Withdrawals	3	
Increase in Capital		2
B. Bass, Capital (ending)		$16

LEARNING UNIT 5-3

The Post-Closing Trial Balance: Step 9 of the Accounting Cycle and the Cycle Reviewed

PREPARING A POST-CLOSING TRIAL BALANCE

The post-closing trial balance helps prove the accuracy of the adjusting and closing process. It contains the true ending figure for capital.

The last step in the accounting cycle is the preparation of a **post-closing trial balance**, which lists only permanent accounts in the ledger and their balances after adjusting and closing entries have been posted. This post-closing trial balance aids in checking whether the ledger is in balance. This checking is important to do because so many new postings go to the ledger from the adjusting and closing process.

The procedure for taking a post-closing trial balance is the same as for a trial balance, except that, since closing entries have closed all temporary accounts, the post-closing trial balance will contain only permanent accounts (balance sheet). Keep in mind, however, that adjustments have occurred.

THE ACCOUNTING CYCLE REVIEWED

Figure 5-6 is the list of the steps we completed in the accounting cycle for Clark for the month of May:

Note: Most companies journalize and post adjusting and closing entries only at the end of their fiscal year. When a company prepares interim reports, it may be that only the first six steps of the cycle are completed. Work sheets allow the preparation of interim reports without the formal adjusting and closing of the books. If this happens, footnotes on the interim report will indicate the extent to which adjusting and closing were completed or not.

STEPS	EXPLANATION
1. Business transactions occur and generate source documents.	Cash register tape, sales tickets, bills, checks, payroll cards.
2. Analyze and record business transactions into a journal.	Called journalizing.
3. Post or transfer information from journal to ledger.	Copying the debits and credits of the journal entries into the ledger accounts.
4. Prepare a trial balance.	Summarizing each individual ledger account and listing those accounts to test for accuracy in recording transactions.
5. Prepare a work sheet.	A multicolumn form that summarizes accounting information to complete the accounting cycle.
6. Prepare financial statements.	Income statement, statement of owner's equity, and balance sheet.
7. Journalize and post adjusting entries.	Refers to adjustment columns of work sheet.
8. Journalize and post closing entries.	Refers to income statement and balance sheet sections of work sheet.
9. Prepare a post-closing trial balance.	Prove the accuracy of the adjusting and closing process of the accounting cycle.

FIGURE 5-6   Steps of the Accounting Cycle.

For example, to prepare a financial report for March, the data needed can be obtained by subtracting the work sheet accumulated totals from the end of March from the work sheet prepared at the end of February. In the situation we have described in this chapter, with Clark's Word Processing Service, we chose a month that would show the completion of an entire cycle.

At this point you should be able to

1. Prepare a post-closing trial balance.   (p. 134)
2. Explain the relationship of interim reports to the accounting cycle.   (p. 134)

SELF-REVIEW QUIZ 5-3

From the ledger of Clark, p. 130, prepare a post-closing trial balance.

SOLUTION TO SELF-REVIEW QUIZ 5-3

Note: No revenue, expenses, or withdrawals are found on the post-closing trial balance.

CLARK'S WORD PROCESSING SERVICE
POST-CLOSING TRIAL BALANCE
MAY 31, 19XX

	Dr.	Cr.
Cash	2 0 9 0 00	
Accounts Receivable	4 1 0 0 00	
Office Supplies	8 0 00	
Prepaid Rent	6 0 0 00	
Word Processing Equipment	8 0 0 0 00	
Accumulated Depreciation Word Processing Equip.		1 0 0 00
Accounts Payable		3 5 7 5 00
Salaries Payable		2 5 0 00
Brenda Clark, Capital		10 9 4 5 00
Totals	14 8 7 0 00	14 8 7 0 00

SUMMARY OF KEY POINTS AND KEY TERMS

LEARNING UNIT 5-1

1. After formal financial reports have been prepared, the ledger has still not been brought up to date.

2. Information for journalizing adjusting entries comes from the adjustments section of the work sheet.

Adjusting journal entries: Journal entries that are needed in order to update specific ledger accounts to reflect correct balances at the end of an accounting period.

LEARNING UNIT 5-2

1. Closing is a mechanical process that aids the accountant in recording transactions for the next period.

2. Assets, liabilities, and capital are permanent (real) accounts; their balances are carried over from one accounting period to another. Withdrawals, revenue, and expenses are nominal (temporary) accounts; their balances are *not* carried over from one accounting period to another.

3. Income Summary is a temporary account in the general ledger and does not have a normal balance. It will summarize revenue and expenses and transfer the balance to capital. Withdrawals do not go into Income Summary, because they are *not* business expenses.

4. All information for closing can be obtained from the work sheet or ledger.

5. When closing is complete, all temporary accounts in the ledger will have a zero balance (to get ready to accumulate the next period's data), and all this information will be updated in the capital account.

6. Closing entries are usually done only at year end. Interim reports can be prepared from work sheets which are prepared monthly, quarterly, etc.

Closing journal entries: Journal entries that are prepared to (a) reduce or clear all temporary accounts to a zero balance, or (b) update capital to a new balance.

Income Summary: A temporary account in the ledger that summarizes revenue and expenses and transfers its balance (net income or net loss) to capital. Does not have a normal balance.

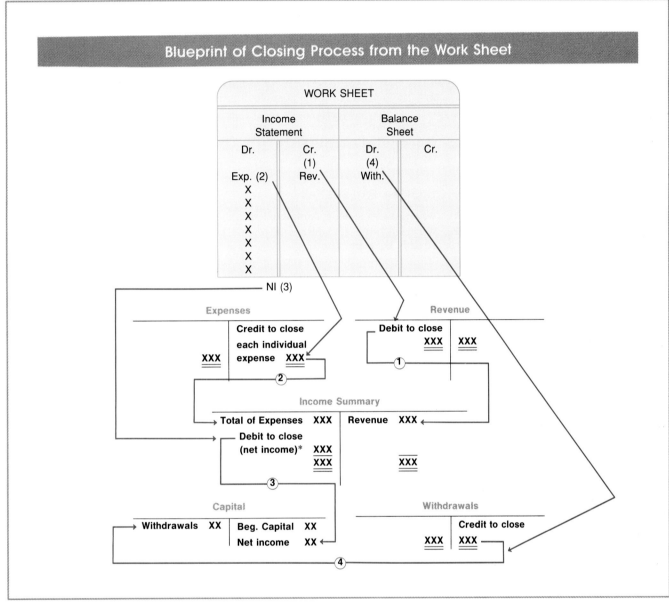

Blueprint of Closing Process from the Work Sheet

* If a net loss, it would be a Credit to Close.

THE CLOSING STEPS

1. Close revenue balance to Income Summary.

2. Close each *individual* expense and transfer *total* of all expenses to Income Summary.

3. Transfer balance in Income Summary (Net Income or Net Loss) to Capital.

4. Close Withdrawals to Capital.

Permanent accounts (real):   Accounts whose balances are carried over to the next accounting period. Examples: assets, liabilities, capital.

Temporary accounts (nominal):   Accounts whose balances at end of an accounting period are not carried over to the next accounting period. These accounts—revenue, expenses, withdrawals—help summarize a new or ending figure for capital to begin the next accounting period. Keep in mind that Income Summary is also a temporary account.

LEARNING UNIT 5-3

1. The post-closing trial balance is prepared from the ledger accounts after the adjusting and closing entries have been posted.

2. The accounts on the post-closing trial balance are all permanent titles.

Post-closing trial balance: The final step in the accounting cycle that lists only permanent accounts in the ledger and their balances after adjusting and closing entries have been posted.

DISCUSSION QUESTIONS

1. When a work sheet is completed, what balances are found in the general ledger?

2. Why must adjusting entries be journalized even though the formal reports have already been prepared?

3. "Closing slows down the recording of next year's transactions." Defend or reject this statement with supporting evidence.

4. What is the difference between temporary and permanent accounts?

5. What are the two major goals of the closing process?

6. List the four mechanical steps of closing.

7. What is the purpose of Income Summary and where is it located?

8. How can a work sheet aid the closing process?

9. What accounts are usually listed on a post-closing trial balance?

10. Closing entries are always prepared once a month. Agree or disagree. Why?

EXERCISES

1. From the adjustments section of a work sheet presented here, prepare adjusting journal entries for end of December.

Journalize adjusting entries.

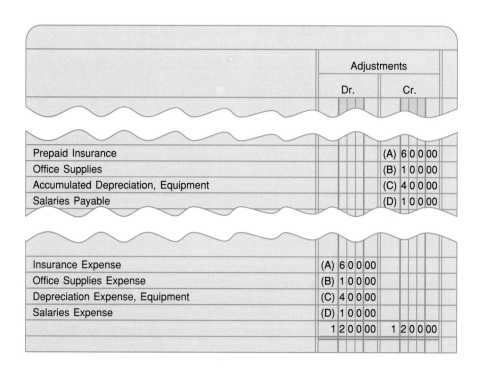

	Adjustments	
	Dr.	Cr.
Prepaid Insurance		(A) 6 0 0 00
Office Supplies		(B) 1 0 0 00
Accumulated Depreciation, Equipment		(C) 4 0 0 00
Salaries Payable		(D) 1 0 0 00
Insurance Expense	(A) 6 0 0 00	
Office Supplies Expense	(B) 1 0 0 00	
Depreciation Expense, Equipment	(C) 4 0 0 00	
Salaries Expense	(D) 1 0 0 00	
	1 2 0 0 00	1 2 0 0 00

2. Complete the following table by placing an X in the correct column.

	TEMPORARY	PERMANENT	WILL BE CLOSED
Ex. Accounts Receivable		X	
1. Withdrawals			
2. Al Jones, Capital			
3. Salary Expense			
4. Income Summary			
5. Fees Earned			
6. Accounts Payable			
7. Cash			

Temporary vs. permanent accounts.

3. From the following T accounts, journalize the four closing entries on December 31, 19XX.

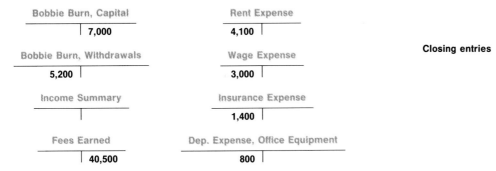

Closing entries

4. From the following posted T accounts, reconstruct the closing journal entries for December 31, 19XX.

Reconstructing closing entries

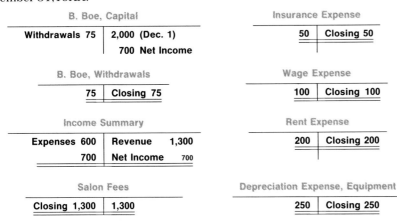

5. From the following accounts (not in order), prepare a post-closing trial balance for Lowe Co. on December 31, 19XX. **Note:** These balances are **before** closing.

Post-closing trial balance.

Legal Fees Earned	$12,000
Accounts Payable	45,000
Cash	22,125
Accounts Receivable	18,750
Legal Supplies	14,250
Office Equipment	59,700
Repair Expense	2,850
Salaries Expense	1,275
A. Lowe, Capital	63,450
A. Lowe, Withdrawals	1,500

5A-1. Given the following data for Sue's Consulting Service:

Review in preparing a work sheet and journalizing adjusting and closing entries.

SUE'S CONSULTING SERVICE TRIAL BALANCE JUNE 30, 19XX	Dr.	Cr.
Cash	17 1 5 0 00	
Accounts Receivable	4 0 0 0 00	
Prepaid Insurance	3 5 0 00	
Supplies	1 2 0 0 00	
Equipment	2 0 0 0 00	
Accumulated Depreciation, Equipment		7 5 0 00
Accounts Payable		6 0 0 0 00
Sue French, Capital		12 7 5 0 00
Sue French, Withdrawals	2 5 0 00	
Consulting Fees Earned		8 2 0 0 00
Salaries Expense	1 2 0 0 00	
Telephone Expense	1 0 3 0 00	
Advertising Expense	5 2 0 00	
	27 7 0 0 00	27 7 0 0 00

Adjustment data:

A. Insurance expired, $100.
B. Supplies on hand, $415.
C. Depreciation on equipment, $150.
D. Salaries earned by employees but not to be paid till July, $150.

Your task is to

1. Prepare a work sheet.
2. Journalize adjusting and closing entries.

5A-2. Enter beginning balance in each account in your working papers from the trial balance columns of the work sheet. From the work sheet on p. 141, (1) journalize and post adjusting and closing entries after entering beginning balance in each account in the ledger, and (2) prepare from the ledger a post-closing trial balance for the month of March.

5A-3. As the bookkeeper of Dorin's Plowing, you have been asked to complete the entire accounting cycle for Tom from the following information:

Comprehensive review of the entire accounting cycle, Chapters 1–5.

Jan. 1 Tom invested $9,000 cash and $6,000 worth of snow equipment into the plowing company.
  1 Paid rent for three months in advance for garage space, $1,500.
  4 Purchased office equipment on account from Regan Corp., $7,200.
  6 Purchased snow supplies for $600 cash.
  8 Collected $12,000 from plowing local shopping centers.
  12 Tom Dorin withdrew $800 from the business for his own personal use.
  20 Plowed North East Co. parking lots, payment not to be received until March, $4,000.
  26 Paid salaries to employees, $1,300.
  28 Paid Regan Corp. one-half amount owed for office equipment.
  29 Advertising bill received from Joyce Co. but will not be paid until March, $700.
  30 Paid telephone bill, $150.

LARSON CLEANING SERVICE
WORK SHEET
FOR MONTH ENDED MARCH 31, 19XX

Account Titles	Trial Balance Dr.	Trial Balance Cr.	Adjustments Dr.	Adjustments Cr.	Adjusted Trial Balance Dr.	Adjusted Trial Balance Cr.	Income Statement Dr.	Income Statement Cr.	Balance Sheet Dr.	Balance Sheet Cr.
Cash	5000.00				5000.00				5000.00	
Prepaid Ins.	4200.00			(A) 1800.00	2400.00				2400.00	
Cleaning Supp.	1440.00			(C) 1000.00	440.00				440.00	
Auto	27200.00				27200.00				27200.00	
Acc. Dep., Auto		8600.00		(B) 1500.00		10100.00				10100.00
Acct. Payable		2240.00				2240.00				2240.00
T. Larson, Cap.		54000.00				54000.00				54000.00
T. Larson, Withd.	4600.00				4600.00				4600.00	
Cleaning Fees		46800.00				46800.00		46800.00		
Sal. Exp.	14400.00		(D) 1600.00		16000.00		16000.00			
Tel. Exp.	2640.00				2640.00		2640.00			
Adv. Exp.	1960.00				1960.00		1960.00			
Gas Exp.	1600.00				1600.00		1600.00			
	63040.00	63040.00								
Ins. Exp.			(A) 1800.00		1800.00		1800.00			
Clean. Supp. Exp.			(B) 1000.00		1000.00		1000.00			
Dep. Exp., Auto			(C) 1500.00		1500.00		1500.00			
Sal. Payable				(D) 1600.00		1600.00				1600.00
			5900.00	5900.00	66140.00	66140.00	26500.00	46800.00	39640.00	19340.00
Net Income							20300.00			20300.00
							46800.00	46800.00	39640.00	39640.00

Adjustment data:

    A. Snow supplies on hand, $250.
    B. Rent expired, $500.
    C. Depreciation on office equip., $120.
        ($7,200 \div 5 \text{ yr.} \doteq \$1,440/12 = \$120$)
    D. Depreciation on snow equip., $100.
        ($6,000 \div 5 = \$1,200/12 \text{ mo.} = \$100$)
    E. Accrued salaries, $260.

Chart of Accounts

Assets
111 Cash
112 Accounts Receivable
114 Prepaid Rent
115 Snow Supplies
121 Office Equipment
122 Accumulated Depreciation,
     Office Equipment
123 Snow Equipment
124 Accumulated Depreciation,
     Snow Equipment

Liabilities
211 Accounts Payable
212 Salaries Payable

Owner's Equity
311 Tom Dorin, Capital
312 Tom Dorin, Withdrawals
313 Income Summary

Revenue
411 Plowing Fees

Expenses
511 Salaries Expense
512 Advertising Expense
513 Telephone Expense
514 Rent Expense
515 Snow Supplies Expense
516 Depreciation Expense,
     Office Equipment
517 Depreciation Expense,
     Snow Equipment

GROUP B PROBLEMS

5B-1.

Review in preparing a work sheet and journalizing adjusting and closing entries.

To:	Ron Ear
From:	Sue French
Re:	Accounting Needs

Please prepare ASAP from the following information (attached) (1) a work sheet along with (2) journalized adjusting and closing entries.

SUE'S CONSULTING SERVICE
TRIAL BALANCE
JUNE 30, 19XX

	Dr.	Cr.
Cash	10 1 5 0 00	
Accounts Receivable	5 0 0 0 00	
Prepaid Insurance	7 0 0 00	
Supplies	3 0 0 00	
Equipment	12 9 5 0 00	
Accumulated Depreciation, Equipment		4 0 0 0 00
Accounts Payable		5 7 5 0 00
Sue French, Capital		15 1 5 0 00
Sue French, Withdrawals	4 0 0 00	
Consulting Fees Earned		5 2 0 0 00
Salaries Expense	4 5 0 00	
Telephone Expense	7 0 00	
Advertising Expense	8 0 00	
	30 1 0 0 00	30 1 0 0 00

Adjustment data:

    A. Insurance expired, $100.
    B. Supplies on hand, $20.
    C. Depreciation on equipment, $200.
    D. Salaries earned by employees but not due to be paid till July, $490.

5B-2. Enter beginning balance in each account in your working papers from the trial balance columns of the work sheet. From the work sheet on p. 144, (1) journalize and post adjusting entries after entering beginning balances in each account in the ledger, and (2) prepare from the ledger a post-closing trial balance at end of March.

Journalizing and posting adjusting and closing entries. Preparing a post-closing trial balance.

5B-3. From the following transactions as well as additional data, please complete the entire accounting cycle for Dorin's Plowing (use the chart of accounts on p. 142).

Comprehensive review of entire accounting cycle. Review of Chapters 1–5.

Jan. 1 To open the business, Tom invested $8,000 cash and $9,600 worth of snow equipment.
     1 Paid rent for 5 months in advance, $3,000.
     4 Purchased office equipment on account from Russell Co., $6,000.
     6 Bought snow supplies, $350.
     8 Collected $7,000 for plowing during winter storm emergency.
    12 Tom paid his home telephone bill from the company checkbook, $70.
    20 Billed Eastern Freight Co. for plowing fees earned but not to be received until March, $6,500.
    24 Advertising bill received from Jones Co. but will not be paid until next month, $350.
    26 Paid salaries to employees, $1,800.
    28 Paid Russell Co. one-half of amount owed for office equipment.
    29 Paid telephone bill of company, $165.

Adjusting data:

    A. Snow supplies on hand, $200.
    B. Rent expired, $600.
    C. Depreciation on office equipment, $125.
        ($6,000/4 yrs = $1,500 ÷ 12 = $125)
    D. Depreciation on snow equipment, $400.
        ($9,600 ÷ 2 = $4,800 ÷ 12 = $400)
    E. Salaries accrued, $300.

PRACTICAL ACCOUNTING APPLICATION #1

Ann Humphrey needs a loan from the Charles Bank to help finance her business. She has submitted to the Charles Bank the following unadjusted trial balance. As the loan officer, you will be meeting with Ann tomorrow. Could you make some specific suggestions to Ann as regards her loan request?

Cash in Bank	770	
Accounts Receivable	1,480	
Office Supplies	3,310	
Equipment	7,606	
Accounts Payable		684
A. Humphrey, Capital		8,000
Service Fees		17,350
Salaries	11,240	
Utilities Expense	842	
Rent Expense	360	
Insurance Expense	280	
Advertising Expense	146	
Totals	26,034	26,034

LARSON CLEANING SERVICE
WORK SHEET
FOR MONTH ENDED MARCH 31, 19XX

Account Titles	Trial Balance Dr.	Trial Balance Cr.	Adjustments Dr.	Adjustments Cr.	Adjusted Trial Balance Dr.	Adjusted Trial Balance Cr.	Income Statement Dr.	Income Statement Cr.	Balance Sheet Dr.	Balance Sheet Cr.
Cash	1724 00				1724 00				1724 00	
Prepaid Insurance	350 00			(A) 200 00	150 00				150 00	
Cleaning Supplies	800 00			(B) 600 00	200 00				200 00	
Auto	1220 00				1220 00				1220 00	
Accumulated Depreciation, Auto		660 00		(C) 150 00		810 00				810 00
Accounts Payable		674 00				674 00				674 00
T. Larson, Capital		2480 00				2480 00				2480 00
T. Larson, Withdrawals	600 00				600 00				600 00	
Cleaning Fees		3700 00				3700 00		3700 00		
Salaries Expense	2000 00		(D) 175 00		2175 00		2175 00			
Telephone Expense	284 00				284 00		284 00			
Advertising Expense	276 00				276 00		276 00			
Gas Expense	260 00				260 00		260 00			
	7514 00	7514 00								
Insurance Expense			(A) 200 00		200 00		200 00			
Cleaning Supplies Expense			(B) 600 00		600 00		600 00			
Depreciation Expense, Auto			(C) 150 00		150 00		150 00			
Salaries Payable				(D) 175 00		175 00				175 00
			1125 00	1125 00	7839 00	7839 00	3945 00	3700 00	3894 00	4139 00
Net Loss								245 00	245 00	
							3945 00	3945 00	4139 00	4139 00

PRACTICAL ACCOUNTING APPLICATION #2

Janet Smother is the new bookkeeper who replaced Dick Burns, owing to his sudden illness. Janet finds on her desk a note requesting that she close the books and supply the ending capital figure. Janet is upset, since she can only find the following:

A. Revenue and expense accounts all were zero balance.

B. **Income Summary**

| 14,360 | 19,300 |

C. Owner withdrew $8,000.

D. Owner beginning capital was $34,400.

Could you help Janet accomplish her assignment?

Comprehensive Review Problem

Valdez Realty— Reviewing the Accounting Cycle Twice

This comprehensive review problem requires you to complete the accounting cycle for Valdez Realty twice. This will allow you to review Chapters 1–5, at the same time reinforcing the relationships among all parts of the accounting cycle. By completing two cycles, you will see how the ending June balances in the ledger are used to accumulate data in July.

In case you want a quick review of the accounting cycle before you start the problem, or if you need to check back when you are in the middle of the problem, the following chart shows the steps of the accounting cycle and the pages in the text where each step is covered:

STEPS IN THE ACCOUNTING CYCLE	PAGE IN TEXT WHERE COVERED
1. Business transactions occur and generate source documents.	**1.** p. 56
2. Analyze and record business transactions into a journal.	**2.** p. 58
3. Post or transfer information from journal to ledger.	**3.** p. 67
4. Prepare a trial balance.	**4.** p. 73
5. Prepare a work sheet.	**5.** p. 88
6. Prepare financial statements.	**6.** p. 105
7. Journalize and post adjusting entries.	**7.** p. 119
8. Journalize and post closing entries.	**8.** p. 124
9. Prepare a post-closing trial balance.	**9.** p. 136

First let's look at the chart of accounts for Valdez Realty.

Valdez Realty
Chart of Accounts

Assets
111 Cash
112 Accounts Receivable
114 Prepaid Rent
115 Office Supplies
121 Office Equipment
122 Accumulated Depreciation,
    Office Equipment
123 Automobile
124 Accumulated Depreciation,
    Automobile

Liabilities
211 Accounts Payable
212 Salaries Payable

Owner's Equity
311 Juan Valdez, Capital
312 Juan Valdez, Withdrawals
313 Income Summary

Revenue
411 Commissions Earned

Expenses
511 Rent Expense
512 Salaries Expense
513 Gas Expense
514 Repairs Expense
515 Telephone Expense
516 Advertising Expense
517 Office Supplies Expense
518 Depreciation Expense,
    Office Equipment
519 Depreciation Expense, Automobile
524 Miscellaneous Expense

On June 1 Juan Valdez opened a real estate office called Valdez Realty. The following transactions were completed for the month of June:

19XX
June 1 Juan Valdez invested $6,000 cash in the real estate agency along with $3,000 of office equipment.
      1 Rented office space and paid three months rent in advance, $2,100.
      1 Bought an automobile on account, $12,000.
      4 Purchased office supplies for cash, $300.
      5 Purchased additional office supplies on account, $150.
      6 Sold a house and collected a $6,000 commission.
      8 Paid gas bill, $22.
     15 Paid the salary of the office secretary, $350.
     17 Sold a building lot and earned a commission, $6,500. Payment is to be received on July 8.
     20 Juan Valdez withdrew $1,000 from the business to pay personal expenses.
     21 Sold a house and collected a $3,500 commission.
     22 Paid gas bill, $25.
     24 Paid $600 to repair automobile.
     30 Paid the salary of the office secretary, $350.
     30 Paid the June telephone bill, $510.
     30 Received advertising bill for June, $1,200. The bill is to be paid on July 2.

Required Work for June:

1. Journalize transactions and post to ledger accounts.
2. Prepare a trial balance in the first two columns of the work sheet and complete the work sheet using the following adjustment data:
    A. One month's rent had expired.
    B. An inventory shows $50 of office supplies remaining.
    C. Depreciation on office equipment, $100.
    D. Depreciation on automobile, $200.
3. Prepare a June income statement, statement of owner's equity, and balance sheet.

4. From the work sheet, journalize and post adjusting and closing entries (p. 3 of journal).

5. Prepare a post-closing trial balance.

During July, Valdez Realty completed these transactions:

July 1 Purchased additional office supplies on account, $700.
2 Paid advertising bill for June.
3 Sold a house and collected a commission, $6,600.
6 Paid for gas expense, $29.
8 Collected commission from sale of building lot on June 17.
12 Paid $300 to send employees to realtor's workshop.
15 Paid the salary of the office secretary, $350.
17 Sold a house and earned a commission of $2,400. Commission to be received on August 10.
18 Sold a building lot and collected a commission of $7,000.
22 Sent a check for $40 to help sponsor a local road race to aid the poor. (This is not to be considered an advertising expense, but it is a business expense.)
24 Paid for repairs to automobile, $590.
28 Juan Valdez withdrew $1,800 from the business to pay personal expenses.
30 Paid the salary of the office secretary, $350.
30 Paid the July telephone bill, $590.
30 Advertising bill for July, $1,400. The bill is to be paid on August 2.

Required Work for July:

1. Journalize transactions in a general journal (p. 4) and post to ledger accounts.

2. Prepare a trial balance in the first two columns of the work sheet and complete the work sheet using the following adjustment data:
   A. One month's rent had expired.
   B. An inventory shows $90 of office supplies remaining.
   C. Depreciation on office equipment, $100.
   D. Depreciation on automobile, $200.

3. Prepare a July income statement, statement of owner's equity, and balance sheet.

4. From the work sheet, journalize and post adjusting and closing entries (p. 6 of journal).

5. Prepare a post-closing trial balance.

SPECIAL JOURNALS:
Sales and Cash
Receipts

In the first five chapters of this book we have analyzed the accounting cycle for businesses that perform personal services for customers, such as word processing or legal services. In this chapter we turn our attention to Art's Wholesale Clothing Company, a merchandise company, which earns revenue by selling goods or merchandise to customers. This will call for some new concepts and procedures. To understand why we need these new concepts and procedures, let's look at some key terms relating to merchandise companies in general.

LEARNING UNIT 6-1

Merchandise Companies: An Overview

Wholesaler buys goods from suppliers and manufacturers for sale to retailers.

Retailer buys goods from wholesalers for resale to customers.

Merchandise is the goods brought into a store by a business for resale to customers. Merchandise companies may be either **wholesalers** (which buy goods from suppliers or manufacturers for resale) or **retailers** (which buy goods from wholesalers for resale to customers). For a service company, net income equals revenue from services minus operating expenses. For a merchandise company much more is involved in figuring net income. One way to see the special concerns of a merchandise company is to look at its income statement:

MERCHANDISE COMPANY	
(1) Gross Sales	$7,000
(2) – Sales Returns and Allowances	1,860
(3) – Sales Discounts	140
(4) = Net Sales	5,000
(5) – Cost of Goods Sold	3,000
(6) = Gross Profit	2,000
(7) – Operating Expenses	600
(8) = Net Income	$1,400

As you can see, there is a lot more going on here than we had looked at in a service company. To begin with we should introduce and define some of the new accounts and concepts we will be dealing with for a merchandise company. We'll take them one by one, as numbered in the chart on p. 150.

1. **Gross sales.** Think of *gross sales* as the total of all the cash and credit sales made by a business over a specific period of time. This is a revenue account with a credit balance.

2. **Sales returns and allowances.** This is a contra revenue account with a debit balance; it shows the effect of customers' returning merchandise or of being given price reductions. This account will help management keep track of customer dissatisfaction. If the balance in this account is higher one month than another, it may mean that customers have been returning goods at a higher rate than usual, or that they have been given price reductions for damaged goods.

3. **Sales discount.** This is also a contra-revenue account with a debit balance; it accumulates the amount of cash discounts that customers are granted for making early payment. Many companies allow a cash discount to encourage early payment of bills; if customers pay within a certain period of time (called the **discount period**), they are granted a discount. Note that a discount period is less time than the **credit period**, which is the length of time allowed to pay back the amount owed on the bill. We will give two examples of discounts and credit periods here:

   2/10, n/30 (Two Ten, Net Thirty). This means that the discount period is the first 10 days, and the credit period is 30 days. In this example, a 2% discount is allowed off the price of the bill if the bill is paid within 10 days. The full amount of the bill is due between days 11 to 30 with *no* discount.

Example:	Total bill, $8,000; terms 2/10, n/30
	Date of sale, 8/3/XX
	Bill paid on 8/7/XX
	Sales discount = .02 × $8,000 = $160

   n/10, EOM. This means that the full amount of the bill is due within 10 days after the end of the month (EOM), and there is no discount.

Example:	Total bill, $6,000; terms n/10, EOM
	Date of bill, 7/16/XX
	Final date to pay bill is August 10

   Credit terms will vary from company to company, and cash discounts will not be taken on sales tax, freight, or goods returned. For now, the key point is that sales discounts provide an incentive to the customer to pay early.

4. **Net sales.** This is the total reached after subtracting sales returns and allowances and sales discounts from gross sales.

5. **Cost of goods sold.** This means the total cost of the goods that are sold to customers (but is *not* the same thing as the selling price). Note in Figure 6-1 (p. 152) how the cost of goods sold is arrived at. Thus cost of goods sold = $3,000 ($200 + $4,000 − $1,200). It costs this company $3,000 to buy merchandise that sells for $5,000.

6. **Gross profit.** This figure represents the amount of revenue from sales that is left to cover the operating expenses and profit of the company. Net Sales − Cost of Goods Sold = Gross Profit. $5,000 − $3,000 = $2,000.

7. **Operating expenses.** These are expenses such as heat, postage, telephone, and all other *expired costs* of operating the company. They are subtracted from gross profit to arrive at net income.

8. **Net income.** Gross Profit − Operating Expenses = Net Income; or, in our example here, $2,000 − $600 = $1,400.

Sales (gross)

Dr.	Cr.
	7,000

Sales Returns and Allowances

Dr.	Cr.
1,860	

Sales Discount

Dr.	Cr.
140	

FIGURE 6-1

	Cost of Goods Sold (\$3,000)	
Beginning Inventory	+ Additional Cost of Goods brought into store	− Ending Inventory
\$200	+ \$4,000	− \$1,200
Cost of **inventory** (merchandise that is *on hand*) at *beginning* of the accounting period	Cost of merchandise that is brought into store *during* the accounting period	Cost of merchandise that is on hand at *end* of the accounting period

There are, of course, many more terms and concepts involved, but this overview should give you the background you need to look at accounting for a merchandise company.

At this point you should be able to

1. Explain the difference between a service company and a merchandise company. (p. 150)
2. Define and explain gross sales, sales returns and allowances, sales discounts, cost of goods sold, and gross profit. (p. 151)
3. Explain the difference between a discount period and a credit period. (p. 151)
4. Calculate sales discounts. (p. 151)
5. Prepare a simplified income statement for a merchandise company. (p. 150)

SELF-REVIEW QUIZ 6-1

Which of the following are false:

1. Sales Returns and Allowances is a contra asset account.
2. Sales Discount has a normal balance of a debit.
3. Net Sales − Cost of Goods Sold = Gross Profit.
4. Ending inventory is added to cost of goods sold.
5. Credit terms are standard in all industries.

SOLUTION TO SELF-REVIEW QUIZ 6-1

1, 4, 5

LEARNING UNIT 6-2

Sales Journal and Accounts Receivable Ledger

Art's Wholesale Clothing Company cannot operate its merchandise business efficiently with just the general journal and general ledger that we discussed in Chapters 1–5. To understand why, let's look first at the purpose of special journals and then at the purpose of subsidiary ledgers.

SPECIAL JOURNALS

Why does Art think that he needs more than just a general journal?

Need division of labor and flexibility to reduce journalizing effort.

1. Using just a general journal means that fewer transactions can be recorded in a work day, since only *one* person can work on a general journal at a time.

2. Using just a general journal means that there will be too many postings, since each line must be posted individually.

Need to reduce posting time.

Art thus feels he needs a set of journals, each of which will record a specific *type* of transaction, as well as reducing the number of postings that have to be completed. These journals are called **special journals**. Art's Wholesale Clothing Company will use the following special journals:

SPECIAL JOURNAL TYPE	WHAT IT RECORDS	
Sales journal	Sale of merchandise on account	Covered in this chapter
Cash receipts journal	Receiving cash from any source	
Purchases journal	Buying merchandise or other items on account	Covered in next chapter
Cash payments journal (cash disbursement journal)	Paying of cash for any purpose	

For a discussion of recording of credit cards in special journals see appendix.

Later in this chapter we will discuss the sales journal and the cash receipts journal, but first let's look at subsidiary ledgers.

SUBSIDIARY LEDGERS

In the same way that he needs more than just a general journal to keep track of his merchandise company, Art needs more than just a general ledger. So far in this text, for example, the only title we have used for recording amounts owed to the seller has been Accounts Receivable. Art could conceivably replace the Accounts Receivable title in the general ledger with the following list of customers who owe him money:

Accounts Receivable, Bevans Company
Accounts Receivable, Hal's Clothing
Accounts Receivable, Mel's Department Store
Accounts Receivable, Roe Company

As you can see, however, this would not work if Art had 1,000 credit customers—the general ledger would not be a manageable size. To solve this problem, Art sets up in alphabetical order an account for each customer in a separate ledger, an **accounts receivable ledger**. Such a special ledger, often called a **subsidiary ledger**, is one that contains accounts of a single type, such as credit customers.

The diagram in Figure 6-2 (p. 154) shows how the accounts receivable ledger fits in with the general ledger. To clarify the difference in updating the general ledger versus the subsidiary ledger we will *post* to the general ledger and *record* to the subsidiary ledger.

The accounts receivable ledger, or any other subsidiary ledger, can be in the form of a card file, a binder notebook, or computer tapes or disks. It will not have page numbers. The accounts receivable ledger is organized alphabetically based on customers' names and addresses; new customers can be added and inactive customers deleted.

The general ledger is *not* in the same book as the accounts receivable ledger.

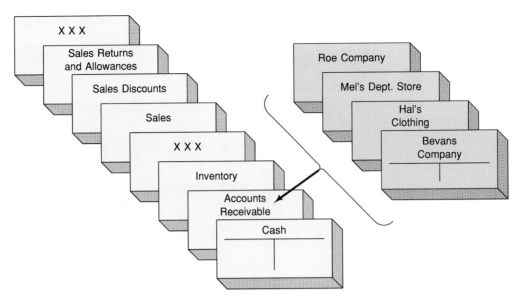

FIGURE 6-2   Partial General Ledger of Art's Wholesale Clothing Company and Accounts Receivable Subsidiary Ledger.

When using an accounts receivable ledger, the title Accounts Receivable in the general ledger is called the *controlling account*, since it summarizes or controls the accounts receivable ledger. At the end of the month the total of the individual accounts in the accounts receivable ledger will equal the ending balance in Accounts Receivable in the general ledger.

Art's Wholesale Clothing Company will use the following subsidiary ledgers:

Accounts receivable ledger	Records money owed by credit customers	Covered in this chapter
Accounts payable ledger	Records money owed by Art to creditors	Covered in next chapter

Let's now look closer at the sales journal, general ledger, and subsidiary ledger for Art to see how transactions are updated in the special journal as well as posted and recorded to specific titles.

THE SALES JOURNAL

The **sales journal** for Art's Clothing records all sales made on account to customers. Figure 6-3 shows the sales journal at the end of the first month in operation, along with the recordings to the accounts receivable ledger and posting to the general ledger. Keep in mind that the reason the balances in the accounts receivable ledger are *debit* balances is that the customers listed *owe* Art's Clothing the money. First study the diagram, and then we'll explain when you post or record and where the information comes from.

Let's take the first transaction listed in the sales journal as our example, the one involving Hal's Clothing. On April 3 Art's Wholesale Clothing Company sold merchandise on account to Hal's Clothing for $800. The bill or **sales invoice** for this sale is shown in Figure 6-4 (p. 156).

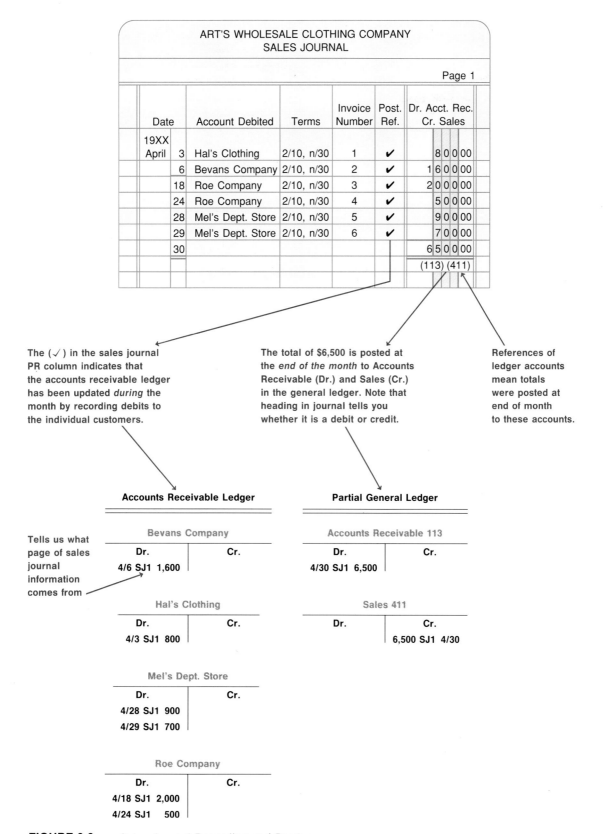

FIGURE 6-3 Sales Journal Recording and Postings.

Normal Balance
- in acct. Rec Ledger
is a debit balance.

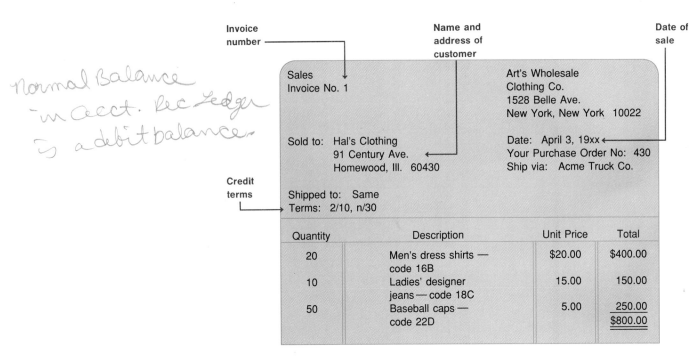

FIGURE 6-4   Sales Invoice.

Recording from the Sales Journal to the Accounts Receivable Ledger

From this invoice we record in the *sales journal* the date (April 3), account debited (Hal's Clothing), invoice number (1), and amount ($800). The *PR column is left blank.* As soon as possible we now update the accounts receivable ledger. We pull out the Hal's Clothing file card and update on the debit side the $800 he owes Art along with the date (April 3) and page of the sales journal (P. 1). When the card of Hal's Clothing is up to date, we go back to the sales journal and place a ✓ in the post reference column of the sales journal. During the month this process continues, and thus at any moment in time we can easily tell Hal his balance outstanding without having to go through all the invoices. Note how the sales journal only needs one line instead of the three lines that would have been required in a general journal.

Recording to the accounts receivable ledger occurs daily.

Hal's Clothing

Dr.	Cr.
4/3 SJ1	
800	

✓ means accounts receivable ledger has been updated.

Posting at End of Month from the Sales Journal to the General Ledger

At the end of the month the sales journal is totaled ($6,500). If you look back to p. 155, you will see that the heading of Art's sales journal is a debit to accounts receivable and a credit to sales. Therefore, at the end of the month the $6,500 total is posted to Accounts Receivable (debit) *and* to Sales (credit) in the general ledger. In the general ledger we record the date (4/30), the initials of the journal (SJ), the page of the sales journal (1), and appropriate debit or credit ($6,500). Once the account in the general ledger is updated, we place below the totals in the sales journal the account numbers to which the information was posted (in this case accounts 113 and 411).

Recording to the general ledger occurs at end of month.

Acc. Rec. 113

Dr.	Cr.
4/30 SJ1	
6,500	

Sales 411

Dr.	Cr.
	6,500 SJ1
	4/30

At this point you should be able to

1. Define and state the purposes of special journals. (p. 153)
2. Define and state the purposes of the accounts receivable ledger. (p. 153)

3. Define and state the purpose of the controlling account, Accounts Receivable. (p. 154)

4. Journalize, record, or post sales on account to a sales journal and its related accounts receivable and general ledgers. (p. 156)

SELF-REVIEW QUIZ 6-2

Indicate which of the following statements is false:

1. Special journals completely replace the general journal.
2. Special journals aid the division of labor.
3. The subsidiary ledger makes the general ledger less manageable.
4. The subsidiary ledger is separate from the general ledger.
5. The controlling account is located in the accounts receivable ledger.
6. The total(s) of a sales journal are posted to the general ledger at the end of the month.
7. The accounts receivable ledger is arranged in alphabetical order.
8. Transactions recorded into a sales journal are recorded weekly to the accounts receivable ledger.

SOLUTION TO SELF-REVIEW QUIZ 6-2

1, 3, 5, 8

LEARNING UNIT 6-3

Sales Tax and the Credit Memorandum

The company we have been using as an example in this chapter, Art's Wholesale Clothing Company, sells goods wholesale and thus does not have to deal with a sales tax. Let's look for a moment at a retail company in order to see how sales taxes affect the sales journal and posting. The company is Munroe Menswear Company; the customer is Jones Company; Figure 6-5 shows Munroe's Sales Journal.

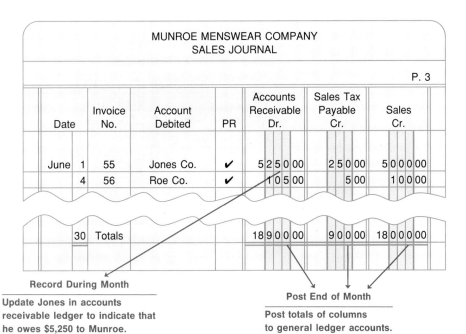

FIGURE 6-5
Munroe Sales Journal.

MUNROE MENSWEAR COMPANY
SALES JOURNAL

P. 3

Date	Invoice No.	Account Debited	PR	Accounts Receivable Dr.	Sales Tax Payable Cr.	Sales Cr.
June 1	55	Jones Co.	✔	5 2 5 0 00	2 5 0 00	5 0 0 0 00
4	56	Roe Co.	✔	1 0 5 00	5 00	1 0 0 00
30		Totals		18 9 0 0 00	9 0 0 00	18 0 0 0 00

Record During Month

Update Jones in accounts receivable ledger to indicate that he owes $5,250 to Munroe.

Post End of Month

Post totals of columns to general ledger accounts.

Sales Tax Payable

	XXX

A liability in general ledger.

The existence of a sales tax means creating a new account, **Sales Tax Payable**, which is a liability account in the general ledger with a credit balance. The customer owes Munroe the sale amount plus the tax.

Keep in mind that if sales discounts are available, they are not calculated on the sales tax. The discount is on the selling price less any returns before the tax. For example, if Jones receives a 2% discount, he pays the following:

$$\$5,000 \times .02 = \$100 \text{ savings} \longrightarrow$$

$5,250	Total owed (tax is $250)
−100	Savings (discount)
$5,150	Amount paid

THE CREDIT MEMORANDUM

At the beginning of the chapter we introduced several new accounts that are used in the merchandising business. One of these was Sales Returns and Allowances, a contra-revenue account with a debit balance. This account handles transactions involving goods that have already been sold. In one transaction the goods are returned, and the money owed for them is credited to the customer. In another type of transaction a customer is given an allowance for damaged goods in the form of a reduction from the original price.

A credit memorandum *reduces* accounts receivable.

Sales Returns and Allowances is called a contra-revenue account because both these transactions *decrease* sales revenue for the company involved in selling the goods, and thus the normal balance is a debit.

Such sales returns and allowances are usually handled by the company by means of a **credit memorandum**, which informs the customer that the amount of the goods returned or the amount allowed for damaged goods has been subtracted (credited) from the customer's ongoing account with the company. A sample credit memorandum from Art's Wholesale Clothing Company is shown here.

Sales Returns and Allowances

Dr.	Cr.
+	−

A contra-revenue account

On April 12 credit memo No. 1 (Figure 6-6) was issued to Bevans Company for defective merchandise that had been returned.

Let's assume that Art's Clothing has high-quality goods and does not expect many sales returns and allowances. Based on this assumption, no special journal for sales returns and allowances will be needed. Thus all returns and allowances will be recorded in the general journal, and all postings and recordings will be done when journalized. Let's look at a transaction analysis chart before we record and post this transaction.

Note that the Sales Returns and Allowances account is increasing, which in turn reduces sales revenue and reduces amount owed by customer (accounts receivable).

Accounts Affected	Category	↑ ↓	Rule
Sales Returns and Allowances	Contra-revenue account	↑	Dr.
Accounts Receivable, Bevans Co.	Asset	↓	Cr.

JOURNALIZING, RECORDING, AND POSTING THE CREDIT MEMORANDUM

The credit memorandum results in two postings and one recording—two postings to the general ledger and one recording to the accounts receivable ledger. This can be seen in Figure 6-7.

Remember, sales discounts are *not* taken on returns.

Note in the PR column next to Accounts Receivable, Bevans Co., that there is a diagonal line with the account number 113 above and a ✓ below. This is to show that the amount of $600 has been credited to Accounts

```
                     Art's Wholesale
                    Clothing Co.    .
                    1528 Belle Ave.
                    New York, NY 10022
Credit
Memorandum No. 1
Date: April 12

Credit to Bevans Company
          110 Aster Rd.
          Cincinnati, Ohio 45227
We credit your account as follows:
Merchandise returned 60 model 8 B men's dress gloves—$600
```

End result is that Bevan owes Art's Wholesale less money.

FIGURE 6-6   Credit Memorandum.

Receivable in the controlling account in the general ledger *and* credited to the account of Bevans Company in the accounts receivable ledger.

SALES TAX AND THE CREDIT MEMORANDUM

Using the same example as above, if a sales tax had been involved, there would have been three postings from the general journal and one recording to the accounts receivable ledger. (After all, the seller no longer owes as much sales tax, since the customer has returned merchandise.)

Seller doesn't owe as much sales tax, since customer has returned merchandise.

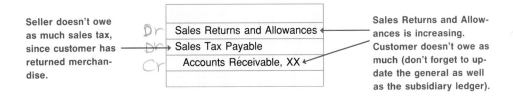

Sales Returns and Allowances is increasing. Customer doesn't owe as much (don't forget to update the general as well as the subsidiary ledger).

FIGURE 6-7   Postings and Recordings for the Credit Memorandum.

					Page 1
Date		Account Titles and Description	PR	Dr.	Cr.
19XX					
April	12	Sales Returns and Allowances	412	600 00	
		Accounts Receivable, Bevans Co.	113 ✔		600 00

412 A debit of $600 is recorded in Sales Returns and Allowances, account no. 412 in the general ledger. When this is done, the account number is placed in the PR column of the journal.

113 The credit of $600 is also posted to Accounts Receivable in the controlling account in the general ledger. When this is done, the account number (113) is placed in the PR column of the journal.

(✓) The check indicates that $600 has been recorded as a credit to the account of Bevans Company in the accounts receivable ledger.

If the accountant for Art's Wholesale Clothing Company at some point decided to develop a special journal for sales allowances and returns, the entry for a credit memorandum such as the one we've been discussing would look like this:

| | | | | | Sales Ret. and Allow. — Dr. |
| | | | | | Accts. |
Date	Credit Memo No.	Account Credited	PR		Rec. — Cr.
19XX					
April 12	1	Bevans Company	✔		6 0 0 00

SALES RETURNS AND ALLOWANCES JOURNAL

At this point you should be able to

1. Explain Sales Tax Payable in relation to Sales Discount. (p. 158)
2. Explain, journalize, post, and record a credit memorandum with or without sales tax. (pp. 158, 159)

SELF-REVIEW QUIZ 6-3

Journalize the following transactions into the sales journal or general journal for Moss Co. Record to the accounts receivable ledger and post to general ledger accounts as appropriate. Use the same journal headings that we used for Art's Wholesale Clothing Company. (All sales carry credit terms of 2/10, n/30.) There is no tax.

19XX
May 1 Sold merchandise on account to Jane Company, invoice No. 1, $600.
     5 Sold merchandise on account to Ralph Company, invoice No. 2, $2,500.
    20 Issued credit memo #1 to Jane Company for $200 due to defective merchandise returned.

SOLUTION TO SELF-REVIEW QUIZ 6-3

MOSS COMPANY
SALES JOURNAL

Page 1

Date	Account Debited	Terms	Invoice Number	Post Ref.	Dr. Accts. Rec. Cr. Sales
19XX					
May 1	Jane Company	2/10, n/30	1	✔	6 0 0 00
5	Ralph Company	2/10, n/30	2	✔	2 5 0 0 00
31					3 1 0 0 00
					(112) (411)

Note: Total of accounts receivable ledger $400 + $2,500 does indeed equal the balance in the controlling account, accounts receivable $2,900 at end of month, in the general ledger.

MOSS COMPANY
GENERAL JOURNAL

Page 1

Date	Account Titles and Description	PR	Dr.	Cr.
19XX May 20	Sales Ret. and Allowances	412	2 0 0 00	
	Acct. Rec., Jane Company	112 ✓		2 0 0 00
	Issued credit memo #1			

PARTIAL GENERAL LEDGER

Accounts Receivable   Account No. 112

Date	Explanation	Post. Ref.	Debit	Credit	Balance Debit	Balance Credit
19XX May 20		GJ1		2 0 0 00		2 0 0 00
31		SJ1	3 1 0 0 00		2 9 0 0 00	

Sales   Account No. 411

Date	Explanation	Post. Ref.	Debit	Credit	Balance Debit	Balance Credit
19XX May 31		SJ1		3 1 0 0 00		3 1 0 0 00

Sales Returns and Allowances   Account No. 412

Date	Explanation	Post. Ref.	Debit	Credit	Balance Debit	Balance Credit
19XX May 20		GJ1	2 0 0 00		2 0 0 00	

Note the unusual balance of $200 due to the return. Why? Because total of sales journal is not posted till end of month.

ACCOUNTS RECEIVABLE LEDGER

NAME Jane Company
ADDRESS 118 Morris Rd., Boston, Mass. 01935

Date	Explanation	Post. Ref.	Debit	Credit	Dr. Balance
19XX May 1		SJ1	6 0 0 00		6 0 0 00
20		GJ1		2 0 0 00	4 0 0 00

ACCOUNTS RECEIVABLE MODULE

NAME Ralph Company
ADDRESS 31 Norris Rd., Boston, Mass. 01935

Date	Explanation	Post. Ref.	Debit	Credit	Dr. Balance
19XX May 5		SJ1	2 5 0 0 00		2 5 0 0 00

Customers owe Moss money and thus have a debit balance.

161

Cash Receipts Journal and Schedule of Accounts Receivable

all receipts of cash go in a cash receipts journal

Besides the sales journal, another special journal often used in a merchandising operation is the cash receipts journal. The **cash receipts journal** records the receipt of cash (or checks) from any source. The number of columns a cash receipts journal will have depends on how frequently certain types of transactions occur. For example, in the cash receipts journal for Art's Wholesale the accountant has developed the headings shown in Figure 6-8. We have added below the heading the purpose of each column and when to update the accounts receivable ledger as well as general ledger.

The following transactions occurred in April for Art's Clothing and affected the cash receipts journal:

19XX
April 1 Art Newner invested $8,000 in the business.
       4 Received check from Hal's Clothing for payment of invoice No. 1 less discount.
      15 Cash sales for first half of April, $900.
      16 Received check from Bevans Company in settlement of invoice No. 2 less returns and discount.

FIGURE 6-8   Cash Receipts Journal.

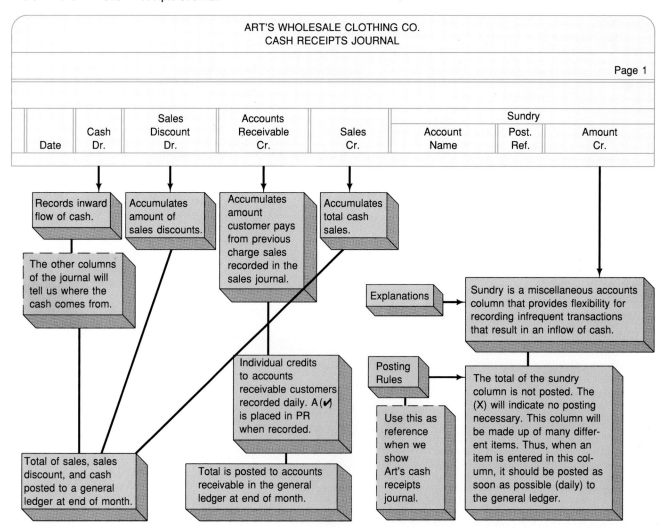

22 Received check from Roe Company for payment of invoice No. 3 less discount.

27 Sold store equipment, $500.

30 Cash sales for second half of April, $1,200.

The diagram in Figure 6-9 shows the cash receipts journal for the end of April along with the recordings to the accounts receivable ledger and posting to the general ledger. Study the diagram, we will review it in a moment.

JOURNALIZING, RECORDING, AND POSTING FROM THE CASH RECEIPTS JOURNAL

On April 4 Art's Wholesale received a check from Hal's Clothing for payment of invoice No. 1 less discount. Remember, it was in the sales journal that this transaction was first recorded (p. 155). At that time we updated the accounts receivable ledger, indicating that Hal's Clothing owed Art $800. Since Hal's Clothing is paying within the 10-day discount period, Art's Wholesale offers a $16.00 sales discount ($800 × .02). (Remember, all credit sales carried terms of 2/10, n/30.)

Now, when payment is received, Art's Wholesale updates the cash receipts journal (see pp. 164–165) by entering the date (April 4), cash debit of $784, sales discount debit of $16, credit to accounts receivable of $800, and which account name (Hal's Clothing) is to be credited. The terms of sale indicate that Hal's Clothing is entitled to the discount and no longer owes Art's Wholesale the $800 balance. *As soon as this line is entered into the cash receipts journal, Art's Wholesale will update* the card file of Hal's Clothing. Note in the accounts receivable ledger of Hal's Clothing how the date (April 4), post reference (CRJ1), and credit amount ($800) are recorded. The balance in the accounts receivable ledger is zero. The last step of this transaction is to go back to the cash receipts journal and put a ✓ in the post reference column.

In looking back at this cash receipts journal, note that:

1. All totals of cash receipts journal *except* sundry were posted to the general ledger at the end of the month.

2. Art Newner, Capital, and Store Equipment were posted to the general ledger when entered in the sundry column. For now in the general ledger it was assumed that the equipment account had a beginning balance of $4,000.

3. The cash sales were not posted when entered (thus the X to show no posting is needed). The sales and cash totals are posted at the *end* of the month.

4. A (✓) means information was recorded daily to the accounts receivable ledger.

5. The use of the Account Name column to describe each transaction.

The last step is to put a ✓ back in the PR of the cash receipts journal to show the accounts receivable ledger is up to date.

We can prove the accuracy of recording transactions of the cash receipts journal by totaling the column with debit balances and the column with credit balances. This process, called **crossfooting**, is done before the totals are posted. Also, if a bookkeeper were using more than one page for the cash receipts journal, the balances on the bottom of one page would be brought forward to the next page. This verifying of totals would result in less work when trying to find journalizing or posting errors at a later date. Let's see how to crossfoot the cash receipts journal of Art's Wholesale (Figure 6-9, pp. 164–165).

Proving the cash receipts journal.

DEBIT COLUMNS   CREDIT COLUMNS

Cash   + Sales Discount = Accounts Receivable + Sales   + Sundry

$14,324 + $76   = $3,800   + $2,100 + $8,500

$14,400 = $14,400

FIGURE 6-9 Cash Receipts Journal and Posting.

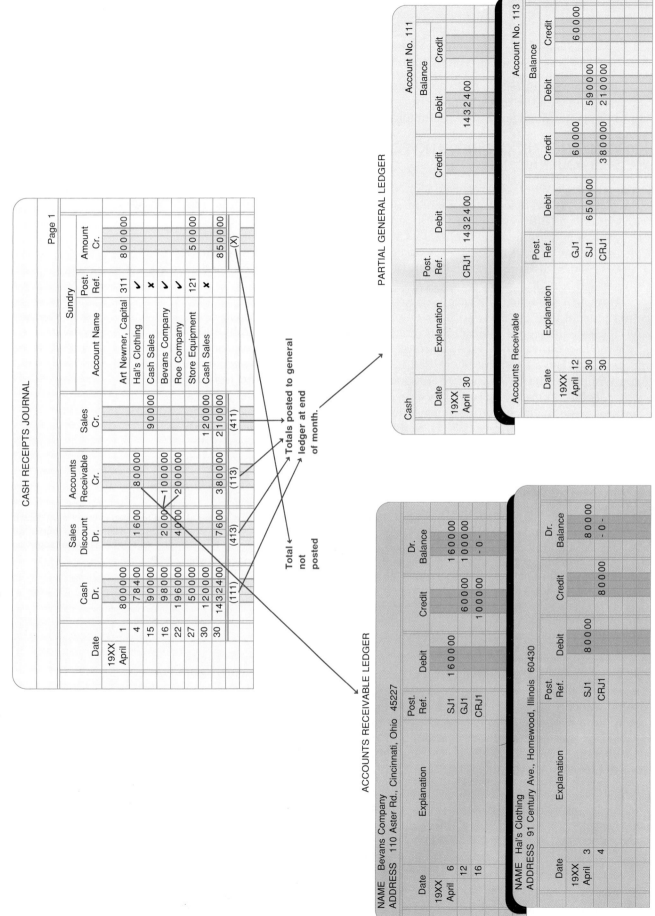

ACCOUNTS RECEIVABLE LEDGER

NAME Mel's Dept. Store
ADDRESS 181 Foss Rd., Swampscott, Mass. 01907

Date	Explanation	Post. Ref.	Debit	Credit	Dr. Balance
19XX					
April 28		SJ1	9000 00		9000 00
29		SJ1	7000 00		16000 00

NAME Roe Company
ADDRESS 18 Rantool St., Beverly, Mass. 01915

Date	Explanation	Post. Ref.	Debit	Credit	Dr. Balance
19XX					
April 18		SJ1	2000 00		2000 00
22		CRJ1		2000 00	- 0 -
24		SJ1	500 00		500 00

PARTIAL GENERAL LEDGER

Store Equipment — Account No. 121

Date	Explanation	Post. Ref.	Debit	Credit	Balance Debit	Balance Credit
19XX						
April 1	Balance	✔			4000 00	
27		CRJ1		500 00	3500 00	

Art Newner, Capital — Account No. 311

Date	Explanation	Post. Ref.	Debit	Credit	Balance Debit	Balance Credit
19XX						
April 1		CRJ1		8000 00		8000 00

Sales — Account No. 411

Date	Explanation	Post. Ref.	Debit	Credit	Balance Debit	Balance Credit
19XX						
April 30		SJ1		6500 00		6500 00
30		CRJ1		2100 00		8600 00

Sales Discount — Account No. 413

Date	Explanation	Post. Ref.	Debit	Credit	Balance Debit	Balance Credit
19XX						
April 30		CRJ1	76 00		76 00	

FIGURE 6-9   Cash Receipts Journal and Posting (Cont.).

The total of sales tax payable would be posted to Sales Tax Payable in the general ledger at the end of the month.

Now let's take a moment to see what sales tax would look like in the cash receipts journal of a business that would need to record sales tax. A typical cash receipts journal might look as follows:

						Sundry		
Date	Cash Dr.	Sales Discount Dr.	Accounts Receivable Cr.	Sales Tax Payable Cr.	Sales Cr.	Account Name	PR	Amount Cr.

CASH RECEIPTS JOURNAL

The total of the sales tax as a result of cash sales would be posted to Sales Tax Payable in the general ledger at the end of the month. It represents a liability of the merchant to forward the tax to the government. Remember, no cash discounts are taken on the sales tax.

Now let's prove the accounts receivable ledger to the controlling account—Accounts Receivable—at the end of April for Art's Wholesale Clothing Company.

SCHEDULE OF ACCOUNTS RECEIVABLE

From pp. 164–165 let's list the customers that have an ending balance in the accounts receivable ledger of Art's Clothing Company. This listing is called a **schedule of accounts receivable**.

Schedule is listed in alphabetical order.

ART'S WHOLESALE CLOTHING COMPANY
SCHEDULE OF ACCOUNTS RECEIVABLE
APRIL 30, 19XX

Mel's Dept. Store	$ 1 6 0 0 00
Roe Company	5 0 0 00
Total Accounts Receivable	$ 2 1 0 0 00

The balance of the controlling account, Accounts Receivable ($2,100), in the general ledger (p. 164) does indeed equal the sum of the individual customer balances in the accounts receivable ledger ($2,100). The schedule of accounts receivable can help forecast potential cash inflows as well as possible credit and collection decisions.

At this point you should be able to

1. Journalize, record, and post transactions using a cash receipts journal with or without sales tax. (pp. 163–165)
2. Prepare a schedule of accounts receivable. (p. 166)

SELF-REVIEW QUIZ 6-4

Journalize, crossfoot, record, and post when appropriate the following transactions into the cash receipts journal of Moore Co. Use the same headings as for Art's Clothing.

ACCOUNTS RECEIVABLE LEDGER		
NAME	BALANCE	INVOICE NO.
Irene Welch	$500	1
Janis Fross	200	2

	ACCT. NO.	BALANCE
Cash	110	$600
Accounts Receivable	120	700
Store Equipment	130	600
Sales	410	700
Sales Discount	420	—

19XX

May 1 Received check from Irene Welch for invoice No. 1 less 2% discount.
    8 Cash sales collected, $200.
    15 Received check from Janis Fross for invoice No. 2 less 2% discount.
    19 Sold store equipment at cost, $300.

SOLUTION TO SELF-REVIEW QUIZ 6-4

MOORE COMPANY
CASH RECEIPTS JOURNAL

Page 2

Date	Cash Dr.	Sales Discount Dr.	Accounts Receivable Cr.	Sales Cr.	Sundry Account Name	Sundry Post Ref.	Sundry Amount Cr.
19XX May 1	490 00	10 00	500 00		Irene Welch	✔	
8	200 00			200 00	Cash Sales	✗	
15	196 00	4 00	200 00		Janis Fross	✔	
19	300 00				Store Equipment	130	300 00
31	1186 00	14 00	700 00	200 00			300 00
	(110)	(420)	(120)	(410)			(X)

Crossfooting: $1,200 = $1,200

PARTIAL GENERAL LEDGER

Cash   Account No. 110

Date	Explanation	Post Ref.	Debit	Credit	Balance Debit	Balance Credit
19XX May 1	Balance	✔			600 00	
31		CRJ2	1186 00		1786 00	

Accounts Receivable   Account No. 120

Date	Explanation	Post Ref.	Debit	Credit	Balance Debit	Balance Credit
19XX May 1	Balance	✔			700 00	
31		CRJ2		700 00	—	—

Store Equipment — Account No. 130

Date		Explanation	Post. Ref.	Debit	Credit	Balance Debit	Balance Credit
19XX May	1	Balance	✔			6 0 0 00	
	19		CRJ2		3 0 0 00	3 0 0 00	

Sales — Account No. 410

Date		Explanation	Post. Ref.	Debit	Credit	Balance Debit	Balance Credit
19XX May	1		✔				7 0 0 00
	31		CRJ2		2 0 0 00		9 0 0 00

Sales Discount — Account No. 420

Date		Explanation	Post. Ref.	Debit	Credit	Balance Debit	Balance Credit
19XX May	31		CRJ2	1 4 00		1 4 00	

ACCOUNTS RECEIVABLE LEDGER

NAME Irene Welch
ADDRESS 10 Rong Rd., Beverly, Mass. 01215

Date		Explanation	Post. Ref.	Debit	Credit	Dr. Balance
19XX May	1	Balance	✔			5 0 0 00
	1		CRJ2		5 0 0 00	—

NAME Janis Fross
ADDRESS 81 Foster Rd., Beverly, Mass. 01915

Date		Explanation	Post. Ref.	Debit	Credit	Dr. Balance
19XX May	1	Balance	✔			2 0 0 00
	15		CRJ2		2 0 0 00	—

SUMMARY OF KEY POINTS AND KEY TERMS

LEARNING UNIT 6-1

1. Sales Returns and Allowances and Sales Discount are contra-revenue accounts.

2. Net Sales = Gross Sales − Sales Returns and Allowances − Sales Discounts.

3. Discounts are not taken on sales' tax, freight, or goods returned. The discount period is shorter than the credit period.

4. Cost of Goods Sold = Beginning + Additional − Ending
Inventory   Cost of   Inventory
Goods
brought
into store

5. Gross Profit = Net Sales − Cost of Goods Sold

6. Net Income = Gross Profit − Operating Expenses

Cost of goods sold: Total cost of the goods that are sold to customers.

Credit period: Length of time allowed for payment of goods sold on account.

Discount period: Period that is shorter than credit period to encourage early payment of bills.

Gross profit: Net sales less cost of goods sold.

Gross sales: The revenue earned from sale of merchandise to customers.

Inventory: Goods or merchandise for resale to customers.

Merchandise: Goods brought into a store for resale to customers.

Net sales: Gross sales less sales returns and allowances less sales discounts.

Retailers: Buy goods from wholesalers for resale to customers.

Sales discount: Contra-revenue account that records cash discounts granted to customers for payments made within a specific period of time.

Sales Returns and Allowances: Contra-revenue account that records price adjustments and allowances granted on merchandise that is defective and has been returned.

Wholesalers: Buy goods from suppliers and manufacturers for sale to retailers.

LEARNING UNIT 6-2

1. A general journal is still used with special journals.

2. A sales journal records sales on account.

3. The accounts receivable ledger, organized in alphabetical order, is not in the same book as Accounts Receivable, the controlling account in the general ledger.

4. At the end of the month the total of all customers' ending balances in the accounts receivable ledger should be equal to the ending balance in Accounts Receivable, the controlling account in the general ledger.

Accounts receivable ledger: A book or file that contains in alphabetical order the individual records of amounts owed by various credit customers.

Controlling account—Accounts Receivable: The Accounts Receivable account in the general ledger, after postings are complete, shows a firm the total amount of money owed to it. This figure is broken down in the accounts receivable ledger, where it indicates specifically who owes the money.

Sales journal: A special journal used to record only sales made on account.

Special journal: A journal used to record similar groups of transactions. Example: The sales journal records all sales on account.

Subsidiary ledger: A ledger that contains accounts of a single type. Example: The accounts receivable ledger records all credit customers.

LEARNING UNIT 6-3

1. The ✓ in the post reference column of the sales journal means a customer's account in the accounts receivable ledger (on the debit side) has been updated (or recorded) during the month.

2. At the end of the month the total(s) of the sales journal is posted to general ledger accounts.

3. Sales Tax Payable is a liability found in the general ledger.

4. When a credit memorandum is issued, the result is that Sales Returns and Allowances is increasing, and Accounts Receivable is decreasing. When we record this into a general journal we assume that all parts of the transaction will be posted to the general ledger and recorded in the subsidiary ledger when the entry is journalized.

Credit memorandum: A piece of paper sent by the seller to a customer who has returned merchandise previously purchased on credit. The credit memorandum indicates to the customer that the seller is reducing the amount owed by the customer.

Sales invoice: A bill reflecting a sale on credit.

Sales Tax Payable account: An account in the general ledger that accumulates the amount of sales tax owed. It has a credit balance.

LEARNING UNIT 6-4

1. The cash receipts journal records receipt of cash from any source.

2. The sundry column records the credit part of a transaction that does not occur frequently. Never post the *total* of sundry. Post items in sundry column to the general ledger when entered.

3. A ✓ in the post reference column of the cash receipts journal means that the accounts receivable ledger has been updated (recorded) with a credit.

4. An X in the cash receipts journal post reference column means no posting was necessary, since the totals of these columns will be posted at the end of the month.

5. Crossfooting means proving that the total of debits and the total of credits are equal in the special journal, thus verifying the accuracy of recording.

6. A schedule of accounts receivable is a listing of the ending balances of customers in the accounts receivable ledger. This total should be same balance as found in the controlling account, Accounts Receivable, in the general ledger.

Cash receipts journal: A special journal that records all transactions involving the receipt of cash from any source.

Crossfooting: The process of proving that the total debit columns of a special journal are equal to the total credit columns of a special journal.

Sundry: Miscellaneous accounts column(s) in a special journal, which records parts of transactions that do not occur too often.

Schedule of accounts receivable: A list of the customers, in alphabetical order, that have an outstanding balance in the accounts receivable ledger. This total should be equal to the balance of the Accounts Receivable controlling account in the general ledger at the end of the month.

Blueprint of Sales and Cash Receipts Journals

SUMMARY OF HOW TO POST AND RECORD
Single-Column Sales Journal

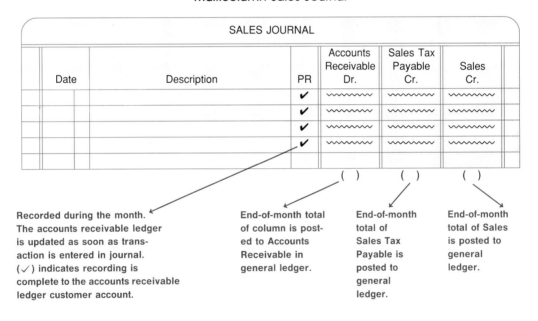

SALES JOURNAL

Date	Description	PR	Accounts Rec.: Dr. Sales: Cr.
		✔	. . .
		✔	. . .
		✔	. . .
		✔	. . .
		✔	. . .
			( )( )

Posted End of Month

Total of column is posted to general ledger accounts, Accounts Receivable and Sales.

Recorded During the Month

Accounts receivable subsidiary ledger is updated as soon as transaction is entered in sales journal. A (✓) indicates that recording is complete to the accounts receivable ledger customer account.

Multicolumn Sales Journal

SALES JOURNAL

Date	Description	PR	Accounts Receivable Dr.	Sales Tax Payable Cr.	Sales Cr.
		✔	~~~~	~~~~	~~~~
		✔	~~~~	~~~~	~~~~
		✔	~~~~	~~~~	~~~~
		✔	~~~~	~~~~	~~~~
			( )	( )	( )

Recorded during the month. The accounts receivable ledger is updated as soon as transaction is entered in journal. (✓) indicates recording is complete to the accounts receivable ledger customer account.

End-of-month total of column is posted to Accounts Receivable in general ledger.

End-of-month total of Sales Tax Payable is posted to general ledger.

End-of-month total of Sales is posted to general ledger.

Issuing a Credit Memo without Sales Tax Recorded in a General Journal

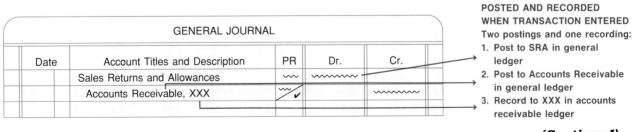

GENERAL JOURNAL

Date	Account Titles and Description	PR	Dr.	Cr.
	Sales Returns and Allowances	~~	~~~~	
	Accounts Receivable, XXX	~~✔		~~~~

POSTED AND RECORDED WHEN TRANSACTION ENTERED
Two postings and one recording:
1. Post to SRA in general ledger
2. Post to Accounts Receivable in general ledger
3. Record to XXX in accounts receivable ledger

(Continued)

Issuing a Credit Memo with Sales Tax Recorded in General Journal

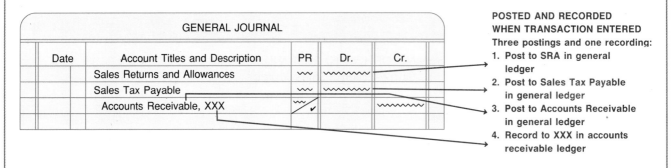

GENERAL JOURNAL

	Date	Account Titles and Description	PR	Dr.	Cr.
		Sales Returns and Allowances	∿	∿∿∿	
		Sales Tax Payable	∿	∿∿∿	
		Accounts Receivable, XXX	∿ ✓		∿∿∿

POSTED AND RECORDED WHEN TRANSACTION ENTERED
Three postings and one recording:
1. Post to SRA in general ledger
2. Post to Sales Tax Payable in general ledger
3. Post to Accounts Receivable in general ledger
4. Record to XXX in accounts receivable ledger

The Cash Receipts Journal

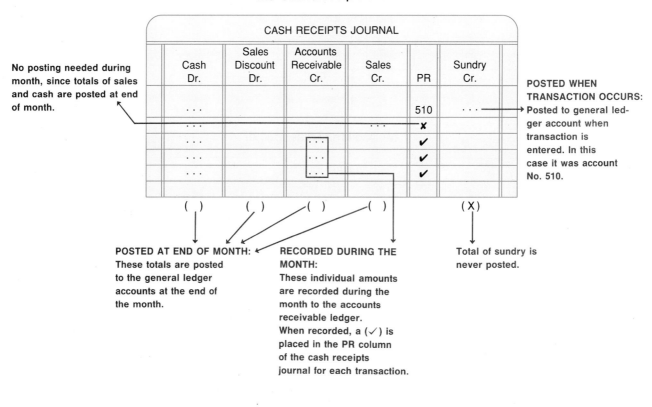

CASH RECEIPTS JOURNAL

Cash Dr.	Sales Discount Dr.	Accounts Receivable Cr.	Sales Cr.	PR	Sundry Cr.
. . .				510	. . .
. . .			. . .	✗	
. . .		. . .		✓	
. . .		. . .		✓	
. . .		. . .		✓	
( )	( )	( )	( )		(X)

No posting needed during month, since totals of sales and cash are posted at end of month.

POSTED WHEN TRANSACTION OCCURS: Posted to general ledger account when transaction is entered. In this case it was account No. 510.

POSTED AT END OF MONTH: These totals are posted to the general ledger accounts at the end of the month.

RECORDED DURING THE MONTH: These individual amounts are recorded during the month to the accounts receivable ledger. When recorded, a (✓) is placed in the PR column of the cash receipts journal for each transaction.

Total of sundry is never posted.

Note: If a Sales Tax Payable column were added, total of column would be posted at end of month.

DISCUSSION QUESTIONS

1. Explain the difference between retailers and wholesalers.
2. Show how you would calculate net sales, cost of goods sold, gross profit, and net income.
3. Give two examples of contra-revenue accounts.
4. What is the difference between a discount period and a credit period?
5. Explain the terms *A.* 2/10, n/30; *B.* n/10, EOM.
6. If special journals are used, what purpose will a general journal serve?

7. Compare and contrast the controlling account Accounts Receivable to the accounts receivable ledger.

8. Why is the accounts receivable ledger organized in alphabetical order?

9. When is a sales journal used?

10. What is an invoice? What purpose does it serve?

11. Why is sales tax a liability to the business?

12. Sales discounts are taken on sales tax. Agree or disagree and tell why.

13. When a seller issues a credit memorandum (assume no sales tax), what accounts will be affected?

14. Explain the function of a cash receipts journal.

15. When is the sundry column of the cash receipts journal posted?

16. Explain the purpose of a schedule of accounts receivable.

EXERCISES

1. From the following sales journal, record to the accounts receivable ledger and post to the general ledger accounts as appropriate.

Recording to accounts receivable ledger and posting to general ledger.

SALES JOURNAL

P. 1

Date	Account Debited	Invoice No.	PR	Dr. Accts. Receivable Cr. Sales
19XX April 18	Kevin Stone Co.	1		4 0 0 00
19	Bill Valley Co.	2		6 0 0 00

ACCOUNTS RECEIVABLE LEDGER   **PARTIAL GENERAL LEDGER**

Kevin Stone Co.   Accounts Receivable 112

Bill Valley Co.   Sales 412

2. Journalize, record, and post when appropriate the following transactions into the sales journal (same heading as Exercise 1) and general journal (P. 1) (all sales carry terms of 2/10, n/30):

19XX
May 16   Sold merchandise on account to Ronald Co., invoice No. 1, $1,000.
    18   Sold merchandise on account to Bass Co., invoice No. 2, $1,700.
    20   Issued credit memorandum No. 1 to Bass Co. for defective merchandise, $700.

Journalizing, recording, and posting that includes credit memorandum.

Use the following account numbers: Accounts Receivable, 112; Sales, 411; Sales Returns and Allowances, 412.

3. From Exercise 2, journalize in the cash receipts journal the receipt of check from Ronald Co. for payment of invoice No. 1 on May 24. Use the same headings as for Art's Wholesale Clothing on p. 164.

Journalizing transaction into cash receipts journal with returns and discounts.

4. From the following transactions for Edna Co., when appropriate, journalize, record, post, and prepare a schedule of accounts receivable. Use the same journal headings (all page 1) and chart of accounts (use Edna Cares, Capital) that Art's Wholesale Clothing used in the text. You will have to set up your own accounts receivable ledger and partial general ledger as needed. All sales terms are 2/10, n/30.

Journalizing, recording, and posting sales and cash receipts journal; schedule of accounts receivable.

19XX

June 1   Edna Cares invested $3,000 in the business.

      1   Sold merchandise on account to Boston Co., invoice No. 1, $700.

      2   Sold merchandise on account to Gary Co., invoice No. 2, $900.

      3   Cash sale, $200.

      8   Issued credit memorandum No. 1 to Boston for defective merchandise, $200.

    10   Received check from Boston for invoice No. 1 less returns and discount.

    15   Cash sale, $400.

    18   Sold merchandise on account to Boston Co., invoice No. 3, $600.

5. From the following facts calculate what Ann Frost must pay Blue Co. for the purchase of a dining room set. Sale terms are 2/10, n/30.

> **A.** Sales ticket price before tax, $4,000—dated April 5.
> **B.** Sales tax, 7%.
> **C.** Returned one defective chair for credit of $400 on April 8.
> **D.** Paid bill on April 13.

(margin note: Sales tax and cash discount calculation.)

GROUP A PROBLEMS

6A-1. Edna Karras opened Max Co., a wholesale grocery and pizza company. The following transactions occurred in July:

19XX

June   1   Sold grocery merchandise to Joe Kase Co. on account, $400, invoice No. 1.

     4   Sold pizza merchandise to Sue Moore Co. on account, $600, invoice No. 2.

     8   Sold grocery merchandise to Long Co. on account, $700, invoice No. 3.

   10   Issued credit memorandum No. 1 to Joe Kase for $150 of grocery merchandise returned due to spoilage.

   15   Sold pizza merchandise to Sue Moore Co. on account, $160, invoice No. 4.

   19   Sold grocery merchandise to Long Co. on account, $300, invoice No. 5.

   25   Sold pizza merchandise to Joe Kase Co. on account, $1,200, invoice No. 6.

Required:

> **1.** Journalize the transactions in the appropriate journals.
> **2.** Record to the accounts receivable ledger and post to general ledger as appropriate.
> **3.** Prepare a schedule of accounts receivable.

6A-2. The following transactions of Ted's Auto Supply occurred in November (your working papers have balances as of Nov. 1 for certain general ledger and accounts receivable ledger accounts):

(margin note: Multicolumn sales journal: Use of sales tax; journalizing and posting to general ledger and recording to accounts receivable ledger; and preparing a schedule of accounts receivable.)

19XX

Nov.   1   Sold auto parts merchandise to R. Volan, $1,000, invoice No. 60, plus 5% sales tax.

     5   Sold auto parts merchandise to J. Seth, $800, invoice No. 61, plus 5% sales tax.

     8   Sold auto parts merchandise to Lance Corner, $9,000, invoice No. 62, plus 5% sales tax.

   10   Issued credit memorandum No. 12 to R. Volan for $500 for defective auto parts merchandise returned from Nov. 1 transaction. (Be careful to record the reduction in sales tax payable as well.)

   12   Sold auto parts merchandise to J. Seth, $600, invoice No. 63, plus 5% sales tax.

Required:

> **1.** Journalize the transactions in the appropriate journals.
> **2.** Record to the accounts receivable ledger and post to general ledger as appropriate.
> **3.** Prepare a schedule of accounts receivable.

6A-3. Mark Peaker owns Peaker's Sneaker Shop. (In your working papers balances as of May 1 are provided for the accounts receivable and general ledger accounts.) The following transactions occurred in May:

Comprehensive Problem: Recording transactions into sales, cash receipts, and general journals. Recording to accounts receivable and posting to general ledger. Preparing a schedule of accounts receivable.

19XX

May 1   Mark Peaker invested an additional $12,000 in the sneaker store.

3   Sold $700 of merchandise on account to B. Dale, sales ticket No. 60, terms 1/10, n/30.

4   Sold $500 of merchandise on account to Ron Lester, sales ticket No. 61, terms 1/10, n/30.

9   Sold $200 of merchandise on account to Jim Zon, sales ticket No. 62, terms 1/10, n/30.

10   Received cash from B. Dale in payment of May 3 transaction, sales ticket No. 60, less discount.

20   Sold $3,000 of merchandise on account to Pam Pry, sales ticket No. 63, terms 1/10, n/30.

22   Received cash payment from Ron Lester in payment of May 4 transaction, sales ticket No. 61.

23   Collected cash sales, $3,000.

24   Issued credit memorandum No. 1 to Pam Pry for $2,000 of merchandise returned from May 20 sales on account.

26   Received cash from Pam Pry in payment of May 20 sales ticket No. 63. (Don't forget about the credit memo and discount.)

28   Collected cash sales, $7,000.

30   Sold sneaker rack equipment for $300 cash. (Beware.)

30   Sold merchandise priced at $4,000, on account to Ron Lester, sales ticket No. 64, terms 1/10, n/30.

31   Issued credit memorandum No. 2 to Ron Lester for $700 of merchandise returned from May 30 transaction, sales ticket No. 64.

Required:

1. Journalize the transactions.

2. Record to the accounts receivable ledger and post to general ledger as needed.

3. Prepare a schedule of accounts receivable.

6A-4. Bill Murray opened Bill's Cosmetic Market on April 1. There is a 6% sales tax on all cosmetic sales. Bill offers no sales discounts. The following transactions occurred in April:

19XX

April 1   Bill Murray invested $8,000 in the Cosmetic Market from his personal savings account.

5   From the cash register tapes, lipstick cash sales were $5,000 plus sales tax.

5   From the cash register tapes, eye shadow cash sales were $2,000 plus sales tax.

8   Sold lipstick on account to Alice Koy Co., $300, sales ticket No. 1, plus sales tax.

9   Sold eye shadow on account to Marika Sanchez Co., $1,000, sales ticket No. 2, plus sales tax.

15   Issued credit memorandum No. 1 to Alice Koy Co. for $150 for lipstick returned. (Be sure to reduce sales tax payable for Bill.)

19   Marika Sanchez Co. paid half the amount owed from sales ticket No. 2, dated April 9.

21   Sold lipstick on account to Jeff Tong Co., $300, sales ticket No. 3, plus sales tax.

24   Sold eye shadow on account to Rusty Neal Co., $800, sales ticket No. 4, plus sales tax.

Comprehensive problem: Using sales tax in recording transactions into sales, cash receipts, and general journals. Recording to accounts receivable and posting to general ledger. Crossfooting and preparing a schedule of accounts receivable.

25 Issued credit memorandum No. 2 to Jeff Tong Co. for $200 for lipstick returned from sales ticket No. 3, dated April 21.

29 Cash sales taken from the cash register tape showed:
(1) Lipstick—$1,000 + $60 sales tax collected.
(2) Eye shadow—$3,000 + $180 sales tax collected.

29 Sold lipstick on account to Marika Sanchez Co., $400, sales ticket No. 5, plus sales tax.

30 Received payment from Marika Sanchez Co. of sales ticket No. 5, dated April 29.

Required:

1. Journalize the above in the sales journal, cash receipts journal, or general journal.

2. Record to the accounts receivable ledger and post to general ledger when appropriate.

3. Prepare a schedule of accounts receivable for the end of April.

GROUP B PROBLEMS

6B-1. The following transactions occurred for Max Co. for the month of June:

Multicolumn column journal: Journalizing and posting to general ledger and recording to accounts receivable ledger and preparing a schedule of accounts receivable.

19XX

June 1 Sold grocery merchandise to Joe Kase Co. on account, $800, invoice No. 1.

4 Sold pizza merchandise to Sue Moore Co. on account, $550, invoice No. 2.

8 Sold grocery merchandise to Long Co. on account, $900, invoice No. 3.

10 Issued credit memorandum No. 1 to Joe Kase for $160 of grocery merchandise returned due to spoilage.

15 Sold pizza merchandise to Sue Moore Co. on account, $700, invoice No. 4.

19 Sold grocery merchandise to Long Co. on account, $250, invoice No. 5.

Required:

1. Journalize the transactions in the appropriate journals.

2. Record to the accounts receivable ledger and post to general ledger as appropriate.

3. Prepare a schedule of accounts receivable.

6B-2. In November the following transactions occurred for Ted's Auto Supply (your working papers have balances as of Nov. 1 for certain general ledger and accounts receivable ledger accounts):

Multicolumn sales journal: Use of sales tax; journalizing and posting to general ledger and recording to accounts receivable ledger; and preparing a schedule of accounts receivable.

19XX

Nov. 1 Sold merchandise to R. Volan, $4,000, invoice No. 70, plus 5% sales tax.

5 Sold merchandise to J. Seth, $1,600, invoice No. 71, plus 5% sales tax.

8 Sold merchandise to Lance Corner, $15,000, invoice No. 72, plus 5% sales tax.

10 Issued credit memorandum No. 14 to R. Volan for $2,000 for defective merchandise returned from Nov. 1 transaction. (Be careful to record the reduction in sales tax payable as well.)

12 Sold merchandise to J. Seth, $1,400, invoice No. 73, plus 5% sales tax.

Required:

1. Journalize the transactions in the appropriate journals.

2. Record to the accounts receivable ledger and post to general ledger as appropriate.

3. Prepare a schedule of accounts receivable.

6B-3. (In your working papers all the beginning balances needed are provided for the accounts receivable and general ledger.) The following transactions occurred for Peaker's Sneaker Shop:

19XX

May 1 Mark Peaker invested an additional $14,000 in the sneaker store.

3 Sold $2,000 of merchandise on account to B. Dale, sales ticket No. 60, terms 1/10, n/30.

4 Sold $900 of merchandise on account to Ron Lester, sales ticket No. 61, terms 1/10, n/30.

9 Sold $600 of merchandise on account to Jim Zon, sales ticket No. 62, terms 1/10, n/30.

Comprehensive Problem: Recording transactions into sales, cash receipts, and general journals. Recording to accounts receivable and posting to general ledger. Preparing a schedule of accounts receivable.

10 Received cash from B. Dale in payment of May 3 transaction, sales ticket No. 60, less discount.

20 Sold $4,000 of merchandise on account to Pam Pry, sales ticket No. 63, terms 1/10, n/30.

22 Received cash payment from Ron Lester in payment of May 4 transaction, sales ticket No. 61.

23 Collected cash sales, $6,000.

24 Issued credit memorandum No. 1 to Pam Pry for $500 of merchandise returned from May 20 sales on account.

26 Received cash from Pam Pry in payment of May 20 sales ticket No. 63. (Don't forget about the credit memo and discount.)

28 Collected cash sales, $12,000.

30 Sold sneaker rack equipment for $200 cash. (Beware.)

30 Sold $6,000 of merchandise on account to Ron Lester, sales ticket No. 64, terms 1/10, n/30.

31 Issued credit memorandum No. 2 to Ron Lester for $800 of merchandise returned from May 30 transaction, sales ticket No. 64.

Required:

1. Journalize the transactions in the appropriate journals.
2. Record and post as appropriate.
3. Prepare a schedule of accounts receivable.

6B-4. Bill's Cosmetic Market began operating in April. There is a 6% sales tax on all cosmetic sales. Bill offers no discounts. The following transactions occured in April:

19XX

April 1 Bill Murray invested $10,000 in the Cosmetic Market from his personal account.

5 From the cash register tapes, lipstick cash sales were $5,000 plus sales tax.

5 From the cash register tapes, eye shadow cash sales were $3,000 plus sales tax.

8 Sold lipstick on account to Alice Koy Co., $400, sales ticket No. 1, plus sales tax.

9 Sold eye shadow on account to Marika Sanchez Co., $900, sales ticket No. 2, plus sales tax.

Comprehensive Problem: Using sales tax in recording transactions into sales, cash receipts, and general journals. Recording to accounts receivable and posting to general ledger, and preparing a schedule of accounts receivable.

15 Issued credit memorandum No. 1 to Alice Koy Co. for lipstick returned, $200. (Be sure to reduce sales tax payable for Bill.)

19 Marika Sanchez Co. paid half the amount owed from sales ticket No. 2, dated April 9.

21 Sold lipstick on account to Jeff Tong Co., $600 sales ticket No. 3, plus sales tax.

24 Sold eye shadow on account to Rusty Neal Co., $1,000 sales ticket No. 4, plus sales tax.

25 Issued credit memorandum No. 2 to Jeff Tong Co. for $300, for lipstick returned from sales ticket No. 3, dated April 21.

29 Cash sales taken from the cash register tape showed:
(1) Lipstick—$4,000 + $240 sales tax collected.
(2) Eye shadow—$2,000 + $120 sales tax collected.

29 Sold lipstick on account to Marika Sanchez Co., $700, sales ticket No. 5, plus sales tax.

30 Received payment from Marika Sanchez Co. of sales ticket No. 5, dated April 29.

Required:

1. Journalize, record, and post as appropriate.
2. Prepare a schedule of accounts receivable for the end of April.

PRACTICAL ACCOUNTING APPLICATION #1

Ronald Howard has been hired by Green Company to help reconstruct the sales journal, general journal, and cash receipts journal, which were recently destroyed in a fire. The owner of Green has supplied him with the following data. Please ignore dates, invoice numbers, etc., and enter the entries into the reconstructed sales journal, general journal, and cash receipts journal.

Accounts Receivable Ledger

P. Bond			M. Raff	
Bal.	100	150 CRJ	Bal.	200
SJ	150	(Entitled to 2% discount)	SJ	100

J. Smooth			R. Venner		
Bal.	300	1,000 GJ	Bal.	200	400 CRJ
SJ	2,000	1,000 CRJ ←	SJ	400	
SJ	1,000	500 GJ			
		(Entitled to 1% discount) ─┘			

Partial General Ledger

Cash		Accounts Receivable			Shelving Equipment		
12,737		Bal.	800	1,000 GJ	Bal.	200	200 CRJ
		SJ	3,650	500 GJ			
				1,550 CRJ			

M. Rang, Capital		Sales		Sales Discount	
	1,000 Bal.		800 Bal.	CRJ 13	
	5,000 (Additional investment this month)		6,000 CRJ←(5,000		
			3,650 SJ and		
			1,000)		

Sales Returns and Allowances	
GJ 1,000	
J 1,500	

PRACTICAL ACCOUNTING APPLICATION #2

The bookkeeper of Floore Company records credit sales in a sales journal and returns in a general journal. The bookkeeper did the following:

1. Recorded an $18 credit sales as $180 in the sales journal.
2. Correctly recorded a $40 sale in the sales journal but posted it to B. Blue's account as $400 in the accounts receivable ledger.

3. Made an additional error in determining the balance of J. B. Window Co. in the accounts receivable ledger.

4. Posted a sales return that was recorded in the general journal to the Sales Returns and Allowance account and the Accounts Receivable account but forgot to record to the B. Katz Co.

5. Added the total of the sales column incorrectly.

6. Posted a sales return to the Accounts Receivable account but not to the Sales Returns and Allowances account. Accounts Receivable ledger was recorded correctly.

Could you inform the bookkeeper as to when each error will be discovered?

SPECIAL JOURNALS:
Purchases and Cash Payments

In this chapter we will cover the following topics:

1. Calculating cost of goods sold. (p. 181)
2. Journalizing transactions in a purchases journal. (pp. 185–187)
3. Posting from a purchases journal to the accounts payable ledger and the general ledger. (p. 187)
4. Recording from the purchases journal to the accounts payable ledger. (p. 187)
5. Preparing, journalizing, recording, and posting a debit memorandum. (pp. 186–188)
6. Journalizing, recording, and posting transactions using a cash payments journal. (pp. 192–193)
7. Preparing a schedule of accounts payable. (p. 194)

In the last chapter we looked at Art's Wholesale Clothing Company as the *seller* of merchandise. In this chapter we will focus on Art's Wholesale as the *buyer* of merchandise and other items. Many of the concepts and rules related to special journals and subsidiary ledgers in Chapter 6 will carry over to this chapter. Before looking at two new special journals that Art's will use, let's introduce some key concepts and terms relating to cost of goods sold that will be helpful in dealing with the content of this chapter.

LEARNING UNIT 7-1

Cost of Goods Sold

We saw in Chapter 6 that net sales less cost of goods sold equaled gross profit. Up to this point we have defined cost of goods sold as follows:

Cost of Goods Sold
↓

Beginning Inventory + Additional cost of goods − Ending Inventory
brought into store

↓	↓	↓
Cost of merchandise on hand to start accounting period	Cost of merchandise that is brought into store *during* the accounting period	Cost of merchandise that is on hand at end of accounting period

The following is a more detailed example of how cost of goods sold is calculated. Let's say that the cost of goods sold is $3,000, as it was in Chapter 6 (p. 152). Note that the bottom line in the accompanying diagram has the same $3,000 total as in Chapter 6 but is arrived at in a more detailed manner.

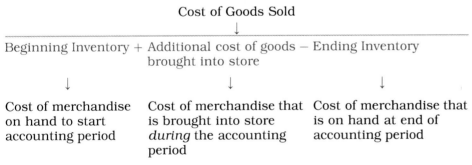

COST OF GOODS SOLD		
(1) Beginning Inventory	$200	Purchases, less
(2) + Net Purchases	3,900	Purchases Returns and Allowances, less
(3) + Freight-In	100	Purchases Discount
(4) − Ending Inventory	−1,200	F.O.B. Shipping Point—
(5) = Cost of Goods Sold	$3,000	Purchaser pays shipping cost

1. Beginning Inventory

At the beginning of the accounting period, the cost of merchandise on hand is $200. (*Note:* Cost of merchandise is *not* the same thing as the selling price of merchandise.)

2. Net Purchases

Purchases

Dr.	Cr.
4,200	

Purchases Returns and Allowances

Dr.	Cr.
	50

Purchases Discount

Dr.	Cr.
	250

Net purchases is the actual cost of bringing additional merchandise for resale into the store before considering freight.

The **Purchases** account accumulates the cost of additional merchandise *bought for resale*. (Anything else purchased, such as supplies or equipment, goes in its own account—the Purchases account is only for goods that will be resold. It represents a cost to the purchaser, and its usual balance is a debit.)

Purchases Returns and Allowances is an account that accumulates the amount the buyer returns for credit, or the amount of price reductions given the buyer for defective merchandise. (This corresponds to the Sales Returns and Allowances account we discussed in the last chapter, but looked at now from the purchaser's point of view rather than the seller's.) Think of the Purchases Returns and Allowances account as a *contra cost*-of-goods-sold account. It represents a savings to the purchaser, and its normal balance is a credit.

Purchases Discount is an account that accumulates the amount of cash discounts the purchaser receives for making payment within the discount period. (This corresponds to the Sales Discount account we mentioned in the last chapter, but looked at now from the purchaser's point of view.) It can represent a substantial savings to the buyer. Think of this account as a *contra cost*-of-goods-sold account.

Thus, net purchases consists of these accounts, as shown here:

Net purchases = Purchases − Purchases Returns − Purchases Discount
and Allowances

$3,900 = $4,200 − $50 − $250

Now we have to look at who pays the shipping costs.

3. Freight-In

Freight-in

Dr.	Cr.
100	

Cost of goods sold account; buyer responsible for shipping costs.

The account **Freight-In** accumulates the shipping costs of the *buyer*. Freight-In is added to the net cost of purchases and thus gives us the true cost of buying additional merchandise. If the *seller* of the goods is responsible for paying the freight, it may be listed as a delivery expense (an operating expense) on the income statement. Let's look at some specific shipping terms that will help us determine who is responsible for the shipping costs.

F.O.B. Shipping Point

F.O.B. is an abbreviation for Free on Board the carrier.

F.O.B. shipping point means that from the point goods are shipped it is the responsibility of the *purchaser* to cover the shipping costs. Seller pays *only* the freight to the shipping point. For example, if a New York company buys goods from a Boston company and shipping terms are F.O.B. Boston, it is the responsibility of the New York company (the buyer) to pay shipping costs from Boston to New York.

F.O.B. Destination

F.O.B. destination means the *seller* is responsible for covering the shipping cost till the goods reach their destination. For instance, if the previous example were F.O.B. New York, the Boston company (the seller) would cover the cost of shipping from Boston to New York.

Sometimes when the shipping terms are F.O.B. shipping point the seller will prepay the freight costs as a matter of convenience and will add it to the invoice of the purchaser.

Seller pays freight to point of destination.

Example:

Bill amount ($800 + $80 prepaid freight)	$880
Less 5% cash discount (.05 × $800)	40
Amount to be paid by buyer	$840

(*Note:* The discount is not taken on the $80 freight.)

If the seller ships goods F.O.B. shipping point, legal ownership (title) passes to the buyer *when the goods are shipped.* If goods are shipped by the seller F.O.B. destination, title will change *when goods have reached their destination.*

When does title change to goods shipped?

At this point you should be able to

1. Explain how cost of goods sold is calculated.   (p. 181)
2. Explain why Purchases is part of cost of goods sold, while Purchases Returns and Allowances and Purchases Discounts are contra cost-of-goods-sold accounts. (p. 182)
3. Explain the difference between Freight-In and Delivery Expense.   (p. 182)
4. Define, compare, and contrast F.O.B. shipping point versus F.O.B. destination. (p. 182)
5. Explain why purchases discounts are not taken on freight.   (p. 183)
6. Explain when title passes to the buyer if goods are shipped F.O.B. destination. (p. 183)

SELF-REVIEW QUIZ 7-1

Which of the following statements are false?

1. Net purchases = Purchases − Purchases Returns and Allowances − Purchases Discount.
2. Freight-In is part of Purchases Discount.
3. F.O.B. destination means the seller covers shipping cost and retains title till goods reach their destination.
4. Purchases discounts are not taken on freight.
5. Purchases Discount is a contra cost-of-goods-sold account.

SOLUTION TO SELF-REVIEW QUIZ 7-1

Number 2 is false.

LEARNING UNIT 7-2

Steps Taken in Purchasing Merchandise and Recording Purchases

Specific steps are taken by any merchandising company when purchasing goods for resale. Let's look at the steps taken by Art's Wholesale Clothing Company in ordering goods from Abby Blake Company on April 3.

Step 1: Prepare a Purchase Requisition at Art's Wholesale

Authorized personnel initiate purchase requisition.

When a low inventory level of ladies' jackets for resale is noted, a request to purchase ladies' jackets is sent to the purchasing department. This document, called a **purchase requisition**, is sent to the purchasing department along with a duplicate copy for the accounting department. The third copy of this requisition remains with the department that initiated the request, to be used as a check on the purchasing department.

Step 2: Purchasing Department of Art's Wholesale Prepares a Purchase Order

Four copies of purchase order: (1) (original) to supplier, (2) to accounting department, (3) remains with department that initiated purchase requisition, (4) to file of purchasing department.

After a check of various price lists, as well as suppliers' catalogs, a business form called a **purchase order** was prepared by the purchasing department of Art's Wholesale, giving Abby Blake Company the authority to ship ladies' jackets ordered (see Figure 7-1).

Step 3: Sales Invoice Prepared by Abby Blake Company

Abby Blake Company receives the purchase order and prepares a *sales invoice*, as we showed in Chapter 6. The sales invoice for the seller is the **purchase invoice** for the buyer. A sales invoice is shown in Figure 7-2.

Note: F.O.B. is Englewood Cliffs. This means Art will cover shipping costs.

Note that the shipping costs are *prepaid* by Abby Blake and thus freight is added on to invoice. Remember, terms are shipping point Englewood Cliffs, and it is Art's responsibility to cover the shipping costs to New York from Englewood Cliffs. Abby pays the cost of shipping as a matter of convenience.

FIGURE 7-1
Purchase Order.

PURCHASE ORDER NO. 1
ART'S WHOLESALE CLOTHING COMPANY
1528 BELLE AVE.
NEW YORK, NY 10022

Purchased From:	Abby Blake Company 12 Foster Road Englewood Cliffs, NJ 07632		Date: April 1, 19XX Shipped VIA: Freight Truck Terms: 2/10, n/60 FOB: Englewood Cliffs
Quantity	Description	Unit Price	Total
100	Ladies' Jackets Code 14-O	$50	$5,000
			Art's Wholesale By: Bill Joy

Purchase order number must appear on all invoices.

```
                    SALES INVOICE NO. 228
                    ABBY BLAKE COMPANY
                     12 FOSTER ROAD
                 ENGLEWOOD CLIFFS, NJ  07632

Sold to:  Art's Wholesale         Date:  April 3, 19XX
          Clothing Co.            Shipped VIA:  Freight Truck
          1528 Belle Ave.        Terms:  2/10, n/60
          New York, NY            Your Order No:  1
          10022                  FOB:  Englewood Cliffs

 Quantity  |       Description       | Price  |  Total
   100     | Ladies' Jackets Code 14-O|  $50  | $5,000
           | Freight                 |       |     50
           |                         |       | $5,050
```

FIGURE 7-2
Sales Invoice.

Step 4: Receiving the Jackets

When goods are received, Art's Wholesale inspects the shipment and completes a **receiving report**.

Step 5: Verifying the Numbers

The accounting department checks the purchase order, invoice, and receiving report to make sure all is in agreement and that no steps have been omitted before the invoice is approved for recording and payment. The form used for checking and approval is an **invoice approval form** (see Figure 7-3).

An important point to keep in mind that Art's Wholesale records this purchase when the *invoice is approved for recording and payment.* Why? The purchase requisition, purchase order, and receiving report are supporting documents. On the other side of the coin Abby Blake Company records this transaction in its records when the sales invoice is prepared.

THE PURCHASES JOURNAL AND ACCOUNTS PAYABLE LEDGER

As we discussed in the last chapter, Art's Wholesale Clothing Company finds it helpful to use special journals as well as the general journal, and subsidiary ledgers as well as the general ledger. Let's look at the purchases journal and

```
           INVOICE APPROVAL FORM

Purchase Order #                         _____
Requisition
check                                    _____
Purchase Order
check                                    _____
Receiving Report
check                                    _____
Invoice
check                                    _____
Approved for Payment                     _____
```

FIGURE 7-3
Invoice Approval Form.

show how to journalize and post to the general ledger and record to the accounts payable ledger. The **purchases journal** is a multicolumn special journal that records the buying of merchandise or other items on account. The **accounts payable ledger** is a book or file that lists alphabetically the amounts owed to creditors from purchases on account.

For example, on April 3 Art's Wholesale Clothing Company records in its purchases journal the following:

Date: April 3, 19XX
Account Credited: Abby Blake Company
Date of Invoice: April 3
Invoice Number: 228
Terms: 2/10, n/60
Accounts Payable: $5,050; Purchases: $5,000; Freight-In, $50

As soon as the information is journalized in the purchases journal (see Fig. 7-4), you should:.

See Fig. 7-4 for complete purchases journal.

Note that the normal balance in the accounts payable ledger is a credit.

1. Record to Abby Blake Co. in the accounts payable ledger to indicate that the amount owed is now $5,050. When this is complete, place a ✓ in the PR column of the purchases journal.
2. Post to Freight-In, account number 514, in the ledger right away. When this is complete, record the 514 in the PR column under sundry in the purchases journal.

The posting and recording rules are quite similar to those in the previous chapter, but here we are looking at the buyer rather than at the seller.

Let's look now at how Art's Wholesale handles returns as a buyer, not a seller.

THE DEBIT MEMORANDUM

A **debit memorandum** is a piece of paper issued by a customer to a seller, indicating that purchases returns and allowances have occurred. On April 6 Art's Wholesale had purchased men's hats for $800 from Thorpe Company (p. 187). On April 9, 20 hats with a value of $200 were found to have defective brims. Art issued a debit memorandum to Thorpe Company, as shown in Figure 7-5. At some point in the future Thorpe will issue Art a credit memorandum, which we discussed in the last chapter. But right now we are

FIGURE 7-5
Debit Memorandum.

A debit memo shows that Art's does not owe as much money as was indicated in his purchases journal.

DEBIT MEMORANDUM		No. 1
Art's Wholesale Clothing Company 1528 Belle Ave. New York, NY 10022		
To: Thorpe Company 3 Access Road Beverly, MA 01915		April 9, 19XX
WE DEBIT your account as follows:		
Quantity	Unit Cost	Total
20 Men's Hats Code 827 — defective brims	$10	$200

FIGURE 7-4   Purchases Journal

ART'S WHOLESALE CLOTHING COMPANY
PURCHASES JOURNAL

Date	Account Credited	Date of Invoice	Inv. No.	Terms	Post Ref.	Accounts Payable Credit	Purchases Debit	Sundry-Dr. Account	PR	Amount
19XX April 3	Abby Blake Company	April 3	228	2/10, n/60	✔	5 0 5 0 00	5 0 0 0 00	Freight-In	514	5 0 00
4	Joe Francis Company	April 5	388		✔	4 0 0 0 00		Equip.	121	4 0 0 0 00
6	Thorpe Company	April 6	415	1/10, n/30	✔	8 0 0 00	8 0 0 00			
7	John Sullivan Company	April 6	516	n/10, EOM	✔	9 8 0 00	9 8 0 00			
12	Abby Blake Company	April 13	242	1/10, n/30	✔	6 0 0 00	6 0 0 00			
25	John Sullivan Company	April 26	612		✔	5 0 0 00		Supplies	115	5 0 0 00
30						11 9 3 0 00	7 3 8 0 00			4 5 5 0 00
						(211)	(511)			(X)

The (✔) in the purchases journal indicates the accounts payable ledger has been recorded *during* the month.

Total of Accounts Payable and Purchases posted to general ledger accounts at *end of month*.

Posted when transaction is entered:

Posted to general ledger account when transaction is entered

Total of sundry *not* posted

ACCOUNTS PAYABLE LEDGER

Abby Blake Co.

Dr.	Cr.
	5,050 PJ1 4/3
	600 PJ1 4/12

Joe Francis Co.

Dr.	Cr.
	4,000 PJ1 4/4

John Sullivan Co.

Dr.	Cr.
	980 PJ1 4/7
	500 PJ1 4/25

Thorpe Co.

Dr.	Cr.
	800 PJ1 4/6

Tells us what page of journal information came from

PARTIAL GENERAL LEDGER

Supplies 115

4/25 PJ1 500	

Purchases 511

4/30 PJ1 7,380	

Equipment 121

4/4 PJ1 4,000	

Freight-In 514

4/3 PJ1 50	

Accounts Payable 211

	11,930 PJ1 4/30

concerned about the accounting records of Art's Wholesale Clothing Company.

Let's look at a transaction analysis chart first.

Accounts Affected	Category	↑ ↓	Rules
Accounts Payable	Liability	↓	Dr.
Purchases Returns and Allowances	Contra cost-of-goods-sold	↑	Cr.

Purchases Returns and Allowances, a credit balance, causes a decrease to the cost of goods for resale.

Journalizing and Posting the Debit Memo

The following is the journal entry for the debit memorandum:

Purchases Returns and Allowances

Dr.	Cr.
−	+

A contra-cost-of-goods-sold account

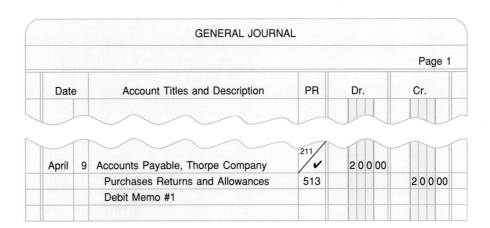

The two postings and one recording are:

1. 211—Post to Accounts Payable as a debit in the general ledger account no. 211. When this is done, place in the PR column the account number, 211, above the diagonal on the same line as Accounts Payable.
2. ✓—Record to Thorpe Co. in the accounts payable ledger to show we don't owe Thorpe as much money. When this is done, place a (✓) in the journal in the PR column below the diagonal line on the same line as Accounts Payable.
3. 513—Post to Purchases Returns and Allowances as a credit in the general ledger (account no. 513). When this is done, place the account number, 513, in the posting reference column of the journal on the same line as Purchases Returns and Allowances. (If equipment was returned that was not merchandise for resale, we would credit Equipment and not Purchases Returns and Allowances.)

At this point you should be able to

1. Explain the relationship between a purchase requisition, a purchase order, and a purchase invoice.   (p. 184)
2. Explain why a typical invoice approval form may be used.   (p. 185)
3. Journalize transactions into a purchases journal.   (p. 187)

4. Explain how to record to the accounts payable ledger and post to the general ledger from a purchases journal. (pp. 186–187)
5. Explain a debit memorandum and be able to journalize an entry resulting from its issuance. (p. 188)

SELF-REVIEW QUIZ 7-2

Journalize the following transactions into the purchases journal or general journal for Munroe Co. Record to accounts payable ledger and post to general ledger accounts as appropriate. Use the same journal headings we used for Art's Wholesale Clothing Company.

19XX

May 5   Bought merchandise on account from Flynn Co., invoice No. 512, dated May 6, terms 1/10, n/30, $900.
      7   Bought merchandise from John Butler Company, invoice No. 403, dated May 7, terms n/10 EOM, $1,000.
     13   Issued debit memo no. 1 to Flynn Co. for merchandise returned, $300, from invoice No. 512.
     17   Purchased $400 of equipment on account from John Butler Company, invoice No. 413, dated May 18.

SOLUTION TO SELF-REVIEW QUIZ 7-2

MUNROE CO. PURCHASES JOURNAL

Page 2

Date	Account Credited	Date of Invoice	Inv. No.	Terms	Post Ref.	Accounts Payable Credit	Purchases Debit	Sundry-Dr. Account	PR	Amount
19XX May 5	Flynn Co.	May 6	512	1/10, n/30	✔	9 0 0 00	9 0 0 00			
7	John Butler	May 7	403	n/10, EOM	✔	1 0 0 0 00	1 0 0 0 00			
17	John Butler	May 18	413		✔	4 0 0 00		Equip.	121	4 0 0 00
31						2 3 0 0 00	1 9 0 0 00			4 0 0 00
						(212)	(512)			(X)

MUNROE CO. GENERAL JOURNAL

Page 1

Date	Account Titles and Description	PR	Dr.	Cr.
19XX May 13	Accounts Payable, Flynn Co.	212 / ✔	3 0 0 00	
	Purchases Returns and Allowances	513		3 0 0 00

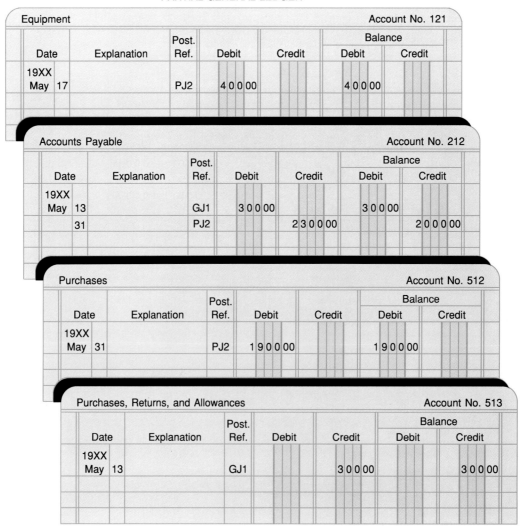

ACCOUNTS PAYABLE SUBSIDIARY LEDGER
JOHN BUTLER COMPANY
18 REED RD.
HOMEWOOD, ILLINOIS 60430

Date	Explanation	Post. Ref.	Debit	Credit	Cr. Balance
19XX May 7		PJ2		1 0 0 0 00	1 0 0 0 00
17		PJ2		4 0 0 00	1 4 0 0 00

FLYNN COMPANY
15 FOSS AVE.
ENGLEWOOD CLIFFS, NEW JERSEY 07632

Date	Explanation	Post. Ref.	Debit	Credit	Cr. Balance
19XX May 5		PJ2		9 0 0 00	9 0 0 00
13		GJ1	3 0 0 00		6 0 0 00

PARTIAL GENERAL LEDGER

Equipment   Account No. 121

Date	Explanation	Post. Ref.	Debit	Credit	Balance Debit	Balance Credit
19XX May 17		PJ2	4 0 0 00		4 0 0 00	

Accounts Payable   Account No. 212

Date	Explanation	Post. Ref.	Debit	Credit	Balance Debit	Balance Credit
19XX May 13		GJ1	3 0 0 00		3 0 0 00	
31		PJ2		2 3 0 0 00		2 0 0 0 00

Purchases   Account No. 512

Date	Explanation	Post. Ref.	Debit	Credit	Balance Debit	Balance Credit
19XX May 31		PJ2	1 9 0 0 00		1 9 0 0 00	

Purchases, Returns, and Allowances   Account No. 513

Date	Explanation	Post. Ref.	Debit	Credit	Balance Debit	Balance Credit
19XX May 13		GJ1		3 0 0 00		3 0 0 00

LEARNING UNIT 7-3

The Cash Payments Journal and Schedule of Accounts Payable

Art's Clothing will record all payments made in cash (or by check) in a **cash payments journal** (which is also called a *cash disbursements journal*). The structure of the cash payments journal in many ways resembles that of the cash receipts journal we discussed in Chapter 6, but now we are looking at the outward flow of cash instead of the inward flow. The following transactions occurred in April and affected the cash payments journal:

April 2 Issued check no. 1 to Pete Blum for insurance paid in advance, $900.
     7 Issued check no. 2 to Joe Francis Company in payment of its April 5 invoice No. 388.
     9 Issued check no. 3 to Rick Flo Co. for merchandise purchased for cash, $800.
    12 Issued check no. 4 to Thorpe Company in payment of its April 6 invoice No. 414 less the return and discount.
    28 Issued check no. 5, $700, for salaries paid.

The diagram in Figure 7-6 on pp. 192–193 shows the cash payments journal for the end of April along with the recordings to the accounts payable ledger and postings to the general ledger. Study the diagram; we will review it in a moment.

Posting and recording rules for this journal are similar to those for the cash receipts journal in Chapter 6.

JOURNALIZING, RECORDING, AND POSTING FROM THE CASH PAYMENTS JOURNAL TO THE ACCOUNTS PAYABLE LEDGER AND THE GENERAL LEDGER

Let's look at the diagram in Figure 7-6 to see how Art's Wholesale recorded the payment of cash on April 12 to Thorpe Company. Back in the purchases journal on April 6, Art had purchased from Thorpe merchandise on account for $800. Now on April 12 Art is paying the amount owed less a purchases discount of 1 percent. As soon as the entry is made into the cash payments journal, the amount owed Thorpe ($800 − $200 returns) is *immediately recorded* in the accounts payable ledger. Note that the payment reduces the balance to Thorpe to zero. Art's Wholesale receives a $6 purchases discount. Be careful not to take a discount on sales tax or freight.

    Now let's review some of the end-of-month posting rules, as well as sundry columns. At the end of the month the totals of the Cash, Purchases Discount, and Accounts Payable accounts are posted to the general ledger. The total of sundry is *not* posted. The accounts Prepaid Insurance, Purchases, and Salaries are posted to the general ledger at the time the entry is put in the journal.

    The cash payments journal of Art's Wholesale can be crossfooted as follows:

$$\text{Debit Columns} = \text{Credit Columns}$$
$$\text{Sundry} + \text{Accounts Payable} = \text{Purchases Discounts} + \text{Cash}$$
$$\$2,400 + \$4,600 \qquad = \$6 \qquad + \$6,994$$
$$\underline{\underline{\$7,000}} = \underline{\underline{\$7,000}}$$

FIGURE 7-6

Cash Payments Journal Recording
and Posting.

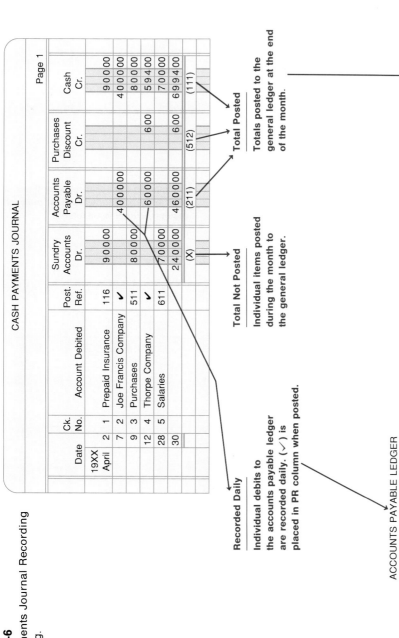

CASH PAYMENTS JOURNAL

Page 1

Date	Ck. No.	Account Debited	Post. Ref.	Sundry Accounts Dr.	Accounts Payable Dr.	Purchases Discount Cr.	Cash Cr.
19XX April							
2	1	Prepaid Insurance	116	9 0 0 00			9 0 0 00
7	2	Joe Francis Company	✓		4 0 0 0 00		4 0 0 0 00
9	3	Purchases	511	8 0 0 00			8 0 0 00
12	4	Thorpe Company	✓		6 0 0 00	6 00	5 9 4 00
28	5	Salaries	611	7 0 0 00			7 0 0 00
30				2 4 0 0 00	4 6 0 0 00	6 00	6 9 9 4 00
				(X)	(211)	(512)	(111)

Recorded Daily

Individual debits to
the accounts payable ledger
are recorded daily. (✓) is
placed in PR column when posted.

Total Not Posted

Individual items posted
during the month to
the general ledger.

Total Posted

Totals posted to the
general ledger at the end
of the month.

PARTIAL GENERAL LEDGER

Cash   Account No. 111

Date	Explanation	Post. Ref.	Debit	Credit	Balance Debit	Balance Credit
19XX April 30		CRJ1	1 4 3 2 4 00		1 4 3 2 4 00	
30		CPJ1		6 9 9 4 00	7 3 3 0 00	

Prepaid Insurance   Account No. 116

Date	Explanation	Post. Ref.	Debit	Credit	Balance Debit	Balance Credit
19XX April 2		CPJ1	9 0 0 00		9 0 0 00	

ACCOUNTS PAYABLE LEDGER

NAME Abby Blake Co.
ADDRESS 12 Foster Rd., Englewood Cliffs, New Jersey 07632

Date	Explanation	Post. Ref.	Debit	Credit	Cr. Balance
19XX April 3		PJ1		5 0 5 0 00	5 0 5 0 00
12		PJ1		6 0 0 00	5 6 5 0 00

NAME Joe Francis Co.
ADDRESS 2 Roundy Rd., Cincinnati, Ohio 45200

Date	Explanation	Post. Ref.	Debit	Credit	Cr. Balance
19XX April 4		PJ1		4 0 0 0 00	4 0 0 0 00
7		CPJ1	4 0 0 0 00		- 0 -

NAME John Sullivan Co.
ADDRESS 18 Print St., Wellesley, Mass. 01980

Date	Explanation	Post. Ref.	Debit	Credit	Cr. Balance
19XX April 7		PJ1		980 00	980 00
25		PJ1		500 00	1480 00

NAME Thorpe Co.
ADDRESS 3 Access Rd., Chicago, Illinois 60430

Date	Explanation	Post. Ref.	Debit	Credit	Cr. Balance
19XX April 6		PJ1		800 00	800 00
9		GJ1	200 00		600 00
12		CPJ1	600 00		- 0 -

Accounts Payable   Account No. 211

Date	Explanation	Post. Ref.	Debit	Credit	Balance Debit	Balance Credit
19XX April 9		GJ1	200 00		200 00	
30		PJ1		11930 00		11730 00
30		CPJ1	4600 00			7130 00

Purchases   Account No. 511

Date	Explanation	Post. Ref.	Debit	Credit	Balance Debit	Balance Credit
19XX April 9		CPJ1	800 00		800 00	
30		PJ1	7380 00		8180 00	

Purchases Discount   Account No. 512

Date	Explanation	Post. Ref.	Debit	Credit	Balance Debit	Balance Credit
19XX April 30		CPJ1		6 00		6 00

Salaries Expense   Account No. 611

Date	Explanation	Post. Ref.	Debit	Credit	Balance Debit	Balance Credit
19XX April 28		CPJ1	700 00		700 00	

FIGURE 7-6
Cash Payments Journal Recording
and Posting (Cont.)

FIGURE 7-7

Schedule of Accounts Payable.

ART'S WHOLESALE CLOTHING COMPANY SCHEDULE OF ACCOUNTS PAYABLE APRIL 30, 19XX	
Abby Blake Co.	$ 5 6 5 0 00
John Sullivan Co.	1 4 8 0 00
Total Accounts Payable	$ 7 1 3 0 00

Now let's prove that the sum of the accounts payable ledger at the end of the month is equal to the controlling account, Accounts Payable, at the end of April for Art's Wholesale Clothing Company.

Schedule of Accounts Payable

From Figure 7-6 let's list the creditors that have an ending balance in the accounts payable ledger of Art's. This listing of amounts owed is called a **schedule of accounts payable**, which is shown in Figure 7-7.

At the end of the month the total owed ($7,130) in Accounts Payable, the controlling account in the general ledger, does indeed equal the sum owed the individual creditors that are listed on the schedule of accounts payable.

If the schedule doesn't agree with the controlling account, (1) check that the journalizing, recording, and posting are completed and (2) double-check the balances of each title.

Trade Discounts

Trade discounts are reductions from the purchase price to customers who buy items to resell or who will use the items to produce other salable goods.

$$\text{Amount of Trade Discount} = \text{List Price} - \text{Net Price}$$

Different trade discounts are available to different classes of customers. These trade discounts are often listed in catalogs that contain the list price as well as the amount of trade discount available. To allow for flexibility, the catalog is usually updated by discount sheets rather than the printing of a new catalog each time a price changes on a certain item.

A key point is that the trade discount has *no relationship* to whether a customer is paying a bill early. Trade discounts and list prices are not going to be shown in the accounts of either the purchaser or the seller of merchandise. Cash discounts are not taken on the amount of trade discount.

For example, let's look at the following:

List price, $800
30% Trade discount
5% Cash discount
Thus: Invoice cost of $560 ($800 − $240) less the cash discount of $28 ($560 × .05) results in a final cost of $532 if the cash discount is taken.

The purchaser as well as the seller would record the invoice amount at $560.

At this point you should be able to

1. Journalize, record, and post transactions utilizing a cash payments journal. (pp. 192–193)
2. Prepare a schedule of accounts payable. (p. 194)
3. Compare and contrast a cash discount to a trade discount. (p. 194)

SELF-REVIEW QUIZ 7-3

Given the following information, journalize, crossfoot, and when appropriate record and post the transactions of Melissa Company. Use the same headings as used for Art's Clothing. All purchases discounts are 2/12, n/30. The cash payments journal is page 2.

ACCOUNTS PAYABLE LEDGER

NAME	BALANCE	INVOICE NO.
Bob Finkelstein	$300	488
Al Jeep	200	410

PARTIAL GENERAL LEDGER

ACCOUNT NO.	BALANCE
Cash 110	$700
Accounts Payable 210	500
Purchases Discount 511	—
Advertising Expense 610	—

19XX
June 1   Issued check no. 15 to Al Jeep in payment of its May 25 invoice No. 410 less purchases discount.
     8   Issued check no. 16 to Moss Advertising Co. to pay advertising bill due, $75, no discount.
     9   Issued check no. 17 to Bob Finkelstein in payment of its May 28 invoice No. 488 less purchases discount.

SOLUTION TO SELF-REVIEW QUIZ 7-3

MELISSA COMPANY
CASH PAYMENTS JOURNAL

Date		Ck. No.	Account Debited	Post. Ref.	Sundry Accounts Dr.	Accounts Payable Dr.	Purchases Discount Cr.	Cash Cr.
19XX June	1	15	Al Jeep	✔		200 00	4 00	196 00
	8	16	Advertising Expense	610	75 00			75 00
	9	17	Bob Finkelstein	✔		300 00	6 00	294 00
		30			75 00	500 00	10 00	565 00
					(X)	(210)	(511)	(110)

$75 + $500 = $10 + $565
$575 = $575

ACCOUNTS PAYABLE LEDGER

NAME Bob Finkelstein
ADDRESS 112 Flying Highway, Trenton, New Jersey 08611

Date		Explanation	Post. Ref.	Debit	Credit	Cr. Balance
19XX June	1	Balance	✔			3 0 0 00
	9		CPJ2	3 0 0 00		- 0 -

NAME Al Jeep
ADDRESS 118 Wang Rd., Saugus, Mass. 01432

Date		Explanation	Post. Ref.	Debit	Credit	Cr. Balance
19XX June	1	Balance	✔			2 0 0 00
	1		CPJ2	2 0 0 00		- 0 -

PARTIAL GENERAL LEDGER

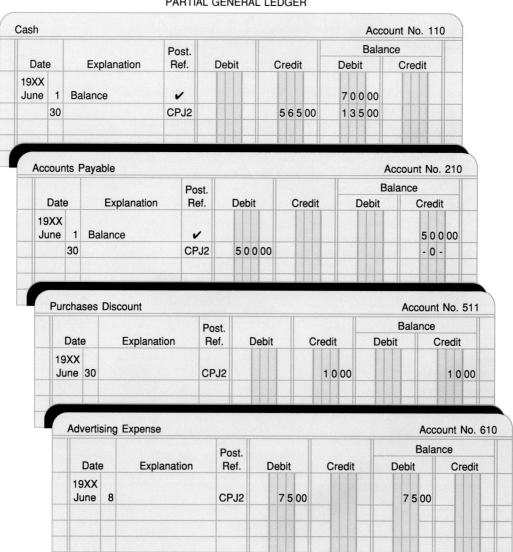

Cash   Account No. 110

Date		Explanation	Post. Ref.	Debit	Credit	Balance Debit	Balance Credit
19XX June	1	Balance	✔			7 0 0 00	
	30		CPJ2		5 6 5 00	1 3 5 00	

Accounts Payable   Account No. 210

Date		Explanation	Post. Ref.	Debit	Credit	Balance Debit	Balance Credit
19XX June	1	Balance	✔				5 0 0 00
	30		CPJ2	5 0 0 00			- 0 -

Purchases Discount   Account No. 511

Date	Explanation	Post. Ref.	Debit	Credit	Balance Debit	Balance Credit
19XX June 30		CPJ2		1 0 00		1 0 00

Advertising Expense   Account No. 610

Date		Explanation	Post. Ref.	Debit	Credit	Balance Debit	Balance Credit
19XX June	8		CPJ2	7 5 00		7 5 00	

SUMMARY OF KEY POINTS AND KEY TERMS

LEARNING UNIT 7-1

1. Purchases is a cost-of-goods-sold account.

2. Purchases Returns and Allowances and Purchases Discount are contra cost-of-goods-sold accounts.

3. Freight-In is a cost-of-goods-sold account that accumulates the amount of shipping costs the buyer is responsible for.

4. *F.O.B. shipping point* means that the purchaser of the goods is responsible for covering the shipping costs. If the terms were *F.O.B. destination*, the seller would be responsible for covering the shipping costs until the goods reached their destination.

5. Purchases discounts are not taken on freight.

F.O.B. Free on Board, which means without shipping charge either to the buyer or seller up to or from a specified location. In the view of one or the other, the shipment is *free* on board the carrier.

F.O.B. destination: *Seller* pays or is responsible for the cost of freight to purchaser's location or destination.

F.O.B. shipping point: *Purchaser* pays or is responsible for the shipping costs from seller's shipping point to purchaser's location.

Freight-In: Cost-of-goods-sold account that records for buyer amount of shipping costs incurred in bringing merchandise into store.

Purchases: Merchandise for resale. It is a cost-of-goods-sold account.

Purchases Discount: A contra cost-of-goods-sold account in the general ledger that records discounts offered by suppliers of merchandise for prompt payment of purchases by buyers.

Purchases Returns and Allowances: A contra cost-of-goods-sold account in the ledger that records the amount of defective or unacceptable merchandise returned to suppliers and/or price reductions given for defective items.

LEARNING UNIT 7-2

1. The steps for buying merchandise from a company may include:

(a) The requesting department prepares a purchase requisition.

(b) The purchasing department prepares a purchase order.

(c) Seller receives the order and prepares a sales invoice (a purchase invoice for the buyer).

(d) Buyer receives the goods and prepares a receiving report.

(e) Accounting department verifies and approves the invoice for payment.

2. The accounts payable ledger, organized in alphabetical order, is not in the same book as Accounts Payable, the controlling account in the general ledger.

3. At the end of the month the total of all creditors' ending balances in the accounts payable ledger should equal the ending balance in Accounts Payable, the controlling account in the general ledger.

4. The purchases journal records the buying of merchandise or other items on account.

5. A debit memorandum (issued by the buyer) indicates that the amount owed from a previous purchase is being reduced because some goods were defective or not up to a specific standard and thus were returned or an allowance requested. On receiving the debit memorandum, the seller will issue a credit memorandum.

Accounts payable ledger: A book or file that contains in alphabetical order the specific amounts owed companies (creditors) from purchases on account.

Debit memorandum: A memo issued by a purchaser to a seller, indicating that some purchases returns and allowances have occurred and therefore the purchaser now owes less money on account.

Invoice approval form: The accounting department uses this form in checking the invoice and finally approving it for recording and payment.

Purchase invoice: The seller's sales invoice, which is sent to the purchaser.

Purchases journal: A multicolumn special journal that records the buying of merchandise or other items on account.

Purchase order: A form used in business to place an order for the buying of goods from a seller.

Purchase requisition: A form used within a business by the requesting department asking the purchasing department of the business to buy specific goods.

Receiving report: A business form used to notify the appropriate people of the ordered goods received along with the quantities and specific condition of the goods.

LEARNING UNIT 7-3

1. All payments of cash (check) are recorded in the cash payments journal.

2. At the end of the month, the schedule of accounts payable, a list of ending amounts owed individual creditors, should equal the ending balance in Accounts Payable, the controlling account in the general ledger.

3. Trade discounts are deductions off the list price that have nothing to do with early payments (cash discounts). Invoice amounts are recorded *after* the trade discount is deducted. Cash discounts are not taken on trade discounts.

Cash payments journal: A special journal that records all transactions involving the payment of cash.

Controlling account: The account in the general ledger that summarizes or controls a subsidiary ledger. Example: The Accounts Payable account in the general ledger is the controlling account for the accounts payable ledger. After postings are complete, it shows the total amount owed from purchases made on account.

Schedule of accounts payable: An alphabetical list of creditors from the accounts payable ledger who have an outstanding balance.

Trade discount: A reduction from the list price; it is the basis for computing and recording the invoice price. Trade discounts have no relationship to cash discounts, which result from early payment.

DISCUSSION QUESTIONS

1. Explain how net purchases is calculated.
2. What is a contra cost-of-goods-sold account? Please give an example.
3. What is the purpose of the Freight-In account?
4. Explain the difference between F.O.B. shipping point and F.O.B. destination.
5. F.O.B. destination means that title to the goods will switch to the buyer when goods are shipped. Agree or disagree. Why?
6. What is the normal balance of each creditor in the accounts payable ledger?
7. Why doesn't the balance of the controlling account, Accounts Payable, equal the sum of the accounts payable ledger during the month?
8. What is the relationship between a purchase requisition and a purchase order?
9. What purpose could a typical invoice approval form serve?
10. Explain the difference between merchandise and equipment.
11. Why would the purchaser issue a debit memorandum?
12. Explain the relationship between a purchases journal and a cash payments journal.
13. Explain why a trade discount is not a cash discount.

Purchase of Merchandise or Other Items on Account

RECORDED DURING THE MONTH: These individual amounts are recorded during the month to the accounts payable subsidiary ledger. When recorded a (✔) is placed in the PR column of the purchases journal for each transaction.

POSTED WHEN TRANSACTION IS ENTERED: Posted to general ledger account when transaction is entered.

The total of sundry is never posted.

END OF MONTH: These totals are posted to the general ledger accounts at the end of the month. Examples: Accounts Payable, Purchases.

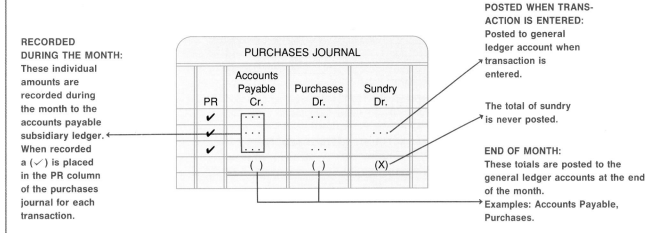

Issuing A Debit Memo (or Receiving A Credit Memo)

POSTED AND RECORDED WHEN TRANSACTION IS ENTERED
Two postings and one recording:
1. Posted to Accounts Payable in the general ledger.
2. Recorded to XXX in the accounts payable ledger. A (✔) indicates recording to the accounts payable ledger is complete.
3. Posted to Purchases Returns and Allowances in general ledger.

	Date	Account Titles and Description	PR	Dr.	Cr.	
		GENERAL JOURNAL				
		Accounts Payable, XXX	✔	. . .		
		Purchases Returns and Allowances	. . .		. . .	

Outward Flow of Cash

Post to general ledger when transaction entered

No posting needed during month, since totals of purchases and cash are posted at end of month.

The total of sundry is never posted.

RECORDED DURING THE MONTH: These individual amounts are recorded during the month to the accounts payable ledger. When recorded, a (✔) is placed in the PR column of the cash payments journal for each transaction.

END OF MONTH: These totals are posted to the general ledger accounts at the end of the month. Examples: Cash, Purchases, Accounts Payable.

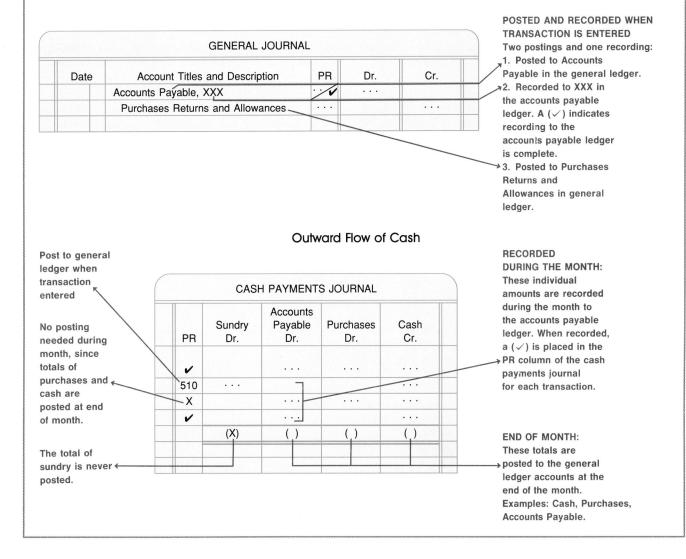

EXERCISES

1. From the accompanying purchases journal, please record to the accounts payable ledger and post to general ledger accounts as appropriate.

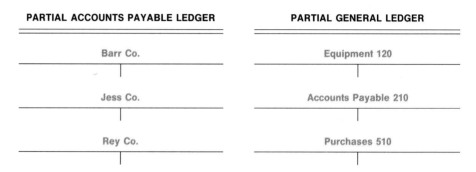

	Date		Account Credited	Date of Invoice	Terms	Post Ref.	Accounts Payable Credit	Purchases Debit	Sundry-Dr. Account	PR	Amount	
	19XX June	3	Barr Co.	May 3	1/10, n/30		6 0 0 00	6 0 0 00				
		4	Jess Co.	May 4	n/10 EOM		9 0 0 00	9 0 0 00				
		8	Rey Co.	May 8			4 0 0 00		Equipment		4 0 0 00	

Page 1

Recording to the accounts payable ledger and posting to the general ledger from a purchases journal.

PARTIAL ACCOUNTS PAYABLE LEDGER

Barr Co.

Jess Co.

Rey Co.

PARTIAL GENERAL LEDGER

Equipment 120

Accounts Payable 210

Purchases 510

Journalizing, recording, and posting a debit memorandum.

2. On July 10, 19XX, Aster Co. issued debit memorandum No. 1 for $400 to Reel Co. for merchandise returned from invoice No. 312. Your task is to journalize, record, and post this transaction as appropriate. Use the same account numbers as found in the text for Art's Wholesale Clothing Company. The general journal is page 1.

Journalizing, recording, and posting a cash payments journal.

3. Journalize, record, and post when appropriate the following transactions into the cash payments journal (p. 2) for Morgan's Clothing. Use the same headings as found in the text (p. 192). All purchases discounts are 2/10, n/30.

ACCOUNTS PAYABLE LEDGER

NAME	BALANCE	INVOICE NO.
A. James	$1,000	522
B. Foss	400	488
J. Ranch	900	562
B. Swanson	100	821

PARTIAL GENERAL LEDGER

ACCOUNT	BALANCE
Cash 110	$3,000
Accounts Payable 210	2,400
Purchases Discount 511	
Advertising Expense 610	

19XX
April 1   Issued check no. 20 to A. James Company in payment of its March 28 invoice No. 522.
     8   Issued check no. 21 to Flott Advertising in payment of its advertising bill, $100, no discount.
    15   Issued check no. 22 to B. Foss in payment of its March 25 invoice No. 488.

4. From Exercise 3, prepare a schedule of accounts payable and verify that the total of the schedule equals the amount in the controlling account.

Schedule of accounts payable.

5. Record the following transaction in a transaction analysis chart for the buyer:

Bought merchandise for $9,000 on account. Shipping terms were F.O.B. shipping point. The cost of shipping was $500.

F.O.B. shipping point.

6. Angie Rase bought merchandise with a list price of $4,000. Angie was entitled to a 30 percent trade discount, as well as a 3 percent cash discount. What was Angie's actual cost of buying this merchandise after the cash discount?

Trade and cash discounts.

GROUP A PROBLEMS

7A-1. Judy Clark recently opened a sporting goods shop. As the bookkeeper of her shop, please journalize, record, and post when appropriate the following transactions (account numbers are: Store Supplies, 115; Store Equipment, 121; Accounts Payable, 210; Purchases, 510):

Journalizing, recording, and posting a purchases journal.

19XX

June 4 Bought merchandise on account from Aster Co., invoice #442, dated June 5, terms 2/10, n/30; $900.

5 Bought store equipment from Norton Co., invoice #502, dated June 6; $4,000.

8 Bought merchandise on account from Rolo Co., invoice #401, dated June 9; terms 2/10, n/30; $1,400.

14 Bought store supplies on account from Aster Co., invoice #419, dated June 14; $900.

7A-2. Mabel's Natural Food Store uses a purchases journal (p. 10) and a general journal (p. 2) to record the following transactions (continued from April):

19XX

May 8 Purchased merchandise on account from Aton Co., invoice #400, dated May 9, terms 2/10, n/60; $600.

10 Purchased merchandise on account from Broward Co., invoice #420, dated May 11, terms 2/10, n/60; $1,200.

12 Purchased store supplies on account from Midden Co., invoice #510, dated May 13, $500.

14 Issued debit memo #8 to Aton Co. for merchandise returned, $400, from invoice #400.

17 Purchased office equipment on account from Relar Co., invoice #810, dated May 18, $560.

24 Purchased additional store supplies on account from Midden Co., invoice #516, dated May 25, terms 2/10, n/30; $650.

Journalizing, recording, and posting a purchases journal as well as recording debit memorandum and preparing a schedule of accounts payable.

The food store has decided to keep a separate column for the purchases of supplies in the purchases journal. Your task is to

1. Journalize the transactions.

2. Post and record as appropriate.

3. Prepare a schedule of accounts payable.

ACCOUNTS PAYABLE LEDGER

NAME	BALANCE
Aton Co.	$ 400
Broward Co.	600
Midden Co.	1,200
Relar Co.	500

ACCOUNT	NUMBER	BALANCE
Store Supplies	110	$ —
Office Equipment	120	—
Accounts Payable	210	2,700
Purchases	510	16,000
Purchases Returns and Allowances	512	—

Journalizing, recording, and posting a cash payments journal. Preparing a schedule of accounts payable.

7A-3. Wendy Jones operates a wholesale computer center. All transactions requiring the payment of cash are recorded in the cash payments journal (p. 5). The account balances as of May 1, 19XX, are as follows:

ACCOUNTS PAYABLE LEDGER

NAME	BALANCE
Alvin Co.	$1,200
Henry Co.	600
Soy Co.	800
Xon Co.	1,400

PARTIAL GENERAL LEDGER

ACCOUNT	NUMBER	BALANCE
Cash	110	$17,000
Delivery Truck	150	—
Accounts Payable	210	4,000
Computer Purchases	510	—
Computer Purchases Discount	511	—
Rent Expense	610	—
Utilities Expense	620	—

Your task is to

1. Journalize the following transactions.
2. Record to the accounts payable ledger and post to general ledger as appropriate.
3. Prepare a schedule of accounts payable.

19XX

May 1 Paid half the amount owed Henry Co. from previous purchases of appliances on account, less a 2% purchases discount, check #21.

3 Bought a delivery truck for $8,000 cash, check #22, payable to Bill Ring Co.

6 Bought computer merchandise from Lectro Co., check #23, $2,900.

18 Bought additional computer merchandise from Pulse Co., check #24, $800.

24 Paid Xon Co. the amount owed less a 2% purchases discount, check #25.

28 Paid rent expense to King's Realty Trust, check #26, $2,000.

29 Paid utilities expense to Stone Utility Co., check #27, $300.

30 Paid half the amount owed Soy Co., no discount, check #28.

Comprehensive Review Problem. All special journals and the general journal. Schedule of accounts payable and accounts receivable.

7A-4. Abby Ellen opened Abby's Toy House. As her newly hired accountant, your task is to

1. Journalize the transactions for the month of March.
2. Record to subsidiary ledgers and post to general ledger as appropriate.
3. Total and rule the journals.
4. Prepare a schedule of accounts receivable and a schedule of accounts payable.

The following is the partial chart of accounts for Abby's Toy House:

Assets
110 Cash
112 Accounts Receivable
114 Prepaid Rent
121 Delivery Truck

Liabilities
210 Accounts Payable

Owner's Equity
310 A. Ellen, Capital

Revenue
410 Toy Sales
412 Sales Returns and Allowances
414 Sales Discounts

Cost of Goods
510 Toy Purchases
512 Purchases Returns and Allowances
514 Purchases Discount

Expenses
610 Salaries Expense
612 Cleaning Expense

19XX

March 1 Abby Ellen invested $8,000 in the toy store.

1 Paid three months' rent in advance, check no. 1, $3,000.

1 Purchased merchandise from Earl Miller Company on account, $4,000, invoice No. 410, dated March 2, terms 2/10, n/30.

3 Sold merchandise to Bill Burton on account, $1,000, invoice No. 1, terms 2/10, n/30.

6 Sold merchandise to Jim Rex on account, $700, invoice No. 2, terms 2/10, n/30.

8 Purchased merchandise from Earl Miller Co. on account, $1,200, invoice No. 415, dated March 9, terms 2/10, n/30.

9 Sold merchandise to Bill Burton on account, $600, invoice No. 3, terms 2/10, n/30.

9 Paid cleaning service $300, check no. 2.

10 Jim Rex returned merchandise that cost $300 to Abby's Toy House. Abby issued credit memorandum No. 1 to Jim Rex for $300.

10 Purchased merchandise from Minnie Katz on account, $4,000, invoice No. 311, dated March 11, terms 1/15, n/60.

12 Paid Earl Miller Co. invoice No. 410, dated March 2, check no. 3.

13 Sold $1,300 of toy merchandise for cash.

13 Paid salaries, $600, check no. 4.

14 Returned merchandise to Minnie Katz in the amount of $1,000. Abby's Toy House issued debit memorandum No. 1 to Minnie Katz.

15 Sold merchandise for $4,000 cash.

16 Received payment from Jim Rex, invoice No. 2 (less returned merchandise) less discount.

16 Bill Burton paid invoice No. 1.

16 Sold toy merchandise to Amy Rose on account, $4,000, invoice No. 4, terms 2/10, n/30.

20 Purchased delivery truck on account from Sam Katz Garage, $3,000, invoice No. 111, dated March 21 (no discount).

22 Sold to Bill Burton merchandise on account, $900, invoice No. 5, terms 2/10, n/30.

23 Paid Minnie Katz balance owed, check no. 5.

24 Sold toy merchandise on account to Amy Rose, $1,100, invoice No. 6, terms 2/10, n/30.

25 Purchased toy merchandise, $600, check no. 6.

26 Purchased toy merchandise from Woody Smith on account, $4,800, invoice No. 211, dated March 27, terms 2/10, n/30.

28 Bill Burton paid invoice No. 5, dated March 22.

28 Amy Rose paid invoice No. 6, dated March 24.

28 Abby invested an additional $5,000 in the business.

28 Purchased merchandise from Earl Miller Co., $1,400, invoice No. 436, dated March 29, terms 2/10, n/30.

30 Paid Earl Miller Co. invoice No. 436, check no. 7.

30 Sold merchandise to Bonnie Flow Company on account, $3,000, invoice No. 7, terms 2/10, n/30.

GROUP B PROBLEMS

Journalizing, recording, and posting a purchases journal.

7B-1. From the following transactions of Judy Clark's sporting goods shop, journalize in the purchases journal and record and post as appropriate:

19XX

June 4 Bought merchandise on account from Rolo Co., invoice No. 400, dated June 5, terms 2/10, n/30; $1,800.

5 Bought store equipment from Norton Co., invoice No. 518, dated June 6; $6,000.

8 Bought merchandise on account from Aster Co., invoice No. 411, dated June 5, terms 2/10, n/30; $400.

14 Bought store supplies on account from Aster Co., invoice No. 415, dated June 13; $1,200.

Journalizing, recording, and posting a purchases journal as well as recording the issuing of a debit memorandum and preparing a schedule of accounts payable.

7B-2. As the accountant of Mabel's Natural Food Store (1) journalize the following transactions into the purchases (P. 10) or general journal (P. 2), (2) record and post as appropriate; and (3) prepare a schedule of accounts payable. Beginning balances are in your working papers.

19XX

May 8 Purchased merchandise on account from Broward Co., invoice No. 420, dated May 9, terms 2/10, n/60; $500.

10 Purchased merchandise on account from Aton Co., invoice No. 400, dated May 11, terms 2/10, n/60; $900.

12 Purchased store supplies on account from Midden Co., invoice No. 510, dated May 13, $700.

14 Issued debit memo No. 7 to Aton Co. for merchandise returned, $400, from invoice No. 400.

17 Purchased office equipment on account from Relar Co., invoice No. 810, dated May 18, $750.

24 Purchased additional store supplies on account from Midden Co., invoice No. 516, dated May 25, $850.

Journalizing, recording, and posting a cash payments journal. Preparing a schedule of accounts payable.

7B-3. Wendy Jones has hired you as her bookkeeper to record the following transactions in the cash payments journal. She would like you to record and post as appropriate and supply her with a schedule of accounts payable. (Beginning balances are in your workbook or Problem 7A-3, p. 202 in the text.)

19XX

May 1 Bought a delivery truck for $8,000 cash, check no. 21, payable to Randy Rosse Co.

3 Paid half the amount owed Henry Co. from previous purchases of computer merchandise on account, less a 5% purchases discount, check no. 22.

6 Bought computer merchandise from Jane Co. for $900 cash, check no. 23.

18 Bought additional computer merchandise from Jane Co., check no. 24, $1,000.

24 Paid Xon Co. the amount owed less a 5% purchases discount, check no. 25.

28 Paid rent expense to Regan Realty Trust, check no. 26, $3,000.

29 Paid half the amount owed Soy Co., no discount, check no. 27.

30 Paid utilities expense to French Utility, check no. 28, $425.

7B-4. As the new accountant for Abby's Toy House, your task is to

1. Journalize the transactions for the month of March.

2. Record to subsidiary ledgers and post to the general ledger as appropriate.

3. Total and rule the journals.

4. Prepare a schedule of accounts receivable and a schedule of accounts payable.

(Use the same chart of accounts as in Problem 7A-4, p. 203. Your workbook has all the forms you need to complete this problem.)

19XX

March 1 Abby invested $4,000 in the new toy store.

1 Paid two months' rent in advance, check no. 1, $1,000.

1 Purchased merchandise from Earl Miller Company, invoice No. 410, dated March 2, terms 2/10, n/30; $6,000.

3 Sold merchandise to Bill Burton on account, $1,600, invoice No. 1, terms 2/10, n/30.

6 Sold merchandise to Jim Rex on account, $800, invoice No. 2, terms 2/10, n/30.

8 Purchased merchandise from Earl Miller Company, $800, invoice No. 415, dated March 9, terms 2/10, n/30.

9 Sold merchandise to Bill Burton on account, $700, invoice No. 3, terms 2/10, n/30.

9 Paid cleaning service, $400, check no. 2.

10 Jim Rex returned merchandise that cost $200 to Abby. Abby issued credit memorandum No. 1 to Jim Rex for $200.

10 Purchased merchandise from Minnie Katz, $7,000, invoice No. 311, dated March 11, terms 1/15, n/60.

12 Paid Earl Miller Co. invoice No. 410, dated March 2, check no. 3.

13 Sold $1,500 of toy merchandise for cash.

13 Paid salaries, $700, check no. 4.

14 Returned merchandise to Minnie Katz in the amount of $500. Abby issued debit memorandum No. 1 to Minnie Katz.

15 Sold merchandise for cash, $4,800.

16 Received payment from Jim Rex for invoice No. 2 (less returned merchandise) less discount.

16 Bill Burton paid invoice No. 1.

16 Sold toy merchandise to Amy Rose on account, $6,000, invoice No. 4, terms 2/10, n/30.

20 Purchased delivery truck on account from Sam Katz Garage, $2,500, invoice No. 111, dated March 21 (no discount).

22 Sold to Bill Burton merchandise on account, $2,000, invoice No. 5, terms 2/10, n/30.

23 Paid Minnie Katz balance owed, check no. 5.

24 Sold toy merchandise on account to Amy Rose, $2,000, invoice No. 6, terms 2/10, n/30.

25 Purchased toy merchandise, $800, check no. 6.

26 Purchased toy merchandise from Woody Smith on account, $5,900, invoice No. 211, dated March 27, terms 2/10, n/30.

28 Bill Burton paid invoice No. 5, dated March 22.

28 Amy Rose paid invoice No. 6, dated March 24.

28 Abby invested an additional $3,000 in the business.

28 Purchased merchandise from Earl Miller Co., $4,200, invoice No. 436, dated March 29, terms 2/10, n/30.

30 Paid Earl Miller Co. invoice No. 436, check no. 7.

30 Sold merchandise to Bonnie Flow Company on account, $3,200, invoice No. 7, terms 2/10, n/30.

PRACTICAL ACCOUNTING APPLICATION #1

Angie Co. bought merchandise for $1,000 with credit terms of 2/10, n/30. Owing to the bookkeeper's incompetence, the 2 percent cash discount was missed. The bookkeeper told Pete Angie, the owner, not to get excited. After all, it was a $20 discount that was missed—not hundreds of dollars. Could you please act as Mr. Angie's assistant and show the bookkeeper that his $20 represents a sizeable equivalent interest cost? In your calculation assume a 360-day year.

Hint: $R = \dfrac{I}{PT}$

PRACTICAL ACCOUNTING APPLICATION #2

Jeff Ryan completed an Accounting I course and was recently hired as the bookkeeper of Spring Co. The special journals have not been posted, nor are *Dr.* and *Cr.* used on the column headings. Please assist Jeff by marking the Dr. and Cr. headings as well as setting up and posting to the general ledger and recording to the subsidiary ledger. (Only post or record the amounts, since no chart of accounts is provided.)

SALES JOURNAL

Account	PR	Amount
Blue Co.		4 8 0 0 00
Jon Co.		5 6 0 0 00
Roff Co.		6 4 0 0 00
Totals		16 8 0 0 00

PURCHASES JOURNAL

Account	PR	Amount
Ralph Co.		4 0 0 0 00
Sos Co.		6 0 0 0 00
Jingle Co.		8 0 0 0 00
Totals		18 0 0 0 00

GENERAL JOURNAL

	Sales Returns and Allowances		1 6 0 0 00	
	Accounts Receivable, Jon Co.			1 6 0 0 00
	Customer returned merchandise			
	Accounts Payable, Jingle Co.		8 0 0 00	
	Purchases, Returns, and Allowances			8 0 0 00
	Returned defective merchandise			

CASH RECEIPTS JOURNAL*

Cash Dr.	Sales Discounts Dr.	Accounts Receivable Cr.	Sales Cr.	Sundry Account Name	PR	Amount Cr.
4 7 0 4 00	9 6 00	4 8 0 0 00		Blue Co.		
1 9 6 0 00	4 0 00	2 0 0 0 00		Jon Co.		
5 0 0 0 00			5 0 0 0 00	Sales		
20 0 0 0 00				Notes Payable		20 0 0 0 00
3 1 3 6 00	6 4 00	3 2 0 0 00		Roff Co.		
4 6 0 0 00			4 6 0 0 00	Sales		
39 4 0 0 00	2 0 0 00	10 0 0 0 00	9 6 0 0 00	Totals		20 0 0 0 00

* Note: This company's set of columns differs from that shown in the chapter.

CASH PAYMENTS JOURNAL

Account	PR	Sundry	Accounts Payable	Purchases Discounts	Cash
Sos Co.			3 0 0 0 00	6 0 00	2 9 4 0 00
Salaries Expense		2 6 0 0 00			2 6 0 0 00
Jingle Co.			4 0 0 0 00	8 0 00	3 9 2 0 00
Salaries Expense		2 6 0 0 00			2 6 0 0 00
Totals		5 2 0 0 00	7 0 0 0 00	1 4 0 00	12 0 6 0 00

BANKING PROCEDURES AND CONTROL OF CASH

The internal control policies of a company will depend on things such as number of employees, company size, sources of cash, etc.

In Chapters 6 and 7 we have developed the special journals of Art's Wholesale Clothing Company. As Art finds his business increasing, he is becoming quite concerned about developing a system of procedures and records for close control over the cash receipts and cash payments of the business. This is called **internal control** and includes control over the store's assets as well as a way of monitoring the company's operations.

Art, his accountant, and a consultant studied the situation and developed the following company policies:

1. Responsibilities and duties of employees will be divided. For example, the person receiving the cash, whether at the register or by opening the mail, will not record this information into the accounting records. The accountant, for his part, will not be handling the cash receipts.
2. All cash receipts of Art's Wholesale will be deposited into the bank the same day they arrive.
3. All cash payments will be made by check (except petty cash, which will be discussed later in this chapter).
4. Employees will be rotated. This allows workers to become acquainted with the work of others as well as to prepare for a possible changeover of jobs.
5. Art Newner will sign all checks after receiving authorization to pay from the departments concerned.
6. At time of payment, all supporting invoices or documents will be stamped paid. That will show when the invoice or document is paid as well as the number of the check used.
7. All checks will be prenumbered. This will control the use of checks and make it difficult to use a check fraudulently without its being revealed at some point.

Let's now look at the checking account of Art's Wholesale along with specific bank procedures.

LEARNING UNIT 8-1

Bank Procedures, Checking Accounts, and Bank Reconciliations

Before Art's Wholesale opened on April 1, Art had a meeting at Security National Bank to discuss the steps in opening up and using a checking account for the company.

OPENING A CHECKING ACCOUNT

The manager of the bank gave Art a signature card to fill out. The signature card includes space for signature(s), business and home addresses, references, type of account, etc. The manager explained that this was for Art to sign (since he would be signing checks for the company) so that the bank could check and validate his signature when checks were presented for payment. The signature card would be kept in the bank's files so that possible forgeries could be spotted.

Purpose of a signature card.

Art also received preprinted **deposit tickets** and a set of checks. The deposit tickets were to be used when Art's Wholesale received cash or checks from any source and deposited them into the checking account. One of the deposit tickets stays with the bank and a duplicate copy remains with the company, so that they can verify that items in the cash receipts journal that make up the deposit have actually been deposited correctly.

Notice on the deposit ticket in Figure 8-1 (p. 210) that much of the information is preprinted. This saves time as well as labor in processing the deposit. Many times when the bank is closed Art will place a locked bag (provided by the bank) in a night depository. Overnight the deposit bag is in a safe place, and the bank will credit (increase) his account balance when the deposit is processed.

When a bank credits your account, it is increasing the balance.

TYPES OF CHECK ENDORSEMENT

Endorsements can be made by using a rubber stamp instead of a handwritten signature.

Before any check can be deposited or cashed, the bank requires that it be *endorsed.* Endorsement is the signing of one's name on the *back left-hand side* of the check. (New regulations require the endorsement to be within the top $1\frac{1}{2}$ inches to speed up the check clearing process.) This process transfers ownership to the bank, which can collect the money from the person or company that issued the check. Figure 8-2 (p. 211) shows several common types of **endorsement** that Art's Wholesale could use.

Drawer—one who writes the check.
Drawee—one who pays money to payee.
Payee—one to whom check is payable.

Now let's look at Art's checkbook to see how payments will be recorded.

THE CHECKBOOK

Figure 8-3 (p. 212) is an example of the type of check used by Art's Wholesale. This **check** is a written order signed by Art Newner (the **drawer** or one who writes the check) instructing Security National Bank (**drawee**) to pay a specific sum of money to Joe Francis Company, the **payee**, the one to whom the check is payable. Note some of the following key points:

1. The number of the check is preprinted, along with Art's address.
2. The check stub is filled out first. The stub will be used in recording transactions as well as for future reference. Note here that the beginning balance is $7,100; a deposit of $784 brought a balance of $7,884 before the check for $4,000 was written, leaving an ending balance of $3,884.
3. The line drawn after XX/100 is meant to fill space up in the check so that changes cannot be made in the amount.
4. The amount written in words should start on the far left and should use only one "and" to signify the decimal position.

FIGURE 8-1
A Deposit Ticket.

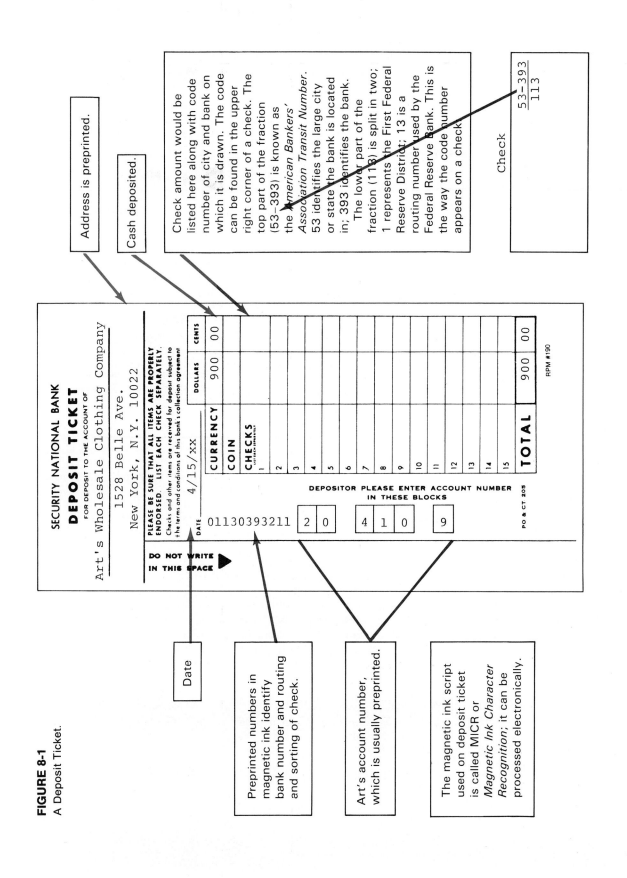

Address is preprinted.

Cash deposited.

Check amount would be listed here along with code number of city and bank on which it is drawn. The code can be found in the upper right corner of a check. The top part of the fraction (53–393) is known as the *American Bankers' Association Transit Number.* 53 identifies the large city or state the bank is located in; 393 identifies the bank. The lower part of the fraction (113) is split in two; 1 represents the First Federal Reserve District; 13 is a routing number used by the Federal Reserve Bank. This is the way the code number appears on a check

Check

53–393
113

SECURITY NATIONAL BANK

DEPOSIT TICKET

FOR DEPOSIT TO THE ACCOUNT OF

Art's Wholesale Clothing Company

1528 Belle Ave.
New York, N.Y. 10022

PLEASE BE SURE THAT ALL ITEMS ARE PROPERLY ENDORSED.   LIST EACH CHECK SEPARATELY.

Checks and other items are received for deposit subject to the terms and conditions of this bank's collection agreement

DATE ___4/15/xx___

	DOLLARS	CENTS
CURRENCY	900	00
COIN		
CHECKS LIST EACH SEPARATELY		
1		
2		
3		
4		
5		
6		
7		
8		
9		
10		
11		
12		
13		
14		
15		
TOTAL	900	00

RPM #190

DO NOT WRITE IN THIS SPACE ▶

DEPOSITOR PLEASE ENTER ACCOUNT NUMBER
IN THESE BLOCKS

01130393211 | 2 | 0 | | 4 | 1 | 0 | | 9 |

PO & CT 205

Date

Preprinted numbers in magnetic ink identify bank number and routing and sorting of check.

Art's account number, which is usually preprinted.

The magnetic ink script used on deposit ticket is called MICR or *Magnetic Ink Character Recognition;* it can be processed electronically.

FIGURE 8-2   Types of Check Endorsement.

Types of Check Endorsement

(A)

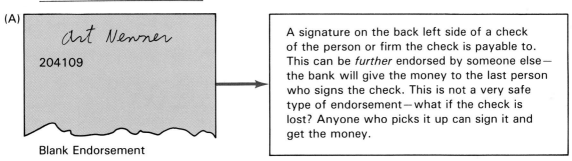

Blank Endorsement

A signature on the back left side of a check of the person or firm the check is payable to. This can be *further* endorsed by someone else—the bank will give the money to the last person who signs the check. This is not a very safe type of endorsement—what if the check is lost? Anyone who picks it up can sign it and get the money.

(B)

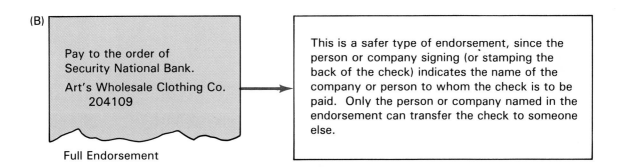

Full Endorsement

This is a safer type of endorsement, since the person or company signing (or stamping the back of the check) indicates the name of the company or person to whom the check is to be paid. Only the person or company named in the endorsement can transfer the check to someone else.

(C)

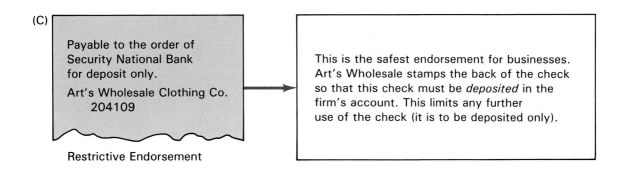

Restrictive Endorsement

This is the safest endorsement for businesses. Art's Wholesale stamps the back of the check so that this check must be *deposited* in the firm's account. This limits any further use of the check (it is to be deposited only).

FIGURE 8-3 A Bank Check.

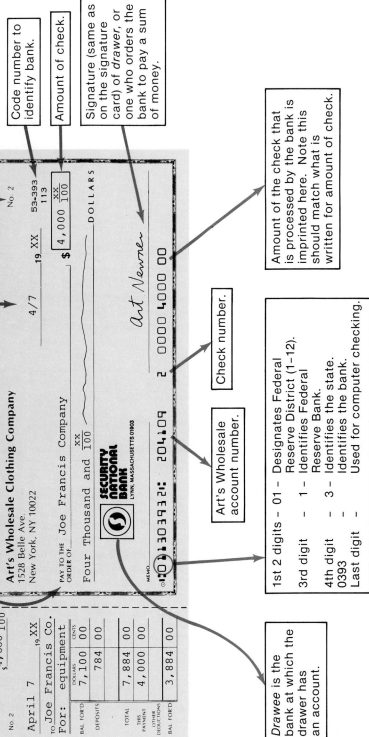

Check stub is used to record journal entries.

To whom check is payable or *payee*.

Check number.

Date check written.

Code number to identify bank.

Amount of check.

Signature (same as on the signature card) of *drawer*, or one who orders the bank to pay a sum of money.

Amount of the check that is processed by the bank is imprinted here. Note this should match what is written for amount of check.

Check number.

Art's Wholesale account number.

1st 2 digits – 01 – Designates Federal Reserve District (1–12).
3rd digit – 1 – Identifies Federal Reserve Bank.
4th digit – 3 – Identifies the state.
0393 – Identifies the bank.
Last digit – Used for computer checking.

Drawee is the bank at which the drawer has an account.

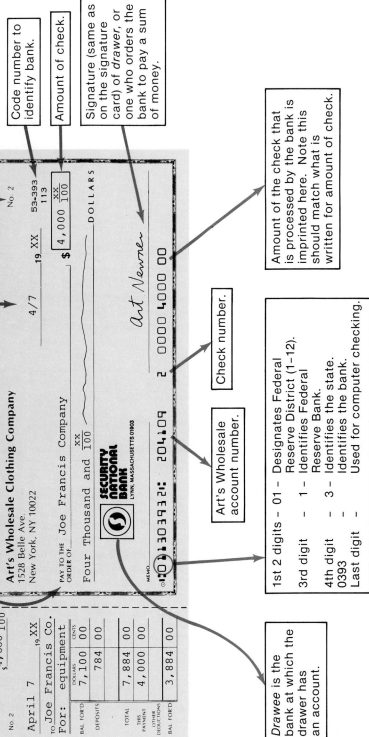

No. 2
$ 4,000 XX/100
April 7 19XX
TO Joe Francis Co.
For: equipment

	DOLLARS	CENTS
BAL. FOR'D	7,100	00
DEPOSITS	784	00
TOTAL	7,884	00
THIS PAYMENT	4,000	00
OTHER DEDUCTIONS		
BAL. FOR'D	3,884	00

Art's Wholesale Clothing Company
1528 Belle Ave.
New York, NY 10022

No. 2
4/7 19 XX
53-393
113

PAY TO THE ORDER OF Joe Francis Company $ 4,000 XX/100

Four Thousand and XX/100 DOLLARS

SECURITY NATIONAL BANK
LYNN, MASSACHUSETTS 01903

Art Newner

MEMO

⑆0⑈1303⑉32⑈ 204⑈09 2 0000 4000 00

If the written amount on the check doesn't match the amount expressed in figures, Security National Bank will pay the amount written in words, will return the check unpaid, or will check with the drawer to see what was meant.

Many companies use checkwriting machines, which type out the amount of the check in figures and words on the check itself. This prevents anyone from making fraudulent changes on the check by hand.

Now let's turn our attention to look at the transactions of Art's Wholesale that affect the checking account.

TRANSACTIONS AFFECTING THE CHECKBOOK

The transactions of Art's Wholesale for the month of April that affect the checking account (p. 214) are the same transactions that were shown in Chapters 6 and 7 in the cash receipts and cash payments journal. Remember, all payments of money are by written check (except petty cash), and all money (checks) received is deposited in the bank account.

Today many checking accounts earn interest. The type of checking account used by Art's Wholesale has a monthly service charge, but we assume

Yvonne James: Office Manager, Bookkeeper

Yvonne James was working as a secretary at a bank when her supervisor suggested that she try bookkeeping. "I learned everything on the job," she says, "and within two months I was a section head. I used to take the manuals home to try to figure out the theory behind what I was doing."

Because she had little experience, Yvonne decided to take some accounting courses at her local community college. "The College Accounting course was helpful because it gave me the fundamental background I needed," she says. "I found that the things I was feeling intuitively were correct. I learned the theory to back up my real life experience."

Yvonne feels that in each of her jobs she has built up her knowledge, and she has reinforced her experience with the courses she needed. For example, a job as a bookkeeper at Nardi Pontiac led her to a course in automotive bookkeeping given by General Motors. "The courses provided a framework, but I also put in a good deal of hard labor. I taught myself," she says. "I was not afraid to make mistakes. I was not afraid to take work home and figure out how to do a task. I also asked a lot of questions."

Yvonne is now Office Manager, Bookkeeper at R. J. Performance Company. As an additional tip for people who want to work in bookkeeping and accounting, she advises, "Learn how to use a computer. It is vital in this field especially if you work for a small company. Knowledge of computers is essential to employers and will make you invaluable."

FIGURE 8-4   Transactions Affecting Checkbook Balance.

BANK DEPOSITS MADE FOR APRIL

DATE OF DEPOSIT	AMOUNT	RECEIVED FROM
April 1	$8,000	Art Newner, Capital
4	784	Check—Hal's Clothing
15	900	Cash sales
16	980	Check—Bevans Company
22	1,960	Check—Roe Company
27	500	Sale of equipment
30	1,200	Cash sales
Total deposits for month:	$14,324	

CHECKS WRITTEN FOR MONTH OF APRIL

DATE	CHECK NO.	PAYMENT TO:	AMOUNT	DESCRIPTION
April 2	1	Peter Blum	$ 900	Insurance paid in advance
7	2	Joe Francis Co.	4,000	Paid equipment
9	3	Rick Flo Co.	800	Cash purchases
12	4	Thorpe Co.	594	Paid purchases
28	5	Payroll	700	Salaries
		Total amount of checks written:	$6,994	

Cash/checks deposited	$14,324
Checks paid	−6,994
Balance in company checkbook	$ 7,330

Differences may result because of timing considerations.

that there is no individual charge for each check written, and the account does not pay interest.

Note in Figure 8-4 that the bank deposits ($14,324) minus the checks written ($6,994) give an ending checkbook balance of $7,330.

At the end of April the bank sends Art a statement that the balance of the cash account is $6,919. How can this be? The following section discusses how this occurs and how it should be handled. Let's now look at the process to reconcile the difference between the bank and checkbook balances.

THE BANK RECONCILIATION PROCESS

The **bank statement** or report shows the beginning balance of the cash at the start of the month, along with the checks the bank has paid and any deposits received (see Figure 8-5). Any other charges or additions to the bank balance are indicated by codes found on the statement. All checks that have been paid by the bank are sent back to Art's Wholesale. These are called **cancelled checks** because they have been processed by the bank and are no longer negotiable.

The problem is that this ending bank balance of $6,919 does not agree with the amount in Art's checkbook, $7,330, or the balance in the cash amount in the ledger, $7,330.

Art's accountant has to find out why there is a difference between the balances and how the records can be brought into balance. This process of reconciling the bank balance on the bank statement vs. the company's check-

FIGURE 8-5 A Bank Statement.

SECURITY NATIONAL BANK

Art's Wholesale Clothing Company
1528 Belle Ave.
New York, New York 10022

ACCOUNT NUMBER 20 410 9

CLOSING PERIOD 4/30/XX

AMOUNT ENCLOSED $ _____

RETURN THIS PORTION WITH YOUR PAYMENT IF YOU ARE NOT USING OUR AUTOMATIC PAYMENT PLAN

Address Correction on Reverse Side ☐

CHECKING ACCOUNT

ON	YOUR BALANCE WAS	NO.	WE SUBTRACTED CHECKS TOTALING	LESS SERVICE CHARGE	NO.	WE ADDED DEPOSITS OF	MAKING YOUR PRESENT BALANCE
	0	3	5,700.00	5.00	5	12,624.00	6,919.00

DATE	CHECKS · WITHDRAWALS · PAYMENTS	DEPOSITS · INTEREST · ADVANCES	BALANCE
4/1		8,000.00	8,000.00
4/2	900		7,100.00
4/4		784.00	7,884.00
4/7	4,000		3,884.00
4/9	800		3,084.00
4/15		900.00	3,984.00
4/16		980.00	4,964.00
4/22		1,960.00	6,924.00
4/25	5.00 SC		6,919.00

REVOLVING CREDIT SUMMARY
OVERDRAFT PROTECTION PLAN/LOAN CHEX/REVOLVING EQUITY LINE OF CREDIT

ACCOUNT NUMBER
CLOSING DATE

① PREVIOUS BAL	② CREDITS	③ PAYMENTS	PAST DUE	CURRENT MINIMUM	TOTAL MINIMUM DUE	⑩ NEW BALANCE	CYCLE DAYS
④ NEW LOANS	⑤ DEBIT ADJ	⑥ AV. DAILY BAL ON WHICH FINANCE CHARGE WAS COMPUTED					

PERIOD RATES APPLICABLE TO ITEM ⑥ ARE AS FOLLOWS:

⑦ FINANCE CHARGE	⑧ NEW BALANCE	⑨ PAYMENT DUE DATE	RANGE OF BALANCE(S) TO WHICH RATES APPLY	**ANNUAL PERCENTAGE RATE**	PERIODIC RATE	AVAILABLE LINE

THE TOTAL MINIMUM DUE WILL BE AUTOMATICALLY DEDUCTED 15 DAYS AFTER THE STATEMENT DATE IF YOU ARE USING OUR AUTOMATIC PAYMENT PLAN.

FINANCE CHARGE is based on the average daily balance.
The Average Daily Balance is determined by dividing the sum of the daily outstanding principal balances by the number of days in the period (Billing Cycle). The total amount of the **FINANCE CHARGE** for the Billing Cycle is computed by multiplying the amount of the Average Daily Balance by the PERIODIC RATE.

NOTICE – SEE REVERSE SIDE FOR IMPORTANT INFORMATION

LYNN AREA 593-6100   LOWELL AREA 459-6111   DANVERS AREA 774-2500

book balance is called a **bank reconciliation**. To prepare the bank reconciliation Art's accountant takes a number of steps.

Deposits in Transit

Relationship of cash receipts journal to bank reconciliation.

Note below how the $500 and $1,200 are not checked off, since they did not appear on the bank statement.

Deposits in transit: These unrecorded deposits could result if a deposit were placed in a night depository on the last day of the month.

In comparing the list of deposits received by the bank with the cash receipts journal (Figure 8-6), the accountant notices that the two deposits made on April 27 and 30 for $500 and $1,200 were not on the bank's statement. The accountant realizes that in order to prepare this statement, the bank only included information about Art's Clothing up to April 25. These two deposits made by Art were not shown on the monthly bank statement, since they arrived at the bank after the statement was printed. This timing becomes a consideration in the reconciliation process. The deposits not yet added onto the bank balance are called **deposits in transit**. These two deposits need to be added to the bank balance shown on the bank statement. Art's checkbook is not affected, since the two deposits have already been added to its balance. The bank has no way of knowing that the deposits are coming until they are received.

Outstanding Checks

Relationship of cash payments journal to bank reconciliation.

Checks #4 and #5 are outstanding.

Checks outstanding: Drawn by depositor but have not reached bank for payment.

The accountant places the checks returned by the bank in numerical order (1, 2, 3, etc.). He opens the cash payments journal (Figure 8-7) and places a checkmark (✓) next to each payment check that was returned by the bank. This indicates that the amount shown in the cash payments journal has been paid and the bank has returned the checks processed (or cancelled after payment). The accountant notices in the cash payments journal that two payments were not made by the bank and these checks, #4 and #5, were not returned by the bank. On Art's books these two checks had been deducted from the checkbook balance; therefore, these **outstanding checks**, or checks that have not been presented to the bank for payment, are deducted from the bank balance. At some point these checks will reach the bank. Keep in

FIGURE 8-6 Cash Receipts Journal.

	Date		Cash Dr.	Sales Discount Dr.	Accounts Receivable Cr.	Sales Cr.	Sundry Account Name	Post. Ref.	Amount Cr.
	19XX April	1	✓8 0 0 0 00				Art Newner, Capital	311	8 0 0 0 00
		4	✓ 7 8 4 00	1 6 00	8 0 0 00		Hal's Clothing	✓	
		15	✓ 9 0 0 00			9 0 0 00	Cash Sales	✗	
		16	✓ 9 8 0 00	2 0 00	1 0 0 0 00		Bevans Company	✓	
		22	✓1 9 6 0 00	4 0 00	2 0 0 0 00		Roe Company	✓	
		27	5 0 0 00				Store Equipment	121	5 0 0 00
		30	1 2 0 0 00			1 2 0 0 00	Cash Sales	✗	
		30	14 3 2 4 00	7 6 00	3 8 0 0 00	2 1 0 0 00			8 5 0 0 00
			(111)	(413)	(113)	(411)			(X)

ART'S WHOLESALE CLOTHING COMPANY
CASH RECEIPTS JOURNAL

Page 1

ART'S WHOLESALE CLOTHING COMPANY
CASH PAYMENTS JOURNAL

Date		Ck. No.	Account Debited	Post. Ref.	Sundry Accounts Dr.	Accounts Payable Dr.	Purchases Discount Cr.	Cash Cr.	
19XX April	2	1	Prepaid Insurance	116	900 00			900 00	✔
	7	2	Joe Francis Company	✔		400 00		400 00	✔
	9	3	Purchases	511	800 00			800 00	✔
	12	4	Thorpe Company	✔		600 00	6 00	594 00	
	28	5	Salaries Expense	611	700 00			700 00	
	30				2400 00	460 00	6 00	699 400	
					(X)	(211)	(512)	(111)	

FIGURE 8-7   Cash Payments Journal.

mind that *Art's* checkbook balance has already subtracted the amount of these two checks; it is the *bank* that has no idea these checks have been written. When they are presented for payment, then the bank will reduce the amount of the balance.

The accountant also notices a bank service charge of $5. This means that Art's checkbook balance should be lowered by $5.

The accountant is continually on the lookout for **NSF (Nonsufficient Funds)** checks. This means that when the company deposits a check, occasionally it will be returned due to lack of sufficient funds. If this happens, it will result in Art's Wholesale having less money than was thought and thus having to (1) lower the checkbook balance and (2) try to collect the amount from the customer. The bank would notify Art's Wholesale of an NSF (or other deductions) check by a **debit memorandum**. Think of a debit memorandum as a deduction from the depositor's balance.

If the bank acts as a collecting agent for Art's Wholesale, say in collecting notes, it will charge Art a small fee, and the net amount collected will be added to Art's bank balance. The bank will send to Art a **credit memorandum** verifying the increase in the depositor's balance.

A bank reconciliation can be done on the back of the bank statement (see Figure 8-8, p. 218). Note that the checkbook balance of $7,330 less the $5 service charge will in fact equal the adjusted balance in Box 5. See the blueprint of a bank reconciliation on p. 229.

A journal entry is also needed to bring the ledger accounts of cash and service charge expense up to date. Any adjustment to the checkbook balance results in a journal entry. The following entry was made to accomplish this:

De bit memorandum:
Deducted from balance

Credit memorandum: Addition to balance

Adjustments to the checkbook balance must be journalized and posted. This keeps the depositor's ledger accounts (especially cash) up to date.

	April	30	Service Charge Expense*			5 00		
			Cash				5 00	

* Could be recorded as miscellaneous expense.

FIGURE 8-8
Bank Reconciliation Using Back
of Bank Statement.

CHECKS OUTSTANDING					
NUMBER	AMOUNT			1. Enter balance shown on this statement.	6,919 00
4	594	00			
5	700	00		2. If you have made deposits since the date of this statement add them to the above balance.	1,700 00
				3. SUBTOTAL	8,619 00
				4. ▶ Deduct total of checks outstanding.	1,294 00
				5. ADJUSTED BALANCE This should agree with your checkbook.	7,325 00
TOTAL OF CHECKS OUTSTANDING	1,294	00			

TO VERIFY YOUR CHECKING BALANCE

1. Sort checks by number or by date issued and compare with your check stubs and prior outstanding list. Make certain all checks paid have been recorded in your checkbook. If any of your checks were not included with this statement, list the numbers and amounts under "CHECKS OUTSTANDING".

2. Deduct the Service Charge as shown on the statement from your checkbook balance.

3. Review copies of charge advices included with this statement and check for proper entry in your checkbook.

IF THE ADJUSTED BALANCE DOES NOT AGREE WITH YOUR CHECKBOOK BALANCE, THE FOLLOWING SUGGESTIONS ARE OFFERED FOR YOUR ASSISTANCE.

- Recheck additions and subtractions in your checkbook and figures to the left.
- Make certain checkbook balances have been carried forward properly.
- Verify deposits recorded on statement against deposits entered in checkbook.
- Compare amount on each checkbook stub.

Keep in mind that both the bank and the depositor can make mistakes that will not be discovered until the reconciliation process.

DM: Remember, a debit memorandum is sent by the bank indicating a reduction in depositor's balance. Examples: NSF, check printing.

CM: A credit memorandum is sent by a bank indicating an increase in depositor's balance. Example: collecting a note.

Example of a More Comprehensive Bank Reconciliation

The bank reconciliation of Art's Wholesale, which we just did, was not as complicated as it might have been for many other companies. Let's take a moment to look at the bank reconciliation for Monroe Company, which is based on the following:

1. Checkbook balance: $3,978.
2. Balance reported by bank: $5,230.
3. Recorded in journal check no. 108 for $54 *more* than should have been when store equipment was purchased.
4. Bank collected a note ($2,000) for Monroe, charging a collection fee of $10.
5. A bounced check for $252 (NSF) has to be covered by Monroe. The bank has lowered Monroe's balance by $252 (see Figure 8-9).
6. Bank service charge of $10.

FIGURE 8-9
Sample Debit Memorandum.

Debit: Monroe Co. 170 Roe Rd. Dallas, Tx. 75208	Valley Bank
2/4-10-60811	Date: 6/30/XX
NSF Check — Alvin Sooth	$252.00
	Approved JS

7. Deposits in transit, $1,084.

8. Checks not yet processed by the bank:

CHECK	AMOUNT
191	$204
198	250
201	100

MONROE COMPANY
BANK RECONCILIATION AS OF JUNE 30, 19XX

Checkbook Balance			Balance per Bank	
Ending Checkbook Balance		$3,978	Ending Bank Statement Balance	$5,230
Add:			Add:	
Error in recording			Deposits in Transit	1,084
Check no. 108	$54			$6,314
Proceeds of a note*				
less collection				
charge by bank	1,990	2,044	Deduct:	
		$6,022	Check no. 191..$204	
			198.. 250	
Deduct:			201.. 100	554
NSF Check	$252			
Bank Service				
Charge	10	262		
Reconciled Balance		$5,760	Reconciled Balance	$5,760

Note the following journal entries needed to update Monroe Company's books. *Every time an adjustment is made in the reconciliation process to the checkbook balance, a journal entry will be needed.*

19XX						
June	30	Cash		1 9 9 0 00		
		Collection Expense		1 0 00		
		Notes Receivable*			2 0 0 0 00	
	30	Cash		5 4 00		
		Store Equipment			5 4 00	
	30	Acct. Rec., Alvin Sooth		2 5 2 00		
		Cash			2 5 2 00	
	30	Miscellaneous Expense		1 0 00		
		Cash			1 0 00	

Remember: If Monroe Company's checking account was the type that earned interest, it would have increased the checkbook balance.

* We will discuss Notes Receivable in a later chapter—for now, think of it as a kind of written Accounts Receivable.

Before summing up this unit, let's look at two interesting trends in the banking field.

See p. 229 for a blueprint of the reconciliation process.

NEW TRENDS IN BANKING

Electronic Funds Transfer

Many financial institutions have developed or are developing a way to transfer funds among parties electronically, without the use of paper checks. The system that does this is called **electronic funds transfer (EFT)**. Let's look at an example.

Jones Company, with appropriate authorization from its employees, deposits their checks directly into the employees' checking accounts, rather than issuing paper checks to the employees. The bank, on receiving computer-coded payroll data, adds each worker's payroll amount to his or her checking account. This saves time and the possible loss or theft of payroll checks.

Another good example is the automatic teller machine (ATM). In some states ATMs now issue postage stamps, railroad tickets, and grocery coupons. In the future we will see bank cards used in fast food chains. (They are now being tested.)

Check Truncation (Safekeeping)

Some banks do not return cancelled checks to the depositor but use a procedure called **check truncation** or **safekeeping**. What this means is that the bank holds a cancelled check for a specific period of time (usually 90 days) and then keeps a microfilm copy handy. In Texas, for example, some credit unions and savings and loan institutions are not sending back checks, but the check date, number, and amount are listed on the bank statement. What happens if a copy of a check is needed? For a small fee the bank provides the company with the check or a photocopy. (Photocopies are accepted as evidence in Internal Revenue Service tax returns and audits.)

Truncation cuts down on the amount of "paper" that is returned to customers and thus provides substantial cost savings. It is estimated that over 50 million checks are written each day in the United States.

At this point, you should be able to

1. Define and explain the need for deposit tickets. (p. 209)
2. Explain where the American Bankers' Association transit number is located on the check and what its purpose is. (p. 210)
3. List as well as compare and contrast the three common types of check endorsement. (p. 211)
4. Explain the structure of a check. (p. 212)
5. Define and state the purpose of a bank statement. (pp. 214–215)
6. Explain the relationship of special journals to the bank reconciliation process. (p. 216)
7. Explain deposits in transit, checks outstanding, service charge, and NSF. (p. 216)
8. Explain the difference between a debit memorandum and a credit memorandum. (p. 217)
9. Explain how to do a bank reconciliation. (p. 219)
10. Explain electronic funds transfer and check truncation. (p. 220)

SELF-REVIEW QUIZ 8-1

Indicate, by placing an X under it, the heading that describes the appropriate action for each of the following situations:

SITUATION	ADD TO BANK BALANCE	DEDUCT FROM BANK BALANCE	ADD TO CHECKBOOK BALANCE	DEDUCT FROM CHECKBOOK BALANCE
1. Bank service charge				X
2. Deposits in transit	X			
3. NSF check				X
4. A $50 check was written and recorded by the company as $60			X	
5. Proceeds of a note collected by the bank.			X	
6. Check outstanding.		X		

SOLUTION TO SELF-REVIEW QUIZ 8-1

SITUATION	ADD TO BANK BALANCE	DEDUCT FROM BANK BALANCE	ADD TO CHECKBOOK BALANCE	DEDUCT FROM CHECKBOOK BALANCE
1				X
2	X			
3				X
4			X	
5			X	
6		X		

LEARNING UNIT 8-2

The Establishment of a Petty Cash Fund

Art realized how time-consuming and expensive it would be to write checks for small amounts to pay for postage, small supplies, etc. What was needed was a **petty cash fund**. It was decided that for the month of May, Art's Wholesale would need a fund of $60 to cover small expenditures. This petty cash was expected to last no longer than one month. A check payable to the order of the custodian was drawn and cashed to establish the fund.

Petty Cash is an asset on the balance sheet.

SETTING UP THE FUND

Shown here is the transaction analysis chart for the establishment of a $60 petty cash fund, which would be entered in the cash payments journal on May 1, 19XX.

Accounts Affected	Category	↑ ↓	Rules
Petty Cash	Asset	↑	Dr.
Cash (checks)	Asset	↓	Cr.

Petty Cash is an asset, which is established by writing a new check. The Petty Cash account is debited only once unless a greater or lesser amount of petty cash is needed on a regular basis.

CASH PAYMENTS JOURNAL

Page 2

Date		Ck. No.	Accounts Debited	PR	Sundry Dr.	Accounts Payable Dr.	Purchases Discount Cr.	Cash Cr.
19XX May	1	6	Petty Cash	112	60 00			60 00

Note the new asset called *Petty Cash*; this new asset was created by writing check no. 6, thereby reducing the asset Cash. In reality, the total assets stay the same; what has occurred is a shift from the asset Cash (check no. 6) to a new asset account called Petty Cash.

The Petty Cash account is not debited or credited again if the size of the fund is not changed. If the $60 fund is used up very quickly, the fund should be increased. If the fund is too large, the Petty Cash account should be reduced.

The check for $60 is drawn to the order of the custodian, cashed, and the proceeds turned over to John Sullivan, the custodian.

But who is responsible for controlling the petty cash fund? Art gives his office manager, John Sullivan, the responsibility and the authority to make payments from the petty cash fund, which is kept in the office safe in a small tin box. In other companies the cashier or secretary may be in charge of petty cash.

MAKING PAYMENTS FROM THE PETTY CASH FUND

John Sullivan has the responsibility for filling out a **petty cash voucher** for each cash payment made from the petty cash fund.

Note that the voucher (shown in Figure 8-10) when completed will include

1. The voucher number (which will be in sequence): 1.
2. The date: May 2.
3. The person or organization to whom the payment was made: Al's Cleaners.
4. The amount of payment: $3.00.
5. The reason for payment: cleaning.
6. The signature of the person who approved the payment: John Sullivan.
7. The signature of the person who received the payment from petty cash: Art Newner.
8. The account to which the expense will be charged.

FIGURE 8-10
Petty Cash Voucher.

Petty Cash Voucher No. 1

Date: May 2, 19XX   Amount: $3.00

Paid To: Al's Cleaners

For: Cleaning Package

Approved By: John Sullivan

Payment Received By: Art Newner

Debit Account No.: 619

The completed vouchers are placed in the petty cash box. No matter how many vouchers John Sullivan fills out, *the total of (1) the vouchers in the box and (2) the cash on hand should equal the original amount of petty cash with which the fund was established* ($60).

Assume that at the end of May the following items are documented by petty cash vouchers in the petty cash box as having been paid by John Sullivan:

Vouchers in box
+ Cash in box
= Original amount placed in petty cash

19XX
May 2 Cleaning package, $3.00.
    5 Postage stamps, $9.00.
    8 First aid supplies, $15.00.
    9 Delivery expense, $6.00.
   14 Delivery expense, $15.00.
   27 Postage stamps, $6.00.

John records this information in the **auxiliary petty cash record** shown in Figure 8-11. It is not a special journal, but an aid to John—an auxiliary record that is not essential but is quite helpful as part of the petty cash system. You may want to think of the auxiliary petty cash as an optional work sheet. Let's look at how to replenish the petty cash fund

Think of the auxiliary petty cash record as a work sheet that gathers information for the journal entry.

HOW TO REPLENISH THE PETTY CASH FUND

No postings will be done from the auxiliary book; it is not a journal. At some point the summarized information found in the auxiliary petty cash record will be used as a basis for a journal entry in the cash payments journal and eventually posted to appropriate ledger accounts to reflect up-to-date balances.

This $54 of expenses (see Figure 8-11) is recorded in the cash payments journal (Figure 8-12, p. 224) and a new check, no. 17, for $54 is cashed and returned to John Sullivan. The petty cash box now once again reflects $60 cash. The old vouchers that were used are stamped to indicate that they have been processed and the fund replenished.

Note that in the replenishment process the debits in the cash payments journal (p. 224) are a summary of the totals (except sundry) of expenses or

In replenishment, old expenses are updated in journal and ledger to show where money has gone.

Auxiliary before replenishment.

FIGURE 8-11   Auxiliary Petty Cash Record.

Date	Voucher No.	Description	Receipts	Payments	Postage Expense	Delivery Expense	Sundry Account	Amount
19XX May 1		Establishment	60 00					
2	1	Cleaning		3 00			Cleaning	3 00
5	2	Postage		9 00	9 00			
8	3	First Aid		15 00			Misc.	15 00
9	4	Delivery		6 00		6 00		
14	5	Delivery		15 00		15 00		
27	6	Postage		6 00	6 00			
		Total	60 00	54 00	15 00	21 00		18 00

CASH PAYMENTS JOURNAL

Establishment

Date	Ck. No.	Accounts Debited	PR	Sundry Dr.	Accounts Payable Dr.	Purchases Discount Cr.	Cash Dr.
19XX May 1	6	Petty Cash	112	60 00			60 00

Replenishment

	31		Postage Expense	616	15 00			
			Delivery Expense	620	21 00			
			Cleaning Expense	619	3 00			
		17	Misc. Expense	617	15 00			54 00

FIGURE 8-12   Establishment and Replenishment of Petty Cash Fund.

other items from the auxiliary petty cash record. Posting of these specific expenses will assure that the expenses will not be understated on the income statement. *The end result is that our petty cash box is filled, and we have justified which accounts the petty cash money was spent for. Think of replenishment as a single, summarizing entry.*

A new check is written in the replenishment process, which is payable to the custodian, cashed by Sullivan, and the cash placed in the petty cash box.

Remember, if at some point the petty cash fund is to be greater than $60, a check can be written that will increase Petty Cash and decrease Cash. If the Petty Cash account balance is to be reduced, we can credit or reduce Petty Cash. But for our present purpose Petty Cash will remain at $60.

The auxiliary petty cash record after replenishment would look as follows (keep in mind no postings are made from the auxiliary):

AUXILIARY PETTY CASH RECORD

Date	Voucher No.	Description	Receipts	Payments	Postage Expense	Delivery Expense	Sundry Account	Sundry Amount
19XX May 1		Establishment	60 00					
2	1	Cleaning		3 00			Cleaning	3 00
5	2	Postage		9 00	9 00			
8	3	First Aid		15 00			Misc.	15 00
9	4	Delivery		6 00		6 00		
14	5	Delivery		15 00		15 00		
27	6	Postage		6 00	6 00			
		Totals	60 00	54 00	15 00	21 00		18 00
		Ending Balance		6 00				
			60 00	60 00				
		Ending Balance	6 00					
31		Replenishment	54 00					
31		Balance (New)	60 00					

	Date		Description	New Check Written	Recorded in Cash Payments Journal	Petty Cash Voucher Prepared	Recorded in Auxiliary Petty Cash Record
	19XX Jan.	1	Establishment of petty cash for $60	X	X		X
		2	Paid salaries, $2,000	X	X		
		13	Paid $10 from petty cash for Band-Aids			X	X
		19	Paid $8 from petty cash for postage			X	X
		24	Paid light bill, $200	X	X		
		29	Replenishment of petty cash to $60	X	X		X

Has nothing to do with petty cash.

In this step the old expenses are listed in cash payments journal and a new check is written to replenish.

FIGURE 8-13   Steps Involving Petty Cash.

The diagram in Figure 8-13 may help you put the sequence together.

Before concluding this unit, let's look at how Art will handle a change fund and problems with cash shortages and overages.

THE CHANGE FUND AND CASH SHORT AND OVER

Change Fund is an asset on the balance sheet.

If a company like Art's Wholesale expects to have many cash transactions occurring, it may be a good idea to establish a **change fund**. This is a fund that is placed in the cash register drawer and used to make change for customers who pay cash. Art decides to put $120 in the change fund, made up of various denominations of bills and coins. Let's look at a transaction analysis chart for this sort of procedure.

Accounts Affected	Category	↑ ↓	Dr./Cr.
Change Fund	Asset	↑	Dr.
Cash	Asset	↓	Cr.

At the close of the business day Art will deposit in the bank the cash taken in for the day but will place the amount of the change fund back in the safe in the office. He will set up the change fund (the same $120) in the appropriate denominations for the next business day.

Now let's look at how to record errors that are made in making change, called cash short and over.

Cash Short and Over

Errors often occur in making change, and so the amount of cash will often be higher or lower than it should be. An account called **Cash Short and Over** will accumulate these shortages or overages. Shortages are debited to

Beg. change fund
+ Cash register total
= Cash should have on hand
− Counted cash
= Shortage or overage of cash

the account; overages are credited. At the end of the accounting period, if there are more shortages than overages (debit balance), the net shortage is shown on the income statement as a miscellaneous expense. If the ending balance is an overage (credit balance), it is reported on the income statement as miscellaneous income.

Cash Short & Over

Shortages	Overages
↑	↑
Misc. Expense	Misc. Income

Example 1: Cash register tapes don't agree with cash receipts.

			SITUATION 1: OVERAGE								SITUATION 2: SHORTAGE			
	Dec.	5	Cash	550					Dec.	15	Cash	600		
			Cash short								Cash short			
			and over		1						and over		5	
			Sales		549						Sales			605

Example 2: Petty Cash has a shortage of $8. The facts are:

$200 Petty Cash account
160 in receipts for expenses
32 in coin and currency

Using Cash Short and Over with Petty Cash.

A general journal entry would look as follows:

Individual Expenses	160	
Cash Short and Over	8	
Cash		168

Keep in mind that in actuality we would use a cash payments journal as well as debit *each* individual expense.

If an auxiliary petty cash record is used to record the cash short and over, it would be recorded as a payment of $8 under the category of payments in the sundry column.

At this time you should be able to

1. State the purpose of a petty cash fund. (p. 221)
2. Prepare a journal entry to establish a petty cash fund. (p. 222)
3. Prepare a petty cash voucher. (p. 222)
4. Explain the relationship of the auxiliary petty cash record to the petty cash process. (p. 223)
5. Prepare a journal entry to replenish Petty Cash to its original amount. (p. 224)
6. Explain why individual expenses are debited in the replenishment process. (p. 224)
7. Explain how a change fund is established. (p. 225)
8. Explain how Cash Short and Over could be a miscellaneous expense. (p. 226)

SELF-REVIEW QUIZ 8-2

As the custodian of the petty cash fund it is your task to prepare entries to establish the fund on October 1, as well as to replenish the fund on October 31. Please keep an auxiliary petty cash record.

19XX
Oct. 1 Establish petty cash fund for $90, check no. 8.
   5 Voucher 11, delivery expense, $21.
   9 Voucher 12, delivery expense, $15.
   10 Voucher 13, office repair expense, $24.
   17 Voucher 14, general expense, $12.
   25 Voucher 15, general expense, $6.
   30 Replenishment of petty cash fund, $78, check no. 108. (Check would be payable to the custodian.)

Checks to establish and replenish Petty Cash would be made out to the custodian.

SOLUTION TO SELF-REVIEW QUIZ 8-2

CASH PAYMENTS JOURNAL

Page 4

Date	Ck. No.	Accounts Debited	PR	Sundry Dr.	Accounts Payable Dr.	Purchases Discount Cr.	Cash Cr.
19XX Oct. 1	8	Petty Cash	*	90 00			90 00
31		Delivery Expense		36 00			
		General Expense		18 00			
	108	Office Repair Expense		24 00			78 00

* The PR would show posting. Deleted for simplicity at this point.

AUXILIARY PETTY CASH RECORD

Date	Voucher No.	Description	Receipts	Payments	Delivery Expense	General Expense	Sundry Account	Sundry Amount
19XX Oct. 1		Establishment	90 00					
5	11	Delivery		21 00	21 00			
9	12	Delivery		15 00	15 00			
10	13	Repairs		24 00			Office Repair	24 00
17	14	General		12 00		12 00		
25	15	General		6 00		6 00		
		Totals	90 00	78 00	36 00	18 00		24 00
		Ending Balance		12 00				
			90 00	90 00				
30		Ending Balance	12 00					
31		Replenishment	78 00					
Nov. 1		New Balance	90 00					

SUMMARY OF KEY POINTS AND KEY TERMS

LEARNING UNIT 8-1

1. Restrictive endorsement limits any further negotiation of a check.

2. Check stubs are filled out first before a check is written.

3. The payee is the person the check is payable to. The drawer is the one who orders the bank to pay a sum of money. The drawee is the bank that the drawer has an account with.

4. The process of reconciling the bank balance with the company's balance is called the bank reconciliation. The timing of deposits, when the bank statement was issued, etc., often results in differences between the bank balance and the checkbook balance.

5. Deposits in transit are added to the bank balance.

6. Checks outstanding are subtracted from the bank balance.

7. NSF means that a check has insufficient funds to be credited to a checking account; therefore the amount is not included in the bank balance and thus the checking account balance is lowered.

8. When a bank debits your account they are deducting an amount from your balance. A credit to the account is an increase to your balance.

9. All adjustments to the checkbook balance require journal entries.

ATM: Automatic teller machines.

Bank reconciliation: This is the process of reconciling the checkbook balance with the bank balance given on the bank statement.

Bank statement: A report sent by a bank to a customer indicating the previous balance, individual checks processed, individual deposits received, service charges, and ending bank balance.

Cancelled check: A check that has been processed by a bank and is no longer negotiable.

Check: A form used to indicate a specific amount of money that is to be paid by the bank to a named person or company.

Check truncation (safekeeping): Procedure whereby checks are not returned to drawer with the bank statement but are instead kept at the bank for a certain amount of time before being first transferred to microfilm and then destroyed.

Credit memorandum: Increase in depositor's balance.

Debit memorandum: Decrease in depositor's balance.

Deposits in transit: Deposits that were made by customers of a bank but did not reach, or were not processed by, the bank before the preparation of the bank statement.

Deposit ticket: A form provided by a bank for use in depositing money or checks into a checking account.

Drawee: Bank that drawer has an account with.

Drawer: Person who writes a check.

Endorsement: *Blank*—could be further endorsed. *Full*—restricts further endorsement to only the person or company named. *Restrictive*—restricts any further endorsement.

EFT (electronic funds transfer): An electronic system that transfers funds without use of paper checks.

Internal control: A system of procedures and methods to control a firm's assets as well as monitor its operations.

NSF (nonsufficient funds): Notation indicating that a check has been written on an account that lacks sufficient funds to back it up.

Outstanding checks: Checks written by a company or person that were not received or not processed by the bank before the preparation of the bank statement.

Payee: The person or company the check is payable to.

LEARNING UNIT 8-2

1. Petty Cash is an asset found on the balance sheet.

2. The auxiliary petty cash record is an auxiliary book; thus no postings are done from this book. Think of it as an optional work sheet.

3. When a petty cash fund is established, the amount is entered as a debit to Petty Cash and a credit to Cash in the cash payments journal.

4. At time of replenishment of the petty cash fund, all expenses are debited (by category) and a credit to Cash (a new check) results. This replenishment, when journalized and posted, updates the ledger from the journal.

5. The only time the Petty Cash account is used is to establish the fund to begin with or bring the fund to a higher or lower level. If the petty cash level is deemed sufficient, all replenishments will debit specific expenses and new checks written. The asset Petty Cash will remain the same.

Blueprint of a Bank Reconciliation

CHECKBOOK BALANCE			BALANCE PER BANK		
Ending Balance per Books	$XXX		Ending Bank Statement Balance (last figure on bank statement)		$XXX
Add:			Add:		
Recording of errors that understate balance	XXX		Deposits in transit (amount not yet credited by bank)	XXX	
Proceeds of notes collected by bank or other items credited (added) by bank but not yet updated in checkbook	XXX		Bank errors	XXX	XXX
		XXX			
Deduct:			Deduct:		
Recording of errors that overstate balance	XXX		List of outstanding checks (amount not yet debited by bank)	XXX	
Service charges	XXX		Bank errors	XXX	
Printing charges	XXX				XXX
NSF, check, etc., or other items debited (charged) by bank but not yet updated in checkbook	XXX				
		XXX			
Reconciled Balance (Adjusted Balance)		$XXX	Reconciled Balance (Adjusted Balance)		$XXX

6. A change fund is an asset that is used to make change for customers.

7. Cash Short and Over is an account that is either a miscellaneous expense or miscellaneous income, depending on whether the ending balance is shortage or overage.

Auxiliary petty cash record: A supplementary record for summarizing petty cash information.

Cash Short and Over: The account that records cash shortages and overages. If ending balance is a debit, it is recorded on the income statement as a miscellaneous expense; if it is a credit, it is recorded as miscellaneous income.

Change fund: Fund made up of various denominations that is used to make change to customers.

Petty cash fund: A fund (source) that allows payment of small amounts without the writing of checks.

Petty cash voucher: A petty cash form to be completed when money is taken out of petty cash.

DISCUSSION QUESTIONS

1. What is the purpose of internal control?
2. What is the advantage of having preprinted deposit tickets?
3. Explain the difference between a blank endorsement and a restrictive endorsement.
4. Explain the difference between payee, drawer, and drawee.
5. Why should check stubs be filled out first, before the check itself is written?
6. A bank statement is sent twice a month. True or false? Please explain.
7. Explain the end product of a bank reconciliation.
8. Why are checks outstanding subtracted from the bank balance?
9. An NSF results in a bank issuing the depositor a credit memorandum. Agree or disagree. Please support your response.
10. Why do adjustments to the checkbook balance in the reconciliation process need to be journalized?
11. What is EFT?
12. What is meant by check truncation or safekeeping?
13. Petty cash is a liability. Accept or reject.
14. Explain the relationship of the auxiliary petty cash record to the cash payments journal.
15. At time of replenishment, why are the totals of individual expenses debited?
16. Explain the purpose of a change fund.
17. Explain how Cash Short and Over can be a miscellaneous expense.

EXERCISES

Bank reconciliation.

1. From the following information, construct a bank reconciliation for Norry Co. as of July 31, 19XX. Then prepare journal entries if needed.

Ending checkbook balance	$420
Ending bank statement balance	300
Deposits (in transit)	200
Outstanding checks	95
Bank service charge (debit memo)	15

2. In general journal form (to keep it simple), prepare journal entries to establish a petty cash fund on July 1 and replenish it on July 31.

Establishing and replenishing petty cash.

July 1   A $40 petty cash fund is established.
    31   At end of month $12 cash plus the following paid vouchers exist: donations expense, $10; postage expense, $7; office supplies expense, $7; miscellaneous expense, $4.

3. If in Exercise 2 cash on hand was $11, prepare the entry to replenish the petty cash on July 31.

Cash overage in replenishment.

4. If in Exercise 2 cash on hand was $13, prepare the entry to replenish the petty cash on July 31.

Cash shortage in replenishment.

5. At the end of day the clerk for Pete's Variety Shop noticed an error in the amount of cash he should have. Total cash sales from the sales tape were $1,100 while the total cash in the register was $1,056. Pete keeps a $30 change fund in his shop. Prepare an appropriate general journal entry to record the cash sale as well as reveal the cash shortage.

Calculate cash shortage with Change Fund.

GROUP A PROBLEMS

8A-1. Rose Company received a bank statement from Macy Bank indicating a bank balance of $6,950. Based on Rose's check stubs, the ending checkbook balance was $5,825. Your task is to prepare a bank reconciliation for Rose Company as of July 31, 19XX, from the following information (please journalize entries as needed):

Preparing a bank reconciliation including collection of a note.

    A. Checks outstanding: no. 124, $600; no. 126, $850.
    B. Deposits in transit, $960.
    C. Bank service charge, $18.
    D. Macy Bank collected a note for Rose, $660, less a $7 collection fee.

8A-2. From the following bank statement, please (1) complete the bank reconciliation for Rick's Deli found on the reverse of the bank statement, and (2) journalize the appropriate entries as needed.

Preparing a bank reconciliation with NSF using back side of a bank statement.

JAMES NATIONAL BANK
RIO MEAN BRAND
BUGNA, TEXAS

RICK'S DELI
8811 2ND ST.
BUGNA, TEXAS

Old Balance	Checks in Order of Payment		Deposits	Date	New Balance
6,000				2/2	6,000
	90.00	210.00		2/3	5,700
	150.00		300.00	2/10	5,850
	600.00		600.00	2/15	5,850
	300.00	NSF	300.00	2/20	5,850
	1,200.00		1,200.00	2/24	5,850
	600.00	30.00 SC	180.00	2/28	5,400

    A. A deposit of $3,000 is in transit.
    B. Rick's Deli has an ending checkbook balance of $6,600.
    C. Checks outstanding: no. 111, $600: no. 119, $1,200; no. 121, $330.
    D. Jim Rice's check for $300 bounced due to lack of sufficient funds.

8A-3. The following transactions occurred in April and were related to the cash payments journal and petty cash fund of Merry Co.:

19XX
April 1 Issued check no. 14 for $80 to establish a petty cash fund.
      5 Paid $5 from petty cash for postage, voucher no. 1.
      8 Paid $10 from petty cash for office supplies, voucher no. 2.
   15 Issued check no. 15 to Reliable Corp. for $200 less a 2% discount for past purchases on account.

Establishment and replenishment of petty cash. Relationship to special journals and auxiliary petty cash record.

   17 Paid $8 from petty cash for office supplies, voucher no. 3.
   20 Issued check no. 16 to Roger Corp., $600, less a 5% discount from past purchases on account.

24　Paid $4 from petty cash for postage, voucher no. 4.

26　Paid $9 from petty cash for local church donation, voucher no. 5 (this is a miscellaneous payment).

28　Issued check no. 17 to Roy Kloon to pay for office equipment, $700.

From the chart of accounts: Petty Cash, 120; Office Equipment, 130; Postage Expense, 610; Office Supplies Expense, 620; Miscellaneous Expense, 630. The headings of the cash payments and auxiliary petty cash records are as follows:

		CASH PAYMENTS JOURNAL						
Date	Check No.	Accounts Debited	PR	Sundry Dr.	Accounts Payable Dr.	Purchases Discounts Cr.	Cash Cr.	

		AUXILIARY PETTY CASH RECORD					Category of Payments	
								Sundry
Date	Voucher No.	Description	Receipt	Payment	Postage Expense	Office Supplies Expense	Account	Amount

Your task is to

1. Record the appropriate entries in the cash payments journal as well as the auxiliary petty cash record as needed.
2. Be sure to replenish the petty cash fund on April 30 (check no. 18).

8A-4.　From the following, record the transactions into Logan's auxiliary petty cash record and cash payments journal (p. 33) as need:

19XX

Oct.　1　A check was drawn (no. 444) payable to Roberta Floss, petty cashier, to establish a $100 petty cash fund.

5　Paid $14 for postage stamps, voucher no. 1.

9　Paid $12 for delivery charges on goods for resale, voucher no. 2.

12　Paid $8 for donation to a church (Miscellaneous Expense), voucher no. 3.

14　Paid $9 for postage stamps, voucher no. 4.

17　Paid $8 for delivery charges on goods for resale, voucher no. 5.

27　Purchased computer supplies from petty cash for $8, voucher no. 6.

28　Paid $4 for postage, voucher no. 7.

29　Drew check no. 618 to replenish petty cash and a $3 shortage.

Establishing and replenishing petty cash including a cash shortage.

GROUP B PROBLEMS

Preparing a bank reconciliation including collection of a note.

8B-1.　As the bookkeeper of Rose Company you received the bank statement from Macy Bank indicating a balance of $9,185. The ending checkbook balance was $8,215. Prepare the bank reconciliation for Rose Company as of July 31, 19XX, and prepare journal entries as needed based on the following:

A.　Deposits in transit, $3,600.

B.　Bank service charges, $29.

C.　Checks outstanding: no. 111, $590; no. 115, $1,255.

D.　Macy Bank collected a note for Rose, $2,760, less a $6 collection fee.

Preparing a bank reconciliation with NSF using back side of a bank statement.

8B-2.　Based on the following, please (1) complete the bank reconciliation for Rick's Deli found on the reverse of the bank statement, and (2) journalize the appropriate entries as needed.

A. Checks outstanding: no. 110, $80; no. 116, $160; no. 118, $52.

B. A deposit of $416 is in transit.

C. The checkbook balance of Rick's Deli shows an ending balance of $798.

D. Jim Rice's check for $40 bounced due to lack of sufficient funds.

Establishment and replenishment of petty cash. Relationship to special journals and auxiliary petty cash record.

JAMES NATIONAL BANK
RIO MEAN BRAND
BUGNA, TEXAS

RICK'S DELI
8811 2ND ST.
BUGNA, TEXAS

Old Balance	Checks in Order of Payment		Deposits	Date	New Balance
718				4/2	718.00
	12.00	36.00		4/3	670.00
	20.00		40.00	4/10	690.00
	80.00		80.00	4/15	690.00
	40.00 NSF		40.00	4/20	690.00
	160.00		160.00	4/24	690.00
	80.00	2.00 SC	24.00	4/28	632.00

8B-3. From the following transactions, (1) record the entries as needed in the cash payments journal of Merry Co. as well as the auxiliary petty cash record, and (2) replenish the petty cash fund on April 30 (check no. 8).

19XX

April 1 Issued check no. 4 for $60 to establish a petty cash fund.

5 Paid $9 from petty cash for postage, voucher no. 1.

8 Paid $12 from petty cash for office supplies, voucher no. 2.

15 Issued check no. 5 to Reliable Corp. for $400 less a 2% discount.

17 Paid $7 from petty cash for office supplies, voucher no. 3.

20 Issued check no. 6 to Roger Corp., $300, less a 5% discount from past purchases on account.

24 Paid $6 from petty cash for postage, voucher no. 4.

26 Paid $12 from petty cash for local church donation, voucher no. 5 (this is a miscellaneous payment).

28 Issued check no. 7 to Roy Kloon to pay office equipment, $800.

Chart of accounts includes: Petty Cash 120; Office Equipment, 130; Postage Expense, 610; Office Supplies Expense, 620; Miscellaneous Expense, 630. Use the same heading as in Problem 8A-3 (p. 232).

8B-4. From the following, record the transactions into Logan's auxiliary petty cash record and cash payments journal (p. 33) as needed:

19XX

Oct. 1 Roberta Floss, the petty cashier, cashed a check, no. 444, to establish a $90 petty cash fund.

5 Paid $16 for postage stamps, voucher no. 1.

Establishing and replenishing petty cash including a cash shortage.

9 Paid $14 for delivery charges on goods for resale, voucher no. 2.

12 Paid $6 for donation to a church (Miscellaneous Expense), voucher no. 3.

14 Paid $10 for postage stamps, voucher no. 4.

17 Paid $7 for delivery charges on goods for resale, voucher no. 5.

27 Purchased computer supplies from petty cash for $9, voucher no. 6.

28 Paid $3 for postage, voucher no. 7.

29 Drew check no. 618 to replenish petty cash and a $4 shortage.

PRACTICAL ACCOUNTING APPLICATION #1

Karen Johnson, the bookkeeper of Hoop Co., has appointed Jim Pool as the petty cash custodian. The following transactions occurred in November:

19XX
Nov. 25 Check no. 441 was written and cashed to establish a $50 petty cash fund.
    27 Paid $8.50 delivery charge for goods purchased for resale.
    29 Purchased office supplies for $12 from petty cash.
    30 Purchased postage stamps for $15 from petty cash.

On December 3 Jim received the following internal memo:

> To: Jim Pool
>
> From: Karen Johnson
>
> Re: Petty Cash
>
> Jim, I'll need $5 for postage stamps. By the way, I noticed that our petty cash account seems to be too low. Let's increase its size to $100.

Could you help Jim replenish petty cash on December 3 by providing him with a general journal entry? Support your answer and indicate whether Karen was correct.

PRACTICAL ACCOUNTING APPLICATION #2

Ginger Company has a policy of depositing all receipts and making all payments by check. On receiving the bank statement, Bill Free, a new bookkeeper, is quite upset that the balance in cash in the ledger is $4,209.50 while the ending bank balance is $4,440.50. Bill is convinced the bank has made an error. Based on the following facts, is Bill's concern warranted? What other suggestions could you offer Bill in the bank reconciliation process?

(a) The Nov. 30 cash receipts, $611, had been placed in the bank's night depository after banking hours and consequently did not appear on the bank statement as a deposit.

(b) Two debit memorandums and a credit memorandum were included with the returned check. None of the memorandums had been recorded at the time of the reconciliation. The first debit memorandum had a $130 NSF check written by Abby Ellen. The second was a $6.50 debit memorandum for service charges. The credit memorandum was for $494 and represented the proceeds less a $6 collection fee from a $500 non-interest-bearing note collected for Ginger Company by the bank.

(c) It was also found that checks no. 942 for $71.50 and no. 947 for $206.50, both written and recorded on Nov. 28, were not among the cancelled checks returned.

(d) Bill found that check no. 899 was correctly drawn for $1,094, in payment for a new cash register. However, this check had been recorded as though it were for $1,148.

(e) The October bank reconciliation showed two checks outstanding on September 30, no. 621 for $152.50 and no. 630 for $179.30. Check no. 630 was returned with the November bank statement, but check no. 621 was not.

PAYROLL CONCEPTS AND PROCEDURES:
Employee Taxes

Payroll can be a significant expense in running a business. Besides the money issue, there are a number of federal and state regulations concerning payroll that a business must comply with.

The use of the computer has taken much of the routine bookkeeping out of day-to-day payroll operations. However, it is quite important for one to completely understand the manual payroll system. There need to be continual checks and balances on the payroll system, as well as strong internal controls, to ensure accuracy.

In this chapter we will take a close look at the employees of Fred's Market and see how their payroll is calculated, how it is affected by federal, state, and local taxes and deductions, and how the accountant for Fred's Market handles a weekly payroll. (In the next chapter, we will continue to look at Fred's Market, but now from the employer's point of view rather than that of the employees.)

LEARNING UNIT 9-1

Introduction to Payroll

A number of laws and regulations at the federal and state level govern payroll. We will look at several of them here.

FAIR LABOR STANDARDS ACT

The **Fair Labor Standards Act** (also called the **Wages and Hours Law**) states that a worker will receive a minimum hourly rate of pay, and that the maximum number of hours a worker will work during a week at the regular rate of pay is 40 hours. Once 40 hours is reached, at least time and a half must be paid the worker. This law also has many amendments that deal with minimum wage, child labor restrictions, and equal pay regardless of sex. It applies to employers who are involved directly or indirectly in interstate commerce. Not all employers must take 40 hours as the standard: restaurants, hotels, and the like have maximum hours of up to 44. Also, many high-level employees in administrative capacities are exempt from the 40-hour requirement.

Following these regulations, there are two methods to use to calculate overtime pay. Let's say that a person worked four hours of overtime and was earning $8 an hour. Pay would be calculated as follows:

METHOD 1			METHOD 2		
44 hr @ $8		= $352	40 hr @ $ 8		= $320
4 hr @ $4		= 16	4 hr @ $12		= 48
Amount of pay received		= $368	Amount of pay received		= $368

Using Method 1, the employer is clearly able to see that pure overtime wages cost him or her $16. Because it is the more common, we will use Method 2, which calculates the overtime rate at time and a half.

FEDERAL WITHHOLDING FOR FEDERAL INCOME TAX (FIT)

Although many rules and regulations govern the federal income taxes that a person must pay, we will not try to discuss them all here. Basically, instead of employees paying their full tax bill on April 15 of the following year, employers withhold taxes for each employee and send them to the government at regular intervals. To do this, employers must have each employee fill out a **Form W–4** (an **Employee's Withholding Allowance Certificate**), which is kept on file by the employer (see Figure 9-1).

Using such a form, along with special withholding tables provided by the Internal Revenue Service, an employer can determine the amount of **federal income tax withholding** by looking at an employee's income, marital status, and number of allowances or exemptions claimed. An **allowance** or **exemption** represents a certain amount of a person's income that will be considered *non*taxable.

FIGURE 9-1   Form W–4, Employee's Withholding Allowance Certificate.

Form **W-4**
Department of the Treasury
Internal Revenue Service

Employee's Withholding Allowance Certificate
▶ **For Privacy Act and Paperwork Reduction Act Notice, see reverse.**

1 Type or print your first name and middle initial	Last name	2 Your social security number
SUSAN	O'REILLY	021-36-9494

Home address (number and street or rural route)
26 ROUNDY ROAD
City or town, state, and ZIP code
MARBLEHEAD, MA 01945

3 Marital Status
☐ Single   ☒ Married
☐ Married, but withhold at higher Single rate.
Note: *If married, but legally separated, or spouse is a nonresident alien, check the Single box.*

4 Total number of allowances you are claiming (from line G above or from the Worksheets on back if they apply) . . . **4** 3

5 Additional amount, if any, you want deducted from each pay . . . . **5** $

6 I claim exemption from withholding and I certify that I meet **ALL** of the following conditions for exemption:
- Last year I had a right to a refund of **ALL** Federal income tax withheld because I had **NO** tax liability; **AND**
- This year I expect a refund of **ALL** Federal income tax withheld because I expect to have **NO** tax liability; **AND**
- This year if my income exceeds $500 and includes nonwage income, another person cannot claim me as a dependent.

If you meet all of the above conditions, enter the year effective and "EXEMPT" here . . . . . ▶ **6** 19

7 Are you a full-time student? (**Note:** *Full-time students are not automatically exempt.*) . . . . **7** ☐ Yes   ☐ No

Under penalties of perjury, I certify that I am entitled to the number of withholding allowances claimed on this certificate or entitled to claim exempt status.

Employee's signature ▶ *Susan O'Reilly*   Date ▶ January 2, 199X

8 Employer's name and address (**Employer:** Complete 8 and 10 **only if sending to IRS**)
9 Office code (optional)
10 Employer identification number

Usually a worker is entitled to an allowance for self, one for his or her spouse (unless the spouse is working and claiming an allowance), and one for each dependent for whom the worker is providing more than half the support in a given year. Other technicalities need not be discussed here; you can find them when you need them on IRS information sheets.

To calculate withholding, the employer uses a wage bracket table found in Circular E of the Employer's Tax Guide, published by the Internal Revenue Service. The **wage bracket tables** found in this publication show the amount of federal tax to be withheld for single and married persons with monthly, semimonthly, biweekly, and weekly payroll periods. Two tables are shown in Figure 9-2.

Let's assume that the employee, who is married, earns $1,250 a week and claims three allowances. Using the table, we go down the left-hand column until we arrive at the $1,250 that says "at least." Since the employee claims 3 allowances, we slide over to the right, and where the 3 allowances intersect with the "at least" $1,250 we see a Federal Withholding Tax of $224. If the employee had earned $1,249, his or her tax would have been $222.

FEDERAL INSURANCE CONTRIBUTIONS ACT (FICA)

Another tax that we pay results from a law called the **Federal Insurance Contributions Act** (better known as **FICA**), which helps fund the payments related to (1) monthly retirement benefits for those over 62 years of age, (2) medical benefits after age 65, (3) benefits for workers who have become disabled, and (4) benefits for families of deceased workers who were covered by the Federal Social Security Act. Under this act, passed in 1933, employees, self-employed persons, and employers all pay a FICA tax. The employer's share of this tax is discussed in Chapter 10.

Each year rates are set for Social Security so that employers match the contributions of each employee. In 1937 the rate for FICA was 1 percent on the first $3,000 of earnings in a calendar year. That meant the most an employee could contribute to Social Security was $30. Since the rate and base continually change, we will assume a FICA rate of 7.65% on the first $52,000 of earnings. That means that before wages are exempt (not taxed) for Social Security, an employee would have to contribute $3,978 (.0765 × $52,000) in a calendar year. (A **calendar year** is a one-year period beginning on January 1 and ending on December 31.)

STATE AND CITY INCOME TAXES (SIT)

There are many other taxes and deductions that we could list here. One tax paid by many employees is the state income tax. The rates vary too much from area to area to give here, but most states publish charts and tables like those of the federal government to allow you to easily calculate the proper amount of **state income tax withholding** from your paycheck. At present two-thirds of all the states require employees to pay a state income tax. In many states there are also city income taxes that must be paid by employees.

WORKERS' COMPENSATION

Employers are required to protect their employees against losses due to injury or death incurred while on the job. This insurance is called **workers' compensation insurance**. Each employer (in cooperation with an insurance

MARRIED Persons—WEEKLY Payroll Period

And the wages are—		And the number of withholding allowances claimed is—										
At least	But less than	0	1	2	3	4	5	6	7	8	9	10
		The amount of income tax to be withheld shall be—										
$620	$630	$85	$79	$73	$67	$61	$56	$50	$44	$38	$33	$27
630	640	86	80	74	69	63	57	51	46	40	34	28
640	650	88	82	76	70	64	59	53	47	41	36	30
650	660	89	83	77	72	66	60	54	49	43	37	31
660	670	92	85	79	73	67	62	56	50	44	39	33
670	680	94	86	80	75	69	63	57	52	46	40	34
680	690	97	88	82	76	70	65	59	53	47	42	36
690	700	100	89	83	78	72	66	60	55	49	43	37
700	710	103	92	85	79	73	68	62	56	50	45	39
710	720	106	95	86	81	75	69	63	58	52	46	40
720	730	108	98	88	82	76	71	65	59	53	48	42
730	740	111	100	90	84	78	72	66	61	55	49	43
740	750	114	103	92	85	79	74	68	62	56	51	45
750	760	117	106	95	87	81	75	69	64	58	52	46
760	770	120	109	98	88	82	77	71	65	59	54	48
770	780	122	112	101	90	84	78	72	67	61	55	49
780	790	125	114	104	93	85	80	74	68	62	57	51
790	800	128	117	106	96	87	81	75	70	64	58	52
800	810	131	120	109	98	88	83	77	71	65	60	54
810	820	134	123	112	101	91	84	78	73	67	61	55
820	830	136	126	115	104	93	86	80	74	68	63	57
830	840	139	128	118	107	96	87	81	76	70	64	58
840	850	142	131	120	110	99	89	83	77	71	66	60
850	860	145	134	123	112	102	91	84	79	73	67	61
860	870	148	137	126	115	105	94	86	80	74	69	63
870	880	150	140	129	118	107	97	87	82	76	70	64
880	890	153	142	132	121	110	99	89	83	77	72	66
890	900	156	145	134	124	113	102	91	85	79	73	67
900	910	159	148	137	126	116	105	94	86	80	75	69
910	920	162	151	140	129	119	108	97	88	82	76	70
920	930	164	154	143	132	121	111	100	89	83	78	72
930	940	167	156	146	135	124	113	103	92	85	79	73
940	950	170	159	148	138	127	116	105	95	86	81	75
950	960	173	162	151	140	130	119	108	97	88	82	76
960	970	176	165	154	143	133	122	111	100	89	84	78
970	980	178	168	157	146	135	125	114	103	92	85	79
980	990	181	170	160	149	138	127	117	106	95	87	81
990	1,000	184	173	162	152	141	130	119	109	98	88	82
1,000	1,010	187	176	165	154	144	133	122	111	101	90	84
1,010	1,020	190	179	168	157	147	136	125	114	103	93	85
1,020	1,030	192	182	171	160	149	139	128	117	106	95	87
1,030	1,040	195	184	174	163	152	141	131	120	109	98	88
1,040	1,050	198	187	176	166	155	144	133	123	112	101	90
1,050	1,060	201	190	179	168	158	147	136	125	115	104	93
1,060	1,070	204	193	182	171	161	150	139	128	117	107	96
1,070	1,080	206	196	185	174	163	153	142	131	120	109	99
1,080	1,090	209	198	188	177	166	155	145	134	123	112	102
1,090	1,100	212	201	190	180	169	158	147	137	126	115	104
1,100	1,110	215	204	193	182	172	161	150	139	129	118	107
1,110	1,120	218	207	196	185	175	164	153	142	131	121	110
1,120	1,130	220	210	199	188	177	167	156	145	134	123	113
1,130	1,140	223	212	202	191	180	169	159	148	137	126	116
1,140	1,150	226	215	204	194	183	172	161	151	140	129	118
1,150	1,160	229	218	207	196	186	175	164	153	143	132	121
1,160	1,170	232	221	210	199	189	178	167	156	145	135	124
1,170	1,180	234	224	213	202	191	181	170	159	148	137	127
1,180	1,190	237	226	216	205	194	183	173	162	151	140	130
1,190	1,200	240	229	218	208	197	186	175	165	154	143	132
1,200	1,210	243	232	221	210	200	189	178	167	157	146	135
1,210	1,220	246	235	224	213	203	192	181	170	159	149	138
1,220	1,230	248	238	227	216	205	195	184	173	162	151	141
1,230	1,240	251	240	230	219	208	197	187	176	165	154	144
1,240	1,250	254	243	232	222	211	200	189	179	168	157	146
1,250	1,260	257	246	235	224	214	203	192	181	171	160	149
1,260	1,270	260	249	238	227	217	206	195	184	173	163	152
1,270	1,280	262	252	241	230	219	209	198	187	176	165	155

FIGURE 9-2 Wage Bracket Tables.

SINGLE Persons–WEEKLY Payroll Period

And the wages are–		And the number of withholding allowances claimed is–										
At least	But less than	0	1	2	3	4	5	6	7	8	9	10
		The amount of income tax to be withheld shall be–										
$0	$25	$0	$0	$0	$0	$0	$0	$0	$0	$0	$0	$0
25	30	1	0	0	0	0	0	0	0	0	0	0
30	35	2	0	0	0	0	0	0	0	0	0	0
35	40	2	0	0	0	0	0	0	0	0	0	0
40	45	3	0	0	0	0	0	0	0	0	0	0
45	50	4	0	0	0	0	0	0	0	0	0	0
50	55	5	0	0	0	0	0	0	0	0	0	0
55	60	5	0	0	0	0	0	0	0	0	0	0
60	65	6	0	0	0	0	0	0	0	0	0	0
65	70	7	1	0	0	0	0	0	0	0	0	0
70	75	8	2	0	0	0	0	0	0	0	0	0
75	80	8	3	0	0	0	0	0	0	0	0	0
80	85	9	3	0	0	0	0	0	0	0	0	0
85	90	10	4	0	0	0	0	0	0	0	0	0
90	95	11	5	0	0	0	0	0	0	0	0	0
95	100	11	6	0	0	0	0	0	0	0	0	0
100	105	12	6	1	0	0	0	0	0	0	0	0
105	110	13	7	1	0	0	0	0	0	0	0	0
110	115	14	8	2	0	0	0	0	0	0	0	0
115	120	14	9	3	0	0	0	0	0	0	0	0
120	125	15	9	4	0	0	0	0	0	0	0	0
125	130	16	10	4	0	0	0	0	0	0	0	0
130	135	17	11	5	0	0	0	0	0	0	0	0
135	140	17	12	6	0	0	0	0	0	0	0	0
140	145	18	12	7	1	0	0	0	0	0	0	0
145	150	19	13	7	2	0	0	0	0	0	0	0
150	155	20	14	8	2	0	0	0	0	0	0	0
155	160	20	15	9	3	0	0	0	0	0	0	0
160	165	21	15	10	4	0	0	0	0	0	0	0
165	170	22	16	10	5	0	0	0	0	0	0	0
170	175	23	17	11	5	0	0	0	0	0	0	0
175	180	23	18	12	6	0	0	0	0	0	0	0
180	185	24	18	13	7	1	0	0	0	0	0	0
185	190	25	19	13	8	2	0	0	0	0	0	0
190	195	26	20	14	8	3	0	0	0	0	0	0
195	200	26	21	15	9	3	0	0	0	0	0	0
200	210	28	22	16	10	5	0	0	0	0	0	0
210	220	29	23	18	12	6	0	0	0	0	0	0
220	230	31	25	19	13	8	2	0	0	0	0	0
230	240	32	26	21	15	9	3	0	0	0	0	0
240	250	34	28	22	16	11	5	0	0	0	0	0
250	260	35	29	24	18	12	6	0	0	0	0	0
260	270	37	31	25	19	14	8	2	0	0	0	0
270	280	38	32	27	21	15	9	3	0	0	0	0
280	290	40	34	28	22	17	11	5	0	0	0	0
290	300	41	35	30	24	18	12	6	1	0	0	0
300	310	43	37	31	25	20	14	8	2	0	0	0
310	320	44	38	33	27	21	15	9	4	0	0	0
320	330	46	40	34	28	23	17	11	5	0	0	0
330	340	47	41	36	30	24	18	12	7	1	0	0
340	350	49	43	37	31	26	20	14	8	2	0	0
350	360	50	44	39	33	27	21	15	10	4	0	0
360	370	52	46	40	34	29	23	17	11	5	0	0
370	380	53	47	42	36	30	24	18	13	7	1	0
380	390	56	49	43	37	32	26	20	14	8	3	0
390	400	58	50	45	39	33	27	21	16	10	4	0
400	410	61	52	46	40	35	29	23	17	11	6	0
410	420	64	53	48	42	36	30	24	19	13	7	1
420	430	67	56	49	43	38	32	26	20	14	9	3
430	440	70	59	51	45	39	33	27	22	16	10	4
440	450	72	62	52	46	41	35	29	23	17	12	6
450	460	75	64	54	48	42	36	30	25	19	13	7
460	470	78	67	56	49	44	38	32	26	20	15	9
470	480	81	70	59	51	45	39	33	28	22	16	10
480	490	84	73	62	52	47	41	35	29	23	18	12
490	500	86	76	65	54	48	42	36	31	25	19	13
500	510	89	78	68	57	50	44	38	32	26	21	15
510	520	92	81	70	60	51	45	39	34	28	22	16
520	530	95	84	73	62	53	47	41	35	29	24	18
530	540	98	87	76	65	54	48	42	37	31	25	19

FIGURE 9-2 Wage Bracket Tables. (Cont.)

agent) will estimate the cost of the insurance and be required to pay the premium in advance. In Chapter 10 we will look at how the premium is calculated along with specific tax responsibilities of the employer.

At this point, you should be able to

1. Calculate overtime pay. (p. 237)
2. Explain the purpose of the Wages and Hours Law. (p. 236)
3. Complete a W-4 form. (p. 237)
4. Explain "claiming an allowance." (p. 237)
5. Define and state the purpose of FICA. (p. 238)
6. Calculate FICA deductions. (p. 238)
7. Utilize a wage bracket table to arrive at deductions from federal income tax. (p. 239)
8. Explain the purpose of workers' compensation insurance. (p. 238)

SELF-REVIEW QUIZ 9-1

John Small, to date this year before the current payroll, has earned $51,900. This week John earned $530. Please calculate the amount for FICA tax, federal income tax, and state income tax, assuming the following facts:

1. FICA rate is 7.65% on $52,000.
2. John is single, claiming one deduction (use table in text).
3. State income tax is 8 percent.
4. No other deductions are taken out by the employer.

SOLUTION TO SELF-REVIEW QUIZ 9-1

FICA: $100 × .0765 = $7.65

Federal income tax: $87 by table

State income tax: $530 × .08 = $42.40

NOTE: Only first $100 of the $530 is taxed for Social Security since John has now gone beyond the $52,000 limit. The other $430 is not taxed for Social Security.

LEARNING UNIT 9-2

The Payroll Process

Fred Stone, owner of Fred's Market, has five employees working for him. They are as follows:

Bob Flynn	$9 per hour
Abby Frost	$7 per hour
Susan O'Reilly	$1,250 salary per week
Paula Rase	$700 salary per week
Al Regan	$1,000 salary per week

Fred does not receive a salary, since he is the owner of the sole proprietorship, but he does plan to eventually withdraw portions of the profit.

FRED'S MARKET
PAYROLL REGISTER
NOVEMBER 18, 19XX

Employee Name	Allowance and Marital Status	Cumulative Earnings	Salary per Week	No. of Hrs.	Wages per Hr.	Earnings			Cumulative Earnings
						Regular	Overtime	Gross	
Flynn, Bob	S-0	6900.00		30	9.00	270.00	—	270.00	7170.00
Frost, Abby	S-1	6500.00		44	7.00	280.00	42.00	322.00	6822.00
O'Reilly, Susan	M-3	56250.00	1250.00			1250.00	—	1250.00	57500.00
Rase, Paula	M-1	31500.00	700.00			700.00	—	700.00	32200.00
Regan, Al	M-2	45000.00	1000.00			1000.00	—	1000.00	46000.00
		146150.00	2950.00			3500.00	42.00	3542.00	149692.00
	*(A)	(B)	(C)			(D)	(E)	(F)	(G)

* The following discussion is keyed to these letters.

FIGURE 9-3 Payroll Register for Fred's Market.

RECORDING PAYROLL DATA IN THE PAYROLL REGISTER

Calendar year: January 1 through December 31.

Fred's Market pays its employees on a weekly basis. The **payroll register** shown in Figure 9-3 contains the payroll information for the week of November 18.

Let's look closely at each column to see how the numbers were arrived at. (Use this as a reference guide for both Chapters 9 and 10.)

(A) Allowance and Marital Status

Employees complete Form W–4 (Figure 9-1) indicating whether they are married or single. Individual workers completing the form are entitled to claim one exemption for themselves and one for each dependent. An employer uses the W–4 form to withhold money for federal income tax (column K) from his workers according to their earnings and number of claimed exemptions. The more exemptions that are claimed, the less is deducted from an employee's earnings for federal income tax at the time the check is issued. The opposite is also true. The fewer the exemptions, the larger the deduction.

> Example: Bob Flynn is single and claims 0 exemptions resulting in more federal income taxes taken out sooner. If Bob overpays FIT, he could receive a refund at year end when his tax return is filed.

(B) Cumulative Earnings

This column represents each employee's cumulative earnings for the calender year *before* the new payroll period. As we will show later, the cumulative figure can be gotten from the employee's individual earnings record.

| | Deductions | | | | Net Pay | Check No. | Distribution of Expense Accounts | |
FICA	Federal Income Tax	State Income Tax	Medical Insurance				Office Salaries Expense	Market Wages Expense
20 66	38 00	13 50	14 00	183 84	822		270 00
24 63	40 00	16 10	14 00	227 27	823		322 00
—	224 00	62 50	20 00	943 50	824	1250 00	
53 55	92 00	35 00	20 00	499 45	825	700 00	
76 50	165 00	50 00	20 00	688 50	826	1000 00	
175 34	559 00	177 10	88 00	2542 56		2950 00	592 00
(J)	(K)	(L)	(M)	(N)	(O)	(P)	(Q)

Example: Abby Frost has earned $6,500 before this payroll in the calendar year.

(C) Salary per Week, Number of Hours, and Wages per Hour

The weekly salary or hours worked with rate of pay per hour provides the basis for computing the gross earnings of the employees.

Example: Bob Flynn is paid $9 per hour and worked 30 hours for this pay period.

(D) Earnings

To calculate the regular earnings for an employee paid by the hour, multiply the number of hours (40 or less) times the rate per hour. Salaried employee amounts are listed with no calculations.

Example: Bob Flynn has earned $270 for this pay period.

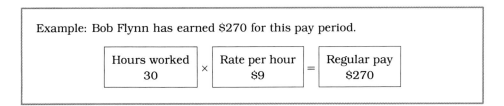

| Hours worked 30 | × | Rate per hour $9 | = | Regular pay $270 |

(E) Overtime

After 40 hours, hourly employees earn time and a half.

Note: salaried employees do not receive overtime.

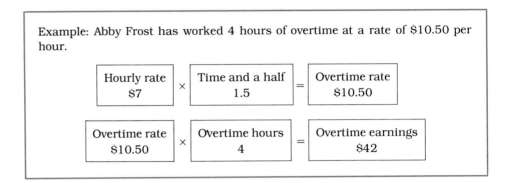

Example: Abby Frost has worked 4 hours of overtime at a rate of $10.50 per hour.

| Hourly rate $7 | × | Time and a half 1.5 | = | Overtime rate $10.50 |

| Overtime rate $10.50 | × | Overtime hours 4 | = | Overtime earnings $42 |

(F) Gross Earnings

Gross earnings is the total amount that has been earned (including overtime) before any deductions. It will be these numbers that we will use to fill columns (P) and (Q).

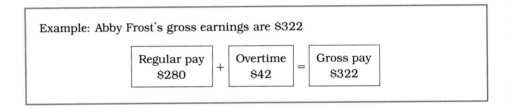

Example: Abby Frost's gross earnings are $322

| Regular pay $280 | + | Overtime $42 | = | Gross pay $322 |

(G) Cumulative Earnings

This column provides an up-to-date picture of how much each employee has earned *after* this pay period for the calendar year (see column B and discussion on page 242).

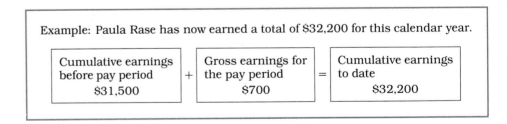

Example: Paula Rase has now earned a total of $32,200 for this calendar year.

| Cumulative earnings before pay period $31,500 | + | Gross earnings for the pay period $700 | = | Cumulative earnings to date $32,200 |

(H) Taxable Earnings: Unemployment Insurance

In the next chapter we will see certain taxes for state and federal unemployment insurance that will be paid only by the employer. These taxes are paid on the first $7,000 of earnings of each employee. *This column doesn't show the tax amount: it shows the earnings that are subject to being taxed.*

Example: Before this payroll, Bob Flynn has cumulative earnings of $6,900. In this pay period, he earns $270. Since the employer pays these unemployment taxes on the first $7,000 of earnings, only $100 will be taxed (we will provide tax rates in next chapter) of the $270.

Total taxable earnings for unemployment taxes per employee	$7,000
Cumulative earnings before pay period for Flynn	6,900
Taxable earnings	$ 100

Only the first $100 of earnings can be taxed since that now puts Bob Flynn over the $7,000 amount.

Note: Abby Frost's entire earnings are taxable since her cumulative earnings plus payroll earnings for this period still do not exceed $7,000. However, look at Paula Rase, Al Regan, and Susan O'Reilly. The earnings of all three are not subject to this tax since each has already earned $7,000 before this pay period.

(I) FICA Earnings

All employees are taxed for Social Security until they have earned $52,000 for the calendar year. This column shows the amount of earnings that will be taxed for Social Security. It *does not* show the tax.

Example: Susan O'Reilly has earned $56,250 before this pay period. Since she has earned more than the maximum of $52,000, none of her present salary is taxable for Social Security.

Note: All the other employees' gross pay is taxable since no one has earned more than $52,000 at end of this pay period.

(J) FICA Rate

The rate for Social Security is 7.65% on the first $52,000 of earnings. In Column I we can see the FICA earnings for which each employee is taxed.

Example: For this pay period, Al Regan pays in $76.50 to cover FICA. All his earnings are taxable since he has earned only $45,000 before this pay period and his new earnings of $1,000 result in cumulative earnings of $46,000, much less than the base of $52,000 for FICA.

Taxable FICA earnings $1,000	×	FICA rate .0765	=	FICA tax $76.50

(K) Federal Income Tax

Federal income tax does *not* have a cutoff point in the calendar year. All earnings will be taxed depending on one's (1) income, (2) marital status, and (3) number of exemptions claimed. Tables are provided in Circular E of the Employee's Tax Guide.

Example: Susan O'Reilly is married, earning $1,250 per week and claims 3 exemptions.

Using Figure 9-2 (p. 239) we get a tax of $224.

(L) State Income Tax

We are assuming a 5% state income tax. There is no cutoff point as there is in Social Security. This tax works like the tax for federal income tax. Individual states have their own tax tables.

Example: Al Regan's state income tax is $50

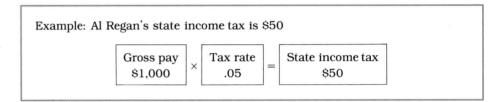

(M) Medical Insurance

A deduction of $14 is taken from hourly workers and $20 from salaried workers to pay for medical insurance.

(N) Net Pay

Net pay, or take home pay, is gross pay less deductions. Gross pay is what we wish we had; net pay is what we are stuck with.

Example: Abby Frost, who is single, has worked a 44-hour week this pay period. Therefore, her gross earnings for the week are $322.00 and her deduction is one. She will take home $227.27 as her net pay. This is what Abby's check showed.

Gross Pay		$322.00
Less: FICA	$24.63	
Federal Income Tax	40.00	
State Income Tax	16.10	
Medical Insurance	14.00	94.73
Net Pay		$227.27

(O) Check Number

When the payroll is paid, the check number is recorded in the Payroll Register.

(P & Q) Distribution of Expense Accounts

These two columns identify the specific accounts to which the total gross earnings of $3,542 (Column F) will be charged. (We will show how this is done in the next unit when data from the Payroll Register is used to journalize and post the payroll entry.)

At this point, you should be able to:

1. Explain as well as prepare a payroll register. (p. 242)
2. Explain the purpose of the taxable earnings columns and how they relate to the cumulative earnings columns. (p. 244)

SELF-REVIEW QUIZ 9-2

Ryan Leter has cumulative earnings of $51,500 before this pay period. This week he earns $990. Calculate his net pay, assuming the following facts:

1. FICA rate is 7.65 percent on $52,000.
2. He is married, claiming one allowance (use table in text).
3. State income tax is 7 percent.
4. No other deductions are made by his employer.

SOLUTIONS TO SELF-REVIEW QUIZ 9-2

1. FICA is $38.25 ($500 × .0765); only first $500 is taxable.
2. Federal income tax is $173.
3. State income tax is $69.30.

Thus his net pay = $709.45 ($990 − $38.25 − $173 − $69.30)

LEARNING UNIT 9-3

Recording and Paying the Payroll

Since the payroll register doesn't have the status of a special journal, we need to take the data from the payroll register and prepare a journal entry to record the payroll and then post to the specific ledger accounts. Refer to the payroll register shown in Figure 9-3, pp. 242–243.

For Fred's Market, the payroll at the end of the first week is recorded in the general journal as follows:

Nov	18	Office Salaries Expense	2 9 5 0 00	
		Market Wages Expense	5 9 2 00	
		FICA Tax Payable		1 7 5 34
		Federal Income Tax Payable		5 5 9 00
		State Income Tax Payable		1 7 7 10
		Medical Insurance Payable		8 8 00
		Wages and Salaries Payable		2 5 4 2 56
		Records payroll from payroll		
		register for week ended Nov. 18		

Note that the debits to **Office Salaries Expense** and **Market Wages Expense** come from the totals of the distribution of expense accounts on the payroll register (p. 243). The credits to **FICA Tax Payable** (a liability account), FIT Payable, SIT Payable, and Medical Insurance Payable are from the totals of these deductions on the payroll register. Keep in mind that these deductions are liabilities. The credit to **Wages and Salaries Payable** (a liability account) is from the total of the net pay column on the payroll register. The ledger of Fred's Market will look as follows after postings are complete:

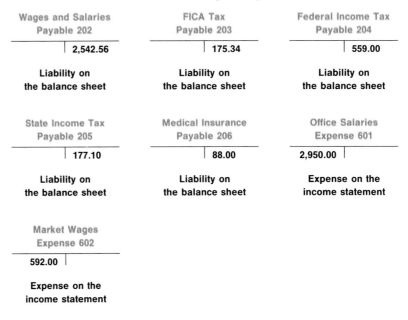

Figure 9-4 summarizes this process.

PAYROLL AND THE CASH PAYMENTS JOURNAL

Since Fred's Market has only five employees, it pays payroll by check from its regular checking account. A larger firm may have a separate payroll checking account as well as a regular checking account. Often the checks are of

FIGURE 9-4   The Payroll Recording and Posting Process.

different colors. A deposit for the full amount of the payroll is placed in this separate payroll account. When all the checks are written, the payroll account should be zero. The check from Fred's Market provides space to list amounts earned along with deductions. Fred also uses the cash payments journal shown here to record the payment to each employee. As we see, each entry reduces the amount of **Wages and Salaries Payable** (a liability account) as well as showing

1. The date of payment.
2. The amount of decrease in cash (check).
3. The payee, or person by whom payment is received.

For example, on November 19, Susan O'Reilly is paid $943.50; the result is to debit Wages and Salaries Payable and credit Cash. No postings will be needed until the end of the month.

Total of Wages and Salaries Payable is posted at end of month as a debit.

CASH PAYMENTS JOURNAL

Page 15

Date	Check No.	Account/ Payment to	PR	Sundry Dr.	Accounts Payable Dr.	Wages and Salaries Payable Dr.	Purchases Discount Cr.	Cash Cr.
Nov. 19	822	Flynn, Bob	x			1 8 3 84		1 8 3 84
	823	Frost, Abby	x			2 2 7 27		2 2 7 27
	824	O'Reilly, Susan	x			9 4 3 50		9 4 3 50
	825	Rase, Paula	x			4 9 9 45		4 9 9 45
	826	Regan, Al	x			6 8 8 50		6 8 8 50

THE EMPLOYEE INDIVIDUAL EARNINGS RECORD

Before concluding this chapter, it is important to look at how Fred keeps an individual record of each person's earnings and deductions, as required to meet state and federal regulations.

Fred maintains a summary of each employee's earnings, deductions and net pay for each payroll period, as well as cumulative earnings during the year. Figure 9-5 (p. 250) is a partial **employee individual earnings record** for Susan O'Reilly. This record will help Fred in gathering information to pay taxes as well as reporting quarterly and yearly payroll amounts. Note in the record for Susan that in the fourth quarter in week 42, she has paid the maximum for FICA. In the next chapter we will see why this record is valuable for the employer. In the diagram in Figure 9-6 (p. 250) we will update the payroll function for Fred's Market. Keep in mind that every quarter has 13 weeks.

NAME OF EMPLOYEE	Susan O'Reilly		SOCIAL SECURITY NUMBER	021-36-9494	
HOME ADDRESS	26 Roundy Road		CITY OR TOWN	Marblehead, MA	ZIP 01945
DATE OF BIRTH 9/6/45	MALE	FEMALE X	MARRIED X SINGLE		NUMBER OF ALLOWANCES 3
POSITION	Manager				
EMPLOYER	Fred's Market		PHONE NO.	631-0233	

Fourth Quarter 19X8

	Hours Worked				Deductions						
Week #	Regular	Overtime	Total Earnings	FICA	Fed. Inc. Tax	State Inc. Tax	Med. Ins.	Net Pay	Check No.	Cumulative Pay
										48 75 0 00
40			1 25 0 00	9 5 63	2 24 00	6 2 50	2 0 00	8 47 87	710	50 00 0 00
41			1 25 0 00	9 5 63	2 24 00	6 2 50	2 0 00	8 47 87	750	51 25 0 00
42			1 25 0 00	5 7 38	2 24 00	6 2 50	2 0 00	8 86 12	780	52 50 0 00
43			1 25 0 00		2 24 00	6 2 50	2 0 00	9 43 50	824	53 75 0 00
44			1 25 0 00		2 24 00	6 2 50	2 0 00	9 43 50	850	55 00 0 00
45			1 25 0 00		2 24 00	6 2 50	2 0 00	9 43 50	890	56 25 0 00
46			1 25 0 00		2 24 00	6 2 50	2 0 00	9 43 50	910	57 50 0 00
Total 4th Quarter			16 25 0 00	2 48 64	2 91 2 00	8 12 50	2 60 00	12 01 6 86		
Total for Year			65 00 0 00	3 97 8 00	11 87 2 00	3 25 0 00	1 04 0 00	44 86 0 00		

FIGURE 9-5   Employee Individual Earnings Record.

FIGURE 9-6   Payroll Function for Fred's Market.

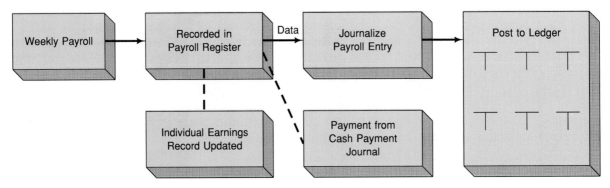

At this point, you should be able to

1. Explain how to enter payroll information into the general journal from the payroll register. (p. 247)
2. Journalize entries to pay a payroll. (p. 248)
3. Update an individual earnings record. (p. 249)

SELF-REVIEW QUIZ 9-3

Indicate which of the following statements are false:

1. All payroll registers must be special journals. This means no payroll entry is ever needed.
2. FICA Tax Payable is a liability on the balance sheet.
3. Wages and Salaries Expense has a normal balance of a credit.
4. Individual earnings records are optional for an employer.
5. Every quarter has 13 weeks.

SOLUTION TO SELF-REVIEW QUIZ 9-3

Statements 1, 3, and 4 are false.

SUMMARY OF KEY POINTS AND KEY TERMS

LEARNING UNIT 9-1

1. The Fair Labor Standards Act states a minimum hourly rate of pay as well as the paying of overtime at time and a half after 40 hours a week.
2. Form W–4, Employee's Withholding Allowance Certificate, determines the amount of federal income tax to deduct from an employee's check.
3. The employee and employer equally contribute to FICA an amount that is based on a given yearly rate and base for a calendar year.
4. Tax tables can be found in Circular E of the Employer's Tax Guide.

Calendar year: A one-year period beginning on January 1 and ending on December 31, used to calculate payroll information.

Fair Labor Standards Act (Wages and Hours Law): Law stating the minimum hourly rate of pay and the maximum number of hours a worker will work before being paid time and a half for overtime.

FICA (Federal Insurance Contributions Act): A tax levied on both the employer and the employee up to a certain maximum rate and base.

Federal income tax withholding: Amount of federal income tax withheld by the employer from the employee's gross pay; the amount withheld is determined by the number of allowances claimed by the employee on the W–4 form and by marital status.

State income tax withholding: Amount of state income tax withheld by the employer from the employee's gross pay.

W–4 (Employee's Withholding Allowance Certificate): A form filled out by employees to supply the employer needed information about the number of allowances claimed, marital status, etc., for determining income tax deductions from an employee's paycheck.

Wage bracket table: Charts in Circular E providing information about deductions for federal income tax based on earnings and data supplied on the W–4 form.

Blueprint for Recording, Posting, and Paying the Payroll

Payroll Transactions for the Period

PAYROLL REGISTER

	Deductions						Distribution of Expense Acccounts	
FICA	Fed. Inc. Tax	State Inc. Tax	Med. Ins.	Net Pay	Ck. No.		Office Salaries	Market Wages
XX	XX	XX	XX	XX			XXX	XXX

GENERAL JOURNAL

Office Salaries Expense	XXX	
Market Wages Expense	XXX	
FICA Tax Payable		XXX
Fed. Inc. Tax Payable		XXX
State Inc. Tax Payable		XXX
Med. Insurance Payable		XXX
Wages and Salaries Payable		XXX

POST TO LEDGER

CASH PAYMENTS JOURNAL

Wages and Sal. Pay. Dr.	〜〜	〜〜	Cash Cr.	
XXX			XXX	
XXX			XXX	
XXX			XXX	
XXX			XXX	

Totals Posted to Ledger at end of Month

W & S Payable		FICA Tax Payable	FIT Payable
XX | XX		XX	XX

SIT Payable	Med. Ins. Payable	Office Salaries Expense
XX	XX	XX

Market Wages Expense

XX

LEARNING UNIT 9-2

1. Gross pay less deductions equals net pay.

2. The taxable earnings columns do not show the tax. They show amount of earnings to be taxed for unemployment taxes and social security.

Gross earnings: Amount of pay received before any taxes.

Medical insurance: A deduction from one's paycheck for health insurance.

Net pay: Gross pay less deductions. Net pay is what the worker actually takes home.

Payroll register: A multicolumn form that can be used to record payroll data. The data in the payroll register is then used to journalize the payroll entry.

Taxable earnings: Shows amount of earnings subject to a tax. Does not show tax amount.

LEARNING UNIT 9-3

1. A payroll register provides the data for journalizing the payroll entry.

2. Deductions for payroll represent liabilities for the employer until paid.

3. The account distribution columns of the payroll register indicate which accounts will be debited to record the total payroll when a journal entry is prepared.

4. Paying a payroll results in debiting Wages and Salaries Payable and crediting Cash.

5. The individual earnings record is updated from the payroll register.

Employee individual earnings record: A record that summarizes the total amount of wages paid, as well as deductions, for the calendar year; it aids in preparing governmental reports.

FICA Tax Payable: A liability account showing the amount owed by an employer (including contributions of employer **and** employee) to the U.S. Treasury for FICA.

Market Wages Expense: An account that records from the payroll register gross earnings for Market Wages.

Office Salaries Expense: An account that records from the payroll gross earnings for Office Salaries.

Wages and Salaries Payable: A liability account that shows net pay for payroll before payment is due.

DISCUSSION QUESTIONS

1. Explain how to calculate overtime.

2. What is the purpose of the Fair Labor Standards Act (Wage and Hours Law)?

3. Define and state the purpose of completing a W–4 form (Employee's Withholding Certificate).

4. Usually, claiming more allowances on a W–4 results in receiving more money per paycheck. Please comment.

5. All payroll registers must be special journals. True or false? Please comment.

6. True or false: the taxable earnings column of a payroll register records the amount of tax due.

7. Define and state the purpose of FICA.

8. The employer doesn't have to contribute to Social Security. Do you agree or disagree?

9. Explain how federal and state income tax withholding are determined.

10. What is a calendar year?

11. Define the purpose of a wage bracket table.

12. What purpose does the employee individual earnings record serve?

13. Why does payroll information center on 13-week quarters?

14. Draw a diagram showing how the following relate: (a) weekly payroll, (b) payroll register, (c) individual earnings, (d) journal entries, (e) cash payments journal.

15. If you earned $120,000 this year, you would pay more FICA than your partner, who earned $60,000. Do you agree or disagree? Explain.

EXERCISES

1. Calculate the total wages earned for each employee (assume an overtime rate of time and a half over 40 hours):

Calculating wages with overtime

EMPLOYEE	HOURLY RATE	NO. OF HOURS WORKED
Bob Role	$ 8	35
Jill West	$10	44
Dale Aster	$12	46

2. Compute the net pay for each employee using the tables in text. (Assume a FICA rate of 7.65 percent on $52,000.) Payroll is paid weekly.

	STATUS	CLAIMS	CUMULATIVE PAY	THIS WEEKS' PAY
Alvin Cell	Married	1	$40,000	$1,150
Angel Lowe	Single	1	$51,850	$ 510

There is no state income tax.

3. Complete the table.

Categorizing accounts.

	CATEGORY	↑	DR./CR.	ACCOUNT APPEARS ON WHICH FINANCIAL REPORT?
Medical Insurance Payable				
Wages and Salaries Payable				
Office Salaries Expense				
Market Wages Expense				
FICA Tax Payable				
Federal Income Tax Payable				
State Income Tax Payable				

Payroll register and the journal entry.

4. The following weekly payroll journal entry was prepared by Luster Co. Which columns of the payroll register has the data come from? How does the taxable earnings column relate to this entry?

Oct.	7	Shop Expense	4 0 0 0 00			
		Factory Wages Expense	2 0 0 0 00			
		FICA Tax Payable			8 1 5 00	
		Federal Income Tax Payable			1 2 0 0 00	
		State Income Tax Payable			9 0 0 00	
		Union Dues Payable			1 1 0 00	
		Wages and Salaries Payable			2 9 7 5 00	

Paying the payroll.

5. From Exercise 4, prepare an entry to pay the payroll from the cash payments journal given the following (on October 9):

	EMPLOYEES' NET PAY	CK. NO.
Dick Right	$1,000	114
Alice Fall	500	115
Jody Reeves	1,475	116

(Use the same headings for the cash payments journal that we have used in the chapter.)

GROUP A PROBLEMS

Calculating gross earnings with overtime.

9A-1. From the following information, please complete the chart for gross earnings for the week. (Assume an overtime rate of time and a half over 40 hours.)

		HOURLY RATE	NO. OF HOURS WORKED	GROSS EARNINGS
A.	Joe Jones	$ 6	40	
B.	Edna Kane	8	47	
C.	Dick Wall	10	42	
D.	Pat Green	12	50	

9A-2. March Company has five salaried employees. Your task is to record the following information into a payroll register.

EMPLOYEE	DEPT.	ALLOWANCE AND MARITAL STATUS	CUMULATIVE EARNINGS BEFORE THIS PAYROLL	WEEKLY SALARY
Kool, Alice	Sales	M–1	$39,800	$ 900
Lose, Bob	Office	S–1	41,900	450
Moore, Linda	Office	M–2	51,800	1,200
Relt, Rusty	Sales	M–3	25,000	700
Veel, Larry	Sales	S–0	29,000	250

Completing a payroll register.

Assume the following:

1. FICA rate is 7.65 percent on $52,000
2. Each employee contributes $25 per week for union dues.
3. State income tax is 6 percent of gross pay.
4. FIT is calculated from tables in text.

Completing a payroll register and journalizing the payroll entry.

9A-3. The bookkeeper of Gore Co. gathered the following data from employees' individual earnings records as well as daily time cards. Your task is to (1) complete a payroll register on Dec. 12 and (2) journalize the appropriate entry to record the payroll.

EMPLOYEE	ALLOWANCE AND MARITAL STATUS	M	T	W	T	F	HOURLY RATE OF PAY	DEPT.	CUMULATIVE EARNINGS BEFORE THIS PAYROLL
Boy, Pete	M–1	5	11	8	8	8	$16	Sales	$52,000
Heat, Donna	S–0	8	10	9	9	4	8	Office	15,000
Pyle, Ray	M–3	8	10	10	10	10	14	Sales	50,000
Vent, Joan	S–1	8	8	8	8	8	6	Office	19,000

Assume the following:

1. FICA rate is 7.65 percent on $52,000.
2. Federal income tax is calculated from tables in text.
3. Each employee contributes $25 per week for health insurance.
4. Overtime is paid at a rate of time and a half over 40 hours.

Payroll register completed; journalizing, posting, and paying the payroll.

9A-4. Gary Nelson, Accountant, has gathered the following data from the time cards and individual earnings records. Your task is to

1. On Dec. 5, 19XX prepare a payroll register for this weekly payroll.
2. Journalize (p. 4) and post the payroll entry.
3. Record the payment of the payroll on Dec. 7 to each employee.

	ALLOWANCE AND MARITAL STATUS	SALARY	CK. NO.	CUMULATIVE EARNINGS BEFORE THIS PAYROLL	DEPT.
Aulson, Andy	M–3	$ 640	30	$29,000	Factory
Flynn, Jacki	M–1	860	31	46,000	Office
Moore, Jeff	M–2	1,100	32	51,000	Factory
Sullivan, Alison	M–1	1,000	33	53,000	Office

Assume the following:

1. FICA rate is 7.65 percent on $52,000.
2. Federal income tax is calculated from tables in text.
3. State income tax is 6 percent.
4. Union dues are $25 per week.

GROUP B PROBLEMS

Calculating gross earnings with overtime.

9B-1. For the following employees, calculate their gross earnings. Assume an overtime rate of time and a half over 40 hours.

	HOURLY RATE	NO. OF HOURS WORKED	GROSS EARNINGS
Joe Jones	$ 5.00	40	
Edna Kane	9.00	47	
Dick Wall	12.00	36	
Pat Green	14.00	55	

Completing a payroll register.

9B-2. As the bookkeeper of March Company, record the following information into a payroll register.

	DEPT.	ALLOWANCE AND MARITAL STATUS	CUMULATIVE EARNINGS BEFORE THIS PAYROLL	WEEKLY SALARY
Kool, Alice	Sales	M–1	$ 9,000	$ 800
Lose, Bob	Office	S–1	12,000	370
Moore, Linda	Office	M–2	51,700	1,050
Relt, Rusty	Sales	M–3	39,800	900
Veel, Larry	Sales	S–0	16,950	480

Assume the followings:

1. FICA rate is 7.65 percent on $52,000.
2. Each employee contributes $30 per week for union dues.
3. State income tax is 5 percent of gross pay.
4. FIT is calculated from tables in text.

Completing a payroll register and journalizing the payroll entry.

9B-3. Ray Cone received a memo requesting him to

1. Complete a payroll register on Dec. 5, 19XX.
2. Prepare a general journal payroll entry. Ray gathered the following data from employees' individual earnings records as well as from daily time cards. Please assist Ray.

EMPLOYEE	ALLOWANCE AND MARITAL STATUS	DAILY TIME M	T	W	T	F	HOURLY RATE OF PAY	DEPT.	CUMULATIVE EARNINGS BEFORE THIS PAYROLL
Boy, Peter	S–1	12	11	7	7	7	$ 8	Sales	$52,000
Heat, Donna	S–0	8	9	9	9	5	10	Office	18,000
Pyle, Ray	M–3	10	10	10	10	10	12	Sales	51,900
Vent, Joan	S–1	6	8	8	8	8	5	Office	8,000

Assume the following:

1. FICA rate is 7.65 percent on $52,000.
2. Federal income tax is calculated from tables in text.

3. Each employee contributes $20 per week for health insurance.

4. Overtime is paid at a rate of time and a half over 40 hours.

9B-4. Gary Nelson has supplied you with the following data that was gathered from time cards and individual earnings records. Your task is to

Payroll register completed; journalizing, posting, and paying the payroll.

1. On Dec. 12, 19XX prepare a payroll register for this weekly payroll.

2. Journalize and post the payroll entry. (Journal is p. 4)

3. Record the payment of the payroll on Dec. 14 to each employee.

	ALLOWANCE AND MARITAL STATUS	SALARY	CK. NO.	CUMULATIVE EARNINGS BEFORE THIS PAYROLL	DEPT.
Aulson, Andy	M–3	$ 660	61	$48,000	Factory
Flynn, Jacki	M–1	900	62	51,600	Office
Moore, Jeff	M–2	1,000	63	52,000	Factory
Sullivan, Alison	M–1	1,200	64	55,000	Office

Assume the following:

1. FICA rate is 7.65 percent on $52,000.

2. Federal income tax is to be calculated from tables in text.

3. State income tax is 6 percent of gross pay.

4. Union dues are $25 per week.

PRACTICAL ACCOUNTING APPLICATION # 1

Small Co., a proprietorship, has two employees, Jim Roy and Janice Alter. The owner of Small Co. is Bert Ryan. During the current pay period, Jim has worked 48 hours and Janice 56. The reason for these extra hours is that both Jim and Janice worked their regular 40-hour work week, plus Jim worked 8 extra hours on Sunday while Janice worked 8 extra hours on Saturday as well as Sunday. Their contract with Small Co. is that they are each paid an hourly rate of $8 per hour with all hours over 40 to be time and a half as well as double time on Sunday. Bert, the owner, feels he is also entitled to a salary, since he works as many hours. He plans to pay himself $425 per week.

As the accountant of Small Co., calculate the gross pay for Jim and Janice and offer some advice to Bert regarding his salary.

PRACTICAL ACCOUNTING APPLICATION # 2

Marcy Moore works for Moose Co. during the day and GTA company at night. Both her employers have deducted FICA taxes at a rate of 7.65 percent on the first $52,000 of earnings. At year end Marcy has earned $48,000 at her job at Moose Co. and $5,000 at her night job at GTA.

At a party she meets Bill Barnes, an accountant, who tells her she has paid too much social security tax and that she is entitled to a refund or credit on the next calendar year's taxes. He tells her to call the Internal Revenue Service's toll-free number and ask for taxpayer assistance.

As Marcy's friend, check to see if Bill Barnes' advice is correct.

THE EMPLOYER'S TAX RESPONSIBILITIES:
Principles
and Procedures

Back in Chapter 9, we looked at how Fred's Market computed and recorded payroll data about its **employees**. This chapter focuses on specific tax responsibilities of the **employer**.

LEARNING UNIT 10-1

The Employer's Payroll Tax Expense

Every employer, when opening a business, has to get a federal **employer indentification number** for purposes of reporting earnings, taxes, etc. To get this number, Fred filled out an SS–4 Form. The SS–4 form asks for the following information:

1. Name.
2. Trade name.
3. Address or place of business.
4. County of business location.
5. Type of organization.
6. Ending month of accounting year.
7. Reason for applying.
8. Date starting business.
9. First date wages will be paid.
10. Number of employees.
11. Nature of business.

If you take over another employer's business, do not use that employer's number. If you don't have your own number by the time a return is due, write "Applied for" and the date you applied in the space shown for the number.

Fred is also responsible for sending in money withheld from employee's paychecks (FICA and federal and state income tax), but these are not taxes that Fred is paying.

Fred's payroll tax responsibilities are recorded in the general journal at the same time the payroll is recorded (as shown in Chapter 9). The three taxes that Fred's Market is responsible for include Social Security (FICA), state unemployment (SUTA), and federal unemployment (FUTA). The sum total of these three taxes is recorded in the **Payroll Tax Expense** account. Let's now look at how Fred calculates the amount of each tax.

CALCULATING THE EMPLOYER'S PAYROLL TAXES

1. FICA (Federal Insurance Contribution Act)

Whatever its employees pay into FICA, it is the responsibility of Fred's Market to match the contribution. The FICA Tax Payable account in the ledger (one we used in Chapter 9) will record the FICA tax for both the employee and the employer. To arrive at FICA tax owned by Fred, we use the FICA taxable earnings column from the payroll register. It is reproduced here for your convenience as Figure 10-1.

For this pay period, employees had earnings subject to FICA taxes of $2,292. Remember this is not the FICA tax but earnings subject to the tax. To calculate the FICA tax, we multiply the FICA taxable earnings times the FICA rate of 7.65%.

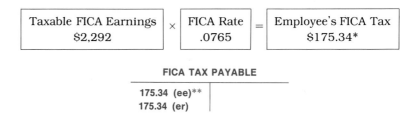

| Taxable FICA Earnings $2,292 | × | FICA Rate .0765 | = | Employee's FICA Tax $175.34* |

FICA TAX PAYABLE

175.34 (ee)**
175.34 (er)

2. FUTA (Federal Unemployment Tax Act)

The federal government and the states are involved in a joint federal-state unemployment insurance program. Each state administers its own unemployment program to its unemployed workers. The state programs are approved by the federal government. To raise money for these unemployment programs, the Federal Unemployment Tax Act (FUTA) levies a tax only on the **employers**. (This **Federal Unemployment Tax** is referred to as **FUTA** tax.) The Act was intended to (1) induce states to create their own unemployment programs and thus receive a credit against the FUTA tax, and (2) allow the federal government to monitor state programs.

Currently the FUTA tax is 6.2 percent of wages paid during the year. The tax applies to the first $7,000 you pay each employee as wages during the calendar year. Generally, you can take a credit against your FUTA tax for contributions you paid into state unemployment funds. This credit cannot be more than 5.4 percent of taxable wages. Employers are responsible for paying FUTA tax; it must not be deducted from employees' wages.

$$\begin{array}{r} 6.2\% \\ -\ 5.4\% \\ \hline .8\% \end{array} \text{ tax for Fred}$$

In Learning Unit 10-3 we will look at how to complete the report and the deposit requirements for the FUTA tax. For now, let's calculate the amount of accumulated federal unemployment tax for Fred based on the unemployment column under taxable earnings in the payroll register. Remember, the figure of $422 represents the amount of earnings taxable for federal unemployment.

To calculate the FUTA tax we multiply the FUTA taxable earnings times the FUTA rate.

| Taxable FUTA Earnings $422 | × | FUTA Rate .008 | = | FUTA Tax $3.38 | | FUTA Tax Payable |
| | | | | | | 3.38 |

* Due to rounding, you might be off a cent or two compared to employees' contribution.

** (ee) is shorthand for *employee* and (er) for *employer*.

FIGURE 10-1 Payroll Register for Fred's Market.

Employee Name	Allowance and Marital Status	Cumulative Earnings	Salary per Week	No. of Hrs.	Wages per Hr.	Earnings		Gross	Cumulative Earnings	Taxable Earnings	
						Regular	Overtime			Unemployment	FICA
Flynn, Bob	S-0	6900 00		30	9 00	270 00	—	270 00	7170 00	100 00	270 00
Frost, Abby	S-1	6500 00		44	7 00	280 00	42 00	322 00	6822 00	322 00	322 00
O'Reilly, Susan	M-3	56250 00	1250 00			1250 00	—	1250 00	57500 00	—	—
Rase, Paula	M-1	31500 00	700 00			700 00	—	700 00	32200 00	—	700 00
Regan, Al	M-2	45000 00	1000 00			1000 00	—	1000 00	46000 00	—	1000 00
		146150 00	2950 00			3500 00	42 00	3542 00	149692 00	422 00	2292 00
	(A)	(B)	(C)			(D)	(E)	(F)	(G)	(H)	(I)

FUTA tax is paid once a year if the total amount owed is less than $100, if the amount owed is more than $100, FUTA Tax is paid quarterly, by the end of the month following the quarter.

Some states charge a higher rate.

3. SUTA (State Unemployment Tax Act)

Most states, under a State Unemployment Tax Act, charge employers 5.4 percent **State Unemployment Tax** (**SUTA** tax) on the first $7,000 paid each employee to support individual unemployment insurance programs.*

States offer employers a **merit-rating plan** that reduces their state unemployment tax rate if they do not lay off employees during slack seasons (such as after Christmas). This inducement to stabilization of employment can provide substantial tax savings to the employer.

The state unemployment tax rate for Fred is 5.4 percent. From the taxable earnings column of the payroll register (p. 261), we multiply $422 by the SUTA rate of 5.4%.

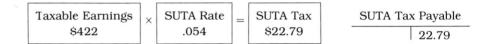

$$\boxed{\begin{array}{c}\text{Taxable Earnings}\\ \$422\end{array}} \times \boxed{\begin{array}{c}\text{SUTA Rate}\\ .054\end{array}} = \boxed{\begin{array}{c}\text{SUTA Tax}\\ \$22.79\end{array}} \qquad \begin{array}{c}\text{SUTA Tax Payable}\\ \hline \qquad | \ 22.79\end{array}$$

SUTA tax is usually paid quarterly.

JOURNALIZING PAYROLL TAX EXPENSE

Before showing the general journal entry to record Fred's Market payroll tax expense, let's review the categories and rules that affect the specific payroll ledger accounts that record this expense.

Account Affected	Category	↑ ↓	Rules
Payroll Tax Expense	**Expense**	↑	**Dr.**
FICA Tax Payable (FICA)	**Liability**	↑	**Cr.**
State Unemployment Tax Payable, (SUTA)	**Liability**	↑	**Cr.**
Federal Unemployment Tax Payable, (FUTA)	**Liability**	↑	**Cr.**

The total of FICA (for employer), SUTA, and FUTA taxes equals the total of Fred's payroll tax expense.

The Journal Entry

The following is the general journal entry recording Fred's payroll tax expense for the weekly payroll ending November 18. (We will look carefully at the ledger in Learning Unit 10-2.)

* For the current rate, check with your state unemployment department. In certain states, employees may have to contribute.

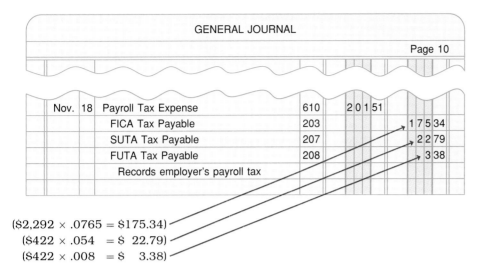

GENERAL JOURNAL

Page 10

Nov.	18	Payroll Tax Expense	610	2 0 1 51	
		FICA Tax Payable	203		1 7 5 34
		SUTA Tax Payable	207		2 2 79
		FUTA Tax Payable	208		3 38
		Records employer's payroll tax			

($2,292 × .0765 = $175.34)
($422 × .054 = $ 22.79)
($422 × .008 = $ 3.38)

In Learning Unit 10-2 we'll look at how to complete the form that goes along with the payment of FICA Taxes of the employee and the employer along with the amounts of federal income tax deducted from employees' paycheck. It is important to keep in mind that SUTA and FUTA taxes also have separate forms to be completed, which we will look at in Learning Unit 10-3.

For now, at this point you should be able to

1. Explain the purpose of form SS-4.   (p. 259)
2. Explain the use of the taxable earnings column in calculating the employer's payroll tax expense.   (p. 260)
3. Calculate the employer's payroll taxes.   (p. 260)
4. Explain the difference between FUTA and SUTA taxes.   (p. 262)
5. Explain when FUTA and SUTA taxes are paid.   (p. 262)
6. Journalize the employer's payroll tax expense.   (p. 263)

SELF-REVIEW QUIZ 10-1

Given the following, prepare the general journal entry to record the payroll tax expense for Bill Co. for the weekly payroll of July 8. Assume: (a) SUTA rate of 5.6 percent on first $7,000 of earnings; (b) FUTA tax rate of .8 percent on first $7,000 of earnings; (c) FICA rate is 7.65 percent on first $52,000.

EMPLOYEE	CUMULATIVE PAY BEFORE THIS WEEK'S PAYROLL	GROSS PAY FOR WEEK
Bill Jones	$6,000	$800
Julie Warner	6,600	400
Al Brooks	7,900	700

SOLUTION TO SELF-REVIEW QUIZ 10-1

July	8	Payroll Tax Expense		2 2 2 15	
		FICA Tax Payable			1 4 5 35
		SUTA Tax Payable			6 7 20
		FUTA Tax Payable			9 60

$$\begin{aligned}\text{FICA:} \quad & \$1,900 \times .0765 = \$145.35 \\ \text{SUTA:} \quad & 1,200 \times .056 = 67.20 \\ \text{FUTA:} \quad & 1,200 \times .008 = \underline{\quad 9.60} \\ & \hphantom{1,200 \times .008 = } \$222.15 \end{aligned}$$

Note. Al Brooks earned more than $7,000; thus his employer takes no SUTA or FUTA taxes on the $700 of Al's gross pay.

LEARNING UNIT 10-2

Form 941: Completing the Employer's Quarterly Federal Tax Return and Paying Tax Obligations for FICA Tax and Federal Income Tax

In this unit, we will look at the last quarter (October, November and December) of the year for Fred's Market.

Our goal is to look at the timing for paying FICA (for employee and employer) and FIT, along with the completion of Form 941, the Employer's Quarterly Federal Tax Return.

Before getting into specific deposit rules and form completions, let's take a look at Figure 10-2 which represents a work sheet that was developed by

FIGURE 10-2

Work Sheet for Payroll at Fred's Market During the Last Quarter.

DEPOSITS DUE

Deposit tax within 3 banking days after end of eighth-monthly period (which ends on the 22nd).

Deposit tax within 3 banking days after end of eighth-monthly period (which ends on the 19th).

Deposit tax within 3 banking days after end of eighth-monthly period (which ends on the 19th).

Due by end of following month.

Amount of taxes owed for:
  FICA (ee)
+ FICA (er)
+ federal income tax (ee)
equals frequency of needed deposits.

Definition of eighth-monthly period follows the summary of deposit rules.

FRED'S MARKET
WORK SHEET
MONITORING DEPOSIT REQUIREMENTS
RELATING TO FORM 941

Payroll Period		Earnings*	FIT	FICA EE and ER	Total Tax	Cumulative Tax
Oct.	7	3 5 4 2 00	5 5 9 00	5 4 1 94	1 1 0 0 94	1 1 0 0 94
	14	3 5 4 2 00	5 5 9 00	5 4 1 94	1 1 0 0 94	2 2 0 1 88
	21	3 5 4 2 00	5 5 9 00	4 6 5 44 **	1 0 2 4 44	3 2 2 6 32
	28	3 5 4 2 00	5 5 9 00	3 5 0 68	9 0 9 68	9 0 9 68
		14 1 6 8 00	2 2 3 6 00	1 9 0 0 00	4 1 3 6 00	
Nov.	4	3 5 4 2 00	5 5 9 00	3 5 0 68	9 0 9 68	1 8 1 9 36
	11	3 5 4 2 00	5 5 9 00	3 5 0 68	9 0 9 68	2 7 2 9 04
	18	3 5 4 2 00	5 5 9 00	3 5 0 68	9 0 9 68	3 6 3 8 72
	25	3 5 4 2 00	5 5 9 00	3 5 0 68	9 0 9 68	9 0 9 68
		14 1 6 8 00	2 2 3 6 00	1 4 0 2 72	3 6 3 8 72	
Dec.	2	3 5 4 2 00	5 5 9 00	3 5 0 68	9 0 9 68	1 8 1 9 36
	9	3 5 4 2 00	5 5 9 00	3 5 0 68	9 0 9 68	2 7 2 9 04
	16	3 5 4 2 00	5 5 9 00	3 5 0 68	9 0 9 68	3 6 3 8 72
	23	3 5 4 2 00	5 5 9 00	3 5 0 68	9 0 9 68	9 0 9 68
	30	3 5 4 2 00	5 5 9 00	3 5 0 68	9 0 9 68	1 8 1 9 36
		17 7 1 0 00	2 7 9 5 00	1 7 5 3 40	4 5 4 8 40	
Total for Quarter		46 0 4 6 00	7 2 6 7 00	5 0 5 6 12	12 3 2 3 12	

* We assume same earnings each week.

** FICA is being reduced since part of O'Reilly's salary is not taxed for FICA. By Oct. 28 her salary is exempt from tax for FICA.

Fred's accountant to monitor Fred's Market deposit requirements regarding FICA and FIT. This work sheet has nothing to do with SUTA or FUTA. Use it as a guide to upcoming information. Do note on the work sheet that the quarter is 13 weeks and FICA payments decreased on Oct. 21 and 28, since Susan O'Reilly had earned more than $52,000 on the latter date. This work sheet can be built from information for each individual's earnings record and payroll register.

Now let's look at the deposit rules Fred's Market must follow regarding FICA and FIT.

DEPOSIT OF TAX DUE

The amount of tax due must be deposited in an authorized depository or a Federal Reserve bank in Fred's area.

Fred's bookkeeper uses the tables of rules that are provided on the back of Form 941. The following is a summary of those rules:

Summary of Deposit Rules

ACCUMULATED
AMOUNT OF UNPAID FICA (EE), FICA (ER), AND FEDERAL INCOME TAX (EE)

LIABILITIES	WHEN DEPOSIT IS REQUIRED
Rule 1. Less than $500 at the end of the calendar quarter.	**Rule 1.** If at the end of the quarter your total undeposited taxes for the quarter are less than $500, you do not have to deposit the taxes. You may pay the taxes to the IRS with Form 941, or you may deposit them by the due date of the return.
Rule 2. Less than $500 at the end of any month.	**Rule 2.** If at the end of any month your total undeposited taxes are less than $500, you do not have to make a deposit. You may carry the taxes over to the following month within the quarter.
Rule 3. $500 or more but less than $3,000 at the end of any month.	**Rule 3.** If at the end of any month your total undeposited taxes are $500 or more but less than $3,000, you must deposit the taxes within 15 days after the end of the month—assuming no eighth-monthly deposits were made during the month.
Rule 4. $3,000 or more at the end of any eighth-monthly period.	**Rule 4.*** If at the end of any eighth-monthly period your total undeposited taxes are $3,000** or more, deposit the taxes within three banking days after the end of the eighth-monthly period. (Do not count as banking days local holidays observed by authorized financial institutions, Saturdays, Sundays, and legal holidays.)

* For exceptions to this rule see back of Form 941.

** The Tax Act of 1989 has mandated a major change in the deposits of payroll taxes made by large firms. Beginning August 1, 1990, employers who have accumulated payroll taxes of $100,000 or more must deposit those taxes on the first banking day after reaching that amount. In 1991 these firms may wait until the second banking day and in 1992 until the third day. The deposit date returns to the first banking day in 1993 and 1994. From 1995 onward, the Treasury Department can establish the dates for depositing six figure payroll taxes.

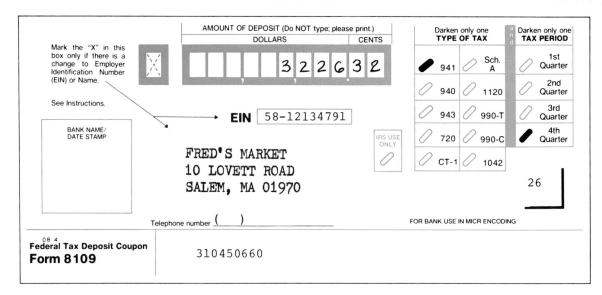

FIGURE 10-3 Form 8109.

Eighth-Monthly Periods

1–3
4–7
8–11
12–15
16–19
20–22
23–25
26–end of month

Eighth-Monthly Periods: Each month is divided into eight deposit periods that end on the 3rd, 7th, 11th, 15th, 19th, 22nd, 25th, and last day of the month.

Using Figure 10-2 (p. 264) we can see that the first deposit will not be due until after the October 21 payroll since the cumulative tax of FICA and FIT was less than $3,000. Thus, by using Rule 4, a deposit of $3,226.32 is made within 3 banking days after the end of the eighth-monthly period (which ends on the 22nd). Thus a deposit is due by October 25th.

Completion of Form 8109 to Accompany Deposits

Fred received a book of federal tax deposit coupons, **Form 8109**. These coupons are completed when the taxes owed are paid to an appropriate Federal Reserve Bank or to an authorized commercial depository (the deposit is not sent directly to the Internal Revenue Service). The coupon shown in Figure 10-3 was prepared by Fred's accountant.

Payments for taxes are recorded in the cash payments journal as follows:

Accounts Affected	Category	↑ ↓	Dr./Cr.
FICA Tax Payable	Liability	↓	Dr.
Federal Income Tax Payable	Liability	↓	Dr.
Cash	Asset	↓	Cr.

			CASH PAYMENTS JOURNAL					
								Page 18
Date	Check No.	Account/Payment to	PR	Sundry Dr.	Accounts Payable Dr.	Purchases Discount Cr.	Cash Cr.	
Oct. 25	218	FICA Tax Payable*	203	1 5 4 9 32				
		Federal Income Tax Payable*	204	1 6 7 7 00			3 2 2 6 32	

* FICA = $541.94 + $541.94 + $465.44 = $1,549.32 (see Fig. 10-2, p. 264)

** FIT = $559 × 3 = $1,677

PARTIAL GENERAL LEDGER

FICA Tax Payable 203

	Date		PR	Dr.	Cr.	Cr. Bal.
	19X8 Oct.	7	GJ8		270 97	270 97
		7	GJ8		270 97	541 94
		14	GJ8		270 97	812 91
		14	GJ8		270 97	1083 88
		21	GJ9		232 72	1316 60
		21	GJ9		232 72	1549 32
		25	CPJ18	1549 32		-0-
		28	GJ9		175 34	175 34
		28	GJ9		175 34	350 68

PARTIAL GENERAL LEDGER

Federal Income Tax Payable 204

	Date		PR	Dr.	Cr.	Cr. Bal.
	19XX Oct.	7	GJ8		559 00	559 00
		14	GJ8		559 00	1118 00
		21	GJ9		559 00	1677 00
		25	CPJ18	1677 00		-0-
		28	GJ9		559 00	559 00

When employer makes deposit on Oct. 25, balance of Federal Income Tax Payable is—0—.

Let's now look at the partial general ledger of Fred's Market to get a better understanding of how specific payroll accounts in the ledger are updated regarding FICA and FIT. Note in the FICA Tax Payable account (above) how postings came from the general journal for the employees' and employer's share of FICA tax. The payment from the cash payments journal is recorded as a debit to FICA Tax Payable on October 25. Also note in the Federal Income Tax Payable account (above) how the balance on October 28 is now $559. Figure 10-2 and p. 263 are good sources to look back at for these figures.

FORM 941: EMPLOYER'S QUARTERLY FEDERAL TAX RETURN

In order to complete Form 941, the bookkeeper has prepared the figures shown in Figure 10-2 (p. 264) from the payroll register and individual earnings record.

Figure 10-4 shows the completed Employer's Quarterly Federal Tax Return that is filed by Fred's Market to the appropriate Internal Revenue Service Center by one month after end of quarter. If all taxes were deposited by Fred during the calendar quarter, the return could be sent in by the tenth of the second month following the end of the quarter. Let's now take a moment to explain how the form was completed.

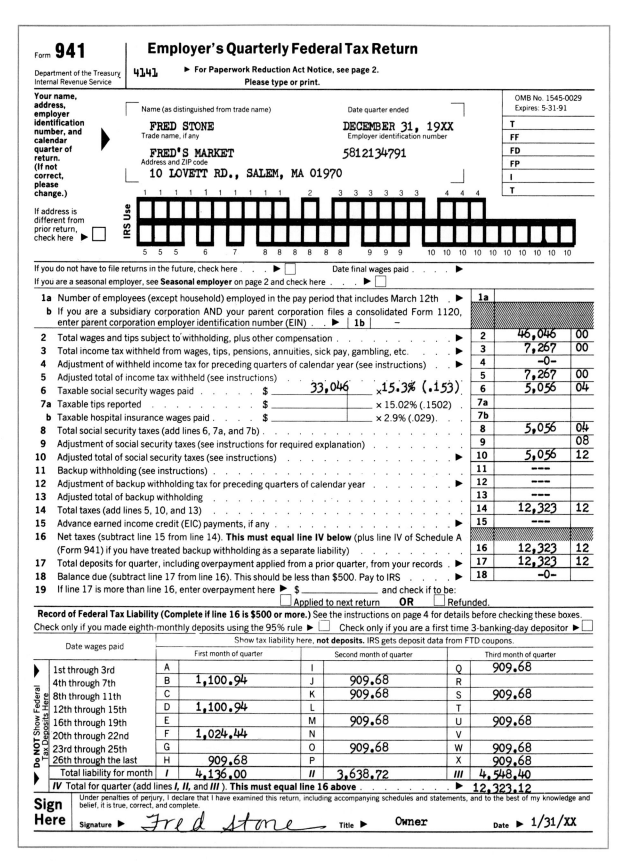

FIGURE 10-4 Completed Form 941: The Employer's Quarterly Tax Return.

Filling Out Form 941

The top section of the form identifies Fred's Market, its address, the date the quarter ended, and Fred's identification number.

LINE

1 Number of employees: 5

2 Total gross pay: $46,046($14,168 + $14,168 + $17,710)
Oct.   Nov.   Dec.

3 Total income tax: $7,267($2,236 + $2,236 + $2,795)

6 The reason Line 6 uses $33,046 rather than $46,046 is that $13,000 of Susan O'Reilly's salary is not taxed for Social Security since she has earned more than $52,000.

9 Owing to rounding, an additional 8 cents is added to Line 9 as an adjustment. The goal is to have Line 16 equal Part IV at the bottom of the form. See marginal note.

14 Total income tax, $7,267, plus adjusted total of Social Security, $5,056.12 equals $12,323.12.

17 Total of deposits is $12,323.12, which Fred has sent in with Form 8109.

18 The total tax obligations for the quarter have been paid in by Fred, resulting in no new tax liability.

Fraction of cents: If there is a difference between the total tax on Line 8 and the total deducted from your employees' wages or tips because of fractions of cents added or dropped in collecting the tax, report the difference on Line 9. If this difference is the only entry, write "Fractions Only" in the margin.

Note on the bottom section that the tax liability for each eighth-monthly period is shown. The amount of federal tax deposits is not shown here. The deposits are shown on the deposit coupons.

At this point, you should be able to

1. Explain which taxes are reported on Form 941.   (p. 264)
2. Explain the summary of deposit rules.   (p. 265)
3. Define an eighth-monthly period.   (p. 266)
4. Prepare, and explain the purpose of, Form 8109.   (p. 266)
5. Record the journal entry to pay FICA and federal income taxes.   (p. 266)
6. Complete an Employer's Quarterly Federal Tax Return.   (pp. 268–269)

SELF-REVIEW QUIZ 10-2

Indicate when the FICA (for employee and employer) and federal income taxes should be deposited based on rules for deposit requirements.

1. Total tax due for quarter, $422.
2. Taxes on wages paid: October, $450; November, $550.
3. Taxes on wages paid from the 1st through the 3rd of the month, $3,600.
4. Taxes on wages paid from the 4th through the 7th, $2,600; from the 8th through the 11th, $2,500.

SOLUTION TO SELF-REVIEW QUIZ 10-2

1. Tax less than $500. Deposit tax by end of month after quarter.
2. Tax due by December 15, $450 + $550 = $1,000.
3. Tax due within three banking days after the 3rd.
4. Add both together ($2,600 + $2,500); total of $5,100 is due within three banking days after the 11th of the month.

W-2, W-3, Form 940, and Workers' Compensation

W-2: WAGE AND TAX STATEMENT

Fred's Market is required by January 31 to give copies of **Form W-2**, **Wage and Tax Statement**, to each person who was employed in the past year. Anyone who stopped working for Fred before the end of that year may be given Form W-2 at any time after the employment ends. If one of Fred's employees (who left before the year end) asks for Form W-2, the employer must give him or her the completed copies within 30 days of the request or of the final wage payment, whichever is later. Employees then use this form to pay their personal income tax to federal, state, and local agencies.

Figure 10-5 is the W-2 that Susan O'Reilly received from Fred's Market. Note that this information was obtained from the individual earnings record. Take a moment to see that boxes 10 and 13 are different; Susan earned more than $52,000 and thus has $13,000 of wages exempt from Social Security tax.

W-3: TRANSMITTAL OF INCOME AND TAX STATEMENTS

The **Form W-3**, **Transmittal of Income and Tax Statements**, which is sent in by the employer, reports the total wages, tips, and compensations paid; the total federal income tax withheld; the total FICA wages; the total FICA tax withheld; and some other information. It is sent to the Social Security Administration along with a copy of each employee's W-2 forms.

FIGURE 10-5   Completed Form W-2.

1 Control number		OMB No. 1545-0008		
2 Employer's name, address, and ZIP code FRED'S MARKET 10 LOVETT ROAD SALEM, MA 01970		3 Employer's identification number 58-12134791 5 Statutory employee ☐ Deceased ☐ Pension plan ☐ Legal rep. ☐ 6 Allocated tips		4 Employer's state I.D. number 621-8966-4 942 emp. ☐ Subtotal ☐ Deferred compensation ☐ Void ☐ 7 Advance EIC payment
8 Employee's social security number 021-36-9494	9 Federal income tax withheld $11,648	10 Wages, tips, other compensation $65,000		11 Social security tax withheld $3,978
12 Employee's name, address, and ZIP code SUSAN O'REILLY 26 ROUNDY ROAD MARBLEHEAD, MA 01945		13 Social security wages $52,000		14 Social security tips
		16		16a Fringe benefits incl. in Box 10
		17 State income tax $3,250	18 State wages, tips, etc. $65,000	19 Name of state MA
		20 Local income tax	21 Local wages, tips, etc.	22 Name of locality

Form **W-2 Wage and Tax Statement**
This information is being furnished to the Internal Revenue Service.   Copy B To be filed with employee's FEDERAL tax return   Dept. of the Treasury—IRS

DO NOT STAPLE

1 Control number	33333	For Official Use Only ▶ OMB No. 1545-0008			

☐ **Kind of Payer** ▶	2 941/941E Military 943 ☐ ☐ ☐ CT-1 942 Medicare gov't. emp. ☐ ☐ ☐	3	4	5 Number of statements attached

6 Allocated tips	7 Advance EIC payments	8

9 Federal income tax withheld $29,068	10 Wages, tips, and other compensation $184,184	11 Social security tax withheld $13,015.58
12 Employer's state I.D. number 281-615	13 Social security wages $171,184	14 Social security tips -0-

15 Employer's identification number 58—12134791	16 Establishment number

17 Employer's name FRED'S MARKET 10 LOVETT ROAD SALEM, MA 01970	18 Gross annuity, pension, etc. (Form W-2P) -0-
	20 Taxable amount (Form W-2P) -0-
	21 Income tax withheld by third-party payer

19 Employer's address and ZIP code (If available, place label over boxes 15, 17, and 19.)

Under penalties of perjury, I declare that I have examined this return and accompanying documents, and to the best of my knowledge and belief they are true, correct, and complete. In the case of documents without recipients' identifying numbers, I have complied with the requirements of the law in attempting to secure such numbers from the recipients.

Signature ▶ *Fred Stine*   Title ▶ Owner   Date ▶ 1/31/XX

Form **W-3** Transmittal of Income and Tax Statements

Department of the Treasury
Internal Revenue Service

FIGURE 10-6   Completed Form W–3.

W–3 is to be sent to Social Security Administration by Feb. 28.

Form W–3 and the attached W–2's allow the Social Security Administration (as well as the IRS at a later date) to check that the withheld taxes reported on the W–2 are the same as reported by Fred on Form 941. The filled-in Form W–3 is shown in Figure 10-6.

The information used to complete the W–3 came from a summary of the individual earnings records that is shown below:

EMPLOYEE	TOTAL EARNINGS	FICA	FIT
Bob Flynn	$ 14,040	$1,074.06	$ 1,976
Abby Frost	16,744	1,200.92	2,080
Susan O'Reilly	65,000	3,978.00	11,648
Paula Rase	36,400	2,784.60	4,784
Al Regan	52,000	3,978.00	8,580
	$184,184	$13,015.58	$29,068

FORM 940: EMPLOYER'S ANNUAL FEDERAL UNEMPLOYMENT TAX RETURN

After the first year that Fred files this form, the IRS sends Fred a preaddressed **Form 940, Employer's Annual Federal Unemployment Tax Return**, near the close of each calendar year (also sent is the Federal Tax Deposit coupon,

Form 8109, discussed on p. 266). Form 940 must be filed no later than January 31 unless all required deposits have been made during the year, in which case the filing of the return can be postponed until February 10th. The completed form is shown in Figure 10-7 on p. 273.

Deposits are considered on time if mailed two days before due date or if bank receives it by due date.

Remember: Form 941 is for FICA tax and federal income tax; Form 940 is for FUTA tax.

As we saw earlier, the FUTA tax rate is .8 percent on the first $7,000 of each employee's gross pay. If Fred's *accumulated* FUTA tax liability is *more than* $100, it must be deposited with a Federal Reserve Bank or an authorized commercial bank on or before the last day of the month following the end of the quarter. As shown earlier, Fred would send payment along with Form 8109, indicating on that form that payment was for FUTA tax. If total tax for the year is less than $100, it can be paid along with the filing of Form 940. Table 10-1 shows how to calculate the tax for the year. Note on the form deposits of $280 have been made resulting in a zero balance owed.

At the end of the first quarter, Fred owes $168 for FUTA taxes. (See Table 10-1 with FUTA tax calculations.) Thus on April 30, Form 8109 is completed and the following journal entry is prepared.

			CASH PAYMENTS JOURNAL						
									Page 29
Date		Check No.	Account/Payment To	PR	Sundry Dr.	Accts. Pay. Dr.	Purch. Disc. Cr.	Cash Cr.	
Apr. 30		391	SUTA Payable		1 1 3 4 00			1 1 3 4 00	
30		394	FUTA Payable		1 6 8 00			1 6 8 00	

Note that Fred also pays the state unemployment tax of $1,134 which is due one month after the end of the quarter ($21,000 × .054).

WORKERS' COMPENSATION INSURANCE

Fred's Market is required to insure its employees against losses due to injury or death incurred during employment. This insurance is called **workers' compensation insurance**. Fred is required to estimate the cost of this insurance and pay the premium in advance.

TABLE 10-1   Computation of FUTA Tax for a Year

	QUARTER 1		
Taxable Earnings* × FUTA Rate			= FUTA Tax Payable
$21,000	.008		$168.00
	QUARTER 2		
$ 3,490	× .008	=	$ 27.92
	QUARTER 3		
$ 2,814	× .008	=	$ 22.51
	QUARTER 4		
$ 7,696	× .008	=	$ 61.57
Proof: $35,000	× .008	= Total FUTA tax liability	$280.00

* Tax is only on first $7,000 of earnings in a calender year for each employee.

Form 940

Department of the Treasury
Internal Revenue Service

Employer's Annual Federal Unemployment (FUTA) Tax Return

▶ For Paperwork Reduction Act Notice, see page 2.

OMB No. 1545-0028

T	
FF	
FD	
FP	
I	
T	

If incorrect, make any necessary change. ▶

Name (as distinguished from trade name)
FRED STONE

Calendar year
19XX

Trade name, if any
FRED'S MARKET

Address and ZIP code
10 LOVETT ROAD, SALEM, MA 01970

Employer identification number
58 - 12134791

A Did you pay all required contributions to state unemployment funds by the due date of Form 940? (See instructions if none required.) . . . ☒ Yes ☐ No

If you checked the "Yes" box, enter the amount of contributions paid to state unemployment funds . . . . . . ▶ $ _____

B Are you required to pay contributions to only one state? . . . . ☒ Yes ☐ No

If you checked the "Yes" box: (1) Enter the name of the state where you are required to pay contributions . . . . ▶ MASS

(2) Enter your state reporting number(s) as shown on state unemployment tax return. ▶ 281-615

C If any part of wages taxable for FUTA tax is exempt from state unemployment tax, check the box. (See the Specific Instructions on page 2.). . . . . ☐

Part I — Computation of Taxable Wages and Credit Reduction (to be completed by all taxpayers)

1	Total payments (including exempt payments) during the calendar year for services of employees	1	184,184 00
2	Exempt payments. (Explain each exemption shown, attaching additional sheets if necessary.) ▶ _____	2 (Amount paid)	
3	Payments for services of more than $7,000. Enter only the excess over the first $7,000 paid to individual employees not including exempt amounts shown on line 2. Do not use the state wage limitation.	3 149,184 00	
4	Total exempt payments (add lines 2 and 3)	4	149,184 00
5	**Total taxable wages** (subtract line 4 from line 1). (If any part is exempt from state contributions, see instructions.) ▶	5	35,000 00

Part II — Tax Due or Refund (Complete if you checked the "Yes" boxes in both questions A and B and did not check the box in C above.)

1	**Total FUTA tax.** Multiply the wages in Part I, line 5, by .008 and enter here	1	280 00
2	Minus: Total FUTA tax deposited for the year, including any overpayment applied from a prior year (from your records)	2	280 00
3	**Balance due** (subtract line 2 from line 1). This should be $100 or less. Pay to IRS . . . ▶	3	-0-
4	**Overpayment** (subtract line 1 from line 2). Check if it is to be: ☐ Applied to next return, or ☐ Refunded . . ▶	4	

Part III — Tax Due or Refund (Complete if you checked the "No" box in either question A or B or you checked the box in C above. Also complete Part V.)

1	Gross FUTA tax. Multiply the wages in Part I, line 5, by .062 . . .	1	
2	Maximum credit. Multiply the wages in Part I, line 5, by .054 . . .	2	
3	**Credit allowable:** Enter the smaller of the amount in Part V, line 11, or Part III, line 2 . .	3	
4	**Total FUTA tax** (subtract line 3 from line 1). . . .	4	
5	Minus: Total FUTA tax deposited for the year, including any overpayment applied from a prior year (from your records)	5	
6	**Balance due** (subtract line 5 from line 4). This should be $100 or less. Pay to IRS . . . ▶	6	
7	**Overpayment** (subtract line 4 from line 5). Check if it is to be: ☐ Applied to next return, or ☐ Refunded . . ▶	7	

Part IV — Record of Quarterly Federal Tax Liability for Unemployment Tax (Do not include state liability.)

Quarter	First	Second	Third	Fourth	Total for Year
Liability for quarter	168.00	27.92	22.51	61.57	$280.00

Part V — Computation of Tentative Credit (Complete if you checked the "No" box in either question A or B or you checked the box in C, on page 1—see instructions.)

Name of state	State reporting number(s) as shown on employer's state contribution returns	Taxable payroll (as defined in state act)	State experience rate period		State experience rate	Contributions if rate had been 5.4% (col. 3 x .054)	Contributions payable at experience rate (col. 3 x col. 5)	Additional credit (col. 6 minus col. 7) If 0 or less, enter 0.	Contributions actually paid to the state
			From—	To—					
1	**2**	**3**	**4**		**5**	**6**	**7**	**8**	**9**

10 Totals . . . . ▶

11 Total tentative credit (add line 10, columns 8 and 9—see instructions for limitations) . . . . ▶

If you will not have to file returns in the future, write "Final" here (see general instruction "Who Must File") and sign the return. ▶

Under penalties of perjury, I declare that I have examined this return, including accompanying schedules and statements, and to the best of my knowledge and belief, it is true, correct, and complete, and that no part of any payment made to a state unemployment fund claimed as a credit was or is to be deducted from the payments to employees.

Signature ▶ *Fred Stone*   Title (Owner, etc.) ▶ Owner   Date ▶ 2/10/XX

Form **940**

FIGURE 10-7   Completed Form 940.

273

The greater the risks on the job, the higher the premium rates.

The premium is based upon the total estimated gross payroll and the rate is calculated per $100 of weekly payroll. At year end, the actual payroll is compared to the estimated payroll, and Fred will receive credit for any overpayment or possibly will pay additional premiums.

This affects Fred in the following ways:

1. Estimated payroll for Fred: $180,000.
2. Two grades of workers: office and stockroom.
3. Rate per $100: Office, $.14; stockroom, $1.90.
4. Estimated payroll: Office, $110,000; stockroom, $70,000.

Let's look at how the estimated premium is calculated:

$$\text{Office:} \quad \frac{\$110,000}{\$100} = 1,100 \times \$ .14 = \$ \ \ 154$$

$$\text{Stockroom:} \quad \frac{\$70,000}{\$100} = \ \ 700 \times \$1.90 = \underline{\ \ 1,330}$$

$$\textit{Total Estimated Premium:} \ \underline{\$1,484}$$

Accounts Affected	Category	↑ ↓	Dr./Cr.
Prepaid Insurance, Workers' Compensation	Asset	↑	Dr.
Cash	Asset	↓	Cr.

The prepaid insurance will be adjusted at year end.

Thus Fred would pay $1,484 in advance. At the end of the year, the actual payroll is as follows:

Office payroll: $105,000   Stockroom payroll: $79,184

Thus the actual premium should be

$$\text{Office:} \quad \frac{\$105,000}{\$100} = 1,050 \quad \times \$ .14 = \$ \ \ 147.00$$

$$\text{Stockroom:} \quad \frac{\$79,184}{\$100} = \ \ 791.84 \times \$1.90 = \underline{\ \ 1,504.50}$$

$$\textit{Total Actual Premium:} \ \underline{\$1,651.50}$$

Since the actual premium is $167.50 higher than the estimate ($1,651.50 − $1,484), Fred will pay this amount in January together with the estimated premium for the next year. This adjustment of $167.50 takes place on December 31 by a debit to Workers' Compensation Insurance Expense and a credit to Workers' Compensation Insurance Payable.

Account Affected	Category	↑ ↓	Dr./Cr.
Workers' Compensation Insurance Expense	Expense	↑	Dr.
Workers' Compensation Insurance Payable	Liability	↑	Cr.

At this point, you should be able to

1. Prepare a W–2. (p. 270)
2. Differentiate between a W–2 and W–3. (pp. 270–271)
3. Explain as well as prepare Form 940. (p. 272)

4. Calculate estimated premium for workers' compensation. (p. 274)

5. Prepare a journal entry to record as well as adjust premiums for workers' compensation. (p. 274)

SELF-REVIEW QUIZ 10-3

Respond true or false to the following:

1. W–4's must be received by employees by January 31 of the following year.

2. Form W–3 is sent to the Social Security Administration yearly.

3. The Employer's Annual Federal Unemployment Tax Return records the employer's FICA tax liability.

4. Tax liabilities for FUTA over $100 must be paid within 10 days at end of quarter.

5. Premiums for workers' compensation may be adjusted.

SOLUTIONS TO SELF-REVIEW QUIZ 10-3

1. False   **2.** True   **3.** False   **4.** False   **5.** True

SUMMARY OF KEY POINTS AND KEY TERMS

LEARNING UNIT 10-1

1. The Payroll Tax Expense for the employer is made up of FICA tax and state and federal unemployment insurance taxes.

2. The maximum amount of credit for state unemployment against the FUTA tax is 5.4 percent.

3. The Payroll Tax Expense is recorded at the time the payroll is recorded.

Employer identification number: Federal identification number of employer for purposes of reporting and paying taxes.

Federal unemployment tax (FUTA): A tax paid by employers to the federal government. The rate in 1990 was .8 percent on the first $7,000 of earnings of each employee.

Merit rating: A percentage rate assigned to a business by the state in calculating state unemployment tax. The lower the rating, the less tax must be paid. The rate is based upon the employment record of the employer.

Payroll Tax Expense: An account that records the total of the employer's FICA, SUTA, and FUTA tax responsibilities.

State unemployment tax (SUTA): A tax usually paid by employers to the state.

LEARNING UNIT 10-2

1. Form 941 is filed by the end of the month following the quarter. Taxes include FICA tax of employee and employer as well as federal income tax of the employee.

2. The amount of tax liability determines the frequency of deposits.

3. An eighth-monthly period means each month is divided into eight deposit periods that end on the 3rd, 7th, 11th, 15th, 19th, 22nd, 25th, and last day of the month.

4. Federal tax deposits are not shown on Form 941. The tax deposits are paid, along with Form 8109, to an appropriate Federal Reserve Bank or in an authorized commercial depository.

Form 941, Employer's Quarterly Federal Tax Return: A report to be completed for each quarter (three months) indicating total FICA owed plus federal income tax for the quarter. If federal tax deposits have been made correctly, the total deposit should equal the amount owed that is indicated on Form 941. If there is a difference, payment may be due.

Form 8109: A coupon that is completed and sent along with payments of tax deposits relating to Forms 940 and 941 (as well as other forms).

LEARNING UNIT 10-3

1. Information to prepare W–2's can be obtained from the individual earnings records of employees.

2. W–3's aid the Social Security Administration in verifying that taxes have been withheld as reported on the W–2's.

3. Form 940 is prepared by January 31st after the end of the calendar year. (Filing of the return can be postponed till February 10 if all required deposits are made during the year.) For FUTA tax, liabilities greater than $100 result in deposits being made before the last day of the month following the end of the quarter.

4. Workers' compensation insurance (the estimated premium) is paid at the beginning of the year by the employer to protect against potential losses to its employees due to injury or death incurred during employment.

Employer's Annual Federal Unemployment Tax Return (Form 940): A form used by employers at the end of the year to pay federal unemployment tax. If more than $100 is cumulatively owed in a quarter, it should be paid quarterly. Normally payment is due January 31 after the calendar year, or February 10 if deposits have already been made by an employer.

Form W–2, Wage and Tax Statement: A form completed by the employer at the end of the calendar year to provide a summary of gross earnings and deductions to each employee. At least two copies go to the employee, one copy to the IRS, and one copy into the records of the business.

Form W–3, Transmittal of Income and Tax Statements: A form completed by the employer to verify the number of W–2's and the amounts withheld as shown on them. The W–2's are attached to the Form W–3.

Workers' Compensation Insurance: Insurance paid for, in advance, by employer to protect its employees against loss due to injury or death incurred during employment.

Blueprint of the Tax Calendar: a Sampling of Due Dates Involving Employer's Tax Responsibilities

The following tax calendar shows a sampling of dates that an employer should be aware of. Although not shown here, an employer may be required to make eighth-monthly deposits if the amount due is over $3,000 for FICA (ee and er) and federal income tax. These deposits are due within three banking days after the 3rd, 7th, 11th, 15th, 19th, 22nd, 25th, and last day of each month. This tax calendar shows monthly and quarterly deposits.

JANUARY

15	Form 8109 Form 941	If tax liability at end of December was $500 or more but less than $3,000 (no eighth-monthly deposit occurred during December), monthly deposit of FICA and federal income taxes are due.
31	Form W–2	Furnish copies of W–2 to employees. (If terminated before year end, they may request

(Continued)

that the W–2 be sent to them within 30 days of last wage payment or the date of their request, whichever is later.)

JANUARY

31	Form 941	From fourth quarter of previous year form is due along with undeposited taxes due. If all tax liabilities were met, form is due on or before February 10.
31	Form 940	This annual form is due along with any undeposited taxes from previous year (less any deposits previously made). If employer has no tax liability, the form is due by February 10.

OCTOBER

31	Form 941	Form due along with tax liability of less than $500 for third quarter. If taxes were paid in full, form can be sent in by the 10th day of the second month following the third quarter.
31	Form 8109 Form 940	If accumulated tax liability exceeds $100, deposit is due.

NOVEMBER

10	Form 941	Form due from third quarter if all deposits were made for third quarter of year on time.
15	Form 8109 Form 941	If tax liability for October was $500 or more but less than $3,000 (no eighth-monthly deposit was made during October) monthly deposit of FICA and federal income taxes are due.

DECEMBER

15	Form 8109 Form 941	If tax liability for November was $500 or more but less than $3,000 (no eighth-monthly deposit was made during November) monthly deposit of FICA and federal income taxes are due.

DISCUSSION QUESTIONS

1. What taxes make up Payroll Tax Expense?
2. Explain how an employer can receive a credit against the FUTA tax due.
3. Explain a merit-rating plan.
4. List the deposit requirements relating to Form 941 if the total tax due is $500 or more but less than $3,000 at the end of the month.
5. What is the purpose of Form 8109?
6. How often is Form 941 completed?
7. Federal tax deposits are always recorded on Form 941. Defend or reject.
8. Bill Smith leaves his job on July 9. He requests a copy of his W–2. His boss tells him to wait until January of next year. Please comment.

9. Explain when the tax liability for FUTA tax is due.

10. Why is a year-end adjusting entry needed for workers' compensation insurance?

EXERCISES

Calculating employer's payroll tax expense.

1. From the following information, prepare a general journal entry to record the payroll tax expense for Asty Company for the payroll of August 9.

EMPLOYEE	CUMULATIVE EARNINGS BEFORE WEEKLY PAYROLL	GROSS PAY FOR WEEK
J. Kline	$3,500	$900
A. Met	6,600	750
D. Ring	7,900	300

FICA tax rate is 7.65 percent. Federal unemployment tax is .8 percent on $7,000. The merit rating for Asty Co. is 5.6 percent.

Merit rating changes: Effect on total payroll tax expense.

2. If in Exercise 1 the merit rating dropped to 4.9 percent, what effect would this have on the total payroll tax expense?

Gross pay change and its effect on payroll tax expense.

3. If in Exercise 1 D. Ring earned $2,000 instead of $300, what effect would this have on the total payroll tax expense?

Determining due date of tax liability and journalizing the entry to record the payment.

4. At the end of January, 19XX, the total amount of FICA tax deductions from employees was $810 for Koon Co. Federal income tax of $3,000 was also deducted from their paychecks. Indicate when this deposit is due and provide a general journal entry to record the payment.

Calculating total payroll tax expense.

5. The total wage expense for Horgan Co. was $150,000. Of this total, $30,000 was not subject to FICA tax and $60,000 was not subject to state and federal unemployment taxes. Calculate the total payroll tax expense for Horgan Co., given the following: FICA tax rate, 7.65 percent; state unemployment tax rate, 5.9 percent; federal unemployment tax rate (after credit), .8 percent.

Recording entries to pay tax liabilities for FICA, federal income tax, SUTA, and FUTA.

6. From the following accounts, record the payment of (a) July 3 payment for FICA and federal income taxes; (b) July 30 payment of state unemployment tax; and (c) July 30 deposit of FUTA tax that may be required. For simplicity, use general journal entries.

FICA Tax Payable		Federal Income Tax Payable	
	June 30 500 (ee)		June 30 3,005
	500 (er)		

SUTA Tax Payable		FUTA Tax Payable	
	June 30 411		June 30 119

7. At the end of the first quarter of 19XX, you have been asked to determine the FUTA tax liability for Oscar Co. as well as to record any payment of tax liability. The following information has been supplied to you: FUTA tax rate is .8 percent on the first $7,000 of earnings.

EMPLOYEES	GROSS PAY PER WEEK
J. King	$400
A. Lane	500
B. Move	600
C. Slade	900

Calculating FUTA tax liability along with entry to record deposit of FUTA tax.

Workers' compensation—calculating estimated premium and recording the journal entry.

8. From the following data, estimate the annual premium and record it (use a general journal entry):

TYPE OF WORK	ESTIMATED PAYROLL	RATE PER $100
Office	$15,000	$ .17
Sales	42,000	1.90

9. Assuming that the actual payroll for the office staff in Exercise 8 was $17,000 and for sales $44,000, calculate the cost of the actual premium, and prepare on December 31 an adjusting entry.

Adjusting entry for workers' compensation.

GROUP A PROBLEMS

10A-1. For the week of April 8 at Kane's Hardware, the partial payroll summary shown below is taken from the individual earnings records. Both Jill Reese and Jeff Vatack have earned more than $7,000 before this payroll.

Your task is to

1. Complete the table.
2. Prepare a journal entry to record the payroll tax expense for Kane's. Please show all calculations.

EMPLOYEE	GROSS	FICA	FEDERAL INCOME TAX
Al Jones	$ 500		
Janice King	600		
Alice Lone	750		
Jill Reese	4,000		
Jeff Vatack	2,000		

Assume: FICA tax rate is 7.65 percent and no one has earned more than $52,000. Federal income tax is assessed at 20 percent. State unemployment tax rate is 5.1 percent on the first $7,000, and federal unemployment tax rate is .8 percent on the first $7,000.

Journalizing the entry to record employers' payroll tax expense.

10A-2. The following is the monthly payroll of Hogan Co., owned by Dean Hogan. All payroll is paid the last day of each month.

Employer's tax responsibilities.

JANUARY

	TOTAL EARNED	FICA TAX	FEDERAL INCOME TAX
Sam Koy	$1,800	$137.70	$ 280
Joy Lane	3,150	240.98	610
Amy Hess	4,100	313.65	890
	$9,050	$692.33	$1,780

FEBRUARY

	TOTAL EARNED	FICA TAX	FEDERAL INCOME TAX
Sam Koy	$1,800	$137.70	$ 280
Joy Lane	3,150	240.98	610
Amy Hess	4,100	313.65	890
	$9,050	$692.33	$1,780

MARCH

	TOTAL EARNED	FICA TAX	FEDERAL INCOME TAX
Sam Koy	$ 3,200	$244.80	$ 615
Joy Lane	4,080	312.12	880
Amy Hess	4,250	325.13	990
	$11,530	$882.05	$2,485

Hogan Co. is located at 2 Roundy Rd., Marblehead, MA 01945. Federal identification number is 29-3458821. FICA tax rate is 7.65 percent. The SUTA tax rate is 5.7 percent on the first $7,000. The FUTA tax rate is .8 percent on the first $7,000.

Your task is to

1. Journalize entries to record the employer's payroll tax expense for each payroll.
2. Journalize entries for the payment of each tax liability including SUTA tax (use a general journal).

10A-3. Ed Ward, accountant of Hogan Co., has been requested to complete Form 941 for the first quarter. Using Problem 10A-2, Ed gathers the needed data. Ed has been called to an urgent budget meeting and has requested you to assist him. (Difference in tax liability, a few cents, should be adjusted in Line 9 due to rounding of FICA calculation.)

10A-4. The following is the monthly payroll for the last three months of the year for Henson's Sporting Goods Shop, 1 Roe Road, Lynn, MA 01945, owned by Bill Henson, federal ID number 28-93118921. All payroll is paid on the last day of the month. Pete Avery is the only employee who has contributed the maximum into Social Security. All other employees will not reach the maximum by year's end. (Assume a rate of 7.65 percent on $52,000.)

OCTOBER

	TOTAL EARNED	FICA TAX	FEDERAL INCOME TAX
Pete Avery	$ 2,950		$ 488
Janet Lee	3,590	$274.64	515
Sue Lyons	3,800	290.70	595
	$10,340	$565.34	$1,598

NOVEMBER

	TOTAL EARNED	FICA TAX	FEDERAL INCOME TAX
Pete Avery	$ 2,950		$ 488
Janet Lee	3,590	$274.64	515
Sue Lyons	3,800	290.70	595
	$10,340	$565.34	$1,598

DECEMBER

	TOTAL EARNED	FICA TAX	FEDERAL INCOME TAX
Pete Avery	$ 4,250		$ 860
Janet Lee	3,800	$290.70	710
Sue Lyons	4,400	336.60	880
	$12,450	$627.30	$2,450

Your task is to

1. Journalize entries to record the employer's payroll tax for each period. Assume that all employees have earned more than $7,000.
2. Journalize entries for the payment of each tax for FICA tax and federal income tax.
3. Complete Form 941.

GROUP B PROBLEMS

10B-1. For the week of Feb. 10 at Kane's Hardware, the following partial payroll summary is taken from the individual earnings records. Both Jill Reese and Jeff Vatack have earned more than $7,000 before this payroll.

Your task is to

1. Complete the table.
2. Prepare a journal entry to record the payroll taxes for Kane. Please show all calculations.

EMPLOYEE	GROSS	FICA TAX	FEDERAL INCOME TAX
Al Jones	$ 400		
Janice King	600		
Alice Lone	800		
Jill Reese	1,400		
Jeff Vatack	1,800		

Assume: FICA tax rate is 7.65 percent and no one has earned more than $52,000. Federal income tax is assessed at 20 percent. State unemployment tax rate is 5.2 percent on the first $7,000. Federal unemployment tax rate is .8 percent on the first $7,000.

10B-2. The following is the monthly payroll of Hogan Co., owned by Dean Hogan. All payroll is paid the last day of each month.

Employer's tax responsibility.

JANUARY

	TOTAL EARNED	FICA TAX	FEDERAL INCOME TAX
Sam Koy	$ 2,900	$221.85	$ 510
Joy Lane	3,850	294.53	790
Amy Hess	4,100	313.65	890
	$10,850	$830.03	$2,190

FEBRUARY

	TOTAL EARNED	FICA TAX	FEDERAL INCOME TAX
Sam Koy	$ 2,900	$221.85	$ 510
Joy Lane	3,850	294.53	790
Amy Hess	4,100	313.65	890
	$10,850	$830.03	$2,190

MARCH

	TOTAL EARNED	FICA TAX	FEDERAL INCOME TAX
Sam Koy	$ 4,040	$309.06	$ 886
Joy Lane	4,200	321.30	910
Amy Hess	4,800	367.20	1,010
	$13,040	$997.56	$2,806

Hogan Co. is located at 2 Roundy Rd., Marblehead, MA 01945. Federal identification number is 29-3458821. FICA tax rate is 7.65 percent. The SUTA rate is 5.7 percent on first $7,000. The FUTA tax rate is .8 percent on the first $7,000.

Your task is to

1. Journalize entries to record the employer's payroll tax expense for each payroll.
2. Journalize the entries for the payment of each tax liability including SUTA tax (use a general journal).

10B-3. As the bookkeeper of Hogan Co. you have been requested to complete Form 941. Gather all needed data from Problem 10B-2. (Make adjustment, due to rounding of FICA, in Line 9 so that total tax liability equals total amount owed.)

Preparing Form 941.

10B-4. The monthly payroll for the last quarter of Henson's Sporting Goods Shop is as follows:

Completing Form 941 with some FICA tax wages exempt; journalizing payments of tax liability.

OCTOBER

	TOTAL EARNED	FICA TAX	FEDERAL INCOME TAX
Pete Avery	$ 2,910		$ 470
Janet Lee	3,500	$267.75	590
Sue Lyons	3,950	302.18	710
	$10,360	$569.93	$1,770

NOVEMBER

	TOTAL EARNED	FICA TAX	FEDERAL INCOME TAX
Pete Avery	$ 2,910		$ 470
Janet Lee	3,500	$267.75	590
Sue Lyons	3,950	302.18	710
	$10,360	$569.93	$1,770

DECEMBER

	TOTAL EARNED	FICA TAX	FEDERAL INCOME TAX
Pete Avery	$ 4,100		$ 770
Janet Lee	4,450	$340.43	810
Sue Lyons	4,600	351.90	990
	$13,150	$692.33	$2,570

Henson's is located at 1 Roe Rd., Lynn, MA 01945, and is owned by Bill Henson; the Federal ID number is 28-93118921. All payroll is paid the last day of the month. Pete Avery is the only employee to have contributed the maximum into Social Security. All other employees will not reach maximum by year's end. Assume a FICA rate of 7.65 percent on $52,000.

1. Journalize entries to record the employer's payroll tax for each period. Assume that all employees have earned more than $7,000.
2. Journalize entries for the payment of each tax for FICA tax and federal income tax.
3. Complete Form 941.

PRACTICAL ACCOUNTING APPLICATION #1

The Moore Company has a significant increase in business each fall—a result of Moore's planning a major advertising campaign for a leading manufacturer of children's clothes. Each fall, consequently, 30 additional workers are hired for a 12-week period, working 40 hours per week at $6 per hour, and then they are laid off. Owing to these yearly layoffs, the state unemployment tax rate for Moore is 5.4 percent, and no merit rating is allowed. The company feels that if temporary help were provided by a temporary employment agency, Moore's state unemployment tax rate could drop to 4.1 percent.

Could you, as the payroll specialist for Moore, identify the pros and cons of using the temporary employment agency? In your analysis, keep in mind the following facts:

1. Five hundred workers (permanent) by fall have earned in excess of $7,000.
2. Temporary employment agencies charge $7.00 per hour for each worker supplied.
3. The federal unemployment tax rate is .8 percent on the first $7,000.
4. Assume that the company pays a FICA tax rate of 7.65 percent on $52,000 and that all wages this calendar year will be taxable.

Please show all calculations. What do you think is the best alternative?

PRACTICAL ACCOUNTING APPLICATION #2

To: Mike Ryan
From: Al Bloom, V.P.
Re: Tax Act of 1989

Next week please provide me with the latest information on any pending legislation that may update the Tax Act of 1989 regarding payroll. Call the IRS, our congressperson, etc. We need the information ASAP!

Please help Mike with this task.

Comprehensive Review Problem

Pete's Market: Completing Payroll Requirements for First Quarter and Preparing Form 941

This comprehensive problem will aid you in putting the pieces of payroll together. In this project, you are the bookkeeper and will have the responsibility of recording payroll in the payroll register, paying the payroll, recording the employer's tax responsibilities, along with payment of tax deposits, as well as completing the quarterly report.

Pete's Market, owned by Pete Reel, is located at 4 Sun Avenue, Swampscott, MA 01970. His employer identification number is 42-4583312. Please assume the following:

1. FICA—7.65% on $52,000.
2. SUTA—4.9% (due to favorable merit rating) on $7,000.
3. FUTA—.8% on first $7,000.
4. Employees are paid monthly. The payroll is recorded the last day of each month and is paid on first day of next month.
5. FIT table provided with problem from Circular E of Internal Revenue publication.
6. State income tax is 8%.

The following are the employees of Pete's Market along with their monthly salary exemptions, etc.

SALARY PER MONTH

		JAN.	FEB.	MARCH	
Fred Flynn	S–0	$1,800	$1,800	$2,100	(Sales Salaries)
Mary Jones	S–2	3,000	3,000	4,000	(Market Salaries)
Lilly Vron	S–1	3,000	3,000	4,260	(Sales Salaries)

Partial Ledger Accounts
as of December 31, 19XX

FICA Tax Payable 210	FIT Payable 220	SIT Payable 225
510.90 (ee)	600	150
510.90 (er)		

FUTA Payable 230	SUTA Payable 240
88	155

As the bookkeeper, please complete the following:

Jan. 15   Record the entry for the deposit of FICA and FIT from last month's payroll, check no. 410. (For simplicity we will not record the payment of state income tax.)

       31   Pay state unemployment tax due from last quarter, check no. 412.

       31   Pay federal unemployment tax owed, check no. 413.

       31   Complete payroll register for January payroll, journalize payroll entry, and journalize entry for employer's payroll tax expense.

Feb.   1   Pay payroll (check nos. 414, 415, and 416).

       3   Pay taxes due for FICA and FIT, check no. 417.

      28   Complete payroll register for February payroll. Journalize payroll entry as well as journalize entry for employer's payroll tax expense.

Mar.   1   Pay payroll (check nos. 510, 511, and 512).

       3   Pay taxes due for FICA and FIT (check no. 515).

      31   Complete payroll register for March payroll. Journalize payroll entry as well as journalize entry for employer's payroll tax expense.

Apr.   1   Pay payroll (check nos. 610, 611, and 612).

       3   Pay taxes due for FICA and FIT (check no. 700).

      30   Pay federal unemployment tax due for quarter 1 (check no. 750).

      30   Pay state unemployment tax due for quarter 1 (check no. 751).

      30   Complete Form 941.

SINGLE Persons—MONTHLY Payroll Period

And the wages are–		And the number of withholding allowances claimed is–										
At least	But less than	0	1	2	3	4	5	6	7	8	9	10
		The amount of income tax to be withheld shall be–										
$1,680	$1,720	$249	$216	$191	$166	$141	$116	$91	$66	$41	$16	$0
1,720	1,760	261	222	197	172	147	122	97	72	47	22	0
1,760	1,800	272	228	203	178	153	128	103	78	53	28	3
1,800	1,840	283	236	209	184	159	134	109	84	59	34	9
1,840	1,880	294	248	215	190	165	140	115	90	65	40	15
1,880	1,920	305	259	221	196	171	146	121	96	71	46	21
1,920	1,960	317	270	227	202	177	152	127	102	77	52	27
1,960	2,000	328	281	234	208	183	158	133	108	83	58	33
2,000	2,040	339	292	246	214	189	164	139	114	89	64	39
2,040	2,080	350	304	257	220	195	170	145	120	95	70	45
2,080	2,120	361	315	268	226	201	176	151	126	101	76	51
2,120	2,160	373	326	279	233	207	182	157	132	107	82	57
2,160	2,200	384	337	290	244	213	188	163	138	113	88	63
2,200	2,240	395	348	302	255	219	194	169	144	119	94	69
2,240	2,280	406	360	313	266	225	200	175	150	125	100	75
2,280	2,320	417	371	324	277	231	206	181	156	131	106	81
2,320	2,360	429	382	335	289	242	212	187	162	137	112	87
2,360	2,400	440	393	346	300	253	218	193	168	143	118	93
2,400	2,440	451	404	358	311	264	224	199	174	149	124	99
2,440	2,480	462	416	369	322	276	230	205	180	155	130	105
2,480	2,520	473	427	380	333	287	240	211	186	161	136	111
2,520	2,560	485	438	391	345	298	251	217	192	167	142	117
2,560	2,600	496	449	402	356	309	262	223	198	173	148	123
2,600	2,640	507	460	414	367	320	274	229	204	179	154	129
2,640	2,680	518	472	425	378	332	285	238	210	185	160	135
2,680	2,720	529	483	436	389	343	296	249	216	191	166	141
2,720	2,760	541	494	447	401	354	307	261	222	197	172	147
2,760	2,800	552	505	458	412	365	318	272	228	203	178	153
2,800	2,840	563	516	470	423	376	330	283	236	209	184	159
2,840	2,880	574	528	481	434	388	341	294	248	215	190	165
2,880	2,920	585	539	492	445	399	352	305	259	221	196	171
2,920	2,960	597	550	503	457	410	363	317	270	227	202	177
2,960	3,000	608	561	514	468	421	374	328	281	234	208	183
3,000	3,040	619	572	526	479	432	386	339	292	246	214	189
3,040	3,080	630	584	537	490	444	397	350	304	257	220	195
3,080	3,120	641	595	548	501	455	408	361	315	268	226	201
3,120	3,160	653	606	559	513	466	419	373	326	279	233	207
3,160	3,200	664	617	570	524	477	430	384	337	290	244	213
3,200	3,240	675	628	582	535	488	442	395	348	302	255	219
3,240	3,280	686	640	593	546	500	453	406	360	313	266	225
3,280	3,320	697	651	604	557	511	464	417	371	324	277	231
3,320	3,360	709	662	615	569	522	475	429	382	335	289	242
3,360	3,400	720	673	626	580	533	486	440	393	346	300	253
3,400	3,440	731	684	638	591	544	498	451	404	358	311	264
3,440	3,480	742	696	649	602	556	509	462	416	369	322	276
3,480	3,520	753	707	660	613	567	520	473	427	380	333	287
3,520	3,560	765	718	671	625	578	531	485	438	391	345	298
3,560	3,600	776	729	682	636	589	542	496	449	402	356	309
3,600	3,640	787	740	694	647	600	554	507	460	414	367	320
3,640	3,680	798	752	705	658	612	565	518	472	425	378	332
3,680	3,720	809	763	716	669	623	576	529	483	436	389	343
3,720	3,760	821	774	727	681	634	587	541	494	447	401	354
3,760	3,800	832	785	738	692	645	598	552	505	458	412	365
3,800	3,840	843	796	750	703	656	610	563	516	470	423	376
3,840	3,880	856	808	761	714	668	621	574	528	481	434	388
3,880	3,920	869	819	772	725	679	632	585	539	492	445	399
3,920	3,960	882	830	783	737	690	643	597	550	503	457	410
3,960	4,000	895	841	794	748	701	654	608	561	514	468	421
4,000	4,040	908	853	806	759	712	666	619	572	526	479	432
4,040	4,080	922	867	817	770	724	677	630	584	537	490	444
4,080	4,120	935	880	828	781	735	688	641	595	548	501	455
4,120	4,160	948	893	839	793	746	699	653	606	559	513	466
4,160	4,200	961	906	851	804	757	710	664	617	570	524	477
4,200	4,240	974	919	864	815	768	722	675	628	582	535	488
4,240	4,280	988	933	878	826	780	733	686	640	593	546	500

ACCOUNTING FORMS SAMPLER

ACCOUNTING FORMS SAMPLER

CHAPTER

INCOME STATEMENT FOR A SERVICE COMPANY

ASSURE REALTY INCOME STATEMENT FOR MONTH ENDED NOVEMBER 30, 19XX		
Revenue:		
Commissions Earned		$ 1 3 6 0 00
Operating Expenses:		
Rent Expense	$ 2 0 0 00	
Advertising Expense	1 5 0 00	
Salaries Expense	9 0 00	
Total Operating Expenses		4 4 0 00
Net Income		$ 9 2 0 00

The income statement is a report written for a specific period of time that lists earned revenue and expenses incurred to produce the earned revenue. The net income or net loss will be used in the statement of owner's equity. There are no debits or credits on financial reports. The inside column is for subtotalling.

STATEMENT OF OWNER'S EQUITY

ASSURE REALTY STATEMENT OF OWNER'S EQUITY FOR MONTH ENDED NOVEMBER 30, 19XX				
Bill Ryan, Capital, November 1, 19XX				$ 5 0 0 0 00
Net Income for November	$ 9 2 0 00			
Less Withdrawals for November	1 0 0 00			
Increase in Capital			8 2 0 00	
Bill Ryan, Capital, November 30, 19XX				$ 5 8 2 0 00

The statement of owner's equity reveals the causes of a change in capital. This report lists any investments, net income (or net loss), and withdrawals. The ending figure for capital will be used on the balance sheet. Any additional investments would go on this report.

BALANCE SHEET FOR A SERVICE COMPANY

ASSURE REALTY
BALANCE SHEET
NOVEMBER 30, 19XX

Assets		Liabilities and Owner's Equity	
Cash	$ 4 7 3 0 00	Liabilities	
Accounts Receivable	6 4 0 00	Accounts Payable	$ 9 0 0 00
Store Furniture	1 3 5 0 00		
		Owner's Equity	
		Bill Ryan, Capital	5 8 2 0 00
		Total Liabilities and	
Total Assets	$ 6 7 2 0 00	Owner's Equity	$ 6 7 2 0 00

The balance sheet uses some of the ending balances of assets and liabilities from the accounting equation and the capital from the statement of owner's equity. Keep in mind that there are no debits or credits on financial reports.

TRIAL BALANCE

	Dr.	Cr.
JANET FOSS ATTORNEY AT LAW TRIAL BALANCE MAY 31, 19XX		
Cash	1 8 0 0 00	
Accounts Receivable	7 5 0 00	
Office Equipment	7 5 0 00	
Accounts Payable		1 2 0 0 00
Salaries Payable		6 7 5 00
Janet Foss, Capital		1 2 7 5 00
Janet Foss, Withdrawals	3 0 0 00	
Revenue from Legal Fees		1 3 5 0 00
Utilities Expense	3 0 0 00	
Rent Epense	4 5 0 00	
Salaries Expense	1 5 0 00	
Totals	4 5 0 0 00	4 5 0 0 00

A trial balance is a list of the ending balances of all accounts, listed in the same order as on the chart of accounts. Note how Withdrawals is listed immediately below Capital.

GENERAL JOURNAL

CLARK'S WORD PROCESSING SERVICES
GENERAL JOURNAL

Page 1

Date			Account Titles and Description	PR*	Dr.	Cr.
19XX May	1		Cash		7 0 0 0 00	
			Brenda Clark, Capital			7 0 0 0 00
			Initial investment of cash by owner			
	1		Word Processing Equipment		8 0 0 0 00	
			Cash			2 0 0 0 00
			Accounts Payable			6 0 0 0 00
			Purchase of equip. from Ben Co.			
	1		Prepaid Rent		9 0 0 00	
			Cash			9 0 0 00
			Rent paid in advance (3 months)			
	3		Office Supplies		4 0 0 00	
			Accounts Payable			4 0 0 00
			Purchase of supplies on acct. from Norris			
	7		Cash		2 5 0 0 00	
			Word Processing Fees			2 5 0 0 00
			Cash received from services rendered			
	15		Office Salaries Expense		4 5 0 00	
			Cash			4 5 0 00
			Payment of office salaries			
	18		Advertising Expense		1 7 5 00	
			Accounts Payable			1 7 5 00
			Bill received but not paid from Al's News			
	20		Brenda Clark, Withdrawals		4 3 0 00	
			Cash			4 3 0 00
			Personal withdrawal of cash			
	22		Accounts Receivable		4 1 0 0 00	
			Word Processing Fees			4 1 0 0 00
			Billed Morris Co. for fees earned			
	27		Office Salaries Expense		4 5 0 00	
			Cash			4 5 0 00
			Payment of office salaries			
	28		Accounts Payable		3 0 0 0 00	
			Cash			3 0 0 0 00
			Paid half the amount owed Ben Co.			

A general journal is a book where transactions are recorded in chronological order. Here debits and credits are shown together on one page. This is the book of original entry. Note that the PR column is left blank in the journalizing process.

GENERAL LEDGER (PARTIAL)

Brenda Clark, Withdrawals   Account No. 312

Date	Explanation	Post. Ref.	Debit	Credit	Balance Debit	Balance Credit
19XX May 20		GJ1	4 3 0 00		4 3 0 00	

Word Processing Fees   Account No. 411

Date	Explanation	Post. Ref.	Debit	Credit	Balance Debit	Balance Credit
19XX May 7		GJ1		2 5 0 0 00		2 5 0 0 00
22		GJ1		4 1 0 0 00		6 6 0 0 00

Office Salaries Expense   Account No. 511

Date	Explanation	Post. Ref.	Debit	Credit	Balance Debit	Balance Credit
19XX May 15		GJ1	4 5 0 00		4 5 0 00	
27		GJ1	4 5 0 00		9 0 0 00	

Advertising Expense   Account No. 512

Date	Explanation	Post. Ref.	Debit	Credit	Balance Debit	Balance Credit
19XX May 18		GJ1	1 7 5 00		1 7 5 00	

Telephone Expense   Account No. 513

Date	Explanation	Post. Ref.	Debit	Credit	Balance Debit	Balance Credit
19XX May 29		GJ1	1 8 0 00		1 8 0 00	

The ledger is a collection of accounts where information is accumulated from the postings of the journal. The ledger is the book of final entry. Note each Ledger Account has an Account Number.

WORK SHEET FOR A SERVICE COMPANY

CLARK'S WORD PROCESSING SERVICES
WORK SHEET
FOR MONTH ENDED MAY 31, 19XX

Account Titles	Trial Balance Dr.	Trial Balance Cr.	Adjustments Dr.	Adjustments Cr.	Adjusted Trial Balance Dr.	Adjusted Trial Balance Cr.	Income Statement Dr.	Income Statement Cr.	Balance Sheet Dr.	Balance Sheet Cr.
Cash	2090 00				2090 00				2090 00	
Accounts Receceivable	4100 00				4100 00				4100 00	
Office Supplies	400 00			(A) 320 00	80 00				80 00	
Prepaid Rent	900 00			(B) 300 00	600 00				600 00	
Word Processing Equipment	8000 00				8000 00				8000 00	
Acct. Payable		3575 00				3575 00				3575 00
B. Clark, Capital		7000 00				7000 00				7000 00
B. Clark, Withdrawals	430 00				430 00				430 00	
Word Processing Fees		6600 00				6600 00		6600 00		
Office Salaries Expense	900 00		(D) 250 00		1150 00		1150 00			
Advertising Expense	175 00				175 00		175 00			
Telephone Expense	180 00				180 00		180 00			
	17175 00	17175 00								
Office Supplies Expense			(A) 320 00		320 00		320 00			
Rent Expense			(B) 300 00		300 00		300 00			
Depreciation Expense W.P. Equip.			(C) 100 00		100 00		100 00			
Accum. Depreciation, W.P. Equip.				(C) 100 00		100 00				100 00
Salaries Payable				(D) 250 00		250 00				250 00
			970 00	970 00	17525 00	17525 00	2225 00	6600 00	15300 00	10925 00
Net Income							4375 00			4375 00
							6600 00	6600 00	15300 00	15300 00

The work sheet is a columnar device used by accountants to aid them in completing the accounting cycle. Not a formal report, it is often called a spreadsheet. With a work sheet all the remaining steps of the accounting cycle can be completed. In a computerized setup a work sheet would not be needed.

SALES JOURNAL

ART'S WHOLESALE CLOTHING COMPANY
SALES JOURNAL

Page 1

Date		Account Debited	Terms	Invoice Number	Post. Ref.	Dr. Acct. Rec. Cr. Sales
19XX April	3	Hal's Clothing	2/10, n/30	1	✔	8 0 0 00
	6	Bevans Company	2/10, n/30	2	✔	1 6 0 0 00
	18	Roe Company	2/10, n/30	3	✔	2 0 0 0 00
	24	Roe Company	2/10, n/30	4	✔	5 0 0 00
	28	Mel's Dept. Store	2/10, n/30	5	✔	9 0 0 00
	29	Mel's Dept. Store	2/10, n/30	6	✔	7 0 0 00
	30					6 5 0 0 00
						(113) (411)

A sales journal records sales on account. Note: Check marks show recordings to the Accounts Receivable Subsidiary Ledger have been completed. Totals will be posted at end of month.

ACCOUNTS RECEIVABLE (SUBSIDIARY) LEDGER (PARTIAL)

ACCOUNTS RECEIVABLE LEDGER

NAME   Bevans Company
ADDRESS   110 Aster Rd., Cincinnati, Ohio   45227

Date	Explanation	Post. Ref.	Debit	Credit	Dr. Balance
19XX					
April 6		SJ1	1 6 0 0 00		1 6 0 0 00
12		GJ1		6 0 0 00	1 0 0 0 00
16		CRJ1		1 0 0 0 00	- 0 -

NAME   Hal's Clothing
ADDRESS   91 Century Ave., Homewood, Illinois   60430

Date	Explanation	Post. Ref.	Debit	Credit	Dr. Balance
19XX					
April 3		SJ1	8 0 0 00		8 0 0 00
4		CRJ1		8 0 0 00	- 0 -

The accounts receivable ledger, organized in alphabetical order, is not in the same book as Accounts Receivable, the controlling account in the general ledger. Subsidiary ledgers have names while general ledgers have account numbers.

CASH RECEIPTS JOURNAL

			CASH RECEIPTS JOURNAL						
									Page 1

Date		Cash Dr.	Sales Discount Dr.	Accounts Receivable Cr.	Sales Cr.	Sundry		
						Account Name	Post. Ref.	Amount Cr.
19XX April	1	8 0 0 0 00				Art Newner, Capital	311	8 0 0 0 00
	4	7 8 4 00	1 6 00	8 0 0 00		Hal's Clothing	✔	
	15	9 0 0 00			9 0 0 00	Cash Sales	✗	
	16	9 8 0 00	2 0 00	1 0 0 0 00		Bevans Company	✔	
	22	1 9 6 0 00	4 0 00	2 0 0 0 00		Roe Company	✔	
	27	5 0 0 00				Store Equipment	121	5 0 0 00
	30	1 2 0 0 00			1 2 0 0 00	Cash Sales	✗	
	30	14 3 2 4 00	7 6 00	3 8 0 0 00	2 1 0 0 00			8 5 0 0 00
		(111)	(413)	(113)	(411)			(X)

The cash receipts journal records receipt of cash from any source. The total of sundry is not posted. Totals of columns are posted at end of month. The checks indicate that recordings to the subsidiary ledger are up-to-date.

SCHEDULE OF ACCOUNTS RECEIVABLE

ART'S WHOLESALE CLOTHING COMPANY
SCHEDULE OF ACCOUNTS RECEIVABLE
APRIL 30, 19XX

Mel's Dept. Store	$ 1 6 0 0 00
Roe Company	5 0 0 00
Total Accounts Receivable	$ 2 1 0 0 00

A schedule of accounts receivable is a listing of the ending balances of customers in the accounts receivable ledger. This total should be same balance as found in the controlling account, Accounts Receivable, in the general ledger.

PURCHASES JOURNAL

ART'S WHOLESALE CLOTHING COMPANY
PURCHASES JOURNAL

Page 1

Date		Account Credited	Date of Invoice	Inv. No.	Terms	Post Ref.	Accounts Payable Credit	Purchases Debit	Sundry-Dr.		
									Account	PR	Amount
19XX April	3	Abby Blake Company	April 3	228	2/10, n/60	✔	5 0 5 0 00	5 0 0 0 00	Freight-In	514	5 0 00
	4	Joe Francis Company	April 5	388		✔	4 0 0 0 00		Equipment	121	4 0 0 0 00
	6	Thorpe Company	April 6	415	1/10, n/30	✔	8 0 0 00	8 0 0 00			
	7	John Sullivan Company	April 6	516	n/10, EOM	✔	9 8 0 00	9 8 0 00			
	12	Abby Blake Company	April 13	242	1/10, n/30	✔	6 0 0 00	6 0 0 00			
	25	John Sullivan Company	April 26	612		✔	5 0 0 00		Supplies	115	5 0 0 00
	30						11 9 3 0 00	7 3 8 0 00			4 5 5 0 00
							(211)	(511)			(X)

The purchases journal records the buying of merchandise or other items on account. The purchases (Debit) column records merchandise bought for resale. The sundry column records items not for resale.

ACCOUNTS PAYABLE (SUBSIDIARY) LEDGER

ACCOUNTS PAYABLE SUBSIDIARY LEDGER

JOHN BUTLER COMPANY
18 REED RD.
HOMEWOOD, ILLINOIS 60430

Date	Explanation	Post. Ref.	Debit	Credit	Cr. Balance
19XX					
May 7		PJ2		1 000 00	1 000 00
17		PJ2		400 00	1 400 00

FLYNN COMPANY
15 FOSS AVE.
ENGLEWOOD CLIFFS, NEW JERSEY 07632

Date	Explanation	Post. Ref.	Debit	Credit	Cr. Balance
19XX					
May 5		PJ2		900 00	900 00
13		GJ1	300 00		600 00

The accounts payable ledger, organized in alphabetical order, is not in the same book as Accounts Payable, the controlling account in the general ledger. Note: There are no account numbers next to each name.

CASH PAYMENTS JOURNAL

		CASH PAYMENTS JOURNAL											

Date		Ck. No.	Account Debited	Post. Ref.	Sundry Accounts Dr.	Accounts Payable Dr.	Purchases Discount Cr.	Cash Cr.
19XX								
April	2	1	Prepaid Insurance	116	9 0 0 00			9 0 0 00
	7	2	Joe Francis Company	✔		4 0 0 0 00		4 0 0 0 00
	9	3	Purchases	511	8 0 0 00			8 0 0 00
	12	4	Thorpe Company	✔		6 0 0 00	6 00	5 9 4 00
	28	5	Salaries	611	7 0 0 00			7 0 0 00
	30				2 4 0 0 00	4 6 0 0 00	6 00	6 9 9 4 00
					(X)	(211)	(512)	(111)

All payments of cash (check) are recorded in the cash payments journal. Totals posted at end of month (except Sundry). Update subsidiary Ledger during the month (✓).

BANK RECONCILIATION WITH JOURNAL ENTRIES

```
                        MONROE COMPANY
              BANK RECONCILIATION AS OF JUNE 30, 19XX
```

Checkbook Balance			Balance per Bank		
Ending Checkbook Balance		$3,978	Ending Bank Statement Balance		$5,230
Add:			Add:		
Error in recording			Deposits in Transit		1,084
Check no. 108	$54				$6,314
Proceeds of a note*					
less collection					
charge by bank	1,990	2,044	Deduct:		
		$6,022	Check no. 191..$204		
			198.. 250		
Deduct:			201.. 100		554
NSF Check	$252				
Bank Service					
Charge	10	262			
Reconciled Balance		$5,760	Reconciled Balance		$5,760

19XX						
June	30	Cash		1 9 9 0 00		
		Collection Expense		1 0 00		
		Notes Receivable*			2 0 0 0 00	
	30	Cash		5 4 00		
		Store Equipment			5 4 00	
	30	Acct. Rec., Alvin Sooth		2 5 2 00		
		Cash			2 5 2 00	
	30	Miscellaneous Expense		1 0 00		
		Cash			1 0 00	

The process of reconciling the bank balance with the company's balance is called the bank reconciliation. The timing of deposits, when the bank statement was issued, etc., often results in differences between the bank balance and the checkbook balance. Whenever the check book is adjusted a journal entry is required.

PAYROLL REGISTER

FRED'S MARKET
PAYROLL REGISTER
NOVEMBER 18, 19XX

Employee Name	Allowance and Marital Status	Cumulative Earnings	Salary per Week	No. of Hrs.	Wages per Hr.	Earnings			Cumulative Earnings	Taxable Earnings	
						Regular	Overtime	Gross		Unemploy-ment	FICA
Flynn, Bob	S-0	6 900 00		30	9 00	270 00	—	270 00	7 170 00	100 00	270 00
Frost, Abby	S-1	6 500 00		44	7 00	280 00	42 00	322 00	6 822 00	322 00	322 00
O'Reilly, Susan	M-3	56 250 00	1 250 00			1 250 00	—	1 250 00	57 500 00	—	—
Rase, Paula	M-1	31 500 00	700 00			700 00	—	700 00	32 200 00	—	700 00
Regan, Al	M-2	45 000 00	1 000 00			1 000 00	—	1 000 00	46 000 00	—	1 000 00
		146 150 00	2 950 00			3 500 00	42 00	3 542 00	149 692 00	422 00	2 292 00
	*(A)	(B)	(C)			(D)	(E)	(F)	(G)	(H)	(I)

1. A payroll register provides the data for journalizing the payroll entry.

2. Deductions for payroll represent liabilities for the employer until paid.

3. The account distribution columns of the payroll register indicate which accounts will be debited to record the total payroll when a journal entry is prepared. Note: These distribution columns represent gross pay, not net pay.

| | Deductions | | | Net Pay | Check No. | Distribution of Expense Accounts | |
FICA	Federal Income Tax	State Income Tax	Medical Insurance			Office Salaries Expense	Market Wages Expense
20 66	38 00	13 50	14 00	183 84	822		270 00
24 63	40 00	16 10	14 00	227 27	823		322 00
—	224 00	62 50	20 00	943 50	824	1250 00	
53 55	92 00	35 00	20 00	499 45	825	700 00	
76 50	165 00	50 00	20 00	688 50	826	1000 00	
175 34	559 00	177 10	88 00	2542 56		2950 00	592 00
(J)	(K)	(L)	(M)	(N)	(O)	(P)	(Q)

HOW COMPANIES RECORD CREDIT CARD SALES IN THEIR SPECIAL JOURNALS

RECORDING BANK CREDIT CARDS

Example: Credit Card Sales of $100 Master Card. It is interesting to note that for bank credit cards (Master Card, Visa) the sales are recorded in the seller's Cash Receipts Journal, since the slips are converted into cash immediately. Bank credit cards are not treated as accounts receivable. The fee the bank charges, $2\frac{1}{4}\%$ to 6%, is usually deducted, and the bank credits the depositor's account immediately for the net. The end result for the seller is:

Accounts Affected	Category	↑ ↓	Rule
Cash	Asset	↑	Dr. $94
Credit Card Expense	Expense	↑	Dr. 6
Sales	Revenue	↑	Cr. 100

			CASH RECEIPTS JOURNAL					
			Credit Card	Accounts		Sales Tax	Sundry	
		Cash	Expense	Receivable	Sales	Payable	Account	Amount
Date		Dr.	Dr.	Cr.	Credited	Cr.	Name	Cr.
		94 00	6 00		100 00			

It is the responsibility of the credit card company to sustain any losses (bad debts) from customers' nonpayment. If the bank waits to take the discount till end of month, the seller makes a nonpayment entry in the cash payment journal to record the credit card expense; the end result would be credit card expense up and cash balance down. Usually, the bank would send the charge on the monthly bank statement. *Remember: bank credit cards are not treated as accounts receivable.*

RECORDING PRIVATE COMPANY CREDIT CARDS

Private companies such as American Express and Diners Club are considered by sellers as accounts receivable. The seller periodically summarizes the sales slips and submits them to the private credit card company for payment (which the company will pay quickly). Let's look at two situations to show how a company would handle its accounting procedures for these credit sales transactions.

Situation 1. On May 4, Morris Company sold merchandise on account $53 to Bill Blank. Bill used American Express. Assume Morris Company has low dollar volume and few transactions.

Note in Figure B-1 (p. 310) how the sale of $53 is recorded in the sales journal. Keep in mind that Morris is treating American Express, not Bill Blank, as the accounts receivable. In Figure B-2 (p. 310) we see on June 8 payment is received from American Express and results in

SALES JOURNAL

Date	Invoice	Description of Accounts Receivable	PR	Accounts Receivable Dr.	Sales Tax* Payable Cr.	Sales Cr.
May 4	692	American Express		5300	300	5000
		(Bill Blank)				

* Assume a 6% sales tax.

FIGURE B-1

CASH RECEIPTS JOURNAL

Date	Cash Dr.	Sales Discount Dr.	Credit Card Expense Dr.	Accounts Receivable Cr.	Sales Tax Payable Cr.	Sundry Account Name	PR	Amount Cr.
June 8	5035		265*	5300		American Express		
						(Bill Blank)		

* Assume credit card expense of 5%. Note the $2.65 is 5% × $53.

FIGURE B-2

1. Cash increasing by $50.35.
2. Credit card expense rising by $2.65.
3. Accounts receivable being reduced by the $53 originally owed by American Express.

Situation 2: On March 31, Blue Company summarized its credit card sales for American Express. Payment was received on April 13 from American Express. Assume Blue Company has high dollar volume and many transactions.

Note in Figure B-3 how each credit company has its own column set up. In the ledger there is an account set up for each as well; the posting to the ledger would be done at the end of the month. With high volume and the need to record many transactions, the use of these additional columns (versus Figure B-1) will result in increased efficiency. Figure B-4 shows the receipt of money from American Express less the credit card expense charge.

BLUE COMPANY SALES JOURNAL

Date	Invoice Number	Description of Accounts Receivable	PR	Accounts Receivable Dr.	Credit Cards American Express Dr.	Credit Cards Diners Club Dr.	Sales Tax Payable Cr.	Credit Card Sales Cr.	Sales Cr.
March 31		Summary of American Express			11970000		57000	11400000	
					(112)	(113)		(401)	

Acc. Receivable American Express **112**

Total of column posted from sales journal at end of month

Acc. Receivable Diners Club **113**

Total of column posted from sales journal at end of month

Credit Card Sales **401**

Total of column posted from sales journal at end of month

These new titles are found in the general ledger. Subsidiary ledgers would not be needed, since a file is kept of all copies submitted for payment.

BLUE COMPANY CASH RECEIPTS JOURNAL

Date	Cash Dr.	Sales Discount Dr.	Credit Card Expense Dr.	Accounts Receivable Cr.	Credit Card Accounts Rec. American Express Cr.	Credit Card Accounts Rec. Diners Club Cr.	Sales Cr.	Sales Tax Payable Cr.	Sundry Account Name	Sundry PR	Sundry Amount Cr.
April 13	11251800		718200		11970000				Summary of American Express payments		

Credit Card Expense **510**

Total of column posted from cash receipts journal at end of month

COMPUTERS
AND ACCOUNTING

Throughout this text we have developed a practical set of procedures to provide accounting information about a business. Increasingly over the last two decades many businesses have found that the same procedures can be performed much more quickly and accurately using a computer. In this chapter we will discuss computers and how they are used to keep accounting information.

LEARNING UNIT C-1

Introduction to Computers in Accounting

The first computerized accounting systems were developed in the 1950s. Only the largest organizations could afford the very expensive computer equipment which was available at that time. Since then the price of computer equipment has dropped dramatically. Today even the smallest business can afford a computer capable of keeping its accounting records.

Computerized systems offer many advantages over manual systems:

Speed. A computerized system can provide information much more quickly than a manual system, because the computer can perform many tasks almost instantaneously that are time consuming when performed manually.

Creation of an audit trail. With a good computerized accounting system the accounting records will be well organized with reports documenting each transaction. This provides a clear audit trail by which each change in an account's balance can be traced back to the transaction that caused it.

Error protection. Using a computer greatly reduces the number of errors, because the computer performs mathematical functions much more accurately than a human. Also, computerized accounting systems have many built-in error protection features. For instance, in most systems the computer would not accept an entry that did not balance.

Automatic posting. In a computerized system posting is automatically performed. This feature alone is an enormous timesaver. Not only is the repetitive task of posting extremely time-consuming, but it is also the source of many errors in a manual accounting system. Using a computerized system ensures that each entry is posted accurately. This prevents such errors as double posting, posting to the wrong account, or posting the wrong amount.

Automatic report preparation. Reports can be generated automatically in a computerized accounting system. All computerized accounting systems provide printouts of journals and ledgers as well as preparing the balance sheet and income statement. In addition, some systems provide many more detailed reports to aid management in the decision-making process. In Learning Unit C-2 we will list some of the reports that a computerized system can prepare at the touch of a button.

Automatic document printing. In addition to printing reports, a computerized system can also provide many of the documents used in a business. Using preprinted forms sold in supply stores, the computer can print documents such as monthly statements for accounts receivable customers and payroll checks with year-to-date information on the stubs.

As you can see, computers can greatly aid the accounting process. You might think that such a powerful tool would require a great deal of expertise to use. On the contrary, it takes very little computer knowledge to use a computerized accounting system. As long as you understand the manual accounting process, computerized methods are not difficult to learn. As we said in Chapter 1, the computer is only a tool to aid you in performing the same bookkeeping operations you have learned to do manually. Basically, the computer is used to do the "drudge" or mechanical work of accounting such as posting. You must still do all of the analysis work, such as deciding which accounts should be debited and credited.

Accounting procedures are basically the same whether they are performed manually or on the computer. In Figure C-1 we review the steps of the accounting cycle as presented in Chapter 5 and compare them with the steps of the accounting cycle in a computerized system.

Computer Basics

A **program** is a set of instructions that tells the computer what to do. Without a program it cannot perform even the simplest of tasks. This does not mean that you must become a **programmer** in order to use a computer for accounting. Since accounting functions are one of the most frequently used computer applications, there are many programs or **applications** already written to handle accounting data. In order to use the computer for accounting, then, you can simply purchase a program that suits the needs of your business and is compatible with your computer. In Learning Unit C-2 we

FIGURE C-1
Comparing Manual and Computerized Accounting Systems.

ACCOUNTING CYCLE IN A MANUAL SYSTEM

1. Business transactions occur and generate source documents.
2. Business transactions are analyzed and recorded in a journal.
3. Information is posted from the journal to the ledger.
4. A trial balance is prepared.
5. A work sheet is completed.
6. Financial statements are prepared and typed.
7. Adjusting entries are journalized and posted.
8. Closing entries are journalized and posted.
9. A post-closing trial balance is prepared.

ACCOUNTING CYCLE IN A COMPUTERIZED SYSTEM

1. Business transactions occur and generate source documents.
2. Business transactions are analyzed and entered in the computer. The computer prints a journal.
3. The computer posts from the journal to the ledger.
4. The computer prepares a trial balance.
5. Adjusting entries are made and the computer posts them. (No work sheet is necessary.)
6. The computer generates and prints financial statements.
7. The computer records and posts closing entries.
8. The computer prepares and prints a post-closing trial balance.

will discuss the types of packages available, and in Learning Unit C-3 we will give guidelines for purchasing a program and converting your records from a manual system to a computer system.

Although you don't need to be a computer expert, you do need to be familiar with some of the computer equipment you will use on a day-to-day basis. Let's look at the various hardware available. Generally, computer equipment is referred to as **hardware** and computer programs are called **software**.

Types of computers are classified according to their speed and the amount of data they can store. Computers can be grouped into three basic classes: mainframes, minicomputers, and microcomputers. In the 1950s the only type of computer available for accounting applications was the mainframe. A **mainframe** computer can handle a large volume of transactions very quickly, but its cost is prohibitive for all but very large businesses. (Today, mainframe computers sell at prices ranging from a quarter million to four million dollars.) In the late 1960's the **minicomputer** was developed. It was less powerful than the mainframe—however, it also was about one-fourth the cost. As technology progressed, a new type of computer was developed— the **microcomputer**. When first developed, microcomputers were not very powerful and were used in large part for playing computer games. However, new ones were soon developed with more memory and speed. Some microcomputers today are more powerful than the mainframes of the 1950s. Best of all, this type of computer is very affordable. A microcomputer capable of keeping business records can be bought complete with monitor and printer for less than $2,000.

Owing to this affordability, programmers have a very large market for their software programs. In the past few years hundreds of software packages have been produced for the microcomputer, making it a very valuable business tool. Since the beginning of the 1980s many comprehensive accounting programs have been written for microcomputers. Some medium and large-size businesses still require mainframes and minicomputers, owing to the volume of data they process, and the number of operators who need to access the system at one time, but microcomputer packages now provide virtually all of the features offered by larger computers and can easily meet the needs of small businesses.

Although we will concentrate here on accounting procedures for microcomputers, basically all procedures are the same no matter what type of computer is used.

Figure C-2 shows the hardware for a typical microcomputer. This computer system consists of three main types of components:

Input devices
Central processing unit
Output devices

Input Devices.   We use **input devices** to feed instructions and data into the computer. An input device usually found on a computer system is a **disk drive**, which reads data and instructions from magnetic disks. The most common form of disk is the floppy **diskette**. This thin, $5\frac{1}{4}$-inch diameter round diskette, which is enclosed in a square plastic envelope and can store approximately 360,000 characters of data, costs under $2. Figure C-3 is a picture of a floppy diskette.

When you want to use the instructions (programs) or data stored on a diskette, you place the diskette in the disk drive, and the computer can

FIGURE C-2
Microcomputer Hardware.

read the information from it. In addition to the $5\frac{1}{4}$-inch diskette, a diskette that measures $3\frac{1}{2}$-inches square is also used to store programs and data. These diskettes can store approximately twice as much data as the $5\frac{1}{4}$-inch diskettes, have a sturdier plastic case for better protection, and cost less than $3 each. In order to use these diskettes, however, your computer must have a disk drive that is designed for a $3\frac{1}{2}$-inch diskette. Disk drives for the $5\frac{1}{4}$-inch diskettes are still more common.

Another type of disk drive is used to read a **hard disk**. This disk is made of metal and can store as much information as dozens of diskettes. Hard drives are permanently mounted in the computer and cost between $300 and $1,000 depending on their storage capacity. As computerized accounting programs for small businesses become more powerful they require more storage space; therefore, many computerized accounting packages can now be run only from a hard disk.

FIGURE C-3
Floppy Diskette.

The other input device usually found in a microcomputer system is the keyboard. Much like a typewriter keyboard, this device lets us enter data and instructions.

Central Processing Unit. The **central processing unit (CPU)** is the "brain" of the microcomputer. The CPU does the "thinking" for the computer—it performs mathematical and logical operations as well as controlling all the other components of the system.

Output Devices. **Output devices** give us the information we want to receive from the computer. There are several ways the computer can present us with this output. The first device we might use is the **cathode ray tube (CRT)** or **monitor**. The monitor looks like a television set. The monitor allows the user to view data as it is being processed and to receive messages or prompts from the program as it is being run.

The printer can provide printed copies of the information after it has been processed. Examples of the printed copies (also called **hard copies**) we might expect to see in an accounting system include printouts of the business's balance sheet and income statement, or payroll checks.

A third common output device is the disk drive (which we also listed as an input device). We can save our records as they have been updated during the day's processing by placing them on a diskette. When the computer is turned off at the end of a work session, the internal memory in the CPU "forgets" the data you have put into it. However, the diskette provides us with extra storage. Here your data can be safely stored until you need it again.

These are the basic hardware components of a microcomputer system. Learning to work with them is not difficult if you have a good program to give instructions to the computer. The types of programs that allow this hardware to be used as a computerized accounting system will be explained in the next unit.

At this point you should be able to

1. State the advantages of using a computerized system.   (p. 313)
2. Define the terms "hardware" and "software."   (p. 315)
3. Differentiate between mainframe computers, minicomputers, and microcomputers.   (p. 315)
4. List the main components of a microcomputer system.   (p. 315)

SELF-REVIEW QUIZ C-1

Respond true or false to the following:

1. Computerized accounting systems are very expensive and are used only by large businesses.
2. Software is the set of instructions that tell the computer how to complete a task.
3. A keyboard is both an input and output device.
4. Hard copy is information from the computer printed on paper.
5. A bookkeeper or accountant who does not know programming can still use a computer effectively to keep accounting records.

SOLUTION TO SELF-REVIEW QUIZ C-1

1. False   **2.** True   **3.** False   **4.** True   **5.** True

Accounting Software Programs

As we said earlier, accounting procedures cannot be performed on a computer unless there is software to tell the computer what to do. Software programs are sold on diskettes. You insert the diskette into the disk drive, and the computer can read the program instructions written on the diskette. Many types of accounting software are available to meet the differing needs of various businesses.

Accounting packages are usually sold in **modules**. Each module handles a particular area of the accounting records. The most common examples of modules would be packages designed to handle the general ledger, accounts receivable, accounts payable, and payroll work of a business. In addition to these modules, many others are available to help with specific functions such as billing, inventory, forecasting, fixed asset management, and job costing. Generally each module is written on a separate diskette, so that one module can be bought to be used alone or several modules can be bought to be used together.

Many small businesses start out using only one module on a **stand-alone** basis. For instance, payroll procedures are often the first accounting

Barbara Woods: Accounting Operations Supervisor

After high school training in business and secretarial skills and involvement in a co-op program, Barbara Woods got a job as a secretary for a CPA. "I learned many aspects of the business," she says, "and I decided I would like to get more involved in accounting."

Barbara got a job as an account analyst with Mutual Benefit Life Insurance Company and became involved with computerized accounting systems. "At the same time," she says, "I decided I needed to enhance my education. If I wanted to work in accounting I needed some courses in the field."

In accounting courses Barbara found very helpful, she learned the reasons for the things she has been doing. "Still," she says, "the best part for me was working while going to school. A lot of accounting courses are theoretical, but reality is sometimes different. I was able to apply the theory to reality in my everyday job."

Now an Accounting Operations Supervisor at Mutual Benefit, Barbara recommends accounting courses for anyone starting out in the field. "I needed the courses to help me move into this field," she says. "I also recommend working in the field while taking classes. The ability to combine theory with practice is invaluable."

function to be converted from a manual system to a computerized system. This area is ideally suited to computerization because of the repetitive nature of payroll activities and the concentration on mathematical calculation. The accountant for a business could therefore save a great deal of time by putting a large payroll on the computer but still maintain the rest of the business's records on a manual basis.

Other businesses find that they can produce accounting records more efficiently if they computerize *several* accounting functions. When several modules are bought to be used together, this is called **integrated software**. In an integrated system each module handles a different function but also communicates with all the other modules. For instance, in order to record a receipt of payment on accounts receivable, you would make an entry using the accounts receivable module. The journal entry would be recorded in the cash receipts journal in this module, and the customer's account would also be automatically updated. In an integrated system this information would also be posted to the general ledger accounts in the general ledger module.

Because all accounting packages vary, it is not possible to list the exact procedures involved in recording transactions. However, most computerized systems have many features in common. For instance, virtually all accounting programs are **menu-driven**. This means that when you turn the computer on and insert the program diskette, a list of options will be displayed for you to choose from. In order to choose a particular function for the computer to perform, you simply enter the number or letter identifying the option or use the arrow keys on the keyboard to highlight your choice and hit the enter key. Menus make the task of learning to use an accounting program much simpler. Each time the program is loaded onto the computer, a menu will come onto the screen listing the functions you can choose from. The first menu you will see is called a master menu. It will guide you to the section of the program that you wish to use. Once you choose an option, the computer will either perform the function or display a new set of menu choices to receive more instructions. A typical master menu is shown in Figure C-4.

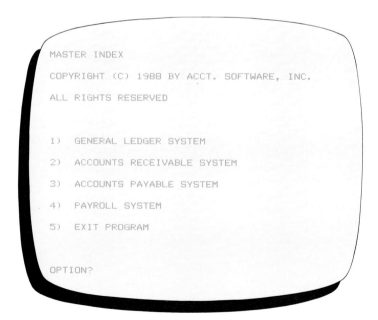

FIGURE C-4
Master Menu.

To choose to work with a particular module of this program you would simply accept the appropriate menu option. For instance, to enter the general ledger section of the program you would simply type a "1".

Generally, in a computerized system (as in a manual system with a large number of transactions) transactions are recorded in batches. Transactions are not recorded the instant they occur. Instead, similar transactions are grouped together and recorded one group at a time. For instance, instead of recording each sale or purchase immediately, we would wait until the end of the day and record all of the sales at one time and then all of the purchases at one time. In the remainder of this unit we will look at four different modules and explain how batches of transactions might be handled by a typical accounting software package.

GENERAL LEDGER MODULE

The general ledger module is the center of an integrated system. In this module all of the general ledger accounts are maintained. Figure C-5 is a typical menu that might be found in a general ledger module.

One option included in this module is the chart of accounts feature. Through this section of the program we can set up the chart of accounts for our business by telling the computer such information as each account's name, number, normal balance, and type (current asset, plant asset, etc.). Since the program will remember this information, we need enter it only once. This chart can be modified whenever necessary. Once the chart has been set up, you can refer to an account simply by listing its account

FIGURE C-5
Typical Menu for General Accounting Program.

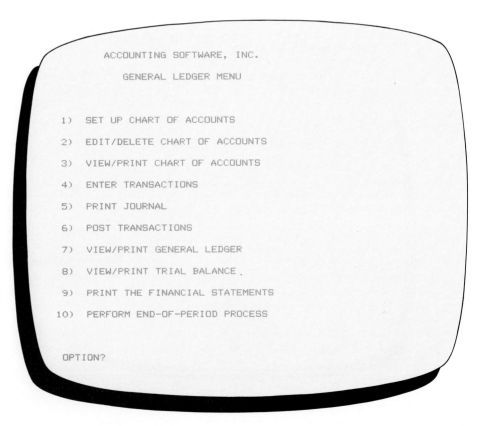

```
          ACCOUNTING SOFTWARE, INC.

              GENERAL LEDGER MENU


     1)   SET UP CHART OF ACCOUNTS

     2)   EDIT/DELETE CHART OF ACCOUNTS

     3)   VIEW/PRINT CHART OF ACCOUNTS

     4)   ENTER TRANSACTIONS

     5)   PRINT JOURNAL

     6)   POST TRANSACTIONS

     7)   VIEW/PRINT GENERAL LEDGER

     8)   VIEW/PRINT TRIAL BALANCE

     9)   PRINT THE FINANCIAL STATEMENTS

    10)   PERFORM END-OF-PERIOD PROCESS


    OPTION?
```

number—given the account number, the program can supply the name and other information by referring back to the chart of accounts.

Journal entries can also be entered through this module. Just as shown in a manual system in Chapters 1–5 of this text, some businesses choose to use the general journal as their only book of original entry. In Chapters 6 and 7 we saw the advantages of a multijournal system for merchandising businesses. The same option exists in a computerized system—the general ledger module can be used on a stand-alone basis, with the general journal as the only book of original entry, or other modules with their special journals can be used in an integrated system.

To enter a journal entry we list the number of each account affected (the computer will supply the account name), the amount of the transaction, and the choice of either debit or credit for the account. Once the transaction has been listed, the program will ask if the entry is correct before recording it. The computer will then check to see if the journal entry balances (if debits equal credits). As an error-protection feature, most programs will not accept the entry if it does not balance.

Once the entries have all been made it is a good idea to print out the general journal. This printout, commonly called a "hard copy," provides a permanent record of the journal entries. It is important that in a computerized system hard copies of all work be kept to document the accounting records. An example of a page of general journal entries is shown in Figure C-6.

FIGURE C-6
General Journal Entries.

```
J&L OFFICE SUPPLY
GENERAL JOURNAL
PAGE 03
-----------------------------------------------------------------
TRANS DATE    ACCT NO.    ACCT. NAME      DR.         CR.
-----------------------------------------------------------------
  32   4/20   1360        STORE EQUIP     1800.00
               2200          ACCOUNTS PAYABLE         1800.00
-----------------------------------------------------------------
  33   4/20   5400        SALARIES EXP    1900.00
               2710          FIT PAYABLE               399.00
               2711          FICA PAYABLE              135.85
               2712          INSUR. PAY                 16.00
               2713          UNION DUES PAY             35.00
               2720          SALARIES PAY             1314.15
-----------------------------------------------------------------
  34   4/20   5410        PAYROLL TAX EXP  212.65
               2711          FICA PAYABLE              135.85
               2718          SUTA PAYABLE               67.20
               2719          FUTA PAYABLE                9.60
-----------------------------------------------------------------
  35   4/21   4130        SALES RET &ALL    86.40
               2370        SALES TAX PAY      6.05
               1200          ACCOUNTS REC               92.45
-----------------------------------------------------------------
  36   4/22   2200        ACCOUNTS PAYABLE 651.00
               5130          PURCH RET & ALL           651.00
-----------------------------------------------------------------
  37   4/23   1370        OFFICE EQUIP     243.20
               2200          ACCOUNTS PAY              243.20
-----------------------------------------------------------------
  38   4/23   4130        SALES RET & ALL  100.00
               2370        SALES TAX PAY      7.00
               1200          ACCOUNTS REC              107.00
-----------------------------------------------------------------
  39   4/26   1360        STORE EQUIP      400.00
               2200          ACCOUNTS PAY              400.00
-----------------------------------------------------------------
                         PAGE TOTALS       5406.30    5406.30
                                           =======    =======
```

After the general journal has been printed out, it should be examined for mistakes. Once this has been done, and any necessary corrections made, the journal can be posted. Posting in a computerized system is a very simple process. Generally, all that is involved is choosing the menu option "Post Transactions." The program will then post and also enter posting references automatically. Obviously this represents a considerable timesaving over the manual method of posting. This method is also much more accurate, because the computer is not likely to make a posting error.

It is also important at times to see (on the screen or printed out) the whole general ledger—in order to check each account, for example. A printout of a few general ledger accounts is shown in Figure C-7. Note that the posting references refer to entries posted from *other* journals besides the general journal. These postings came from the other modules, which will be explained later in this unit.

At the end of the financial period, the program will produce the trial balance. We can use this trial balance as a guideline for making our adjusting

FIGURE C-7 Sample Printout of General Ledger Entries.

```
  J&L OFFICE SUPPLY
  GENERAL LEDGER
  AS OF 04-30-XX

  ---------------------------------------------------------------------
  CASH                                          ACCOUNT NO.  1100
  ---------------------------------------------------------------------
  DATE        EXPLANATION      REF      DEBIT       CREDIT      BALANCE
  ---------------------------------------------------------------------
  19XX
  0401        BEG. BAL.        ----                             35540.00 DR
  0430        TOTAL            CR12     23671.00                59211.00 DR
  0430        TOTAL            CP08                 31437.23    27773.77 DR
  ---------------------------------------------------------------------

  CHANGE FUND                                   ACCOUNT NO.  1110
  ---------------------------------------------------------------------
  DATE        EXPLANATION      REF      DEBIT       CREDIT      BALANCE
  ---------------------------------------------------------------------
  0401        BEG. BAL.        ----                               300.00 DR
  ---------------------------------------------------------------------

  PETTY CASH                                    ACCOUNT NO.  1120
  ---------------------------------------------------------------------
  DATE        EXPLANATION      REF      DEBIT       CREDIT      BALANCE
  ---------------------------------------------------------------------
  0401        BEG. BAL.        ----                               100.00 DR
  ---------------------------------------------------------------------

  ACCOUNTS RECEIVABLE                           ACCOUNT NO.  1200 DR
  ---------------------------------------------------------------------
  DATE        EXPLANATION      REF      DEBIT       CREDIT      BALANCE
  ---------------------------------------------------------------------
  0401        BEG. BAL.        ----                              8743.00 DR
  0421                         J03                   92.45       8650.55 DR
  0423                         J03                  107.00       8543.55 DR
  0430        TOTAL            S06      19872.00                28415.55 DR
  0430        TOTAL            CR12                 25112.00     3303.55 DR
  ---------------------------------------------------------------------
```

entries. Adjusting entries would be recorded using the "Enter Transactions" option like any other general journal entry. These entries would then be posted using the posting option on the menu. Once this is done, the account balances wil be updated and ready to be used on the financial statements.

An important element in using a computerized system is that you do *not* have to prepare a work sheet. The reason that we use a work sheet in a manual system is to organize and check data before preparing the financial statements. (By showing the adjustments on the same sheet as the trial balance, we are less likely to make errors in posting and calculating balances.) Since in a computer system we can post very quickly and the computer does the math, the potential for error is reduced and there is no need for a work sheet.

In order to print the financial statements, all that is necessary is to select the option from the menu, the statement will be created automatically.

As we stated in Chapter 5, the closing process is a purely mechanical one. Therefore, most accounting packages include an option allowing you to request at the end of each fiscal period that the temporary accounts be automatically cleared to the proper account. Once this is done, a post-closing trial balance can be prepared by choosing the "View/Print Trial Balance" option in the general ledger menu. Just as in a manual system, this completes the accounting cycle, and our balances are updated and ready to be used in the next accounting period.

Figure C-8 is a chart of the flow of information in a system using a general ledger module.

As you can see from this figure, the entire accounting cycle can be completed using the general ledger module of the accounting program. However, many businesses find that they can derive even greater benefit from their computerized system if they use one or more of the other modules in coordination with the general ledger module. Let's examine three common modules.

ACCOUNTS RECEIVABLE MODULE

The accounts receivable module allows us to keep track of our accounts receivable ledger as well as providing special journals to record transactions that affect accounts receivable. In Chapter 6 we discussed the need many businesses had for the sales journal and the cash receipts journal. By using an accounts receivable module a business using a computerized system can also record entries in these special journals. A typical menu for the accounts receivable module is shown in Figure C-9 (p. 325).

When a business first converts its records to a computerized basis, all of the information in the manual accounts receivable ledger must be transferred to this program. Each customer's name and balance will be put on the computer. In addition, it is generally necessary to assign account numbers to the accounts receivable accounts. This makes the task of referring to an account on the computer much easier, since only the account number need be entered and not the entire name. Many businesses assign A/R account numbers that begin with an alphabetic character. In this way they can still keep accounts listed in alphabetic order. For instance, the account number for Ralph's Hardware might be R2020, and the number assigned to Rose's Florist Shoppe would be R3080. As new customers are added, the accountant can use the option to modify the accounts receivable ledger to set up new accounts for them.

FIGURE C-8

Flow of Information Using
a General Ledger Module.

GENERAL LEDGER MODULE

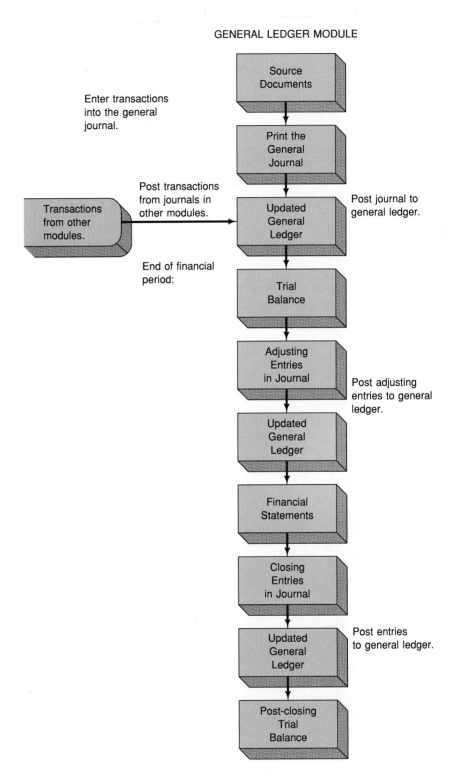

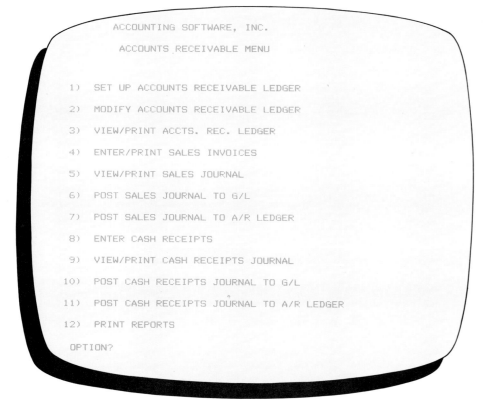

```
          ACCOUNTING SOFTWARE, INC.

          ACCOUNTS RECEIVABLE MENU


    1)   SET UP ACCOUNTS RECEIVABLE LEDGER

    2)   MODIFY ACCOUNTS RECEIVABLE LEDGER

    3)   VIEW/PRINT ACCTS. REC. LEDGER

    4)   ENTER/PRINT SALES INVOICES

    5)   VIEW/PRINT SALES JOURNAL

    6)   POST SALES JOURNAL TO G/L

    7)   POST SALES JOURNAL TO A/R LEDGER

    8)   ENTER CASH RECEIPTS

    9)   VIEW/PRINT CASH RECEIPTS JOURNAL

    10)  POST CASH RECEIPTS JOURNAL TO G/L

    11)  POST CASH RECEIPTS JOURNAL TO A/R LEDGER

    12)  PRINT REPORTS

    OPTION?
```

FIGURE C-9
Typical Menu for an Accounts
Receivable Module.

As stated earlier, transactions would be recorded in batches. The sales for the day would be recorded at one time using this module. In some programs the sales would be entered in the same format as a manual sales journal. Other programs will allow the accountant to enter each sale in the form of a sales invoice. Not only will the program create a sales journal from these entries but also it can print out actual sales invoices to be sent to customers, thus eliminating the need to prepare these invoices manually. An example of a computer-generated sales invoice is shown in Figure C-10.

Once the sales for the day have been entered, a sales journal can be printed out. A hard copy will be checked for correctness and then saved as a permanent record. This journal can now be posted. Just as in a manual system, the sales journal should be posted to two ledgers—both the accounts receivable ledger in the A/R module and the general ledger in the G/L module.

The other journal found in the A/R module is the cash receipts journal, where all transactions involving a receipt of cash are recorded. A batch of cash receipt transactions will be entered into the computer in the same format in which the entries would be recorded manually. As with the other journals, a hard copy would be printed out and checked for correctness. This journal would also be posted to both the general ledger and the accounts receivable ledger.

In some programs the computer not only will keep a running balance of the A/R ledger accounts but also can print out monthly statements to be sent to customers with their present account balance. An example of a monthly statement is shown in Figure C-11 (p. 327).

These programs can also automatically assign finance charges to overdue accounts and prepare an aging of accounts receivable report. If a business

FIGURE C-10   Computer-Generated Sales Invoice.

J&L Office Supply
1200 Poydras Street
New Orleans, LA 70130

INVOICE

INVOICE NO. 2081
INVOICE DATE 4-23-XX
ACCOUNT NO. H01000

PAGE 1

SOLD TO: Shaw Engineering Consultants   SHIP TO: Same
1400 Veteran's Blvd.
Metarie, LA 70123

PURCHASE ORDER NO.	SALESPERSON	SHIP VIA	FREIGHT	DATE SHIPPED	TERMS
628		Your Truck		April 23	2/10,N/30

QUANTITY	STOCK ITEM	UNIT	DESCRIPTION	UNIT PRICE	DISC %	AMOUNT
10	24X914		Staplers	7.00		70.00
50	87A827		Mechanical Pencils	1.25		62.50
20	24X820		Staples	1.50		30.00
100	42B191		Memo Pads	.25		25.00

SALE AMOUNT	187.50
MISC. CHARGES SALES TAX FREIGHT	13.13
TOTAL	200.63

ORIGINAL INVOICE

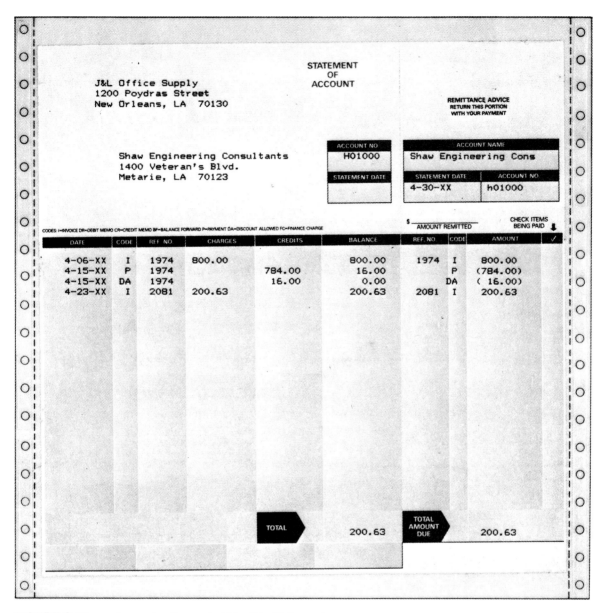

FIGURE C-11 Computer-Generated Monthly Statement.

is also using an inventory module in its system, each item sold can automatically be subtracted from the inventory. Obviously these functions can save accounting personnel a great deal of time. Figure C-12 shows how information flows in a system using an accounts receivable module.

ACCOUNTS PAYABLE MODULE

Using this module a business can maintain its accounts payable ledger, issue checks to pay off accounts payable, and generate both the purchases and cash payments journals. A typical accounts payable module menu is shown in Figure C-13.

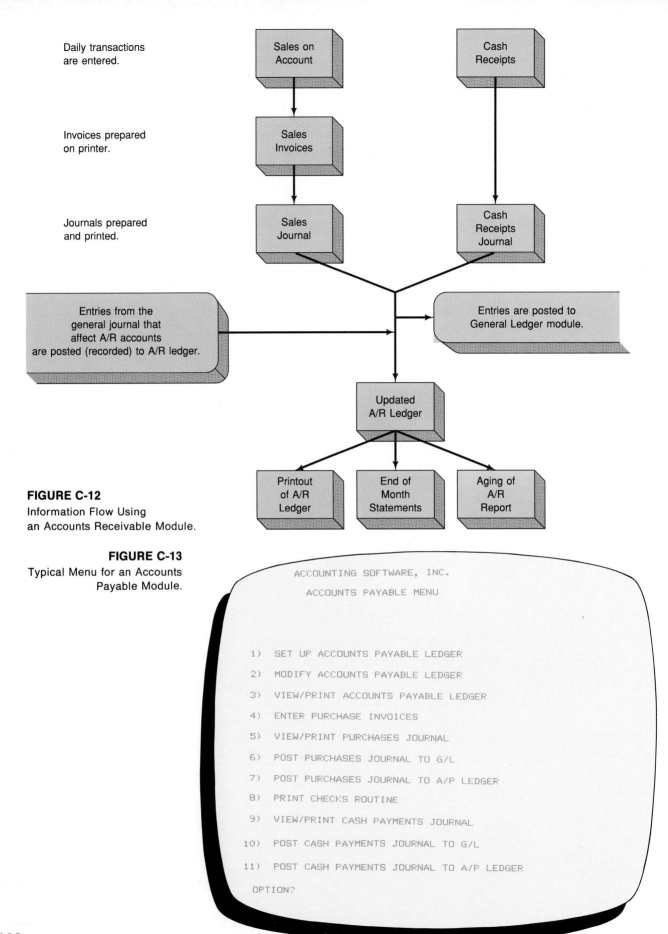

Daily transactions are entered.

Sales on Account

Cash Receipts

Invoices prepared on printer.

Sales Invoices

Journals prepared and printed.

Sales Journal

Cash Receipts Journal

Entries from the general journal that affect A/R accounts are posted (recorded) to A/R ledger.

Entries are posted to General Ledger module.

Updated A/R Ledger

Printout of A/R Ledger

End of Month Statements

Aging of A/R Report

FIGURE C-12

Information Flow Using an Accounts Receivable Module.

FIGURE C-13

Typical Menu for an Accounts Payable Module.

```
         ACCOUNTING SOFTWARE, INC.

          ACCOUNTS PAYABLE MENU



  1)  SET UP ACCOUNTS PAYABLE LEDGER

  2)  MODIFY ACCOUNTS PAYABLE LEDGER

  3)  VIEW/PRINT ACCOUNTS PAYABLE LEDGER

  4)  ENTER PURCHASE INVOICES

  5)  VIEW/PRINT PURCHASES JOURNAL

  6)  POST PURCHASES JOURNAL TO G/L

  7)  POST PURCHASES JOURNAL TO A/P LEDGER

  8)  PRINT CHECKS ROUTINE

  9)  VIEW/PRINT CASH PAYMENTS JOURNAL

  10) POST CASH PAYMENTS JOURNAL TO G/L

  11) POST CASH PAYMENTS JOURNAL TO A/P LEDGER

  OPTION?
```

When first setting up the accounts payable module we will transfer all of the vendor information from the manual A/P ledger. As we did with accounts receivable, it will be necessary to assign account numbers to each account.

When a purchases invoice is received from a vendor, it is entered into the accounts payable module. From each batch of invoices entered the program will create a purchases journal. From this journal the purchases can be posted to both the accounts payable ledger and the general ledger.

When the time comes to pay invoices, the computerized system can provide a list of each invoice that is due on a particular date. The accountant can list the numbers of each invoice he wishes to pay and the amount of the payment. Using preprinted forms, the computer can actually print out the checks. Figure C-14 is an example of a computer-generated check along with its stub showing information about the invoice paid.

The program will record each check as an entry in the cash payments journal. This journal can then be posted to both the accounts payable and general ledgers. The accounts payable module not only keeps an accurate accounts payable ledger but also keeps track of every purchase invoice, when it is due, and the outstanding balance. Even fully paid invoices will be shown along with the date of payment. Occasionally, we will wish to print out a list of all paid invoices for the records and delete them from the computer files. Computerized accounts payable systems are generally very efficient and pre-

FIGURE C-14   Computer-Generated Check and Stub.

OUR REF. NO.	YOUR INVOICE NO.	INVOICE DATE	INVOICE AMOUNT	AMOUNT PAID	DISCOUNT TAKEN	NET CHECK AMOUNT
P1028	5673	6-10-XX	3080.00	3080.00		3080.00
P1264	5823	6-17-XX	1420.00	1420.00	28.40	1391.60
					TOTAL	4471.60

J&L Office Supply--1200 Poydras Street--New Orleans, LA   CHECK   005074

GUARANTY NATIONAL BANK

CHECK   005074

J&L Office Supply
1200 Poydras Steet
New Orleans, LA 70130

DATE   CONTROL NO   AMOUNT
6-23-XX   4813   4471.60

PAY TO THE ORDER OF   FOUR THOUSAND SEVENTY ONE AND 60/100---------------------------------

Franklin Paper Co.
2120 Essen Lane
Baton Rouge, LA 70810

J&L Office Supply

AUTHORIZED SIGNATURE

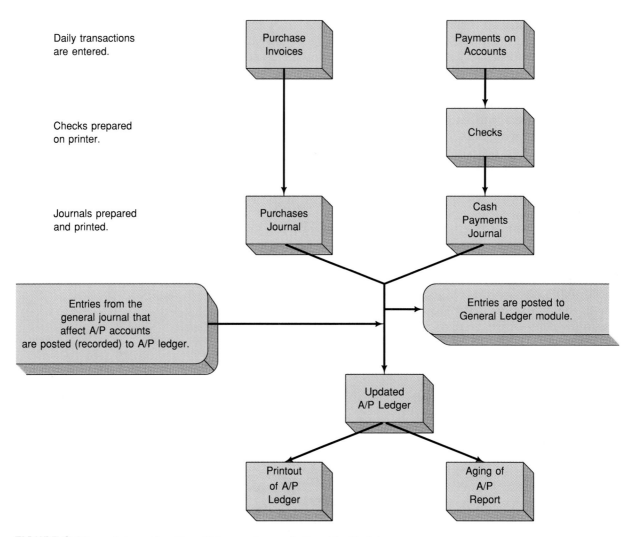

FIGURE C-15   Information Flow Using an Accounts Payable Module.

vent many errors—such as paying an invoice twice, paying the wrong amount, or mistakenly paying too late to receive the discount. Also, if an inventory module is added to this system, each purchase of merchandise can automatically be added into the inventory list. Figure C-15 shows how information flows in a system using an accounts payable module.

PAYROLL MODULE

As stated earlier, payroll activities are ideally suited for a computerized system. A typical payroll module menu is shown in Figure C-16 (p. 331).

In order to use the payroll program, we will have to set up a file on each employee of the firm. These files will contain such information about each employee as name, address, pay rate (if hourly), salary (per pay period), marital status, withholding allowances, and voluntary deductions. This information can be modified at any time (for instance when an employee moves or receives a raise, or when a new employee is hired).

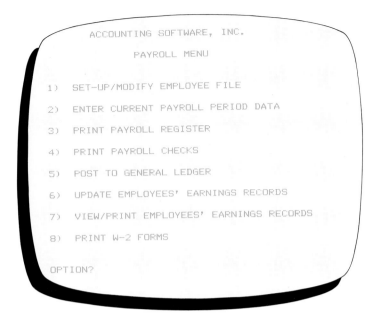

```
          ACCOUNTING SOFTWARE, INC.

               PAYROLL MENU

    1)   SET-UP/MODIFY EMPLOYEE FILE

    2)   ENTER CURRENT PAYROLL PERIOD DATA

    3)   PRINT PAYROLL REGISTER

    4)   PRINT PAYROLL CHECKS

    5)   POST TO GENERAL LEDGER

    6)   UPDATE EMPLOYEES' EARNINGS RECORDS

    7)   VIEW/PRINT EMPLOYEES' EARNINGS RECORDS

    8)   PRINT W-2 FORMS


    OPTION?
```

FIGURE C-16
Typical Menu for a Payroll Module.

On each payday we will use the "Enter Current Payroll Data" option in the menu to give the computer the necessary information to calculate the payroll. The program will list each employee in order of employee number and show information that was last entered to calculate payroll. This information would consist of number of regular and overtime hours worked, bonuses or commissions to be received, and any special deductions to be taken from this paycheck. For most employees this information does not change from pay period to pay period and will not have to be modified. After the information for the current payroll is entered, the computer will automatically calculate each paycheck. The program will calculate regular pay, overtime pay, gross pay, each deduction, and net pay. The current tax tables should be built into the program so that both federal and state taxes can be calculated. Also the computer knows year-to-date earnings for each employee and can calculate FICA taxes.

Next, we will instruct the program to print the payroll register. After we verify that all information is correct, the payroll checks can be printed. Using preprinted checks, the program can print out checks and the accompanying stubs. Figure C-17 is an example of a computer-generated paycheck.

Once the payroll checks have been printed, all that is left to be done for the current payroll is to post the payroll register information to the general ledger and to update the employee's individual earnings records. Both of these tasks can be performed by simply choosing the appropriate menu option.

Whenever year-to-date payroll information is needed on an employee, a menu option can be chosen to print out the employees' earnings records. At the end of each calendar quarter the information in the employees' earnings records can be used to prepare Form 941. Supply stores sell 941 forms that will feed through your printer. Many programs have an option letting the computer print the forms for you. At the end of the calendar year you must also prepare W-2 forms for each employee. You can also buy W-2 forms that will fit into your printer and have the computer fill out the W-2's. An example of a computer-generated W-2 is shown in Figure C-18.

J&L Office Supply--1200 Poydras Street--New Orleans, LA 70130

J&L Office Supply
1200 Poydras Street
New Orleans, LA 70130

	CHECK NO.	DATE
	000004	12-28-XX

TO THE
ORDER OF   Melissa L. Thomas

AMOUNT
$ 428.71

PAY   · Four hundred twenty-eight and 71/100------------------------

AUTHORIZED SIGNATURE

HOURS	RATE	TYPE OF PAY	EARNINGS
40	12.50	REGULAR	500.00
6	18.75	O/T	112.50

EMPLOYEE NAME

Melissa L. Thomas

CHECK NO.	DATE	SOCIAL SECURITY NUMBER
000004	12-28-XX	435-21-9393

GROSS EARNINGS ▶   612.50

NET PAY ▶
THIS PERIOD ▶   428.71

DEDUCTIONS ▶	FEDERAL W/H	F.I.C.A.	STATE W/H			
AMOUNT ▶	116.00	43.79	24.00			

YEAR TO-DATE ▶	GROSS	FEDERAL W/H	F.I.C.A.	STATE		
	30650.00	5826.52	2277.28	1429.20		

FIGURE C-17   Computer-Generated Paycheck.

FIGURE C-18   Computer-Generated W-2 Form.

1 Control Number	22222	For Paperwork Reduction Act Notice, see back of Copy D. OMB No. 1545-0008	For Official Use Only ▶	
2 Employer's Name, Address, and ZIP Code		3 Employer's Identification Number 72-1214782	4 Employer's State I.D. Number 54-7699-4	
J&L Office Supply 1200 Poydras Street New Orleans, LA 70130		5 Statutory Employee ☐ Deceased ☐ Legal Rep. ☐ 942 Emp. ☐ Subtotal ☐ Void ☐		
		6 Allocated Tips	7 Advance EIC Payment	
8 Employee's Social Security Number 435-21-9393	9 Federal Income Tax Withheld 5826.52	10 Wages, Tips, Other Compensation 30,650.00	11 Social Security Tax Withheld 2277.28	
12 Employee's Name (First, Middle, Last) Melissa L. Thomas		13 Social Security Wages 30,650.00	14 Social Security Tips	
23 Rue De La Place Avenue New Orleans, LA 70124		16 *	16a Fringe Benefits Incl. in Box 10	
		17 State Income Tax 1429.20	18 State Wages, Tips, Etc. 30,650.00	19 Name of State LA
15 Employee's Address and ZIP Code		20 Local Income Tax	21 Local Wages, Tips, Etc.	22 Name of Locality

Form **W-2 Wage and Tax Statement**
36-2515832 I.R.S. APP.

COPY A For Social Security Administration
*See Instructions for Form W-2 and W-2P

Department of the Treasury
Internal Revenue Service

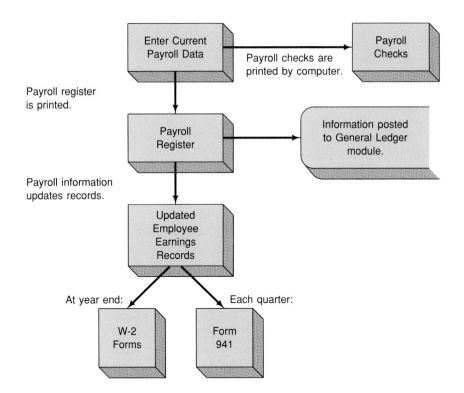

FIGURE C-19
Information Flow Using a Payroll Module.

To begin a new year all of the year-to-date totals on the employees' earnings records will be zeroed out. It is always a necessary to make a hard copy of the final employees' earnings records at the end of the year before starting all of the balances over, since the law requires that payroll information be kept a minimum of four years.

Figure C-19 shows how information flows in a system using a payroll module.

It is not necessary to memorize the procedures used in this unit. Each software package is slightly different and will not follow these exact procedures. What is important is that you have enough confidence to pick up the manual for a software package and learn how to use the program in your business. As you can see, the procedures followed in a computerized accounting system are almost identical to those in a manual system. Because of this, it is not difficult for someone who understands a manual system to use a good computer accounting program. The next unit will explain how to make sure that the accounting package you buy is easy to use, reliable, and suits the needs of your business.

At this point you should be able to

1. Define and contrast stand-alone modules and integrated software. (p. 319)
2. Explain the term "menu-driven program." (p. 319)
3. Discuss how closely computerized procedures follow manual procedures. (p. 320)
4. List various documents that the computer can generate for the accountant. (pp. 319–333)

SELF-REVIEW QUIZ C-2

Respond true or false to the following:

1. It is possible to computerize just one area of the accounting records such as the A/R ledger and not computerize the other areas.

2. No special journals are used in a computerized system.

3. In order to prepare financial statements in a computerized system you must first complete a work sheet.

4. It is necessary to assign account numbers to A/R and A/P accounts in the subsidiary ledgers in a computerized system.

5. Transactions are recorded on the computer in batches of similar transactions rather than in order of occurrence to improve efficiency.

SOLUTION TO SELF-REVIEW QUIZ C-2

1. True   **2.** False   **3.** False   **4.** True   **5.** True

LEARNING UNIT C-3

How to Choose and Use Accounting Software

You have seen in the previous unit that if a business has a good software package, it is not difficult to perform accounting tasks on the computer. The problem most small businesses face when they decide they need to convert to a computerized system is how to buy a good software package. There are dozens of accounting software packages available.

Some of the considerations important when buying an accounting package are discussed below.

Similarity to Present Procedures.   When purchasing a software package, you should carefully analyze the procedures you are using in your manual accounting system. Although you probably won't find a system that handles every task exactly as you have done in the past, you should be able to find one that will fit your present procedures.

Software Compatibility.   Make sure that the software you buy is **compatible** with (will run on) the computer you own. Since different computers have different operating systems, a software package must be written for that computer (or one that it is compatible with) for the software and computer to be able to communicate. If you are not sure whether the program is compatible with your computer—ask the software dealer.

Minimum Requirements.   You should carefully analyze your business to determine whether a particular accounting program is able to meet its needs. For instance, if your business has 300 credit accounts, a program that could carry a maximum of 250 accounts would not meet your minimum requirements. Limits in such areas as the number of transactions in a financial period, accounts receivable accounts, accounts payable accounts, general ledger accounts, inventory items, and employees on the payroll should be considered.

Cost.   There is a wide range of prices in accounting software today. Prices for good software range from as low as $60 for a fully integrated package with seven modules to as much as several hundred dollars per module. Unlike many other products, price is not necessarily an indicator of quality with software packages. Recently, many software producers have found that by lowering their prices they increase their sales so dramatically that they can still make a good profit. Many of the lower-priced packages are of the highest quality.

Documentation.   A very important factor when setting up a computerized system is how well the program **documentation** is written. Documentation comes in the form of a manual. Unfortunately, many software packages come with complicated or badly organized manuals. Even the best software, if it has a poor instruction manual, can be completely unusable (or at least underutilized). Before purchasing a package you should ask to examine the manual carefully. It is important to make sure it guides you step-by-step through each procedure. The manual should be thorough enough to answer questions that will arise in use of the program.

User Support.   Another important factor to consider is what kind of **user support** is provided by the company that produced the software. Occasionally you will have questions or problems not covered in the manual. When this happens, you should be able to call a user support line where your questions can be answered. Some software manufacturers provide free support for a limited time after purchase of the program or "sell" support for a stated period of time. You should also be sure that the software producer will provide updates of the program when payroll rates change.

Employee Training.   For some software packages training classes are available through either the makers of the software, the software vendor, or local colleges. For a firm whose employees don't have the time to teach themselves how to use a particular program these classes can be very helpful.

Error Protection.   You should examine the software to determine whether it has adequate **error protection**—built-in controls to prevent errors. Examples would be a feature whereby the program requires the debits to equal the credits before it will accept a journal entry, or a feature that requires you to confirm that a command to delete a file was indeed intentional. This type of protection is virtually essential to a smoothly running accounting system.

Demonstration.   When considering the purchase of a particular software package you should request the software dealer to give you a demonstration of the package. A demonstration can reveal much about the ease of use of the program.

References.   One of the most revealing checks that you can make on an accounting package is to ask the software vendor for references. You should request the names of other businesses that have used this software. Just as you would check the references of a new employee, you should ask questions of someone who has used the program. After all, this package will be a significant "member" of your accounting staff. Although it is not always possible, it is particularly helpful if they have been using the software for an entire fiscal period. Often problems with software are not evident right away. By speaking to someone who has used the system you can verify its ease of use, reliability, and the quality of the user support.

VERTICAL, MODIFIED, AND CUSTOM SOFTWARE

Some companies find that owing to the unusual nature of their accounting procedures standard accounting packages do not suit their needs. In addition to packages that are designed to meet the needs of businesses in general, which are called **horizontal accounting packages**, there are packages that are available for specific types of businesses. For instance, there are programs designed to be used in a dentist's office and packages designed to fit the accounting done in a law firm. These are referred to as **vertical accounting packages**. Since these packages are designed to fit the procedures in a particular type of office, it might be possible to find one that matches a specialized business's needs more closely than a general package would.

If a business can find no ready-made software that is adequate, it still has two options. One option is to have a programmer write a custom program specifically for the company's needs. The other is to buy a ready-made program and have a programmer modify it. Owing to the large variety of software available today, however, these steps are generally not necessary. The vast majority of small businesses are able to buy a ready-made software package that suits their requirements and provides distinct advantages over their manual method.

SETTING UP THE SYSTEM

Once you have purchased an accounting package, the next consideration is setting up the system. This is often the most difficult part of using a computerized system. However, a good program with a well-written manual can make this task relatively easy if the business's books are in good shape before the conversion.

Most software packages require that you perform several tasks in order to set up the system. Though this may be a time-consuming procedure, it is only a one-time job and will be more than worth the trouble in the long run. Many brands of software even make the task of setting up the system much easier by providing a diskette called a *tutorial*. This program leads you step-by-step through normal setup procedures with messages on the monitor. Typical procedures required to be performed before the program can be used are

- Entering general information about the business, such as name, address, fiscal year, etc.
- Setting up a chart of accounts. This will be the same list of account numbers and names you used in the manual system.
- Setting up a general ledger file for each account. If the business is not new and manual records have been kept, then it is also necessary to enter present account balances for each account. In many packages this is done by means of an opening journal entry in the general journal.
- Setting up a customer file. This is equivalent to an accounts receivable ledger. Besides listing the name, address, and balance owed by each customer, it is often necessary to assign account numbers to each accounts receivable account—even if they were not used in the manual system.
- Setting up a vendor file. This is equivalent to an accounts payable ledger. As with accounts receivable, the vendor's name, address, and the balance we owe each vendor will be transferred from the manual system; in addition, account numbers should be assigned.

- Setting up an employee information file. In order to do payroll calculations the program must have data about each employee to work with. This information would include their name, address, social security number, pay rate, marital status, and number of withholding allowances.
- Formatting of financial statements. Some of the more versatile packages allow you to design the financial statements to suit your needs.
- Defining hardware configuration. This simply means that a program may need to be told what brand of monitor and printer you are using before it can be used. Generally, excellent guidelines for this one-time procedure will be given in the manual

Although a computerized system will generally run smoothly, once it has been set up and you have become accustomed to it, it is always advisable to continue performing the manual procedures alongside the computerized ones for the first two to three months. By using the two systems in parallel, you can detect problems in the conversion and also confirm the accuracy of the accounting records under the new system.

CONTROLS IN A COMPUTERIZED ACCOUNTING SYSTEM

When using a computerized system there are some controls that a business must consider. Perhaps the most important new controls are those that prevent the loss of accounting information and those that ensure the continuance of accounting operations.

In a computerized system all records are stored on diskettes. Care should be taken with these diskettes so that the accounting records on them will not be lost. Sometimes, however, despite careful handling, data will be damaged or erased. For this reason it is essential that duplicate copies, called *backups*, be made of the diskettes fairly often. If a backup diskette is made of the accounting information on a daily basis, then at most only one day's worth of transactions would have to be reconstructed in the event of a damaged diskette.

We have noted several times that hard copies of all journals and ledgers should be kept. Just as in a manual system, it is always a good idea to place an up-to-date copy of the ledgers in a fireproof safe or somewhere off the premises at least once a week to protect against the loss of all accounting records.

So that there will not be any disruptions in accounting work, proper care should be taken of all computer equipment. Many businesses buy maintenance contracts from computer repair companies that will make any necessary repairs to hardware during the period it is under contract. Diskettes should be handled carefully and stored properly so that they are not damaged.

Other controls in computerized accounting systems are aimed at maintaining the confidentiality of accounting records.

In a manual accounting system the checkbooks and payroll information would not be left where unauthorized employees had access to them. The same care must be taken in a computerized office. Unused checks should be locked safely away. Since these checks come in a cardboard box like regular printer paper, many offices forget to protect them from theft.

Information in a computerized system can be viewed in several ways. If confidential records (such as payroll) are being entered on the computer, the computer should be located where only the accountant can see the monitor. As in a manual system, confidential information in a printed form should be stored in a place where only authorized personnel have access. In addition, since all accounting information is recorded on the diskettes we discussed in Learning Unit C-1, these diskettes should also be locked safely away.

Once the conversion is complete and the accounting personnel are comfortable with the new accounting system, efficiency will be greatly increased. There are some businesses that would not benefit from using a computerized system. However, only the very smallest of businesses with only a few transactions a month would fall into this category. In the past, owing to the high cost of computers, many businesses sent their accounting work out to computer service centers. These centers keep the accounts of hundreds of businesses. Obviously, though, this type of arrangement involved time lags when information was sent out and had to be processed and then returned. For a small business that does not have an accountant on staff it is still a viable alternative. For the majority of the country's businesses, however, accounting on a microcomputer has become a very affordable and beneficial alternative.

At this point you should be able to

1. Discuss what factors are important when purchasing accounting software. (p. 334)
2. Define and contrast horizontal and vertical accounting packages. (p. 336)
3. List several tasks performed during the conversion from a manual system to a computerized system. (p. 336)
4. Explain several of the controls that a business should consider when using a computerized system. (p. 337)

SELF REVIEW QUIZ C-3

Respond true or false to the following:

1. Low-priced software packages are not as powerful as the higher-priced packages.
2. A user-support line allows you to find out the answer to questions not covered in the manual.
3. Vertical software packages are valuable for businesses such as law offices that have unique accounting procedures.
4. It is important to make backups of all information stored on diskettes to protect against the loss of data.
5. Once the computerized system has been set up, it is no longer necessary to keep any manual records.

SOLUTIONS TO SELF-REVIEW QUIZ C-3

1. False   **2.** True   **3.** True   **4.** True   **5.** False

SUMMARY OF KEY POINTS AND KEY TERMS

LEARNING UNIT C-1

1. Many mechanical accounting functions can be performed more quickly and accurately on a computer than manually.

2. Accounting procedures are virtually the same whether they are performed manually or on the computer.

3. Computer equipment is called hardware. The programs or instructions that tell the computer what to do are called software.

4. Until the 1980s the cost of computer equipment was so high that small businesses could not afford to use a computer for their accounting information.

5. Microcomputers are small, inexpensive computer systems powerful enough to keep track of the accounting information of a small business.

6. Input devices allow us to feed information into the computer. Common input devices include the disk drive and the keyboard.

7. The CPU (central processing unit) is the brain of the computer.

8. We get information out of the computer by means of output devices. Common output devices include the monitor, the printer, and the disk drive.

9. Information can be stored on small, thin disks called floppy diskettes.

Applications software: Programs designed to perform specific tasks such as accounting.

Audit trail: Notations and references that allow each entry in the accounting records to be traced back to the transaction that generated it.

Central processing unit (CPU): The "brain" of the computer that performs all mathematical and logical functions.

Diskette: A thin magnetic disk in a flexible plastic envelope used to store data.

Disk drive: The input/output device used to read information off a magnetic diskette and to record information onto it.

Hard copy: A printed version of information on the computer.

Hard disk: A disk made of metal which is mounted permanently in the computer and used to store data.

Hardware: The physical components of the computer equipment.

Input devices: Components of the computer designed to feed information into the CPU.

Mainframe: A large, multiuser computer capable of processing large amounts of data.

Microcomputer: A small, inexpensive computer that serves one user at a time.

Minicomputer: A medium-size computer capable of serving many users but less powerful than a mainframe.

Monitor (CRT): An output device that resembles a television monitor.

Output device: Components of the computer designed to send information from the computer to the user.

Program: A set of instructions that tell the computer what to do.

Programmer: An individual who writes a computer program.

Software: The program, or set of instructions that tell the computer how to complete a task.

LEARNING UNIT C-2

1. In order to perform accounting on the computer you must have a software program to tell the computer what to do.

2. Accounting packages are sold in modules. Each module handles a different accounting function.

3. A stand-alone system is one in which only one accounting module is being used.

4. An integrated system is one in which two or more modules are used together.

5. Accounting packages are menu-driven.

6. Transactions are generally grouped so that similar transactions are recorded at one time. This is called batching.

7. Besides recording journal entries, posting, and providing financial statements, some software packages actually print many forms such as checks and invoices.

Integrated software: A system in which two or more modules are used in conjunction with one another.

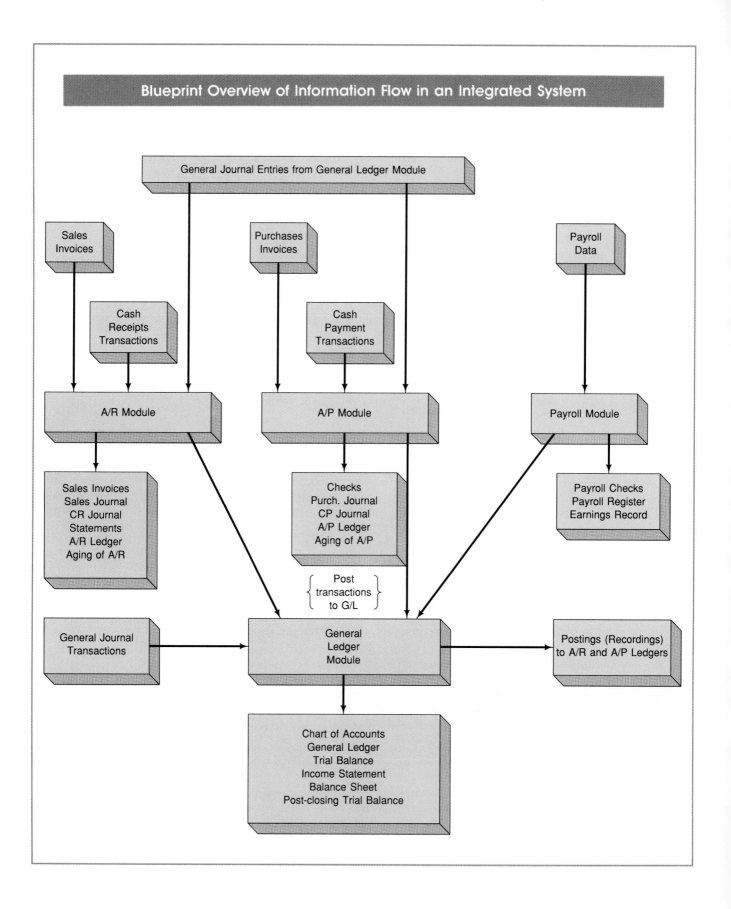

Blueprint Overview of Information Flow in an Integrated System

General Journal Entries from General Ledger Module

Sales Invoices

Cash Receipts Transactions

Purchases Invoices

Cash Payment Transactions

Payroll Data

A/R Module

A/P Module

Payroll Module

Sales Invoices
Sales Journal
CR Journal
Statements
A/R Ledger
Aging of A/R

Checks
Purch. Journal
CP Journal
A/P Ledger
Aging of A/P

Payroll Checks
Payroll Register
Earnings Record

Post transactions to G/L

General Journal Transactions

General Ledger Module

Postings (Recordings) to A/R and A/P Ledgers

Chart of Accounts
General Ledger
Trial Balance
Income Statement
Balance Sheet
Post-closing Trial Balance

Menu-driven: A program that guides the user with a series of choices called menus, which give the user the option of functions he wants performed.

Module: A section of a program that performs a certain function or set of functions and can communicate with other modules.

Stand-alone: A system in which only one module is used.

LEARNING UNIT C-3

1. When purchasing an accounting package you should carefully analyze the needs of your business to define what you need from your software.

2. In order for software to work on a computer, the hardware and software must be compatible.

3. A good manual, user support, and employee training programs are beneficial in learning to use a software package.

4. Horizontal accounting packages are software designed to meet the accounting needs of businesses in general.

5. Vertical accounting packages are written to meet the needs of a particular type of business.

6. In order to first set up the accounting software for a business it is necessary to enter information from the manual system into the computer.

7. Controls are needed to protect the privacy of information and to make sure that extra copies of all information (in the form of printouts and backup diskettes) are available in the event data is lost.

Documentation: Information written about a program to aid the user, often in the form of a manual.

Error Protection: A set of controls written into a program and designed to prevent errors such as a transaction where debits do not equal credits.

Horizontal accounting packages: Software packages designed to meet the accounting requirements of a typical business.

Software compatibility: The ability of a software package to communicate with a particular brand of computer.

User support: A service provided by the producers of a software program designed to answer user questions not covered in the manual.

Vertical accounting packages: Software packages designed to meet the accounting requirements for a specialized business such as a law firm or a construction firm.

DISCUSSION QUESTIONS

1. A business that purchases a good accounting software package does not need a trained accountant or bookkeeper. Agree or disagree. Explain.

2. Name three time-consuming accounting functions that the computer can perform automatically.

3. An accountant or bookkeeper must be knowledgeable about programming in order to use an accounting program. Agree or disagree.

4. Explain the differences in the accounting cycle for a manual system and a computerized system.

5. Define a program.

6. Explain the relationship between mainframes, minicomputers, and microcomputers.

7. Name two common input devices.

8. Name two common output devices.

9. Define a module.

10. Contrast an integrated accounting system and a stand-alone system.

11. What is meant by the term "menu-driven" program?

12. Explain why account numbers are assigned to A/R and A/P ledger accounts in a computerized system.

13. Price is probably a significant indication of the quality of a software package. Agree or disagree. Explain.

14. Explain why it is important to ask for references when purchasing a software package.

15. Why do we need to make backup diskettes of our work when using a computerized accounting system?

PRACTICAL ACCOUNTING APPLICATION #1

Michael Tremont, your boss, told you today that although he knows that putting the accounting records on a microcomputer would improve efficiency, he is still reluctant to do so. He is afraid that if a diskette were damaged all of the accounting records would be lost and could not be reconstructed. Since the business you work for has a large volume of transactions and hundreds of credit accounts, you know that a computer would really be beneficial. Research some methods of protecting accounting information from loss. Write a memo to your boss listing these methods and reassuring him of the safety of a computerized system.

PRACTICAL ACCOUNTING APPLICATION #2

A friend of yours, Lauren LeVaul, runs an alteration business out of her home. She has had some training as a bookkeeper and keeps all of her accounting records herself on a manual basis. She has asked you if she should purchase a computer so that she can keep her accounting records on it. Upon examining her records, you find that she has only about fifteen transactions a week and that they are all recorded in a general journal. Also, since she provides her service on a cash basis only, she sends out no invoices and does not maintain an accounts receivable ledger. She prepares financial statements once a year for tax purposes. Does Lauren need to computerize her records? Please explain to her why or why not.

INDEX